D0408693

WITHDRAWN
UTSA LIBRARIES

COMPLICATED SHADOWS

SHADOWS

The Life and Music of

ELVIS COSTELLO

GRAEME THOMSON

CANONGATE

Edinburgh · New York · Melbourne

Copyright © 2004 by Graeme Thomson

All rights reserved. No part of this book may be reproduced in any
form or by any electronic or mechanical means, including
information storage and retrieval systems, without permission in
writing from the publisher, except by a reviewer, who may quote
brief passages in a review. Any members of educational institutions
wishing to photocopy part or all of the work for classroom use, or
publishers who would like to obtain permission to include the work
in an anthology, should send their inquiries to Canongate,
841 Broadway, New York, NY 10003.

First published in Great Britain in 2004 by
Canongate Books Ltd., Edinburgh, Scotland

Printed in the United States of America

FIRST AMERICAN EDITION

ISBN 1-84195-650-3

Canongate
841 Broadway
New York, NY 10003

05 06 07 08 09   10 9 8 7 6 5 4 3 2 1

Library
University of Texas
at San Antonio

For my own 'Three Distracted Women':
Jen, Kat – and my mother, Kathleen.

Contents

Acknowledgements

THERE ARE NUMEROUS PEOPLE TO THANK for their contributions to the writing of this book. Like Blanche DuBois in *A Streetcar Named Desire*, the biographer also finds himself relying on 'the kindness of strangers' to a slightly worrying degree. As such, the most significant input came from the memories, opinions, insights and revelations of those who know or have known Elvis Costello, and who provided the raw material for much of this biography in hundreds of hours of taped interviews conducted between August 2002 and April 2004.

Everyone I spoke to gave their time freely and generously, and in particular I would like to thank: Robert Azavedo, Roger Bechirian, Bebe Buell, Marianne Burgess, Brian Burke, Paul Cassidy, Philip Chevron, John Ciambotti, Alex Cox, Chris Difford, Charlie Dore, Paul Du Noyer, Steve Earle, Dale Fabian, Jem Finer, Bill Frisell, Mitchell Froom, Bob Geldof, Charlie Gillett, Ian Gomm, Eric Goulden, Richard Harvey, Philip Hayes, Steve Hazelhurst, Larry Hirsch, Carole Jeram, Allan Jones, Clive Langer, Andrew Lauder, Allan Mayes, John McFee, Sean O'Hagan, Marc Ribot, Nick Robbins, Dave Robinson, Jerry Scheff, Paul Scully, David Sefton, Ricky Skaggs, Ken Smith, Mat Snow, Bruce Thomas and Ron Tutt.

Not all of these interviewees are quoted directly in the book, but I thank them all individually, reserving special mention – for dedication above and beyond the call of duty – to: Brian Burke, Allan Mayes, Ken Smith, Steve Hazelhurst, Bruce Thomas and Philip Chevron.

In addition, the input, interest and unwavering assistance of Richard Groothuizen at the *Elvis Costello Information Service* and Mark Perry and Mike Bodayle at the now sadly defunct *Beyond Belief* fanzine was invaluable, especially in the early research stages and in assisting with photographs; indeed, I can scarcely imagine where I would have been without them. I would also like to thank John and Martin Foyle and the numerous – and therefore, by necessity nameless – journalists, writers, record company employees and photographers who made the path of my research all the easier with their help and suggestions. Special thanks to Pennie Smith and Starfile (starfileonline.com) for their patience and flexibility.

At the typeface, reliable and invaluable transcription help was provided by Dawn Hucker. Kate Beveridge also helped out with various time-consuming and hugely helpful tasks, running the gamut from tape transcription to correcting my spelling, a task she has been performing since I was old enough to write. For ploughing their way through the work in various draft stages and making numerous winning suggestions in bright ink, I would also like to thank my brother Gordon and my partner Jen.

At Canongate, I tip my hat to Jamie Byng, Marney Carmichael, Jim Hutcheson and Andy Miller, whose collective input – and patience – aided the book in numerous ways, both technically and creatively. Thanks also to Deborah Kilpatrick for her meticulously efficient copy editing. Above all, I raise a glass to my editor Colin McLear for sterling work in the face of adversity. His contribution to the finished text is incalculable. Finally, I must also acknowledge the role Clare Pierotti played in getting the whole thing going – I think I still owe you a drink.

To my colleagues and employers at all the publications I write for, for showing (varying, it must be said) degrees of understanding and patience while I finished the book – thank you. Special mentions to Michael Hodges, Mat Snow, Hugh Sleight, Gordon Thomson, Gavin Newsham and Bill Borrows, for help, guidance and wildly distracting e-mails.

On a personal note, I pass my thanks back through the years to Chris Gaffney for lighting the Elvis torch, to Bevis Hughes for his help in keeping it burning, and to Martin Baker, my musical friend and foil before the flood. As ever, the lion's share of love and thanks is reserved for my family – especially Mum and Gordon – for endless and ongoing support in all manner of ways. And to Jen, who was there at the beginning and still there at the end: for allowing me to frequently go emotionally AWOL, and for tolerating my obsessive jabberings on the occasions when I was present, always with humour, understanding and love – thank you most of all.

Elvis faces his inquisitors during the combative press conference
at CBS headquarters, New York, 30 March 1979.
Credit: Starfile/Chuck Pulin

'Drunken Talk Isn't Meant To Be Printed in the Paper'*

THE BAR OF A HOLIDAY INN is as good a place as any to die. Stranded in the nowhere lands between Cleveland and Cincinatti, Elvis Costello finally pulled the trigger in the game of Russian roulette he had recently been playing with his career. Drunk, wired and coiled tight with aggression, a one-sided, after-hours slanging match with Stephen Stills and his entourage escalated to the point where Elvis branded James Brown 'a jive-ass nigger' and Ray Charles as 'nothing but a blind, ignorant nigger'. Never keen on half-measures, Elvis also described the British as 'original white boys' and Americans as 'colonials'.

Initially, the incident seemed like just another example of the increasingly desperate escapades that Elvis and The Attractions were making their speciality: too much attitude, too much of *everything*, swapped insults, a scuffle. But while Elvis emerged the following morning remembering little of what he had said or done, he would soon be reminded in intimate detail. The sorry tale that spilled out from the bar in Columbus, Ohio would slam the brakes on his swift ascendance in the United States. It was the story the circling US media had been waiting for, and they would make sure they seized their opportunity with both hands.

* * *

It had been going so well. Of all the loosely-labelled British punk and new wave hopefuls of the late 1970s, Costello alone had struck gold prospecting across the Atlantic. With a band that could swing and punch in a way which everyone – even the Americans, *especially* the Americans – could instinctively understand, he had managed to bully and inveigle his way into the hearts and minds of the critics and music-buying public with a trio of best-selling albums that had invited comparison with the best of Dylan, Springsteen and The Beatles.

I

By March 1979, he was poised to go the extra yard, right up to the big league. *Armed Forces* had lodged in the US Top 10 as Elvis and The Attractions were marauding through the country on the 'Armed Funk' tour, their fourth US trip in a little over a year and, by far, the most important and intensive: fifty-seven dates in barely two months. With Elvis up for a Grammy for Best New Artist, CBS viewed *Armed Forces* in much the same way as they had regarded Bruce Springsteen's third album, *Born To Run* in 1975: it was the record intended to make the artist not just a star, but a superstar.

'We either make it all the way with *Armed Forces* or we don't,' said Elvis's manager Jake Riviera on the eve of the tour. 'If this album doesn't break us in America then Columbia will still keep us, but we'll be considered pretty much a spent force.'[1]

Elvis was feeling the pressure. Uneasy about the way fame was making him feel and allowing him to behave, he seemed a heavily fuelled mixture of nerves, paranoia and arrogance. The tour matched his mood. Characterised by a series of nasty stand-offs and set-tos, the slow-burning sense of menace finally ignited on 15 March, following a show at The Agora Club in Columbus.

It took more than a week for details of the Holiday Inn incident to spread. Stills' backing singer Bonnie Bramlett had been a witness to the outburst, and wasn't inclined to dismiss Elvis's behaviour on the grounds that it had arrived in a moment of private, drunken idiocy. She began relaying details to the local press, and within a few days the *Village Voice*, New York's highly influential and righteously liberal commentator, was running the story, openly accusing Elvis of racism. *People* magazine and other nationals rapidly picked up the baton, with the result that the records began disappearing from radio playlists, and even from some shops.

As the furore gathered pace, Elvis adhered to his long-standing *omerta* towards the press. But by the time he arrived in New York on 30 March, he – and more significantly CBS – realised that something had to be done to counter-act the tide of negative publicity and ill-feeling. As well as the material damage to his career, an estimated 150 death threats came flooding in. In the circumstances, Elvis was left with no other option but to accede to Columbia's insistence for an emergency press conference. It was finally time for him to face his pursuers. And himself.

The conference was conducted in the appropriately soulless surroundings of the fourteenth floor of CBS headquarters on 57th Street in Manhattan. Part suicide, part mass-execution, it was witnessed by a throng of journalists who had been roundly ignored, alienated, and, at times, physically threatened by the Elvis camp over the course of the tour. Summoned with only a couple of hours' notice, over fifty New York journalists had made the trip to the press conference, relishing the chance to take a retaliatory swipe at the man who had declared himself virtually untouchable.

'Because of the attitude he'd had previously towards the press, he really set himself up,' *Rolling Stone* writer Kurt Loder later said. 'Here he is touring America, putting down Americans. There were some people – definitely – who were ready to push him on this one.'[2] And push him they did, right over the edge.

Elvis arrived expecting a rough ride. 'I never – ever – thought I'd be in this position,' he began nervously, and from the outset the articulacy so evident in his songs deserted him. He appeared to the world jumpy, wired, still trying to punch his way out of a corner despite the odds being stacked so heavily against him. It was standard practice for Elvis to up-the-ante whenever he felt he was under attack, and here he opted for a combative approach rather than a conciliatory one. Snapping at photographers and journalists alike, at no point did Elvis ever try to deny his remarks about James Brown and Ray Charles, although he did question whether they were reported verbatim.

'In the course of the argument, it became necessary for me to outrage [Stills and his people] with the most obnoxious and offensive remarks that I could muster,' he explained. 'I said the most outrageous thing I could possibly say to them – that I knew, in my drunken logic, would anger them more than anything else. It was in the context of an argument that I used certain words and that is not my opinion, and that's what I've come here to say.'

He then expressed regret 'if people got *needlessly* angry about it', but made it clear he was offering no apology to Stephen Stills or Bonnie Bramlett, 'who now seem to have chosen to seek publicity at my expense by making it a gossip item'. Nor was he going to say sorry to anybody else. 'As I'm not a racist, why do I have to apologise?' he asked.

The press corps were quick to pick up on the overtones of the statement, which echoed the 'please don't ask me to apologise' stance from *This Year's Model's* 'Hand In Hand'. Inevitably, having spent such a long time being denied access to Elvis, they were not especially inclined to believe that he went around in private saying things that he didn't believe.

Playing such a dangerously high-handed game with the media throughout the tour had left little room for manoeuvre. When Elvis complained that his words had been quoted out of context, that nobody had bothered to contact him for an explanation, the full pent-up resentment of the press corps came back at him.

'You weren't available for comment,' shouted Richard Goldstein from

3

the *Village Voice*. 'I tried for hours to reach you. *You* made yourself unavailable! Don't blame it on the press. It's not the press, it's *you*! You said it and you were unavailable to clarify it.'

If there was more than a hint of *schadenfreude* in the room, it was only to be expected. To many present, the remarks tallied neatly with the kind of bully-boy attitude that the Costello camp had made their speciality. Indeed, his behaviour in the Holiday Inn seemed to complement the withering contempt of much of his music, and soon the lyrics of *Armed Forces* were being artlessly picked over – particularly the references to 'darkies' in 'Sunday's Best' and 'white niggers' and 'itchy triggers' in 'Oliver's Army' – in the hope that they might take on more sinister connotations in the current context. As ever, Elvis showed no appetite for debate or dissection, which did little to help his cause. He simply kept repeating his mantra, over and over. 'I am not a racist. It ain't the truth, and that's all I'm gonna say.'

Even those members of the press who accepted his explanation still couldn't understand why it was so necessary to offend Stills and his friends. Where did all this hostility come from? When asked why he didn't just leave the bar and walk away, Elvis pondered: 'I *suppose* you can always get up and leave,' as if the thought of avoiding confrontation had only just occurred to him. Maybe it had. There were a lot of 'whys' flying around the room, but they could all be distilled down to one essence: '*Why are you so angry?*'

Elvis didn't really have an answer. Increasingly trapped in a persona that was so rigidly and aggressively combative it barely gave him room to breathe, he seemed almost consumed by the need to express rage. What he would previously do only for effect, he now did by instinct. What had once been a defined image was now – perhaps – the person he believed he really was.

The initial impression of the man facing his inquisitors that March afternoon in Manhattan was of someone who couldn't quite grasp what all the fuss was about, and who possessed neither the patience nor the inclination to explain himself fully to people he obviously despised. Only later did it become clear that not only the incident in Columbus and his desperate, back-to-the-wall last stand at the press conference, but indeed the entire 'Armed Funk' tour, had been an exercise in subconscious self-sabotage, destroying much of what he and The Attractions had spent two years creating.

Perhaps he had simply become disgusted at what he saw and at what it allowed him to be. With a wife and child back in England, a glamourous model girlfriend, an excess of alcohol and cocaine in his bloodstream and a record at the top end of the charts on both sides of the Atlantic, Elvis had become a very mainstream exemplar of everything he had once professed to loathe. By the time he left CBS headquarters to return to the hyper-reality of the streets of New York, Elvis Costello – global rock star in waiting – was effectively dead. As he later admitted: 'The press were looking for something to crucify me with and I fed myself to the lions.'[3]

Now he could be whatever he wanted.

---

* Ray Charles was later asked for his opinion on Elvis Costello's comments, and showed the kind of maturity and restraint that few on either side of the battle-lines had been able or willing to display. 'Anyone could get drunk once in his life,' said Charles. 'Drunken talk isn't meant to be printed in the paper.'

PART ONE
The Great Unknown

Chapter One
1954-73

IT IS ALWAYS HARD TO DETERMINE exactly where genetic inheritance ends and destiny begins. Declan Patrick MacManus may have been raised in a household filled with music, but he was never groomed to play the role of professional musician. There was no formal tuition or education. From birth, he was simply immersed in an ocean of wide-ranging sounds as an integral part of a rounded, liberal and socially aware upbringing.

Among the first half-dozen or so words that Declan ever uttered, according to his mother Lillian, were 'Siameses' and 'skin, mummy'; straightforward requests for Peggy Lee's 'Siamese Cat Song' and – more often – Frank Sinatra's definitive version of 'I've Got You Under My Skin'.

'I used to request it before I could form proper sentences,' he would later reflect. 'I guess that's a pretty young appreciation of Cole Porter.'[1]

But it would be entirely wrong to suggest that there wasn't also pedigree in the MacManus genes. Born on 25 August, 1954, in St Mary's Hospital, Paddington, west London, the new arrival would – given time – simply become the greatest exponent of the family business.

The musical bloodline can be traced back to the early 1900s. Declan's paternal grandfather Patrick Matthew McManus* was an accomplished trumpet player who learned his craft as a teenager at the Royal Military School of Music at Kneller Hall. The son of Irish emigrants, Pat was born in 1896 in the working-class, shipbuilding town of Birkenhead, directly across the river Mersey from Liverpool, and almost exclusively Irish in character in the latter part of the nineteenth century.

There is little known or to be told about Pat's parents. They hailed from the Ulster town of Dungannon, and there were later hints within the

---

* The family's surname was originally spelt with the Mc- prefix, rather than Mac-, but by the time Declan's father Ross married in 1952 it had morphed into the latter spelling, traditionally Scottish rather than Irish. This may have been an attempt to escape anti-Irish prejudice.

family that Pat's father – a coal merchant by trade – was embroiled in activities which may have eventually resulted in his murder. Whatever the exact truth, Pat was raised in an orphanage in Southall, north-west London, before being sent on to Kneller Hall near Twickenham, about ten miles south-west of central London.

While there he learned to read music and became an accomplished player on the coronet. He also acquired an English accent. While still only eighteen, Pat was sent to France during the Great War. He was shot and injured in action, and returned to recuperate at Beggar's Bush Barracks in Dublin. It's a supreme irony that the grandfather of the author of 'Oliver's Army' – that deceptively jaunty indictment of the English military's brutalisation of Ireland – didn't return to the Front upon his recovery, but instead found himself as a non-combative soldier in the British Army in Ireland at the time of the rising Republican tide in 1916.

With many Irish friends and a strong Irish heritage, Pat was caught in the middle, a quirk of fate that didn't sit easily with the McManus family, and indeed caused ripples and repercussions much further down the generational line.

'I was brought up with this anti-attitude,' remembers Declan. 'My father got that from his father, who was anti-English. He passed that on to my dad and my dad passed it onto me.'[2]

Pat became a military bandmaster in the army. Following de-mob, he made a living playing the trumpet in ships' orchestras on the White Star Line cruise liners that made regular traffic between Liverpool and America. Apparently – and we must always be aware of the traditional Irish enthusiasm for turning a good story into a great one – Pat had quite a time of it in 1920's New York.* He socialised with boxers, bootleggers, and even shared a house with the gangster 'Legs' Diamond, an East Coast demilegend whose colourful past included army desertion, hijacking and car theft, and whose presence in Prohibition-era New York principally involved sating the public's illicit thirst for alcohol.

Pat's ocean travels throughout the '20s and '30s also took in Japan and India, before he returned to England to become a pit musician with conventional orchestras. His home base was 282 Conway Street, Birkenhead, where he lived with his wife Mabel McManus (*nee* Jackson), known as Molly, and whose middle names of Josephine Veronica would one day also inspire Declan into song.

* * *

* Pat's stint in the US is celebrated in the final verse of 'American Without Tears' on *King Of America*, where the singer tenderly evokes his grandfather 'walking the streets of New York'.

Ronald Patrick Ross McManus arrived on 20 October 1927, born at home in Birkenhead, a town where religious choices were still an important issue. 'As a child I lived in an area where bigotry was rife,'3 he later recalled, which served only to fan the flames of that 'anti' feeling that Declan felt was part of his genetic inheritance.

Ross was gifted both his father's passion and talent for music. In time, he learned to read music and later mastered the trumpet, emulating the jazz records he loved. Ross was something of a pioneer: according to local musical history sources, he was perhaps the first musician brave enough to blow his beloved be-bop in Birkenhead.

Learning his trade in the myriad swing bands that flourished in Britain around the time of the Second World War, Ross augmented his musical work with a job as a shipping clerk. Although principally a trumpet player, he would occasionally sing with the band, and found he had both reasonable technique and immense power. 'I have a memory of him singing and the door rattling in the frame,'4 recalled Declan, who inherited a considerable percentage of his father's vocal punch.

Ross settled down in 1952, marrying Lilian Alda Ablett in Bromley Registry Office, south-west London. Both bride and groom were twenty-four at the time and living – at separate addresses, naturally – in Sidcup, Kent. The daughter of Jim and Ada, Lilian was another product of a displaced Irish Catholic family from Smithdown Road in Liverpool's Toxteth, a tough, multi-racial dockside neighbourhood flanking the Mersey.

The couple's similar upbringings cemented their relationship and informed their left-wing social and political values, but it was music that really brought them together; Lilian had helped run some of the jazz clubs where Ross played early in his career, and, at the time of her marriage, was working as a gramophone record assistant at Selfridges department store in London's Oxford Street.

'She had to sell all different kinds of music,' said Declan. 'So she was knowlegable about lots of records.'5 Lilian's enthusiasm for music existed independently of her husband, grounded firmly in the classic ballad singing of Ella Fitzgerald and Frank Sinatra. She would become an invaluable source for Declan.

Young, versatile and good-looking enough when dressed for action, Ross's hum-drum musical career took a quantum leap in 1954, when a talent scout for Joe Loss spotted him singing with a band in Nottingham. At the time, Loss was the leader of the most famous big band in the UK, the closest thing Britain had to Glenn Miller. His fourteen-piece orchestra played sell-out seasons in every major dance hall in the country, when they weren't entertaining royalty or making one of their constant radio or television appearances. They were *the* band to be in. Ross was signed as one of the three principal vocalists, alongside Rose Brennan and Larry Gretton. It was the biggest of breaks.

By the time of Declan's birth on 25 August 1954, Lilian and Ross had moved to 46a Avonmore Road in Olympia, west London. Home was a rented ground-floor flat just off the intersection of Hammersmith Road and Kensington High Street, on a quiet, cosmopolitan street which had once boasted Edward Elgar among its residents. The flat in Avonmore Road was the setting for the photographs which later appeared as part of the *Brutal Youth* artwork, and also inspired the flickering childhood shadowplays of 1986's 'Battered Old Bird', although in reality the young Declan was taught to swear in Welsh, not French, by the live-in landlady.

The child was taken home and almost immediately enveloped in music. Ross was already an integral part of the Joe Loss Orchestra, quickly settling into a fourteen-year-long residency at the Hammersmith Palais, the famous London ballroom only a short distance away from Avonmore Road. The band were required to turn around the hits of the day week-in, week-out at the Palais, embarking on short national tours during the summer. Sometimes, Declan would hop on the tour bus to see a couple of shows and catch up with his dad, but most of the early memories of watching his father come from the Hammersmith Palais.

As well as playing to paying punters, the Joe Loss Orchestra also performed a live radio broadcast every Friday lunchtime, churning out faithful approximations of all the current hits.* Declan was listening to all of this – and learning.

'I knew the names of jazz musicians before I went to school,' he recalled. '[Dizzy] Gillespie, Charles Mingus, I really loved Peggy Lee; and that comes from the broad-mindedness that was fostered in my household from an early age.'[6]

Charlie Parker, Miles Davis and Clifford Brown were among the other frequent and welcome guests on the MacManus turntable, providing a far more fruitful education than school. Declan began attending the local Catholic primary in 1959, but he didn't linger long. In 1961, the family moved from the bustle of west Kensington to the leafier locale of 16 Beaulieu Close in Twickenham Park, just over the river from Richmond and a stone's throw from the banks of the Thames.

The family were doing well. They went to Spain on holiday every year – certainly not the common occurrence then that it is now – and the new

* The perennially popular Joe Loss Show ran on the BBC light service and later Radio One between 1933 and 1968.

house was comfortably middle-class: a medium-sized, modern maisonette, one in a semi-detached block of four in a pleasant cul-de-sac just outside London's city limits in Middlesex.*

The change of address meant a change of school. Aged seven, Declan started at St Edmund's primary school in Nelson Road in the suburb of Whitton, a couple of miles west of his new house, near where the England Rugby Union stadium now stands and literally around the corner from where he would establish his first marital home nearly fifteen years later.

With a total pupil roll of around 150, St Edmund's was a small parish school in a sedate suburban area, run by nuns and attached to St Edmund's Church. An utterly ordinary example of its type, with its one-storey buildings, fenced-in asphalt play area and small grass playing field, it was a friendly enough environment, although in keeping with most institutions which involve nuns, there was inevitably an aggressively religious atmosphere coursing through it. 'I didn't like it very much,' Declan said later. 'I don't think anybody likes school very much.'7

The feeling wasn't necessarily mutual. He was popular with the nuns, partially because most of them were of Irish extraction and anyone with Irish links and an obviously Irish heritage was regarded favourably, but above all because he was very little trouble to anyone. School friend Robert Azavedo remembers him as 'a quiet lad', and this seemed to personify his primary school days.

Brian Burke was another friend from Declan's class at St Edmund's who recalls random snapshots of him from that time: taking their first Holy Communion together, working on a piece of basketwork during craft classes, and one striking vignette which hinted that his future ambitions lay not merely in consuming music, but in performing it.

'The one thing that has always stuck in my mind is him singing 'The Little White Bull' in class one day,' says Burke, painting a slightly unsettling picture of the boy who went on to write 'Tramp The Dirt Down' sneering through a Tommy Steele number. 'He still has this sort of nasal singing style which I recognise as being the way he sang back then, just from this single song.'

It was perhaps the first public exhibition of a stubborn, single-minded determination and a certain immunity to ridicule, core characteristics which to date have shown no sign of diminishing. Physically, Declan was on the plump side, and one vital ingredient was missing. 'He wasn't

* Beaulieu Close was firmly within the west London/Middlesex axis within which, two teenage years in Liverpool notwithstanding, Declan would spend the remainder of his formative years and continue well into adulthood: Twickenham, Whitton, Hounslow, Roehampton, Richmond, Chiswick.

wearing glasses,' says Burke. 'But you could recognise him in old photographs that I have as Elvis Costello. You can see the facial resemblance.'

Ross's status as a local celebrity with the Joe Loss Orchestra did Declan no harm at school either. 'The nuns would go crazy when his father came to collect him,' recalls Robert Azavedo. 'He used to come to school dressed in white trousers, blue socks and white Italian shoes. Drove the nuns clucking mad like giggly schoolgirls.'

His father's career was becoming more and more important, and not just to excitable women under strict religious orders. By the age of nine or ten, Declan was taking every opportunity to capitalise on the benefits of Ross's job, especially keen to catch the preparations for the weekly radio show whenever he could.

'Fridays during the [school] holidays were something that I really used to look forward to,' he recalls. 'I used to see bands rehearse. I would get there at nine in the morning and see The Hollies, then Billy J. Kramer, then Engelbert Humperdinck or whoever it was.'[8]

Regularly observing the stars of the day first-hand over a number of years was an invaluable learning experience, even if it did drain most of the romance from the idea of being a professional musician. 'A lot of the instinctive things I have about being onstage come from watching my dad and the discipline of that band, but I saw that it wasn't actually glamourous, that it was sort of a job.'[9]

There was precious little 'sort of' about it. By the mid-'60s the glamour of the big-band era had long since ebbed away, along with most of the groups that had helped create it. Even the Joe Loss Orchestra needed to be increasingly adaptable to survive. The band had evolved into an amazingly versatile if somewhat eccentric beast, album releases like *Go Latin With Loss!* – featuring a booming Ross singing 'La Bamba' – with performances combining everything from straight renditions of the latest Tony Bennett 45 to full treatments of The Beach Boys' 'God Only Knows' and 'See Emily Play' by Pink Floyd.

Where some might have scoffed, the polished diversity of what Ross and the Joe Loss Orchestra were able to do was not lost on Declan. Nor was the effort it required: there's no question that his work ethic was forged from an observance of his father in those days. Penning a tribute to the recently deceased Joe Loss in the *Guardian* in 1990, Ross recalled: 'I still travel 50,000 miles a year entertaining people and every night I operate to the same principles as everyone who has passed through Joe's hand: discipline, punctuality, hard work and value for money.' It's an ethos that clearly made an impact on his son. Declan would always be a worker, perhaps deferring only to James Brown for the title of hardest working man in the business.

There was little sense of any generational divide in the MacManus household. Ross's work ensured he had no need to make the kind of excruciating – if well-intentioned – attempts to understand or appreciate his son's tastes that wrought divisions in many other families. The two males were close, and when Declan later grew into adulthood it would become possible to identify several shared father-son characteristics.

'I remember that the woman my dad sang with for a number of years, Rosie Brennan, told me that my dad was always flirting with the tallest, best-looking woman in the room or trying to pick a fight with the biggest guy, depending on his mood,' said Declan. 'He was a terror! I think that's where I get some of it from.'[10] Ross was also a very loving father, articulate, passionate, loquacious and witty, and passed on many of these attributes to his son. He also bequeathed the mighty MacManus nose.

It was an unusually tight father-son relationship, made all the more unique by the fact that Declan's mother also defied stereotype. Allan Mayes played with Declan in Liverpool in the early '70s and remembers Lilian well from those days: '[She] was hipper than my mother, hipper than any other mother. She was like, "Have you heard the new Band album, Declan? I heard Neil Young on the radio this afternoon." She knew stuff like that, and she had stories to tell about life on the road with the Joe Loss Band. And she was a very nice lady.'

Declan himself noted that his parents were a bit beatnik, and later sensed that Ross had sacrificed most of his own artistic ambitions to be a serious jazz artist as a young man by throwing in his lot with the middle-of-the-road stability of the Joe Loss Orchestra. Although there was never any parental pressure on Declan to be a musician, the legacy of his father's compromised career stayed with him. Later, when he realised he had the privilege of an audience that was prepared to follow him down some of his more experimental avenues, he would seize the opportunity to cover every inch of musical territory he possibly could. Ross would expect no less. As contemporary composer and some-time Costello collaborator, Richard Harvey notes: 'I think Declan is very much aware of being the son his father would want him to be.'

* * *

In August 1965, Declan turned eleven and moved up to Catholic secondary school. Archbishop Myers, now re-named St Mark's, was situated on Bath Road in Hounslow, north-west of Whitton and a trip which necessitated a ride on the No. 281 bus. Life required some adjustment. It was a secondary modern school, much bigger than St Edmund's, above average in standard, and Declan was by no means part of the social or academic elite. However, he was beginning to make an impression as an individual character, if a bit of a loner.

'I liked him, he was very independent,' remembers Marianne Burgess, who was in Declan's class at Myers. 'He wasn't bothered by what people thought of him. I remember him wearing a bow tie to the school dance, which was quite unusual. We girls could have sensible chats with him because he seemed very mature.'

He may have been mature, but maturity is seldom what teenage girls are really interested in. Declan was very chunky, serious-minded and stubbornly individual, and by all accounts was not a particularly big hit with the opposite sex. However, there was the perennial teenage boy's consolation prize: he was a 'solid footballer', according to Robert Azavedo.

'I was fanatical about [football] in those days,' Declan later recalled. 'I was always a Liverpool supporter. I suppose my hero was Roger Hunt.'[11]

Hunt was soon fighting for heroic status with those other Scouse legends, The Beatles. The first single Declan had bought with his own money was 'Please Please Me', released in March 1963.* It was the beginning of an obsession, and not merely with the Fab Four. Although *With The Beatles* was his first LP purchase and he joined The Beatles' fan club in 1965, he was avidly consuming all kinds of pop music.

'From the time I was eleven to sixteen – only five years, but five pretty important years in your life – I concentrated on pop music and the changing trends,'[12] he recalled. He could afford to be choosy. His tastebuds, already sharpened on jazz and the classic American songbook, were highly sophisticated for one so young. Initially it was The Kinks, The Who, Merseybeat and classic Motown sides, rather than Buddy Holly, Cliff Richard or Chuck Berry. In his mid-teens his tastes became even more refined, encompassing reggae and the songs of Burt Bacharach, Aretha Franklin, Marvin Gaye and Dusty Springfield.

Ross's position with the Joe Loss Orchestra ensured that Declan had access to many record company acetate copies of the very latest singles before they were officially released to the public. As Declan moved into his teens and became more aware of the inherent *nowness* of the classic pop single, it became a genuinely thrilling experience to get his hands on copies of the newest sounds a couple of weeks before anyone else, made all the more exhilarating due to his good fortune in being a teenager slap-bang in the middle of the pop single's peak years.

---

* The purchase is celebrated in the mathematical autobiography of '45', from 2002's *When I Was Cruel*.

His record collection was soon far larger than the standard pocket money allowance of a child his age would normally permit, and unlike most people's fathers Ross knew all the hip songs spinning on his turntable. Not just the songs, but often the chords and the lyrics as well; he might even have been on nodding terms with the band. It was this innate good fortune that fostered Declan's sense of musical superiority, which endured through thick and thin. He didn't look for – nor did he require – approval for what he was going to do with his life.

'He was a big dreamer,' recalls Myers schoolmate Dale Fabian. 'All he was interested in was his beloved Liverpool FC and becoming a famous musician. This didn't ever seem likely to his classmates, who frequently ridiculed him.'

The jeers of his classmates would not go unfelt or unforgotten, but the sense of otherness wouldn't distract Declan from his vocation; indeed, it fuelled him over and over and over again. 'When it comes down to it, *they* don't know what *I* know,' he would say years later. 'It sounds arrogant, but that happens to be the way it is.'[13]

The transition into secondary education coincided with Declan beginning to take a much more serious interest in playing music. Initially, he toyed with the school's formal music classes, but found them stifling.

'The music teaching was laughable. I could sing, so I sang in the school choir, but then my voice got too loud and they threw me out. Then I became an altar boy because of the solemn face, but I got thrown out at fourteen for laughing, because the priest used to mumble everything except the church plate takings.'[14]

Perhaps understandably, the lack of spontaneity and excitement in these mundane experiences would put him off formal music training for the best part of twenty-five years. Instead, he started to get to grips with things on his own terms. He had had an acoustic guitar since he was nine years old, a gut-stringed Spanish guitar his father had bought him; it had all but been ignored until his early teens. Now he began tinkering, and despite an initial reluctance to follow in Ross's footsteps, he quickly came to the conclusion that this was his calling; he also realised, with typical self-assurance, that he was potentially very good at it. 'I knew I had a career when I was fourteen,' he later claimed. 'It just took a long time for me to work out how to do it. But I knew exactly what I wanted to do.'[15]

Although he was far from a natural on the guitar, he worked around his limitations with characteristic determination, and began writing his own songs straight away. The first one was called 'Winter', a cheery little

17

number kicking off in E-minor. It has long since been consigned to the dustbin of musical history.

*　*　*

Life was changing. The final two years of the '60s saw the security and assurance of family life begin to break apart. Already something of a loner with a growing awareness that life could be a melancholy experience, Declan became even more self-sufficient, and a little more cynical.

'I wouldn't say I was raised on romance,' he would sing just a few years later in 'Pay It Back', a rueful nod back to the events of 1969 when his parent's marriage reached the end of the road. Around the same time, his father fell in love with a singer called Sara Thompson, many years his junior, which marked the final and most significant of all the changes Ross had made to his life. He had left the Joe Loss Orchestra in 1968 after fourteen years' service, finally ready to go it alone. From then on, he effectively became a solo cabaret artist, continuing to make a very comfortable living by singing and playing the trumpet all over the country, augmented with regular TV and radio work.

Ross had already scored a No. 15 hit in Germany in 1966 with the self-penned ska tune 'Patsy Girl', backed by The Joe Loss Blue Beats. Later, he caused a minor stir with a version of The Beatles' 'The Long And Winding Road', released under the name Day Costello, the surname taken from Ross's maternal grandmother. But the staples of his solo career were themed albums concentrating on one particular genre or artist: these included *Ross MacManus Sings Frank Sinatra; Day Costello Sings Elvis Presley's Greatest Hits;* and *Ross MacManus Sings Roy Orbison.* Predictable fare, perhaps, but at last he was getting the opportunity to map out his own career.

Meanwhile, Declan was laying the foundations for a solo career of his own. During these domestic upheavals he had continued to persevere with the guitar, writing and improving with typical fortitude. There was even the odd appearance – including one at Archbishop Myers – with his dad, usually consisting of him sitting in unobtrusively on guitar while Ross played his set.

Both Ross and Lilian had been full of quiet encouragement, despite understandable misgivings. 'My parents were aware of the dangers and pitfalls and disappointments of [the music business],' said Declan. 'But they never discouraged me. They were very conscious of not putting me off it.'[16]

An important part of their level-headed support was allowing their son the time to find his feet. They had little choice. Declan heavily discouraged Ross and Lilian from attending his first-ever solo public appearance, which came early in the summer of 1970. The Crypt at St Elizabeth's in Richmond was a fixture in the London folk scene, with a welcome lack of ceremony. 'If you played acoustic guitar you could basically get up there,' Declan recalled. 'It was very open.'[17]

The Crypt became a weekly outing for Declan during the school summer holidays, first to watch a parade of folk talent and then later to play. The night of his first appearance he happened to perform in front of Ewan MacColl, the author of such folk standards as 'Dirty Old Town' and a rather austere presence by all accounts. MacColl wasn't necessarily impressed with Declan's set of 'little sensitive teenage songs'.[18]

'He sat there, head bowed all the way through my set,' he recalled. 'I'm sure he just nodded off. I had a traumatic first appearance; [it] was pretty crushing.'[19] However, he remained undeterred, and spent the remainder of the summer confirming over and over again what he already knew in his heart: that this was what he wanted to do with his life.

* * *

At the end of the summer he moved to Liverpool. 'It was question of going home, really,'[20] he later claimed. 'I was born in London but I was christened in Birkenhead. My mother's from Liverpool and my father's from Birkenhead. I went to school in London for most of my life, but all my holidays were in Merseyside.'[21]

This was putting a brave face on things. The notion of 'going home' was rather fanciful. In reality, Declan may have felt he had little option but to leave London. He had just turned sixteen, and planned to go onto sixth form at school and complete his final two years of education. And although Declan had great affection for Liverpool and knew the city and Birkenhead well, living there was a different proposition: as an only child he was pained by the break up of his parent's marriage and the enforced separation from his father, his musical mentor and friend, as much as a parental figure. He felt the absence keenly.

Declan and Lilian moved to the West Derby area of Liverpool, only a stone's throw from where the now-defunct Channel Four soap opera *Brookside* was filmed. As an added boon for Declan, West Derby also bordered Anfield, home of Liverpool FC, and he would take every available opportunity to go there, often alone. The house was new, a semi-detached brick building in a neat suburban area that was neither upmarket nor dowdy. Although relations between Lilian and Ross were understandably distant, Ross and Declan's close relationship survived the marital strife.* His father was a frequent visitor to Merseyside, to see his son, naturally, but also to visit his own mother in Birkenhead, and to play the odd gig at British Legions and similar venues.

On occasion, Declan would join the band and play a little guitar, once venturing as far afield as Blackpool. It afforded him a low-key but tempting taste of the professional musician's life.

Liverpool would be Declan's home for over two years. In late August 1970, he started at Campion School in Salisbury Street, Everton, a lay Catholic school previously known as St Francis Xavier Bi-Lateral School and still often referred to in Liverpool as SFX. He entered the sixth form to sit his A-Levels, and found the atmosphere entirely different from his experiences in the capital.

'It was very much two years behind London,' he later recalled. 'I'd gone to school in Hounslow, and you had to like Tamla and reggae otherwise you were dead. But then I went [to Liverpool] and you didn't dare say you liked Tamla, you had to like Deep Purple or something.'[22]

Ross was going through a psychedelic phase in his early forties, growing his hair long and reading Herman Hesse. Perhaps in sympathy, Declan adopted the Grateful Dead as his personal group. 'Nobody else liked them and you had to have a group that you liked,' he remembered. 'I used to sit at home going, "Please make me like the Grateful Dead!".'[23] He eventually talked himself into it.

Declan made little effort to integrate socially, and as a result had few friends, mainly by choice rather than design. A stubbornly independent youngster, he began to devour books and newspapers, forming the rather idealistic social consciousness typical of many intelligent teenagers. He also drew increasingly close to his immediate family: his mother in Liverpool, his father in London, and his grandmother in Birkenhead.** He was a frequent visitor to her house, and the area made a permanent imprint on his brain, providing the geographical location for many of his songs: the shipyards of Cammell Laird in 'Shipbuilding'; the 'sedated homes' of 'Little Palaces'; the departing émigré of 'Last Boat Leaving'; and the enduringly affectionate tribute of 'Veronica' are but four examples of dozens of lyrical snapshots which have their emotional heart in the tight terraced streets and docks around his grandmother's house in Conway Street.

Football and music were the twin cornerstones. Aside from going along to watch Liverpool play on the odd Saturday, Declan busied himself by making tentative forays into the less-than-happening local music scene. The

---

* Ross and Sara finally married in 1975, and went on to have four children: Ruari, Ronan, Liam and Kieran, who currently play in London group Riverway.
** By the time Declan moved to Liverpool, his grandfather Pat had passed away.

Merseybeat boom had long gone, the demise of The Beatles a symbolic sign that times had changed. Now it was heavy rock and folk music. However, the more progressive, intuitive folk culture which Declan had tentatively dipped a toe into in London was made of much grimmer stuff up north, and he was floundering in his attempts to find a foothold in a music scene which was all but moribund. 'I found a scene dominated by Jacqui & Birdie and sub-Spinners people and it was like running into a brick wall,' he said. 'It was horrendous.'24 The clubs wanted folk music of the most traditional kind: Ralph McTell's 'Streets Of London', Ewan MacColl's 'Dirty Old Town', the usual crowd-pleasers. There was little appetite for original songs and it was a harsh, unforgiving atmosphere for anyone who wanted to play contemporary music or try something individual.

Aware of Declan's frustration, Ross tried to help his son by introducing him to a rock band/art collective called The Medium Theatre, who also ran a poetry magazine called *Medium*. Well, it *was* the early '70s. Ross had some vague Liverpool links with members of the band and had also donated something along the lines of £10 to the magazine to help with publishing costs. The members of the group were slightly older than Declan, and his father hoped that they might help the sixteen-year-old integrate into whatever was happening in Liverpool at the time.

Allan Mayes was one of the boys involved with The Medium Theatre, and much more interested in playing music than getting embroiled in the group's loftier artistic pretensions. A year older than Declan, Mayes first bumped into him at one of the band's get-togethers. 'I think he was just very uncomfortable; basically his dad had forced him into it,' he recalls.

It proved to be a blind alley, but Declan slowly sought out the right places to be seen; sympathetic environments such as Thursday nights at The Songwriter's Club in Broad Street, and the Remploy or Lamplight in Wallasey.

If he was playing at all during this period it was infrequently, but he was continuing to write. Perhaps influenced by the local beat-poet boom which was still going strong, he became involved with the school's sixth form magazine throughout 1971, contributing the occasional poem* and helping out on the editorial side.

But still Declan was having trouble finding his musical feet – until he bumped into Allan Mayes again at a party at mutual friend Zinnie Flynn's house on New Year's Eve, 1971. Mayes arrived at the party clutching his guitar and bumped into Declan, clutching his. Mayes had left Medium Theatre earlier that year, over what he rather grandly remembers as musical

---

* One poem ran, in part: 'If you want to be the King/Lying on a bed of gold/Take the sceptre of the Old/Take the sword and wear the crown/You're in your robes and on the stairway/ Looking down.'

differences. 'I wanted to be Crosby, Stills and Nash and [Medium Theatre] were still arty-farty,' he recalls, so he left and took the bass player with him, forming a drumless three-piece with bassist David Jago and harmony singer Alan Brown, labouring under the name of Rusty. Mayes began gigging around Liverpool, sometimes playing solo gigs in folk clubs, but more often working up a set with Rusty that included original material and cover songs by Crosby, Stills and Nash, Neil Young, Van Morrison and Bob Dylan.

It was the same kind of music that Declan had grown into. Having tentatively discovered country-flavoured American music via his rather reluctant immersion in the Grateful Dead's two 1970 albums – *Workingman's Dead* and *American Beauty* – he was growing to love The Byrds' *Sweetheart Of The Rodeo*, a record which would lead him to the door of Gram Parsons and untold country music riches. He was also feeling his way into The Band's *Music From Big Pink*, the debut offering from Bob Dylan's erstwhile backing band and an object lesson in the enduring musical arts of harmony, mystery and simplicity. 'When I was about eighteen, The Band were *it* for me,' he would later say. 'It was like receiving a letter from the other side of the world, a world you couldn't possibly understand, let alone visit.'[25]

Declan also loved Neil Young's debut album; Crosby, Stills, Nash and Young's *Deja Vu*; Van Morrison's *His Band And The Street Choir*; Joni Mitchell's *Blue*. Perhaps the most obscure – and downbeat – records on his turntable at the time were David Ackles' *The Road To Cairo* and *Subway To The Country*, both of which had a profound influence on Declan; he later rated Ackles as 'the greatest unheralded American song-writer of the late '60s'.[26] More conventionally, he favoured some of the less whimsical singer-songwriters of the time such as Randy Newman, Loudon Wainwright, Jackson Browne, Jesse Winchester – whose eponymous 1970 album had been produced by The Band's Robbie Robertson – and even James Taylor. It was either that or glam rock, and Declan had neither the physique nor the eyelashes for that.

The Medium Theatre encounter, though awkward and brief, served as an ice-breaker between Mayes and Declan, before the two got down to business. 'It was a matter of "Oh, here's a guy with a guitar who knows two Van Morrison songs",' says Mayes. '"He's my new best friend and to hell with drinking cider and chasing women".' As Declan later admitted, this 'wasn't the carousing crowd'.[27]

Instead, the two new friends ushered in 1972 sitting in an unoccupied bedroom for three hours, playing Neil Young's 'Heart Of Gold' 'a hundred times' and most of the first Crosby, Stills and Nash album. According to Mayes, almost every sentence they uttered started with 'Do you know?'

'"Do you know 'Brown Eyed Girl'?" "Do you know anything off the first Neil Young album?" "Do you know 'The Night They Drove Old Dixie Down'?" We weren't trying to impress anybody, we weren't trying to impress each other, it was just the fact that we had each found a soulmate.'

At the end of the night, the two swapped telephone numbers. Keen to keep the momentum going, Mayes called the next day to make arrangements to meet up again. This time, Declan was introduced to David Jago and Alan Brown, and Rusty had a new member.

Declan's guitar style may have left more to luck than chance, and his flirtation with open tuning was simply disastrous, but he and Mayes found they could harmonise instinctively. Like any young man trying to find his voice – both literally and figuratively – he was trying on different hats as both a vocalist and songwriter; his style would change from week to week depending on who he was listening to. 'He had all the Americanised phrasing,' says Mayes. 'He could sing like Robbie Robertson and Neil Young.'

Just three weeks into the New Year, on 21 January, 1972, the new Rusty line-up was unveiled at the Wallasey Lamplight. They played eleven songs, including Bob Dylan's 'The Mighty Quinn', 'Dance Dance Dance' by Neil Young, and Van Morrison's 'I've Been Working', as well as some original Rusty material written before Declan joined the band. They also played a new song by Declan, called 'Warm House', and took home £7 between the four of them.

It was the beginning of a concerted onslaught on the less glamourous venues of the north-west of England. Though Declan was still in sixth form, the band naturally claimed precedence over his academic work, but not everyone shared his view. Within a few months, both David Jago and Alan Brown left for college and Rusty became just Allan Mayes and Declan.

They weren't necessarily the greatest-looking duo on earth. Declan was still noticeably overweight, with scraggly long hair and a bizarre misunderstanding of what constituted style. 'He was always pretty geeky and even then he dressed like shit,' says Mayes. 'None of us was exactly snappy, but he dressed to the point where we'd both be laughing at him; these terrible chequered jackets and red shoes, big red Doc Martens.'

The duo played bars, clubs, schools, libraries, hotels, community centres, colleges, arts centres and even a cathedral; anywhere that would have them. Their packed schedule wasn't really a reflection on their talents. The local scene was more the 1970's equivalent of karaoke: virtually anybody could walk in with a guitar and play a few songs.

Declan didn't drive, so Mayes would pick him up. Mostly it was Liverpool, but there were regular visits to Birkenhead, and occasional trips out of town to pubs in Widnes, Wigan, Manchester and even London. If they were playing at a poetry night, their musical intervention was tolerated as long as they didn't play anything too poppy; gentler numbers by The Band, Neil Young, Bob Dylan, Randy Newman, Simon and Garfunkel and Loudon Wainwright were the order of the day, interspersed with original songs from both Mayes and MacManus and usually topped off with their show-stopping version of the Crosby, Stills and Nash classic, 'Wooden Ships'.

If they were playing somewhere like the Crow's Nest Hotel in Widnes or the Fox and Grapes in Birkenhead, a slightly less sensitive side would be required. On these occasions, Allan and Declan included songs that people recognised from the charts and could sing along to: a Slade or a Rod Stewart number, or a '60s favourite such as 'Happy Together' by The Turtles.

Rusty played eighty-eight gigs in 1972, the year in which Declan could justifiably claim to have first become a working musician. But it was never a band based on a great social bond. 'We never did the girl thing,' says Mayes. 'I don't remember him ever drinking. I don't remember any rock 'n' roll camaraderie, but then I don't remember us ever having an argument, either.'

They played mostly to sympathetic audiences where people would listen, or at least not interrupt, but they quickly became used to a kind of polite apathy. 'Ninety per cent of the room when we were playing was full of other musicians,' reckons Mayes. 'The only people who weren't musicians were wives, girlfriends or someone who was a friend of somebody. There was no one booking us. We'd just go and play for nothing. There was no actual drawing power of people on the street.' It was essentially background music.

* * *

In the early summer of 1972, Declan sat his final exams and left Campion. He escaped with one A-level in English, insufficient for college or university even if he had shown the inclination. Virtually everybody who has ever worked with him over the years picks up on his daunting brainpower and ability to assimilate information at an astounding rate; The Brodsky Quartet's Paul Cassidy describes his brain as 'turbo charged', while composer Richard Harvey even goes as far as to rate him as 'one of the three or four most intelligent people I've ever met'. Clearly, he would have done better in his exams had he been inclined to put the hours in.

But life was overtaken by music. At the same time as he was enduring his final exams, Rusty secured a weekly Tuesday night residency at the Temple Bar on Liverpool's Dale Street, which would have been far bigger news to Declan. The venue became a home-from-home for Rusty, their weekly spots continuing virtually uninterrupted from 6 June right up until Christmas.

The end of school meant the beginning of a greater sense of freedom. Over the Thursday, Friday and Saturday of 13–15 July, he and Allan drove down to London, staying with Ross and Sara. It was the first time Allan had met Declan's dad, and he remembers him being 'off the radar' compared to other people's fathers.

'He had a copy of *Playboy* on the coffee table and loads of LPs and could talk about 'King Of The Road'. It was just too bizarre for me. Dads were supposed to be: "Get your bloody hair cut," yet this guy was: "Grow your hair, son, and have you heard the new Grateful Dead album?" It was just too weird.'

While in London, Rusty played gigs at the New Bards Folk Club, the Half Moon in Putney and the Troubabdour in south Kensington, supporting Ralph McTell, Bridget St John and Swan Arcade for free. Significantly, over the same long weekend they also took in an all-nighter in London featuring Lou Reed and Brinsley Schwarz.

In 1972, Brinsley Schwarz had just released their third album, *Silver Pistol*. Their first two records – *Despite It All* and *Brinsley Schwarz* – had been lumpen, progressive affairs, and the band were looking to change direction and take on board a neater, sharper sound. They were managed by the garrulous, no-nonsense Irishman Dave Robinson, who worked as tour manager for Jimi Hendrix in the late '60s. Robinson subsequently went into PR, and 'masterminded' the Brinsleys' disastrous launch in New York in 1970, when a planeload of British journalists were flown over to watch the band play at the Filmore East and had returned distinctly unimpressed. Despite that blip, in his capacity as manager and a promoter, Robinson was an essential component in creating the nascent pub-rock scene in London in the early '70s, helping to turn Brinsley Schwarz into the movement's leading band and their singer and bassist Nick Lowe into perhaps its finest songwriter.

One night in 1971, Robinson had stumbled upon a San Franciscan band called Eggs Over Easy playing at the Tally Ho! pub in Kentish Town, north London. In such inauspicious surroundings, they had shown him the light. 'It was Eggs Over Easy who I essentially stole the idea of pub-rock from,' he admits. 'Here were four guys playing three-minute songs, one after the other, great singers, great playing, great style.'

Knocked out by what he heard, Robinson whisked the band off to meet Brinsley Schwarz at the group's communal house in Northwood, Middlesex. Eggs Over Easy played for – and with – the Brinsleys all night, and by the morning they had passed on the torch. 'The penny dropped that here were people who were real musicians, real songwriters and they could teach the Brinsleys,' says Robinson. 'I was doing my best to drag them out of the Stone Age of English prog music. And they did learn. Nick Lowe learned very quickly, and it came from that.'

Robinson helped Eggs Over Easy build a following at the Tally Ho! and spread the word around town. He began getting the Brinsleys gigs, then another outfit called Ducks Deluxe, until the Tally Ho! swiftly became the hub of the new scene. In this way, the classic pub-rock prototype of the band who could play a bit of everything that was deemed right-eous and good – country, R&B, blues, rock, funk – was born.

Soon there were hundreds of them, but the rejuvenated Brinsley Schwarz were at the top of the tree. From the goodtime, bar-room piano roll of 'Dry Land' through the Hammond-soaked 'Merry Go Round' to the final, slipper-wearing lilt of 'Rockin' Chair', *Silver Pistol* was a laid-back, home-cooked slice of whimsy and charm, very much of its time. It hasn't dated particularly well, and yet placed in context its Anglo take on the rural American sound was significant.

For Declan – hopelessly smitten with The Band and the charms of Americana, and looking for something closer to home about which to get excited – *Silver Pistol* was a watershed. 'If you really want to know the album that changed Declan's life, it was *Silver Pistol*,' says Mayes. 'We played everything off that album live.' Indeed. At the final Rusty gig in June 1973, the duo played no less than eight Brinsley Schwarz covers, including four from the record.

The band became Declan's new obsession. He went to see the Brinsleys whenever he could, both in London and Liverpool, and some time in 1972 he bumped into Nick Lowe, as he was preparing for a show at The Cavern Club in his favoured fashion. 'We were playing at the Cavern, and we were in The Grapes across the road, sitting there having a cock-tail before getting ourselves set,' Lowe later recalled. 'He came in, and somebody said, "Look, there's that weird-looking geezer who's been at a few of our shows." And I thought, "Well, it's about time I bought him a pint and I introduced myself," because he never used to come back stage or anything.' [28]

The two hit it off, talking exclusively about music. 'I seem to remember at that time, Jesse Winchester we were keen on, and Bobby Charles & The Amazing Rhythm Aces. When you meet someone and you shove a couple of names out and they react to it, you think, "Oh, this is a pretty decent guy".' [29] Declan frequently looked Nick up at Brinsleys' gigs there-after. It was to become a key friendship.

* * *

Wherever Rusty performed they would play several of Declan's own compositions: 'Warm House'; 'Sleeper At The Wheel'; 'Sunflower Lancers'; 'Two Day Rain'; 'Dull Echoes'; 'Are You Afraid Of Your Children'; 'Sweet Deceiver' and many more* poured out around this time.

Although he was really only cutting his teeth as a writer, it was quickly apparent to Allan Mayes that this was somebody with an unusual amount of talent. 'It was staggering, really. Every time he played a new song I knew that the songs I were writing were just a joke. He'd sit down and go into this intense shit, shut everything else off, play the damn song and immediately I loved it. But I have no memory of anybody ever saying, "God! His songs are stunning, aren't they?". I was the only one who ever thought that.'

Lyrically, the tracks were staunchly impenetrable, and read today the words tend to sit awkwardly on the page: 'Sunflower lancers, where do you go/Out in the morning, out in the cold/Rings of silver, rings of gold/ These I will bring to save me,' is the creaking opening salvo to 'Sunflower Lancers'. It doesn't get much better. Later, he muses: 'Old night-time story's endless refrain/"Lady, have you come to save me?".'

'Dull Echoes' – not perhaps the most tempting of song titles – evokes similarly pastoral images, again with a distinctive, early '70s hippy flavour: 'My mandolin picks out of time/And out of tune as well/A simple song I learnt a while ago/ While you were sleeping.' And later: 'Go down to the water/And lay down at the water's edge/My waterfall is endless/But I also have a fountain.'

'Two Day Rain' is at least a little more promising. 'Do you fit your situation to someone else's song?' he asks in the middle, and it's tempting to hear a soon-to-be characteristic sneer in the voice; while the concluding bitter-sweet flourish is genuinely affecting in a way that the future, invented Elvis Costello persona would no doubt have scoffed at: 'Look at what you had to sell/Because you said goodbye/ No sweeter than you said farewell.'

Allan Mayes admits to having absolutely no idea what Declan was trying to say, with one exception. 'Warm House' was one of the best things we ever did,' he says. 'It was about thinking he was going to get beaten up while walking the streets on the way to a gig. This was back in the skinhead days, when it was not unknown in Liverpool to get jumped for no reason. I remember him saying, "God, I was so glad when I got to the club, because I was sure these guys were going to beat me up and steal my guitar".' Declan himself has long been dismissive and characteristically unrevealing of his earliest attempts at songwriting. 'Like

* One of them 'Maureen And Sam', co-written with Mayes, would later turn up in rewritten form as 'Ghost Train' on the *New Amsterdam* EP, released in March 1980.

anybody's first steps at doing anything, you wouldn't want to put them under the microscope,' he has reflected. 'They were probably pretty awful.'[30]

* * *

No longer tied to school, Declan began seeking out employment. He wasn't looking for any long-term career outside of music, but with the work ethic and the idea of earning his keep already firmly instilled in him, he went for anything that was going in the newspaper. With his A-level in English, he was thought unsuited for the role of tea boy. He was briefly considered for the arcane job of Admiralty Chart Corrector in a 'Dickensian office', but his handwriting wasn't up to scratch. Eventually he got a job working with computers in a large centre run by the Midland Bank.

When he finally broke through in 1977, Declan's work with computers – along with the glasses – would be one of the major incriminating factors adding fuel to the flames of his carefully cultivated geek persona, but the truth was far more prosaic. It was not the hi-tech, highly-attuned vocation that it is today, and required little skill. 'I knew nothing about computers,' he said in the '80s, back in what was still the dark ages of that particular type of technology. 'But really all that's irrelevant. It's just button-pushing and dealing with tapes and printers. It's manual work, really, but it has a sort of status attached to it because it's modern technology.'[31]

His new job also revealed a problem with his eyes. Until the age of sixteen his sight had been fine, but working every day with computers made him realise it had deteriorated. He started wearing glasses to correct astigmatism, although at first it was only to read or watch television. 'He'd wear glasses occasionally,' says Allan Mayes. 'These trendy, *Easy Rider*-types.' The famous horn rims wouldn't come until much later on.

Employment made little impact on Rusty's rounds of folk clubs, schools and *ad hoc* poetry meetings. There were occasional appearances at a concert hall as part of a one-off event, but they were few and far between. Nevertheless, the duo got to tread the boards at such notable venues as Liverpool University and St George's Hall. A poster advertising the entertainments on offer at a charity folk concert at the College Hall, Widnes on Friday, 15 December, 1972 lists Rusty as fifth – or if you prefer, bottom – of the bill, beneath such luminaries as Bullock Smithy Folk Group and Cyder Pye. Admission was 40p.

Declan's parents continued to encourage the young singer in his musical ambitions, with the clear proviso that he did most of the legwork himself. But Ross wasn't averse to using his connections in the music business to give Declan a nudge in the right direction. One night, as Rusty were setting up to play in the Yankee Clipper club in Liverpool, Declan mentioned to Allan that Ross had got them a job accompanying him in the studio to record a song for a lemonade commercial.

'I remember almost doing a lap of honour around that club, thinking "Oh, studio!",' says Mayes. 'As far I was concerned, it was the most glorious moment of my life.' As the months went by, Allan kept pestering his partner about the advert, until one day Declan simply turned around and said: 'I did it last weekend.'

'I've never been so dejected in my life and I have never forgotten it,' Mayes recalls. The song that Ross and Declan recorded for the R. Whites lemonade advert became somewhat legendary, running on British television between 1973 and 1984. The ridiculously catchy jingle – 'I'm a, I'm a, I'm a, I'm a secret lemonade drinker' – marked Declan's studio debut, adding his already distinctive backing vocals behind Ross's voice of the drinker.* He would have made only a little pocket money from the recording session, but it was another invaluable experience, and one he clearly had little inclination to share.

Soon afterwards, in early 1973, Declan decided to move back to London. 'I came back to London after two years because I realised there wasn't any scene in Liverpool to get into,' he later remembered. 'It was completely dead.'[32]

The dreary combination of traditional folk music and serious rock based on a love of Yes, Caravan or Led Zeppelin were the twin alternatives in Liverpool, and held little appeal. Meeting Nick Lowe had made a profound impact on the way he perceived his own music. While Allan Mayes' later claim that Declan 'went chasing Nick Lowe' to London is perhaps rather overstating the case, the rapport with a like-minded soul and the possibilities of the kind of music he could play in London was highly significant in his move back south.

Declan rather half-heartedly sounded out Allan as to whether he was also willing to make the move, but Mayes was reluctant. 'I was going on twenty, but still way too scared to take that kind of chance,' he says. 'I wasn't prepared to starve for my art.' Rusty's unlamented last stand was two shows supporting Steve Harley and Cockney Rebel on 24 June, 1973

* So successful was the commercial that a Secret Lemonade Drinker fan club was set up, a R. Whites football team played their matches in pyjamas, and there was even a Secret Lemonade Drinker handicap horse race held at Lingfield Park. In 2000, it was voted the seventh favourite advert ever in the UK.

at Warwick University in Coventry, booked months previously. Declan travelled north from London and Allan travelled south, before they finally went their separate ways. They would keep in touch – with increasing infrequency – up until the early 1980s.

So Declan went to London alone: to his dad; to the heart of the music business; to a burgeoning pub-rock scene. He was ready for something new. There were probably a hundred good reasons for going back home.

Chapter Two
1973–75

MARY BURGOYNE WAS JUST EIGHTEEN at the time she became Declan's first serious girlfriend. Although the exact circumstances of their initial introduction are unclear, the couple met in 1973 and were very much an item by the end of the year. Mary lived on the Redwood Estate, Cranford Lane in Heston, just off the M4 motorway and a few miles from Heathrow airport, where she worked.

They had much in common. Her Irish roots were stronger than Declan's: although she may have had an English accent, she had been born in the Republic of Ireland, but had moved to Britain as a child. Mary was also an avid music fan, a factor which would have played a significant part in the attraction. Although her father – Patrick Victor Burgoyne, known as Vic – was a salesman by trade, he had been a veteran of the thriving Irish dance band culture back home.

Allan Mayes recalls meeting Mary briefly when she accompanied Declan on one of his family forays back to Liverpool and being impressed. 'I clearly remember thinking, didn't you overachieve!' he says. Mary was very pretty, with a passing resemblance to the actress Jenny Agutter, a favourite of Declan's. She was also bright, loquacious, funny, temperemental, with a bouyant sense of humour, and by all accounts could give as good as she got in the intense battles which tended to characterise her time with Declan.

'The two of them were that classic thing: couldn't live with each other, couldn't live without each other,' recalls Steve Hazelhurst, who began playing with Declan in 1974. 'When they were together they were always scrapping.' The relationship quickly became serious.

Declan had returned to London in the early spring of 1973, having arranged a transfer to Midland Bank's computer centre in Putney. He moved in with Ross and Sara, with whom he had apparently established an amiable relationship, at 16 Beaulieu Close in Twickenham Park.

His first gig back on home turf took place on 18 April, a mixed set of covers and originals in the Barmy Army pub in Twickenham. Although he was still going out solo, he was already beginning to forge the friendships that would help him establish Flip City, the first significant band of his career. Ken Smith – who now runs the Elsubsta record label in south London – became their *de facto* manager by virtue of booking gigs, having a few budding contacts in the record industry, organising occasional recordings and being singularly unable to play any musical instrument.

Smith first bumped into Declan in the late spring or early summer of 1973, at The Royal Charter in Kingston upon Thames, a music pub better known to its regulars as The Three Fishes. Declan had some new friends in tow: the first was Michael Kent – known to all as Mich* – whom Declan had met at a Brinsley Schwarz gig in St Pancras Town Hall not long before. The other was Malcolm Dennis, who knew Mich from school. A bass player and drummer respectively, they were slightly older than Declan, but soon came together, united by their similar tastes.

The DJ at The Three Fishes played a lot of San Franciscan music: everyone was into the Grateful Dead, while Clover – who eventually backed Declan on his first album – were also popular. Bruce Springsteen had just recently appeared, and Declan took to his first two records – *Greetings From Astbury Park, NJ* and *The Wild, The Innocent & The E Street Shuffle* – with relish, probably because they were wordy, musically rich and clearly influenced by Van Morrison. He also still loved The Band,** and indeed all the future members of Flip City bonded over their mysterious, timeless sound and the superlative songwriting of Robbie Robertson. On the British side of the Atlantic, pub-rock was burgeoning in the capital. 'I was totally into the pub-rock scene at the time,' recalls Ken Smith. 'Going off to see Kilburn & The High Roads, Ducks Deluxe and all those bands. Brinsley Schwarz were my favourites and Dec had seen the Brinsleys in Liverpool and London, so there was kind of common ground.'

Declan went to see the Brinsleys on so many occasions, that by 1974 he was regarded by the band as 'a part-time' roadie. Maybe he was 'chasing' Lowe after all. Certainly, following the band at close quarters made him take a long, hard look at his own songwriting. If Liverpool had been a time of melancholy and meandering poetic musings, London brought him back down to earth with a satisfying bump.

---

* Pronounced 'Mish'

** 'Declan loved that set-up, as we all did,' says Ken Smith. 'I always thought The Band were the most convincing white band doing music based on deep soul,' Declan later agreed. 'I thought they were the best. They kind of invented their own version of it, almost by accident. They were men, and yet they weren't dressing up as cowboys or anything. The sexuality was taken for granted. It wasn't phoney.'[1]

He was trying to write cleaner, crisper songs with a snappier musical accompaniment, moving away from the gentler acoustic sound of Rusty. Following long nights listening to Declan talk a good game in The Three Fishes, Ken Smith was eager to check out his mettle as a musician. He knew little about Rusty. Much as he would remain staunchly guarded about his past when he finally became successful in 1977, Declan was typically cagey with his London friends in 1973. 'We didn't really know anything about [Liverpool],' remembers Ken Smith. 'We knew he lived there but I never quite got the whole story.'

Smith first caught up with Declan at Southlands College in Wimbledon, playing a repertoire covering everything from Gerry Rafferty's 'Can I Have My Money Back?' to Hank Williams classics like 'You Win Again'. He kicked off the set solo, before being joined by Mich Kent and Malcolm Dennis.

As with many fledgling bands, the music was secondary: finding a name was the most pressing problem. The first gig at Southlands was billed as The Bizzario Brothers. Another mooted name – the even less inspired Mother Truckers, mercifully never used – was soon jettisoned in favour of Flip City. The inspiration came from Joni Mitchell's version of the Annie Ross song 'Twisted', where in the background the listener can hear Cheech & Chong babbling inanely about 'Flip City'. It was Mary Burgoyne who suggested using it and it stuck. She had good ears. 'Mary knew what she was talking about as far as music was concerned,' says Ken Smith. 'And she was way into the country [music] thing.'

Although it was one of the few musical forms that he hadn't had immediate access to as a boy, country music was becoming more and more important to Declan. '[It] had never really got into our household,' he says. 'So I discovered it for myself.'[2]

Allan Mayes has no recollection of Declan having a passionate interest in country in Liverpool; he certainly never saw any George Jones or Hank Williams records in the house. But through his love of The Band, the Grateful Dead and The Byrds, Declan had discovered what could loosely be called Americana, and was gradually tracing a rich seam of musical history back towards its source. Thus, Gram Parson's involvement on The Byrds' *Sweetheart Of The Rodeo* album lead him to the Flying Burrito Brothers' *Gilded Palace Of Sin*, and later the first two Parsons solo records: *GP* and *Grevious Angel*, released in 1973 and 1974 respectively. These in turn led him back to the even more elemental, traditional music of legends like George Jones, Hank Williams and Merle Haggard. 'I was curious to find out who these country singers were that these people were covering,' he later said.[3]

What he discovered was not the glitzy, rhinestone-clad kitsch of Kenny Rogers or the faux-authenticity of Boxcar Willie, but raw, powerful music steeped in simple, emotional phrasing. The central tenets of country music – the romanticising of the mundane realities of domesticity; the elevation of the simple man and woman to mythical status; the way that heartfelt and often painful emotions were laid out plainly and unashamedly; the unique mixture of bar-room machismo and bedroom self-deprecation – all appealed to Declan and would slowly start to inform his songwriting. Mary, hailing from a family steeped in the showband culture of Ireland in which country music is revered, knew her Hank Williams from her Hank Snow and would have been something of a kindred spirit along the way. And with Declan and Mary embarking on a relationship which some-times seemed to echo that of George Jones and Tammy Wynette in terms of its emotional volatility, the music must have made just that little bit more sense.

* * *

Flip City continued to progress. By 1974, the band and the friendships within it had developed sufficiently for Declan to leave Ross and Sara's home in Twickenham and move in with the rest of the group, who were living together at a shared cost of £32 a month in a semi-detached house at 3 Stag Lane, Roehampton, on the fringes of Wimbledon Common in south-west London.

By now, Declan was working at the Elizabeth Arden cosmetics company on Wales Farm Road, north Acton,* operating an IBM 360 computer in a small office next to the factory. He was generally left to his own devices, trying to stave off the more dispiriting bouts of boredom the job brought on.

Although he had slowly become a competent guitar player, especially adept at working out particular parts and sticking to them, Declan was not confident when it came to improvising; the band decided they needed another guitarist to fill out the sound and began holding auditions.

Steve Hazelhurst had moved to London from Cumbria in 1971, seeking the gold-paved road to rock 'n' roll glory. He failed to find it, to the extent that he was even passed over in the first Flip City audition. However, when the guitarist initially chosen didn't work out, the band called Hazelhurst back to see if he was still interested. He was, and with Mich's

* The factory building was directly off the Western Avenue, and his trip on the 105 bus to and from work every day took him past an art deco building which housed a factory that made vacuum cleaners, a journey which later found itself literally transposed into 'Hoover Factory'.

34

workmate Dickie Faulkner also joining on harmony vocals and percussion in early 1974, the five-piece band started to click.

The vibe Flip City were searching for was a uniquely American alchemy, a laid-back, seamless groove which bands like Little Feat, Clover and The Band could produce with deceptive ease, and of which Brinsley Schwarz were the leading British practitioners. This particular collection of young, pale Englishmen, however, found it somewhat less easy to replicate. They were just one of hundreds of pub-rock bands in London at that time, and their setlist reflected their lack of originality. 'We totally copied the blueprint of the Brinsleys,' said Declan. 'You had to have one R&B song, one country song, a few songs you had written yourself, a Dylan song. It was totally nicked from that.'[4]

Under Ken Smith's guidance, Flip City began finding gigs around London: the North Pole pub in North Pole Road, W10; Southland College in Wimbledon; a street festival in Fitrozvia; even a residency at the highly sought-after Kensington Tavern in Russell Gardens. A true landmark, the Kensington was where future Attraction Pete Thomas first laid eyes on Declan, when he came to see Flip City play at the behest of his friend Ken Smith. The drummer of London pub-rock stalwarts Chilli Willi and The Red Hot Peppers, Thomas walked out after about thirty seconds. 'I think he came to see our worst-ever gig,' said Declan.[5]

They would often open with 'Pontiac Blues' from The Youngbloods *Good 'N' Dusty* LP. 'Loverman' by Redwing was also a regular, alongside Clover's 'Sound Of Thunder'. More conventionally, there were usually a couple of Sam Cooke songs – often 'Bring It On Home To Me' and 'Another Saturday Night' – sitting cheek by jowl alongside Dylan's 'It Takes A Lot To Laugh, It Takes A Train To Cry.' The songbooks of Smokey Robinson, Mose Allison, Chuck Berry and Jesse Winchester were all plundered; the only overtly country song – played in tongue-in-cheek, bluesy call-and-response style – was Hank Williams' 'You Win Again'. There was no image. In keeping with the ethos of the day, it was simply five scruffy working boys in jeans and shirts who wanted to let the music do the talking.

As well as continuing to immerse himself in the deep well of classic American music, throughout 1974 Declan continued to improve his writing. Very few of the songs that he had played with Rusty had survived the transition; now he was writing with a band in mind, simpler songs driven by smart words, kiss-off sentiments and a tougher rhythmic dynamic. The first MacManus original most of the band recall hearing was an older song called 'Exile's Road', a sparky travelling narrative with a sweet uptempo tune and swift chord changes. Lyrically, it was inspired by his grandfather's travels and touched on the émigré themes that Declan would later return to in 'The Deportees Club', 'American Without Tears' and 'Last Boat Leaving': 'My best friend he took a trip/ While playing for his money on a cruising ship/He sailed across the ocean on a big ol' liner/ All the way to Rio and across to China.'

While 'Exile's Road' had its distinctive moments – the pay-off line concludes, 'You gotta sell the saddle when the horse is dying' – it didn't amount to much, glued together by a clunking introductory guitar riff which kept returning to the fray with all the subtlety of a day time game-show theme tune. Nonetheless, it was suitably accomplished in both construction and execution to impress his peers.

Like Allan Mayes before them, his new band members were immediately aware that Declan's songwriting talent had already developed far beyond the conventional case of the aspiring singer-songwriter whose ambition heavily outweighed his ability. And indeed, heard next to Flip City's other original material, such as Steve Hazelhurst's lumpen, derivative 'On The Road', 'Exile's Road' started to shine just a little brighter.

It was jauntier than the majority of Declan's more recent material. The hit-and-miss poetic images of the year before were almost entirely gone, and the beginning of a more caustic world view was beginning to creep in. The Springsteen-fronts-The-Drifters groove of 'Please Mister, Don't Stop The Band' was crammed with screeds of words, some of which he managed to assemble into clever lines: 'They took away all of your paper money/Better learn to laugh if you wanna be funny,' he snaps, and nearer the end he chides again: 'Better take your chances 'cos you don't get many/ Better take your turn or you don't get any.' But despite the welcome fuck-you tenor of the lyrics and the tone, the overall result was directionless.

'Sweet Revival' was better, based around the slick funk riff of Van Morrison's 'I've Been Working' and featuring Declan urging the object of his attentions to seize the day: 'Better do some of your living before you get old and grey.' The tone is bullying here, rather than cajoling. And later, 'The only time that you got is the time that you got now.' There was even a memorably uplifting chorus.

Other songs written around this period included the rambling 'Wreck On The Slide' (containing the line 'I feel like a juggler running out of hands,' later to surface on 'Welcome To The Working Week'), 'Flatfoot Hotel', 'Baseball Heroes' and 'Imagination (Is A Powerful Deceiver)'. Furthermore, Declan was already writing the material that would end up on his first two records: 'Pay It Back', 'Miracle Man', 'Living In Paradise' and 'Radio, Radio' were all taking shape in one form or another.

'Miracle Man', which appeared as the second track on *My Aim Is True*, was originally called 'Baseball Heroes', a fast-paced, humourous tale recounting the escapades of a struggling baseball team who are 'Sitting on the edge of a hometown ledge/Always waiting for that final run.' 'Baseball Heroes' had been suggested as a title by Ken Smith; Declan took it and ran all the way to home base. With wisecracking, Chandler-esque lines like: 'He pulled a Lucy from a Lucky Strike pack,' he was happily indulging his love affair with Americana and American English, and the song is a short slice of fun.

Later, he changed the words completely and announced to the band that 'Baseball Heroes' was now 'Miracle Man'. The opening stanzas are virtually the same, but this time around the mood is darker. Now the tongue-in-cheek scenario of a struggling baseball team has been transposed to signify a struggling relationship ('I put my best foot forward and fell on my face'). Only the chorus refrain and the line 'I never knew that so much trouble was resting upon reply' would survive the final transition to the *My Aim Is True* version. Alongside the change of words, the song had now been turned into a criminally slow shuffle, a fairly straight imitation of The Band in 'Up On Cripple Creek'-mode.

'Radio, Radio', meanwhile, started life as 'Radio Soul', a title which again came from Ken Smith, along with a few scrappy lyrics which Declan worked into something 'singable and meaningful'. 'Radio Soul' was as close as Flip City had to a signature tune; people who came to see the band would often identify it as the one song that stood out. It also sums up the basic differences between Declan MacManus and Elvis Costello, and between Flip City and The Attractions.

Although melodically virtually identical to the '78 version of 'Radio, Radio', the '74 incarnation of 'Radio Soul' is lyrically very different and moves at a gentler pace, with a Spanish-style sway and a rhythmic acoustic guitar underpinning it. More crucially, the early version is a straightforwardly affectionate nod to the wireless, rather than the withering attack it later became: Here, the celebration of 'the sound salvation' is distinctly non ironic. 'One thing we've got too much of/Is trouble, guess you know that's true/What we need is a little music/So we're here to entertain you.' The music tries to match the sentiments by contriving to conjure up a laid-back, good-time, west-coast feel. All very mellow, *very* mid-'70s.

In contrast, the '78 version is a snarling riot of guitars and organ underpinning Costello's vehement anti-establishment jibes. This time the band is fighting tooth-and-nail to cut Costello sufficient slack to contain his outpouring of disgust at the fools 'trying to anaesthetise the way that you feel'. The stuttering, characteristically new wave intro bookends the whole thing for added drama. It is effectively the same song as it was in 1974,

37

only this time very conciously manipulated and choreographed – contrived, even – to tie in with a new public persona and the prevailing mood of the times. And with an absolutely white-hot band behind him.

It would be an exaggeration to claim chameleon-like qualities on his behalf, but Declan MacManus became very aware of the best way to present his material for maximum impact at each stage in his career. He would later claim to have written songs such as 'Different Finger', 'Watch Your Step' and 'New Lace Sleeves' – all three appeared on *Trust* in 1981 – in the mid-'70s, although no Flip City member recalls hearing them. It could be that Declan was already consciously compartmentalising his musical life, stockpiling his more sophisticated or genre-specific material and only handing over songs he felt would suit the band's more straight-forward style. If this was the case, it certainly wouldn't be the last time he kept his choicest cards close to his chest.

The songs were strong, but still derivative. He was listening to Randy Newman's *Sail Away* and *Good Ol' Boy*, Van Dyke Parks's *Discover America*, Little Feat's *Sailing Shoes* and *Feats Don't Fail Me Now*, Joni Mitchells' *Blue* and *Court And Spark*, Lee Dorsey's *Yes We Can*, Steely Dan's *Countdown To Ecstasy*; Allan Touissant, Gram Parsons, John Prine's epnoymous 1972 album, The Band, Van Morrison and Bruce Springsteen, among many others. Vocally, he had developed a characteristic and highly stylised American drawl, which contained trace elements of Van Morrison and The Band's Rick Danko* in particular, both singers who placed the emphasis on soul-baring emotional resonance rather than technique or a detached stand-offishness. '"We gotta sound desperate!",' Ken Smith recalls Declan saying. 'He really loved that desperate sort of sound. If he heard it on a record, he'd really pick up on it. I remember one afternoon down at the house, me and him sat and played a load of albums, and we dissed about everybody apart from Bruce Springsteen and Van Morrison.'

Indeed, a live version of one of Flip City's best original songs, 'Imagination (Is A Powerful Deceiver)', recorded at the band's penultimate gig at the Red Cow in Hammersmith in November 1975, shows the extent to which Declan was apeing Morrison, right down to the extended, declaimed repetition – 'Turn out the light!' – at the song's conclusion, a characteristic Morrison trait which can be heard to full effect on his 1973 live masterpiece, *It's Too Late To Stop Now*. At the Red Cow, Declan's impassioned imitation merely earns him a smattering of polite applause,

---

* 'Rick Danko was my absolute hero. He had a unique style,' Declan later said. 'It was kind of nasal and it had a little bit of what I now realise to be country in it, but at the same time it was just so unusual to me.'[6] He could be describing himself.

a fair barometer of the kind of fervour that Flip City were failing to generate.

He also went to see one of Bruce Springsteen's now legendary 1975 shows at the Hammersmith Odeon. Joining him was Ken Smith, who remembers how Declan was immediately impressed by the emotional impact of the music. 'Springsteen started off with "Thunder Road", and after that first number Declan turned to me and he said, "He's done it. He's done it!". Straight away. That was it.'

Aside from playing and attending gigs, most of the activity centred around the house in Stag Lane, propelled by the kind of intense, late-night arguments common in most shared households. Declan quickly became the in-house *agent provocateur* on all subjects from politics, abortion, football and – of course – music. He loved to talk, and could argue the rest of the house under the table, but the atmosphere was usually lighthearted. 'It was a laugh,' says Hazelhurst. 'He had a great sense of humour. We always used to joke about Declan's taste in food. He'd suddenly emerge from the kitchen with a peanut-butter sandwich with blackberry jam with tomatoes on it. Really weird stuff.'

The behaviour was pretty restrained for a group of young men in their late teens and early twenties living together and playing music, but Declan – along with everyone else – was working full-time and it seems that partying was far from uppermost in his mind. He could never handle his drink, anyway. 'We used to go out and have a pint occasionally, but it wasn't an inspiration,' says Ken Smith. 'He sometimes used to like drinking Jamesons [Irish whiskey], but he needed watching after that. Drugs I never saw him take. Ever. He was more interested in getting an album by somebody and listening to it. He got quite worked up about Steely Dan at one point.' Some might argue that this was indulging in an altogether more dangerous pastime than excessive drinking.

In stark contrast to the subsequent Stiff-styled image of the tweed-suited, horn-rimmed, eight-stone weakling who'd had not just sand, but an entire beach, kicked in his face, Declan was actually a keen swimmer and still a fanatical football fan, physical interests none of the other members of the band shared. He had shed the excess weight of his Liverpool days and now had an athletic physique, favouring over-sized denim dungarees and sporting medium-length hair with small, rimless glasses.

Into this fraternal atmosphere, the arrival of Mary at Stag Lane began to cause some serious inter-band conflict. According to both Ken Smith and Steve Hazelhurst, Mary was a fixture in the house by early 1974, but at some point broke off with Declan and starting having a relationship with Mich Kent, who was also living at Stag Lane. Then in April 1974, Mary fell pregnant. 'There was this thing going on with Mich which was all a bit hush-hush at the time,' recalls Hazelhurst. 'Then Declan and Mary got together again, and she became pregnant. Mich and Declan were thick as thieves, but there was this triangle, and it ended up with Dec the victor and the father of the child.'

Some time after these emotional upheavals, Declan wrote his most heartfelt song to date, the pained 'Imagination (Is A Powerful Deceiver)'. A clear attempt to write a ballad that would do justice to The Band, it was his most straightforward effort to date to write from the soul, a stark look at a three-way love affair which – as would soon become common – portrayed Declan in the role of the embittered victim. Evoking himself as the man who got 'caught up in a whirlwind' and 'got blown right out the door', 'Imagination' seemed to be a pointed reflection upon the tangled relationship between Declan, Mary and Mich.

The song was also the first clear manifestation of the themes that would become more and more prominent as Declan MacManus moved towards becoming Elvis Costello. 'I'm Not Angry' from *My Aim Is True* takes the same dark, domestic territory as its direct inspiration. Given that Mary was Declan's first serious relationship, the mother of his child, and later his wife, an argument could be made that his weary view of relationships and his antipathy towards particular women (as opposed to women in general) as expressed in his early records could reasonably be said to stem from the events of 1974. With Mary, it would simply never be an easy relationship. 'They used to have pretty strong arguments,' recalls Ken Smith. 'She had a pretty strong temper, as did he.'*

The somewhat inevitable end result of the pregnancy came on 9 November, 1974, when Declan Patrick MacManus and Mary Martina Burgoyne married at St Margaret's Catholic Church in Richmond-Upon-Thames. She was nineteen, he was twenty. The groom listed his occupation as computer operator, the bride as airline stewardess. Bizarrely, Mich Kent was best man, all previous differences apparently forgotten, and the rest of the band also attended.

Mary was nearly seven months pregnant on her wedding day. For two young Catholics in the early '70s, a termination had probably never been a serious option. Indeed, Declan was vocally opposed to abortion and has remained that way.

By the time their son Matthew – named in honour of Declan's grand-

* One night at Dingwalls, Mary had a fight with Pretender's vocalist Chrissie Hynde. One source claims that 'Mary could start a fight in a telephone box', while Bruce Thomas agrees that 'they used to go at it a bit, sometimes in restaurants and whatever'.

father, whose middle name he shared – was born at Queen Mary's Hospital in Roehampton on 21 January, 1975, the newlyweds had moved into the flat below Declan's father's house; Ross and Sara remained at 16 Beaulieu Close, while Declan, Mary and Matthew occupied No. 15. Around the same time, Flip City made their second foray into the recording studio.

The band's studio debut had been back in the summer of 1974, when one of Ken Smith's music biz contacts had got them some 'downtime' at the BBC's Maida Vale studios. They cut through three MacManus originals – 'Baseball Heroes', 'Radio Soul' and 'Exile's Road', as well as Steve Hazelhurst's 'On The Road' – under the auspices of a well-heeled BBC engineer, decked out in a bright orange shirt and cravat, who would count the band in with a click of the fingers and 'OK boys, let's take a trip! One, two, three!'

Heard today, the tapes of the three MacManus songs illustrate clearly both his individual strengths and the weaknesses in the component parts of the band's sound. The voice is instantly recognisable: strong, expressive, perhaps slightly more nasal than it would become but containing the same idiosyncratic stylings as the one that kicked off *My Aim Is True* three years later.

With the benefit of hindsight, there's no particular gulf in the standard of his songwriting between 1974 and 1977; although lyrically he would develop considerably, Declan was already gifted and confident enough to be making records. However, unlike many other artists who make a rapid and definable creative leap between their early amateur days and a professional career, his artistic arc would be a steady upward ascent rather than a steep and sudden climb. The reason for this was almost certainly Flip City. The band was ragged, enthusiastic but amatuerish. They sounded like what they were: a pub band playing for drinks and kicks.

As a means of getting the band gigs, the BBC demo tape was certainly adequate, but by the time they ventured into the studio above the Hope and Anchor pub in Islington in early 1975, Declan in particular was looking for much more. 'He was absolutely dead serious about what he was doing,' says Steve Hazelhurst. 'He wanted the band to be successful.'

The Hope was a regular stop in Flip City's London itinerary. On the afternoon before a Saturday evening gig, Ken Smith had managed to secure some studio time from proprieter Dave Robinson, who in between inventing pub-rock, managing bands and promoting gigs, ran a makeshift studio there.

Having helped Robinson move a piano up to the top floor, Flip City were rewarded with the chance to put down three tracks. Original drummer Malcolm Dennis had now left and a replacement had yet to be found for the drum stool, so Flip City recorded with a long-forgotten session drummer from a band called Phoenix, whose talents were supplied by Robinson. The results – 'Pay It Back', 'Imagination (Is A Powerful Deciever)' and 'Radio Soul' – were intended to showcase Declan's prowess as a songwriter as much as present the band itself as an entity.

In any event, the former aim was probably better realised than the latter: driven by enthusiastic but rudimentary saxophone, a driving soul beat and a structure clearly pinched virtually wholesale from Van Morrison's 'Domino', 'Pay It Back' was lyrically and structurally very similar to the later version that appeared on *My Aim Is True,* but entirely different in feel. Lacking the album version's loose-limbed swagger, the band instead attempted a fluid blue-eyed soul swagger in an early Springsteen style which they couldn't pull off, and which sat awkwardly against the vengeful sentiments of the song.

The assured – if slightly plodding – recording of 'Imagination (Is A Powerful Deciever)' was more successful, and can be heard on the bonus disc of the *My Aim Is True* CD reissue. It was Declan's finest song to date, and Ken Smith remembers an attempt to get the American blues singer and songwriter Bonnie Raitt to listen to it, with the aim of persuading her to record it.

'We went to Browns Hotel in Kensington with this reel-to-reel tape, but she had a cold and couldn't come down, so we left it with the clerk at the desk with a strong promise that he would give this to Bonnie. [The tape] might have had other tracks on it, but it certainly had 'Imagination' on it, because that was the one we were trying to sell.'

If Raitt ever did get the tape, she made no use of it, but it's clear that Declan saw his future career as a songwriter as much as a performer, with ambitions and a drive which far exceeded what he was doing with Flip City. From an early age he would have been fully aware of the financial rewards of song publishing, not least because both his parents were well versed in the intricacies of the music business. The final track recorded at the session was 'Radio Soul'. It remained both melodically and lyrically strong, but the band were still searching for the right musical setting. It would take The Attractions to find it.

As Flip City continued to gig into 1975, it became more and more apparent that Declan's attitude and improving songwriting was increasingly at odds with the laid-back, happily amateur philosophy of the rest of the band. He knew what he wanted – and it wasn't Flip City.

'They were just the weirdest fucking band,' recalls Dave Robinson. 'I booked Flip City because I liked their manager Ken – very eager, very keen – but the band couldn't play at all. They never actually played as a unit ever, and you didn't have to play that great in those days for people to feel it was all right. They were just musically dyslexic.'

The inability of the band to adequately express his ideas teased the hostility out of Declan. During one live rendition of 'Pay It Back', Steve Hazelhurst's light-hearted introduction – 'This is a song for all you thieves in the audience'* – was cut dead in its tracks by the furious singer: 'He just looked at me with this glower on his face. Obviously I'd said the wrong thing.'

Another case in point was 'Flatfoot Hotel', a set regular, and a long, labyrinthine and less-than-melodic trek through some obscure personal preoccupation: 'And there's no forgiveness/And there's no relief/'Cos I start off as the good guy and I end up as the thief.' The end result sounded like a cross between 'Hotel California' and something by Santana, only even less appetising than that sounds. It even featured a drum solo. Declan was obsessed with getting the song absolutely right, but the band had little enthusiasm for the track and never really got to grips with it.

Apparently based on real life characters at either the Three Fishes pub in Kingston or the band's household at Stag Lane, it's tempting to read the line: 'So you came looking for sweet romance/Did you find out what you were missing?' as a dig at Mich Kent. The song piled allegory upon allegory until its eight-minute trek became not just tedious, but effectively meaningless.

The numbing qualities of 'Flatfoot Hotel' were utilised to full effect on the night that Flip City played a private party at an expensive house in Purley in London. The partygoers were a young, well-to-do media crew, merely looking for an excuse to dance and have fun. In other words, the kind of people that Declan instinctively mistrusted. In a typically single-minded – or simply contrary – mood, he started the band off into the long trawl through 'Flatfoot Hotel'. 'It was always a set closer, but for some reason he wanted to start the set with it, to shock the people who were all waiting to party,' says Ken Smith. 'I looked at people's faces and I was worried about whether they were going to pay us!'

Declan had no intention of being dismissed as another run-of-the-mill pub rocker, filling in time before promotion and a paunch set in. If the audience didn't recognise his talents, then he certainly wasn't going to pander to them. 'The attitude was already there,' says Steve Hazelhurst. 'It was like a stage persona, but it was more than that. The word entertainment was anathema to him: "I'm not an entertainer. I'm not here to entertain people." He used to go on and on that the whole world was

* The song's first line is 'Stop thief, you're gonna come to grief.'

full of apathy. He'd say things like: "My ambition is to shake people out of their apathy. I want us to be so good that we scare people!". I don't think you could quite call it punk, but it was very fortuitous the way it all came together.'

While the original Hope and Anchor tape was primarily an exercise in showcasing Declan's talents as a songwriter, the band decided to reconvene on the fourth floor of Dave Robinson's Islington studio in the late spring of 1975 with humbler aims: to put down the staples of their live set in order to secure more gigs. This time there were no heavy musical instruments that needed moving, so they paid the priapic Robinson something along the lines of '£20 and a bottle of port'. With new drummer Ian Powling in place, the tape was a live, first-or-second-take bash through four MacManus originals and four covers.

They breezed through the original songs: 'Exile's Road', 'Sweet Revival', a messy 'Please Mister, Don't Stop The Band' and 'Wreck On The Slide', before adding an energetic, call-and-response cover version of Chris Kenner's 'Packin' Up' and a jokey canter through the hardy Hank perennial 'You Win Again'. The two songs of note, however, were Bob Dylan's 'Knockin' On Heaven's Door' and Jesse Winchester's* 'Third Rate Romance'. The Dylan song had been released on the *Pat Garrett & Billy The Kid* soundtrack album in 1973, and was a recent addition to the Flip City live set, first aired at a disco party in Charing Cross where the band had supported a miming Desmond Dekker. It was slightly out of the ordinary for the band's style, but if the song's rudimentary, circular chord sequence never quite suited their tempo and the lyrics sat oddly with Declan's sardonic vocal, then 'Third Rate Romance' was much more successful.

A recent US pop hit, 'Third Rate Romance' ('low rent rendezvous') was a sly tale of two strangers meeting in a restaurant, cutting their losses and having a one-night stand. A grown-up, unsentimental slice of sexual reality, it had at its heart a subject matter that Declan would go on to explore in minute and lacerating detail in later years. Even in 1975 he does not disappoint, singing it beautifully with the kind of wry smile which indicates he is revelling in unravelling this slightly seedy sexual encounter. 'She said, "You don't look like my type, but I guess you'll do",' he sings, adding, 'And he said, "I'll tell you I love you if you want me to".'

For Dave Robinson, it was a turning point. 'Him doing a cover of "Third Rate Romance", that's what attracted me to him. I thought, "Fuck me, this guy is good. Why don't you find a real band?". But he stuck with

* Declan had been a fan of singer-songwriter Jesse Winchester since his Liverpool days, and Ken Smith recalls accompanying him to see Winchester play in London and meeting the singer afterwards.

them.' For the time being at least. While Steve Hazelhurst recalls that Robinson was slightly more ambivalent about Declan – 'He liked him, but he wasn't 100 per cent. He did use the phrase "verbal diarrhoea" at one point,' – Robinson was keen enough on 'Third Rate Romance' to agree to put it out as a single on his fledgling Street Records. It was a break.

While contemplating their luck, Flip City continued gigging around London and sometimes beyond through the summer of 1975. Gigs at The Lord Nelson on Holloway Road, The Brecknock in Camden Road, The Greyhound in Fulham, The Hope and Anchor, and a late-night residency at the Howff in Primrose Hill, were slotted in alongside higher profile appointments: an open-air festival in Stepney; two gigs at the famous Marquee in central London supporting Dr Feelgood and National Flag respectively; an out-of-town engagement in Dudley, near Birmingham; and two memorable performances at Wandsworth Prison.

The prison shows were held in the chapel on Sunday afternoons, where the band was requested not to smoke on stage or bring their girlfriends in case it should incite the inmates. The audience were also threatened with solitary confinement should they not display sufficient enthusiasm. The ruse worked. As Flip City soundchecked with Commander Cody's 'Looking At The World Through A Windshield', one prisoner was particularly impressed with Declan's guitar-playing talents: 'He can really tickle them strings, can't he?'

But despite the approval of the cons at Wandsworth, Flip City were treading water. The most they ever earned collectively was £25. They had no fans as such, and most of the time they barely even registered. There had been one professional photo shoot for the gig guide in London's *Time Out* magazine, but no reviews, and certainly nobody was misguided enough to be touting them as the next big thing in the music papers. The same prominent UK music journalists that created such a ballyhoo when Elvis Costello eventually got his first record on the shelves had encountered Declan MacManus and Flip City and gone away unimpressed.

'Noboby wanted to know back then!' he complained only a couple of years later. 'I remember the time [Nick Kent] came down to the Marquee when we were supporting Dr Feelgood. [He] didn't even bother to check us out. And I really resented that, you know.'[7]

With a man as determined and musically ambitious as Declan at the helm, such a sidelined role was never going to be satisfactory. Aged twenty-one, he was getting restless at the many possibilities of musical achievement that he believed were passing him by, and increasingly eaten up by the gnawing sensation that he was being ignored or unappreciated. There was a lot at stake. Self-belief and sheer determination can only take a person so far, and even somebody as sure in his heart of his talents as Declan couldn't help but ponder whether he was destined to a life of mundanity. 'I did sometimes wonder whether I was going mad,' he said later. 'That maybe it wasn't any good. But I kept on thinking it was they who were wrong and not me. It turned out to be the best way to think about it.'[8]

Or perhaps the only way. He could hardly contemplate the idea of not being successful; having invested so much energy and commitment into his music, in the certainty that he was somehow ahead of the pack, much of his self-esteem was hanging in the balance. He desperately wanted out of the nine-to-five suburban routine before it got him by the lapels and wouldn't let go – before it *defined* him.

This transparent and unashamed hunger for success led to charges of greed by some of his fellow band members. '[One] thing that annoyed me about Declan: he wanted money,' recalls Steve Hazelhurst. 'Vast amounts of it.' Although one of his few comments about his Flip City days acknowledged that 'we never had any money, we played for peanuts',[9] there is scant evidence that it was the quest for cash which spurred Declan's ambition.*

What he wanted most was the freedom to concentrate on his music rather than his unfulfilling job as a computer operator. But with a wife and young child, he couldn't take the kind of calculated career risks that many of his peers were able to take. Little wonder then that money simply provided the most tangible means of escape from the constrictions of life in the suburbs. As he agonised in a new song written around this time: 'How much longer?'

As it transpired, not too long.

* * *

Largely without rancour, Flip City broke apart. After some deliberation, Dave Robinson had decided not to pursue the idea of releasing 'Third Rate Romance' as a one-off single, a decision that battered the morale of the band. The gigs were failing to make any waves, and the dynamic of the band had changed. Declan was now living with Mary and Matthew in Twickenham, and the remaining members had been evicted from Stag Lane. They were all growing up, and into other things.

* Early on, Declan stated that: 'I don't want to be successful so that I get a lot of money and retire. I'm just interested in playing.'[10] Indeed, he has never been prone to the traditional rock star trappings of mansions in the country, or fleets of flash cars. 'I don't think money has ever been his motivating force,' says ex-Attraction Bruce Thomas.

A sense of futility finally overwhelmed the group and in the autumn of 1975 Declan told the other band members he was leaving. It had run the gamut as far as he was concerned. They had been together for over two years, and it was abundantly clear that Flip City were not a band who were going to make it. It was equally clear that a nice bunch of guys who had fun playing in a bar band was never going to be enough for him.

It was an amicable enough parting of the ways. With an afternoon and evening residency at the Red Cow in Hammersmith and a final gig booked at Ewell College, the band agreed to fulfil their remaining engagements. The penultimate gig at the Red Cow took place on 30 November, 1975, preserved for posterity on bootleg. It is clear from listening to the recording that Declan is in charge. He changes the setlist at one point to throw Sam Cooke's 'Bring It On Home To Me' into the mix – to the mild irritation of some of the band – and introduces Steve Hazelhurst's 'On The Road' with the only slightly patronising aside, 'Finally, the world is ready for Steven Hazelhurst – the reluctant hero!'

There is muted audience response, and only on 'Radio Soul' and a reworked version of the Smokey Robinson classic 'One More Heartache' do they finally show their mettle. Through the smoke and stale beer, it's possible to catch a tantalising glimpse of what Declan would later go on to achieve. But as quickly as it appears, it's gone.

The end came soon after, supporting an incarnation of the Climax Blues Band, on this occasion called Climax Chicago, at Ewell College. Flip City limped to the finishing post on something of a sour note. They had opted to end their set and bring down the curtain on the band with 'Third Rate Romance', but Declan decided to ignore both the setlist and the wishes of the rest of the band by launching into an impromptu version of the R&B classic 'Money' instead.

'He just walked up to the mic and [sang]: "The best things in life are free" and went straight into it,' says Steve Hazelhurst. 'There was no real nastiness afterwards, but it was like: "We didn't want you to do that. Why did you do it?" It was a bit sad.'

Declan wasn't overly concerned, either by the slightly bitter ending or the demise of the band. Indeed, he later dismissed Flip City virtually out of hand. '[We were] just a regular bar band, on the periphary of the dying embers of the pub-rock scene. There was no focus to it; it was aimless. With no offence to the guys, we weren't very good.'[11]

Harsh, perhaps, but true. Within a matter of months Declan would have a record deal. Within twelve months he would be recording his debut album as a solo artist with one of his favourite bands backing him and one of his heroes at the mixing desk. He knew it was time to move on.

Chapter Three
1976–77

BY EARLY 1976, THE YOUNG MACMANUS family had left Twickenham Park and moved to Palgrave House, a modern block of Housing Association flats on the corner of Cypress Avenue in Whitton.* Their new home was situated in the sole block of flats in a neat, well-maintained road of two-up-two-downs, literally just around the corner from Declan's old primary school in Nelson Road. Whitton would not have been his area of choice. 'It's a very boring area,' he later admitted. 'It's a terrible place. Awful. Nowhere. Nothing happens.'[1] Its very blankness and sense of creeping claustrophobia became in itself a kind of negative inspiration for many of the early songs: his music would always be particularly effective when imagining the sinister and sometimes nightmarish underbelly of the most outwardly unremarkable places – and faces. Of the early songs, 'Blame It On Cain', 'Waiting For The End Of The World', and 'I'm Not Angry' in particular are driven by the motor of suburban paranoia.

Flip City may have flopped to a fittingly lacklustre end, but the break-up in no way signalled defeat or lowered expectations. On the contrary, with a band who couldn't meet his escalating requirements, Declan regarded his departure as a necessary step towards a bona fide career. Now, he felt that the best way to present the songs he was writing was by singing them loud and direct to the audience, without any fancy guitar embellishment. 'I'd really got the volume up by then,' he recalled later. 'I was so fucking loud. I'd abandoned all attempts at playing subtle guitar. The style came from having to cover myself in noisy clubs.'[2]

He played whenever he could, at The White Lion in Putney, The Swan in Mill Street, Kingston upon Thames, even at a charity fete in Chiswick in early 1976, where he supported his father by playing Sam Cooke's 'A Change Is Gonna Come' on piano, before Ross rounded off an eccentric

---

* The significance of the address would not have been lost on Declan. 'Cypress Avenue' is a key track on Van Morrison's classic 1968 album *Astral Weeks*.

48

evening of entertainment with a version of Rod Stewart's 'Sailing'. The appearances at The Swan were more conventional. It was a rocker's pub, with a backroom where Ken Smith and his friend Scott Giles ran The Amarillo Club on a Saturday night. Declan played there on 'numerous' occasions in 1976, usually a forty-minute acoustic set supporting the headlining act.

'It was a pretty rowdy place,' says Smith. 'I remember introducing him as "The man Randy Newman should take his hat off to!" before he belted some of his songs out. [By then] he was a very forceful performer.'

As evidenced by his performances at Smith's Amarillo Club, Declan was still in contact with some of his old friends from Flip City, and there remained a degree of solidarity. Following the demise of the band, Steve Hazelhurst had recorded a demo of his own songs which he had sent to several record companies, with little luck. One rejection letter he received in reply was particularly scathing in its assessment of his musical talents. Despondent, Steve showed the letter to Declan. 'He actually wrote me a letter back saying, "Don't take any notice of this, keep on, you've got to keep doing it",' recalls Hazelhurst. 'Furthermore, he did one of my songs [the sadly non-prophetic 'You Ain't Seen Nothing Yet'] at one of his solo gigs. He suddenly said "This is for my mate Steve," and played it, which was a nice little touch. I've always appreciated it.'

Declan's most regular haunt was the Half Moon in Putney, where he played at least a couple of times a month through to April 1976, usually for 50p and a plate of sandwiches. Charlie Dore, a singer with the group Hula Valley who befriended Declan at the time, recalls first seeing him perform at the Half Moon in late 1975 or early in 1976. 'Ralph McTell told me to come and check this guy out. I was expecting this folkie type thing and was very much surprised. He looked normal, there was nothing particularly distinctive about him, but I was just impressed by his range, the whole [musical] package.'

Declan occasionally supported Hula Valley at the Half Moon and elsewhere, and as Dore got to know him better it became abundantly clear how driven and self-contained he had become. 'He was very self-assured, very much a one-man band,' she says. 'He was intense, utterly focused and single-minded. He didn't suffer fools gladly. He would get very frustrated with people who stood in his way or didn't get it.'

Often, the entire audience seemed to be full of such types and the aggression would be raised a notch or two. On one occasion, Declan supported Hula Valley at a London pancake house called the Obelisk, a recipe for disaster if ever there was one. 'People would be stuffing their faces with pancakes or asking for more syrup as he was singing about wringing someone's neck,' says Dore. 'He hated that. I remember him moaning about playing "while those fuckers eat!". The attitude was definitely already there.'

Some nights he was practically seething. There was rarely any attempt made at ingratiating his audience, little in the way of 'I wrote this song about' repartee. At one performance at a traditional London folk club – probably either the Grail Folk Club in Hounslow or Centrefolk, both semi-regular gigs – there were a couple of chairs on stage that had been used by the previous act. When Declan strolled on for his set, he swung his foot as hard as he could and kicked one of the chairs over. It was hardly on a par with Jimi Hendrix burning his guitar, but it struck many observers as a rather odd way to behave.

Partly, these kind of antics stemmed from his desire to make an impression, the same canny impulse which later recognised that taking the name of Elvis might not be such a bad career move. They could also be attributed to a genuine build-up of nerves; but mostly they were an expression of sincere contempt. 'I wasn't going up to people meekly and saying, "Look, with your help and with all your expertise and knowledge of the world of music we might have a moderate success on our hands." I was thinking: "You're a bunch of fucking idiots who don't know what you're doing." It didn't *make* me bitter. I was already bitter.'[3]

By now, he had a stage name. Like Ross before him, Declan had taken the maiden name of his great-grandmother, then initialised his two forenames, and became D.P. Costello. It was primarily convenience. MacManus didn't really trip off the tongue, although part of him would have been happy to be continuing where his father had left off. Declan insisted that his stage name was pronounced COS-tello – rhyming with 'Manilow', with the emphasis firmly on the first syllable in the traditional Irish manner – rather than Cos-TELLO, as it would become. He later dropped this attempt at authentic pronounciation when it became clear that Anglo tongues weren't prepared to make the required effort.

Lack of effort was not something D.P. could be accused of. He was writing prodigiously. Unshackled by the demands of getting a band to learn and perform the songs, his imagination was running riot. Newly penned numbers like 'Hoover Factory', 'Jump Up', 'Wave A White Flag', 'Dr Luther's Assistant', 'Call On Me', 'I Hear A Melody', 'Blue Minute' and 'Ghost Train' were wildly different to what he had being doing with Flip City; baroque, musically much more adventurous and experimental, with a nod to the classic American songwriters from Hoagy Carmichael to John Prine and Randy Newman, and an equally large nod to country music, which was increasingly taking a hold on him. The old Hank Williams favourite 'You Win Again' was still making an appearance in his live set, as it would for many, many years to come.

Declan recorded once again at Dave Robinson's Hope and Anchor Studios, and was sending reams of acoustic and vocal demo tapes off to every record company and song publisher he could think of. 'I didn't know enough to realise that no publisher has the patience to listen to twenty songs in the hope that the eighteenth one is the one that's good,'4 he later recalled. He tried a more direct approach, landing up outside publisher's offices, guitar in hand, to sing directly to them in the hope that the immediacy of his performance – and a desperate Costello at full throttle could be a pretty immediate experience – would rouse them from their day-to-day office distractions long enough to give him a second, more attentive listen. It may have worked for Judy Garland and Mickey Rooney, but it didn't work for Declan.

Finally sensing that he needed to muster a supreme effort and make a concise, professional and unified presentation of his best songs, in the early summer of 1976 Declan borrowed a Revox recorder from a friend and taped a number of tracks with just voice and acousic guitar in his bedroom at the flat in Cypress Avenue. He then selected the best of the bunch and sent them off to record companies, publishers, radio stations and DJs. The songs he recorded were all recent compositions: 'Mystery Dance', 'Cheap Reward', 'Jump Up', 'Wave A White Flag', 'Blame It On Cain' and 'Poison Moon'.

It was no coincidence that the two most melodically immediate and musically most straightforward numbers – 'Mystery Dance' and 'Blame It On Cain' – would survive Declan's blitzkreig writing jag of 1976 to finally make the cut on *My Aim Is True*. The former was a true wonder, a '50s-style rocker with a persona-defining lyrical portrait of a young man caught between sexual desire, frustration and confusion. 'Both of us were willing, but we didn't know how to do it', he yelped, not without humour. It was a rare thing indeed to hear such straightforward admissions of inadequacy and embarassment in a pop song. 'Blame It On Cain' on the other hand, was a confident, chugging, bluesy number that harked back to the Flip City days, with the traditional taxpayer's groan against 'government burglars' thrown in for good measure.

The other four songs were discarded quite quickly. 'I later realised that most of the songs on the tape just didn't speak up enough to be heard,'5 he said. In other words, in accordance with the harsh punk diktats of 1976, they were a little too sophisticated and complicated for popular consumption. But that didn't mean they weren't any good.

No matter how much Declan later dismissed the tape,* in the main the songs were undeniably impressive. 'Cheap Reward' was a breezy uptempo country tune with a sly lyric, while one could imagine a band taking hold of the short, sombre 'Poison Moon' and twisting it into something remarkable. Only 'Jump Up' was a misfire, veering off into a disjointed, rambling jazzy structure, with very little resembling a verse or a chorus.

'Wave A White Flag' was the pick of the litter, a caustic, Randy Newman-esque tale of two lovers in love with their domestic disharmony. It pointed to a soon-to-be enduring lyrical obsession of the dark discord that goes on behind closed doors, admitting that 'something deep inside me wants to turn you black and blue'. He sings it sweetly, with a smile in his voice, but given the tempestuous nature of his marriage, the listener can only hope that it's a character study.

The combination of the carefree vocal, happy tempo and nasty lyrics was undoubtedly commanding, and it's not hard to see why it was this track that pricked up a few ears. The opening coda in particular sounds so musically sophisticated and vocally rich that it could have turned up on *Spike* or *Mighty Like A Rose* without sounding out of place. However, it was clearly too strong a brew for *My Aim Is True*. The rest of the song skips into a neat, pre-war jazz-guitar styling, which only just fails to avoid falling into pastiche with its final, tongue-in-cheek lament of 'gee whiz, baby!'.

The demo finally prompted some genuine interest in Declan and his songs. Most significantly, it got him played on the radio, courtesy of Charlie Gillett, a highly influential DJ on BBC Radio London whose Sunday afternoon *Honky Tonk* show had recently brought Graham Parker to public notice and would later break the career of Dire Straits. Gillett had been aware of the existence of Flip City through his acquaintance with Ken Smith, who sometimes helped out on the radio show by volunteering to answer phones. Indeed, Gillett had plugged Flip City gigs on his show and had once made a specific effort to see the band in 1975, which ended in vain when he couldn't find the venue. Perhaps fortuitously, having failed to hear the band, when Gillett received Declan's tape in the post he made no connection between Flip City and D.P. Costello. 'I knew nothing about [him],' he recalls. 'This little three-inch reel-to-reel tape came through with

* In part, this was because he later raided many of the lyrics for future songs and wasn't particularly keen for anyone to trace the link. 'Cheap Reward' would later yield the key chorus phrase for *This Year's Model*'s 'Lip Service'. 'Jump Up' was also plundered for lyrics later in his career, when the phrase 'last night's obituaries' turned up amidst the two-minute riot of 'Luxembourg' on 1981's *Trust*. The lasting legacy of 'Poison Moon' was again a snatch of lyrics – 'starts with fascination, it ends up like a trance' – which finally surfaced on 'Party Girl', while 'Call On Me' was used as a launchpad for both 'Moods For Moderns' and 'Lipstick Vogue'.

D.P. Costello written on the outside, which – when I played – I just liked the sound of.'

Interestingly, for someone who would be lauded primarily for his song-writing and his lyrical invention, what struck Gillett most immediately about Declan was the voice. That 'desperate' sound which had attracted Declan to the likes of Van Morrison, Bruce Springsteen and Rick Danko now immediately drew Charlie Gillett to D.P. Costello. 'The strongest vocal association I made at the time was that he sounded a bit like Tim Hardin, which is not a name I've ever heard mentioned in association with him. Hardin had that slight quaver in his voice of somebody on the edge of crying.'*

And just because Declan's voice was the immediate hook, it didn't mean that Gillett didn't also appreciate the songs and the intellectual craft behind them as well. His particular favourite was 'Wave A White Flag'. 'It was a fantastic song,' he says. 'Everything about it: the use of words, like when he sings "Til you ca-pit-u-late". Even right back in those days he had that thing of picking out words that you rarely heard in pop songs. The songs were essentially not that unusual, [but] a few unusual words would jump up at you, and it really made a difference.'

Over the course of a few weeks, Gillett played two or three songs from the demo tape on his show. Declan was a regular listener and was uncharacteristically excited when he heard his own songs coming over the airwaves for the first time without any prior warning. 'Mary later told me that it was one of the big moments of his life,' says Gillett. 'Because I didn't tell him I was going to play it. I just did.'

The radio exposure finally began to stir up some interest. Virgin Records put a 'really pitiful deal'[6] on the table, according to Declan, while Island – who later distributed My Aim Is True – sniffed around and then turned him down. They said they couldn't hear a hit. An A&R man at America's CBS Records, who were looking for British talent, was also unimpressed when Gillett played him the tape. 'He just didn't get it at all,' says Gillett. 'I was very surprised and disappointed. I said to him, "You're wrong, you're wrong! This will do well in America". And he said, "Well, my brief is to get things that work in the UK. If somebody else gets him and he does well, we can still pick him up in America".'**

Gillett also talked to Declan about putting out a single on his own Oval label. It was less a formal approach than a loose meeting to sound out

* Declan certainly would have been aware of the American singer-songwriter; indeed, he nominated Hardin's 1966 album *Hang On To A Dream* in his '500 Essential Albums' list for *Vanity Fair* magazine in November 2000.
** Ironically, that is exactly what happened. A little over a year later, CBS were alerted by the success of Elvis Costello in the UK and signed him to an American deal.

what Declan felt he needed to move forward. The sticking point came when everybody agreed that some kind of backing band was required.

Although he was playing solo gigs and accompanying himself on the *Honky Tonk* demos, Declan was essentially a rhythmic songwriter whose style of playing and singing suggested the cadences of a band. 'He had a lot of dynamics just as a one-man act,' says John McFee, who later played guitar on *My Aim Is True*. 'A lot of the stuff like the drum build-ups, he was doing on his guitar.' D.P. Costello wasn't going to be the next Donovan, but unfortunately Oval didn't have a core of session musicians who they could just call in to make some recordings.

It wasn't to matter. In August 1976, Declan came across an advert in *Melody Maker* for a a small independent record company looking for new acts. It looked interesting. The label was called Stiff.

* * *

Stiff was the brainchild of Dave Robinson and Jake Riviera. A handsome, whip-smart impressario in the tough, no-nonsense managerial mould of Peter Grant or Don Arden, Jake in particular was absolutely key to the development of Declan. Born Andrew Jakeman, Jake had managed pub-rock par-celebs Chilli Willi and The Red Peppers before they split in 1975, and was now tour manager for Dr Feelgood. In addition, he co-managed Dave Edmunds and Graham Parker as part of the Advancedale Management group he ran with Dave Robinson, who had previous managerial experience with such London luminaries as Ian Dury's Kilburn and The High Roads and Brinsley Schwarz.

Those who met Riviera were often split between admiration and disgust. His attitude towards journalists, photographers and even fans was often described as aggressive and hostile, and from the very start he seemed intent on creating an atmosphere of surly suspicion around his charge which sounded out an implicit – and sometimes not so implicit – keep-your-distance warning to unwelcome inquisitors. However, there is no doubting that Jake's utter determination and loyalty, often-inspired marketing, and tightrope tactical ruses were a major factor in Declan's initial propulsion into fame. 'Jake could be very difficult sometimes and irritating, but at the same time he was totally devoted to Declan,' says Roger Bechirian, a recording engineer and colleague of Nick Lowe's who was also managed by Riviera. 'If Jake believed in something, he went with it with every cell of his body.'

Together, Dave and Jake set up Stiff. Their credo was an all-encompassing, wildly eclectic love for music rooted in live performance, strong songwriting and more than a passing fascination with the eccentric. Having spent years trying to make tone-deaf A&R men sit up and listen to their acts, Robinson and Riviera's combined hatred of the cartels of major labels was the driving force behind the label, which harboured a distinctly malevolent, anti-establishment streak behind its carefree exterior. 'Jake and I had the same kind of attitude,' says Robinson. 'We thought if you had a good songwriter and he or she could sing their own songs, you were ahead of the game. We saw the record company as a partner to the artist, rather than an employer.'

Although it has been posthumously reclaimed as a punk label, the Stiff house style was all over the place, but was primarily spawned in the melting pot of pub – rather than punk – rock. It was a style built up by Robinson booking literally hundreds of bands into pubs over a long period, focusing on musicians who could play their instruments and who knew their way around a decent song. And The Damned.

During the initial, frenetic twelve months of its existence in particular, Stiff was propelled forwards by bright, passionate, slightly out-of-control people who ripped up the rule book and did more or less what they wanted. It was all topped off with an unprecedented zeal for clever marketing strategies and a healthy degree of unhinged madness. Stiff may have been a miss at least as often as it was a hit, but from their tiny offices in London's Alexander Street, the likes of Ian Dury, Nick Lowe and Wreckless Eric all made their haphazard assaults on the music world.

In late July 1976, the label was readying itself for combat with its debut single, Nick Lowe's 'So It Goes', due for release on 13 August. Around the same time, Declan handed in his demo tape at Stiff's offices.

There has always been something slightly convenient about the legend of how D.P. Costello became a Stiff artist. The official party line runs thus: Declan had read about Stiff being open for business in *Melody Maker* and promptly took a 'sickie' from work to hand his demo in to the secretary. On the way home, he coincidentally bumped into Nick Lowe at Royal Oak tube station, and told him he'd just been up to Stiff to buy a copy of 'So It Goes' and to leave his demo tape with Jake. The two shook hands, Lowe wished Declan luck and then went up to Alexander Street, where he found an excited Jake Riviera raving about Declan's tape.

Jake's immediate impulse was to sign Declan as a writer, because he felt 'Mystery Dance' would be a perfect song for Dave Edmunds. However, because Declan's was the first demo tape the label had received, Riviera decided to wait until some other examples arrived so he could make a meaningful comparison. When a 'load of real dross' subsequently dropped through the Alexander Street letterbox, Jake offered Declan a deal on the spot, as a performer rather than merely a writer.

While this may indeed have been the genuine sequence of events, in the small world of the London pub-rock scene it would have taken a frankly astonishing series of coincidences for Declan to arrive on Stiff's doorstep as a completely unknown quantity. Nick Lowe, of course, knew him well from his regular appearances at Brinsley Schwarz gigs. Robinson's connection was stronger. He had booked Flip City at the Hope and Anchor on several occasions, had also recorded them, and indeed had planned to release a single of 'Third Rate Romance' the previous year, largely on the strength of Declan's distinctive voice. He had also recorded D.P. Costello earlier in the year, and frequently used Charlie Gillett as a sounding board. How could Stiff not have known about Declan MacManus?

Robinson states today that he had Declan in his sights long before the demo tape arrived at Stiff's offices, but had struggled to convince Jake. 'I knew quite a bit about Declan and put him on my list. Jake was difficult though, because he wanted to sign everybody himself. I remember mentioning Declan MacManus and Jake going, "Urrrgh! Flip City, fuck that".'

Only when Jake heard Declan's songs on the Charlie Gillett show was he finally persuaded of the talents of D.P. Costello. 'I knew Charlie quite well,' states Robinson. 'We asked Charlie, Charlie told Declan and Declan sent in a tape. He wanted to be on Stiff, and I think Charlie Gillett also said to him, "This would be the label".'

Whatever the exact details of his signing to Stiff in August 1976, it was not immediately a life-changing event for Declan. His signing-on fee consisted of £150, a cassette recorder and a Vox battery-powered amplifier, not quite enough to quit his day job. It would be nearly another full year before he could give up work at Elizabeth Arden and turn professional. However it was a real, bona fide record deal with a vibrant new label who were not likely to try to mess with his artistic sensibilities. It was also a happy place to be. 'It was a family atmosphere,' recalls Dave Robinson. 'It was good fun, there was a vibe. We used to go in the pub whenever things got a bit boring. Not that Declan was a drinker, but you had Wreckless Eric falling in the door and Nick Lowe always liked a quick sharpener.'

Soon, Declan was making the Stiff office in Alexander Street a regular stopping-off point on his way home from work, hatching plans, helping with slogans. It made him feel he was finally getting somewhere, but what he really needed was a backing band. Luckily, there was one virtually on the doorstep. Clover consisted of guitarist John McFee, bassist John Ciambotti, drummer Mickey Shine, keyboardist Sean Hopper and singer and harmonica player Huey Lewis, later to shoot to stardom in Huey Lewis & The News. Hailing from Marin County in California, Clover had been brought over to the UK in the wake of one of Dave Robinson's 'fact-finding' trips to California, their similarity to the laid-back, consumately accomplished style of Eggs Over Easy convincing him they were worth investigating.

He and Jake signed Clover to their Advancedale roster and set them up in a dilapidated old country house in Headley Grange, a village not far from Guildford and within easy distance of London. Although they had a record deal with Polygram and toured constantly, the mood of the times meant that it wasn't really happening for them in the UK. They were left at a loose end, simply hanging around much of the time, until eventually they became a kind of house band for Stiff.

Clover were by no means unknown or unloved by Declan: both Rusty and Flip City had played their songs, so when the time came for him to enter the studio to make his first recordings, Nick Lowe's suggestion that he use Clover seeemed inspired. And the band were more than amenable to the idea.

'The closest thing Jake could compare him to was a Van Morrison type,' says John McFee, who had played with Morrison on his *Saint Dominic's Preview* album. 'I got a little demo of Declan and his guitar, and I was blown away. It was pretty scary to hear somebody with so much conviction and such a sense of how to use the language. Great voice. He just had a lot going for him.'

After an initial break-the-ice meeting at Advancedale's London offices, a rehearsal was set up with Clover at Headley Grange to run through two or three songs. This time, it was John Ciambotti's turn to be bowled over. 'He dragged out this green Fender Jaguar electric guitar, played it without plugging it in and just started singing these songs. And each new song was better than the last. It was kinda mindblowing, actually.'

Clover were a favoured band of his from the early '70s, and Nick Lowe something close to a hero, but Declan was taking it all in his stride. 'I don't think being intimidated is in his nature!' laughs Ciambotti. 'Intimidation, maybe, although I don't think consciously he ever tried to intimidate anybody, but feeling intimidated? No.' Declan simply felt that his talents were at last getting due recognition from his peers.

Originally, the plan was simply for Declan to cut a single, because Stiff were operating on severely limited resources. With house producer Nick Lowe also moonlighting on bass duties, a stripped-down line-up of Declan, John McFee and Mickey Shine went into the tiny eight-track Pathway Studio in Islington, north London, to record 'Radio Sweetheart' – intended as the first single – and 'Mystery Dance', the song from the *Honky Tonk* demo which both Jake and Lowe had taken a particular shine to. Pathway was a glorified box. 'No bigger than the average front room, with a control booth barely able to contain two people and the mixing board,' recalled Declan. 'It was rather like recording in a telephone booth.'[7]

It was all distinctly home-made. Nick Lowe banged a drum stick for the trills on 'Mystery Dance', while Declan hammered the piano. The fact that – to all intents and purposes – he couldn't play piano didn't appear to concern him.

The sessions turned out so well that Stiff rethought their intial plans for simply cutting a 45. Instead, the label proposed a split album in the style of Chess Records' legendary *Chuck Meets Bo* record, where Chuck Berry and Bo Diddley had shared a side each. The plan was for Declan to split his debut with Wreckless Eric, aka Eric Goulden, another recent Stiff signing.

'Declan meets Eric' didn't have quite the same buzz, and neither artist was particularly keen on the idea – or each other for that matter – and to most observers and certainly to Declan himself, it quickly became apparent that even half an album was not going to do justice to his talents. 'I cut enough demos to make nonsense of this idea [of a side each],'[8] he later recalled. Thus, *My Aim Is True* became an album made by both accident and increment, as the scope of the record steadily expanded, creeping from 7 inches towards 12, from 45 rpm towards the full $33^{1}/_{3}$ as Declan and the band put down more and more tracks.

As a full-time worker, not to mention a father and husband, Declan began cutting corners in all aspects of his life to ensure he was able to spend as much time on the music as he could. He would skip work, go down to Headley Grange, rehearse a few songs with Clover, then the ensemble would travel up to London the following day to put the results on tape.

Everything was moving at a frantic pace. He was writing all the time, later claiming that he wrote much of *My Aim Is True* in little over a fortnight. 'Waiting For The End Of The World' popped up 'when riding on the underground. [It was] a fantasy based on a real late night journey.'[9] In actual fact, Declan claimed the song was partly inspired by watching legendary *NME* scribe Nick Kent – 'obviously pretty out of it'[10] – get on a tube bound for Osterley, oblivious to the mayhem he was causing around him. 'Red Shoes' was another train song, written on a British Rail timetable on an inter-city between Runcorn Bridge and Lime Street stations in Liverpool, the tune held in his head for the duration of the ten-minute journey and then bashed out on an old guitar at his mother's house in West Derby.

'Pay It Back' came from the Flip City days, while 'Less Than Zero' took the elderly British fascist Oswald Mosely to task, written after Declan fumed over a television programme which allowed Mosley to reminisce about his blackshirt days in the east End of London. It was recorded three days later. 'That was unbelievable,' admits John Ciambotti. 'Less Than Zero' was pretty amazing. Once we recorded it, I can remember hearing John McFee playing it about 150 times on his ghetto blaster in his room.'

But the pick of the bunch was 'Alison', a bitter-sweet love song with a chorus taking its inspiration from the unlikely source of The Detroit Spinner's 'Ghetto Child'. Despite several contradictory theories over the years regarding the inspiration for the song, many fuelled by its author, 'Alison' is for and about Mary, plain and simple. It was cut at the second session, and finally alerted Nick Lowe to the true depths of Declan's talents. 'That was the day when I thought this is something seriously happening,' he recalled. 'He gave off something. You could tell that here was somebody different. For someone as young as he was to be so clear and so in control of what he was trying to portray and get across was maturity beyond his years. Unsettling and very soulful. I'm not ashamed to admit that I cried.'[11]

All those who worked on the record emphasise the importance of Lowe in the producer's chair as the catalyst for bringing everyone together and keeping enthusiasm at a peak. At the age of twenty-seven, he was very much the senior partner in the Costello-Lowe relationship, a veteran of the music industry with albums and hit singles under his belt. Because Declan had little studio experience, he was happy to let Lowe take the lion's share of the responsibility, even if Lowe often felt he was making it up as he went along. 'The people I was working with then were all in their teens or very early twenties,' said Lowe. 'As far as they were concerned, I was this real experienced old cove, but I didn't really know anything about anything.'[12]

But he did know instinctively what a good record should sound like – and that making it should be fun. The essence of the Lowe production technique was to wind up the energy levels to fever pitch and then ensure that that Delphic factor known as 'the feel' was right. He wasn't interested in technical perfection, but had an astute ear for a great performance and a gift for creating an atmosphere that suited the mood of each song. He was also smart and secure enough to recognise that the songs were the most important part of the recording process, and he had sufficient faith in Declan's ability to want to keep things simple. Less romantically, with a tight budget to adhere to, Lowe also had one eye firmly on the studio clock. 'They came into the studio and set up and played, and all I did was just switch everything on and watch them do it,'[13] he later claimed, with no small degree of self-deprecation.

Most of the album was recorded live, in first takes, with Declan singing and playing guitar to Clover's backing. There were a few overdubs of background vocals here and there, but very little polish, to the extent that Clover were originally a little concerned by the rawness of the final takes. If any of the band came to him wanting to re-do their bass part or have another go at their guitar line, the standard Lowe response was: 'Ach, nobody will hear it in the morning!' And he was right.

The songs that would eventually make up *My Aim Is True* were recorded in about sixteen hours, between October 1976 and January 1977, with the final mix being made in a five-hour session at Pathway on 27 January, with Nick Lowe and Declan in attendance, at a cost of £43.20. In total, the album cost about £800, mainly because the speed of recording and the budget studio – basic rates were £8 an hour – ensured expenses stayed very low. Clover were already on a retainer from Robinson and Riviera, and were therefore paid very little for their services. 'If the group know what they're doing and they're ready to make a record it shouldn't cost very much money and it should be made quickly,' says Dave Robinson.

The songs were an intriguing mixture of the personal and the persona-building. While there is no reason to doubt Declan when he said that 'whatever lyrical code or fancy was employed, the songs came straight out of my life plain enough',[14] it's also equally certain that with songs like 'Mystery Dance', 'Miracle Man', 'No Dancing' and 'Sneaky Feelings', Declan had, not entirely accidentally, hit upon a unique rock 'n' roll creation.

He admitted as much to Nick Kent in the infamous interview conducted for the *New Musical Express* in August 1977, best remembered for his oft-repeated quote: 'The only two things that matter to me, the only motivating points for me writing all these songs, are revenge and guilt. Those are the only emotions I know about.'

Although those were to be the lines that stuck fast in people's minds, elsewhere in the interview he was unambiguous about the way in which he consciously tailored a lyrical style and means of expression that combined his own – undoubtedly genuine – painful personal experiences with a keen eye for a gap in the rock market.

'[Those] are the only songs in a rock idiom where a guy is admitting absolute defeat,' he told Kent in 1977, referring to the tracks on *My Aim Is True*. 'I'm talking about being a *complete* loser. That's something totally new to the rock idiom, which by its very nature is immature and totally macho-orientated in its basic attitude. Only in country music can you find a guy singing about that kind of deprivation honestly.'

It was a lesson he had learned from the likes of George Jones and Charlie Rich, and it was perhaps the most significant factor in allowing Declan to make such a dramatic early impact as a lyricist. At a time when most pop and rock idols were expected to brag about how they were – in the words of Bruce Springsteen – gonna 'Prove It All Night', a skinny little man confessing to being a wimp and a loser was something quite out of the blue. It was a neat ruse, and along with the soon-to-be unveiled new name and image, it ensured that Declan arrived on the scene with a ready-made persona so strong that it virtually guaranteed him a shot at the big time.

It was all rather more contrived than many might have imagined. The context, of course, was punk, which for all its claims at having no boundaries was as strict and unforgiving in its membership rites as any other social or musical movement. Elvis's style of both dress and music, his background and tastes, were in reality far removed from the punk ethic, but he saw that this was not the time to be singing country ballads in Great Britain.

The plight of Clover had not been lost on him: superb musicians who could write, record and perform their own music to an exceptional standard, they had wilted in the hothouse environment of the UK – and more specifically London – in the summer of 1976 and the eighteen months that followed. 'All those qualities were the worst thing [Clover] could have had going for them then,' he said. 'I could see that.'[15] As such, he allowed himself to be swept along in the slipstream of punk and kept his more ambitious musical ideas in check until he had established himself. 'There was a whole bunch of things I could have done even back then. However, I tailored my songs and style very purposefully because I knew which way the prevailing winds were blowing. I was shrewder than most people.'[16]

A telling admission, but nothing particularly new. Bob Dylan had jumped on the 'protest' bandwagon in the early '60s to gain a foothold in the music business, courtesy of a highly conservative folk scene he instinctively knew he would outgrow and outlast. Declan was merely doing the same, sophisticated enough to realise that punk was far too narrow to hold him, yet astute enough to know that it gave him the perfect opportunity to make his mark.

Later, he reasoned, he could do what he *really* wanted to do, but for the time being, if people were going to get excited about a seething young man in glasses ramming tales of inadequacy, 'revenge and guilt' down their throats, then he would give them what they wanted. It almost backfired, to the point where it would later take him all his creative energy to try and shake off the image. Like Woody Allen's more benign cinematic creation, the grudge-bearing, bespectacled nerd on a losing streak was a winner from the start, but would prove rather more difficult to set in reverse.

* * *

With Declan's debut single, 'Less Than Zero' b/w 'Radio Sweetheart', scheduled for release on 25 March 1977, both Robinson and Riviera took the view that D.P. Costello was too prosaic a name for their new Stiff protégé. The label already had a reputation for marketing nous, taking pride in their sloganeering and gimmicky advertising ruses. Their principal slogan – 'If It Ain't Stiff It Ain't Worth A Fuck' – was a fairly straightforward statement of intent regarding the unapologetic, swaggering manner in which the label presented itself, while others such as 'We're Not The Same, You're Not The Same' tapped into the timely thirst for a paradoxical sense of 'collective individuality'.

Declan also enjoyed that side of the label, the product of heavily fuelled get-togethers at Alexander Street. Now Stiff went to work on him. The legend states that the change of name took place during a drunken meeting in a restaurant on the Fulham Road early in 1977, although John Ciambotti recalls Jake Riviera bursting into the studio and shouting 'Elvis! That's it. Elvis!', which is at least a nice story, albeit one from the Vincente Minelli school of narrative.

Whatever the exact circumstances, the idea was a piece of quintessential Riviera inspiration/idiocy. It was risky. 'I was amazed that [Declan] took it,' admits Dave Robinson. 'He was keen to get going, and it would seem looking back that he committed himself to the idea of it, so he accepted everything. He felt Jake and I or some combination of the two knew everything and he would do what we wanted.'

'Jake and Dave would come at you like good-cop, bad-cop,' Declan recalled. ' "*This'll be great*", Jake just said, "We're going to call you Elvis. Ha ha ha ha!". And I thought it was just one of these mad things that would pass off, and of course it didn't. Then it became a matter of honour as to whether we could carry it off.'[17]

In March 1977, Elvis Presley was still alive and nobody had any idea at that time that he was so ill; to many, he was still the reigning 'King of Rock 'n' Roll'. Within a few months Presley would be dead, his demise bizarrely coming within weeks of the release of *My Aim Is True*. Then, Costello's name came to inherit a harder edge, and also embodied a little more the mood of the zeitgeist.

But all this was merely luck. At the time it occurred, the change from Declan to Elvis represented some of the less inventive aspects of the punk era: a juvenile jab at shocking the establishment which could be traced directly back to the Sex Pistols and myriad other, more jokey punk acts. Declan taking on the name of Elvis rendered the multi-faceted arrogance so obvious in his music bluntly explicit rather than cunningly implicit. It could have gone badly wrong.

Some people had huge problems with the name. Charlie Gillett for one was appalled, and claims it took him a long time to say the name aloud without it leaving a bitter taste in his mouth; while both John McFee and John Ciambotti thought Declan would 'get stoned' if he toured America. Other people just found it funny. The fledgling Boomtown Rats handed their demo tape into Stiff in early '77 and met Dave Robinson, who introduced Declan to the band, at the same time telling them they were changing his name to Elvis. 'We all went, "fucking hell!",' recalls Bob Geldof. 'Everyone started pissing themselves, and we went [sarcastically], "Oh! *That's* good!".'

In the US, some journalists felt it was disrespectful, especially after Presley's death, and Declan even felt the need to offer a rare explanation: 'It wasn't meant as an insult to Elvis Presley,' he said towards the end of 1977. 'It's unfortunate if anyone thinks we're having a go at him in any way.'[18] However, he was not immune to the sense of drama the name provoked. It simply stopped people dead in their tracks. 'It meant people would pause just that little bit longer,' he said. '"He can't be called *that*! He is called that!" By that time, they'd noticed me more than the bloke called Joe Smith.'[19]

To complete the striking picture, Declan was now decked out in tight thrift shop suit jackets, turned-up jeans, and big, Buddy Holly-style spectacles. It was a cartoon caricature of his existing look, with everything blown up large for effect. He already wore glasses, but they were discreet and rimless rather than black-framed and over-sized; there are pictures of Declan from 1974 with his jeans turned up, but now he turned them up six inches rather than two. He had always been physically slightly awkward; now he was gawky and comically knock-kneed.

Dave Robinson takes the plaudits for the exaggerated glasses. 'I said "Can you try these on?" So he put them on, he was wearing some funny grey suit, we looked at him and thought "Elvis Costello!" And he didn't tell us to fuck off, he just said, OK. I remember thinking, "Have we made a big mistake here or what?".' Ian Gomm of Brinsley Schwarz recalls walking into the Stiff office in Alexander Street and meeting Declan 'flying out of the door' on his way out. 'He was wearing these stupid glasses. Jake was behind him, shouting: "And don't fucking take them off!".'

At the age of twenty-two, Elvis Costello was born.

PART TWO
Don't Come Any Closer,
Don't Come Any Nearer

Chapter Four
1977-78

ELVIS COSTELLO MADE HIS LIVE DEBUT with two short, unscheduled guest slots supporting The Rumour at London's Nashville Rooms on Friday, 27 and Saturday, 28 May. The acoustic guitar had gone, regarded as a relic of the D.P. days; instead, he backed himself with the crisp, biting tones of a Fender electric. Nattily turned out in shades, jacket, waistcoat and loosened tie, over the two nights Elvis played urgent solo sets which included 'Red Shoes', 'Waiting For The End Of The World', 'Mystery Dance', 'Hoover Factory' and 'I'm Not Angry'.

The gigs provided the only break in a long, frustrating lull in proceedings following the adrenalin rush of making *My Aim Is True*. The release of 'Less Than Zero' in March 1977 was intended to herald the imminent launch of the album, but the record was delayed until the end of July while Stiff resolved a dispute with Island over a distribution deal that the two labels were finalising.

In the meantime, a further two singles were released to proclaim Elvis's talents to the world, but the world wasn't necessarily interested. Like their predecessor, both 'Alison' and 'Red Shoes' failed to do any business in the charts or on mainstream radio, despite their obvious strengths. Elvis's career effectively remained on hold. He was still trudging into Elizabeth Arden every day to earn a living, trooping back to Whitton in the evening to be with his wife and two-year-old son.

The feeling of being left in limbo brought his desire to get going bubbling somewhere close to boiling point. He remained in occasional touch with some of his Flip City friends, and they noticed a definite gear change in his attitude when they all attended a gig at Kingston Polytechnic. 'He turned up with the drainpipe jeans and the jacket and the stupid black glasses, and by then you could tell,' says Steve Hazelhurst. 'The attitude was: "Yeah, I'm Elvis now. Hiya, but no thank you".'

However, progress was being made. The shows at the Nashville Rooms had marked the beginnings of a print media buzz that rapidly built up a considerable head of steam. 'The very wonderful Elvis Costello spells Major New Talent,' raved Allan Jones' review in *Melody Maker*. 'You'd better believe it.' Others had admired the singles and been highly impressed by advance copies of the album.

The hiatus had another positive side-effect: it gave Elvis the chance to write. By the time of *My Aim Is True*'s release in the summer of 1977, much of the follow-up record had already been written. 'He was writing two songs a minute,' says Dave Robinson. 'He never stopped. He drove everyone potty around him. He was driven, just totally and utterly fixated.'

Elvis revisted old Flip City and D.P. Costello songs such as 'Radio Soul' and 'Cheap Reward', moulding them into 'Radio, Radio' and 'Lip Service'. 'He was such a cannibal,' says Robinson, 'that he cannibalised his own stuff.' He dusted down 'Living In Paradise' and stripped it of its country flavour, and added several more: 'Crawling To The USA', 'The Beat', 'Lipstick Vogue', 'Night Rally', 'No Action', 'Watching The Detectives', '(I Don't Want To Go To) Chelsea' and 'Less Than Zero (Dallas Version)'* were all written around this time, an extraordinarily focused period of creativity.

Perhaps most crucially of all, the delay gave Elvis the time to get a band together. Clover had done a laudable job on *My Aim Is True*, especially considering the time constraints and the fact that they had their own career to worry about, but their laid-back look and polished sound would have set Elvis back to square one had he used them as his permanent backing band. 'I would have been happy to do it, but I don't think it was ever really a serious consideration,' says John McFee. Elvis was astute enough to know he needed something considerably sharper and harder behind him, more attuned to the mood of the times. And preferably with shorter hair.

With Elvis keen to keep the guitars down to one – 'there'll be no fucking soloists in my band',[1] he decreed – he opted for providing all the parts himself, dispensing with the need for a lead guitarist. The sound would be filled out with bass, drums and keyboards.

The drum stool had already been claimed by Pete Thomas, who had been playing with John Stewart in Los Angeles ever since the demise of Chilli Willi and The Red Hot Peppers in 1975. Now he was coming home.

---

* A companion piece to 'Less Than Zero', inspired by a late-night discussion with John Ciambotti at the Nashville Rooms. With its 'Calling Mr Oswald' refrain, Ciambotti was convinced that 'Less Than Zero' was about Lee Harvey Oswald and the assassination of JFK. Suitably inspired by this misreading, Elvis wrote 'Less Than Zero (Dallas Version)'. Ciambotti later heard the 'Dallas Version' in concert and allowed himself a small amount of credit. 'Maybe I put a bug in his ear.'

Ostensibly, Pete was returning to Britain to join ex-Dr Feelgood guitarist Wilko Johnson's new band. In reality, Jake – Dr Feelgood's former tour manager – merely used Johnson as a means of getting another record company to pay for Thomas's flight back to the UK. In a piece of classic Riviera audacity, within a week he had poached the lanky drummer for Elvis's new band. So much for pub-rock loyalties.

Just a couple of weeks older than Elvis, Pete was an inspired choice, unshowy but ruthlessly rhythmic, as comfortable sitting back and keeping time on 'Alison' as laying down the pounding pulse of 'Lipstick Vogue'. Thomas was – and remains – one of the few great 'song' drummers around, with a genuine love and instinctive understanding of how best to complement the nuances of great writing. He has even been known to ask for the lyrics of a song before recording a session, emphatically not standard practice for a drummer. In his humour, appetites and penchant for partying, however, Pete was much closer to the standard stereotype, and would become the chief source of mischief in the band.

On 4 June a small advert for a big band appeared in the back pages of *Melody Maker*: 'Stiff Records Require Organist/Synthesizer Player and Bass Player – both able to sing for rocking pop combo. Must be broad-minded. Young or old.' Bass player Bruce Thomas was broad-minded enough, old-ish, and was certainly interested. He recalls Elvis taking a typically hands-on approach to the selection procedure: 'I remember ringing up for the audition, and the girl who answered the phone [Stiff secretary Suzanne Spiro, whom Thomas would later marry] said hello. And then this other voice came over the line: "Who are your favourite bands?" "Well, um, Graham Parker and Steely Dan." "Get rid of him!" But thankfully the secretary said, "Oh no, give him a chance! He sounds quite nice".'

Despite Elvis's terse interventions, Bruce Thomas got his chance. Born in Stockton on Tees on 14 August, 1948 and unrelated to Pete, Bruce was a full six years older than Elvis and had a wealth of professional experience, both on the road and in the studio. He had been part of future Free vocalist Paul Rodgers' earliest band, The Roadrunners, in 1967, before playing with numerous groups, including Village and country rockers Quiver, whom he left in 1973 when they joined forces with The Sutherland Brothers. Bruce then turned to session work, playing for the likes of Ian Matthews, Al Stewart and Bridget St John and touring and recording as part of Baz and Moonrider in 1974 and 1975.

Although a cursory glance at his age and CV – not to mention his flares and earth shoes – placed Bruce firmly on the wrong side of the all-important hippy/punk divide, his attitude was not at all 'peace and love'. By nature, he was a temperamental type: moody, sensitive, often quick to take offence and slow to forgive, with a famously sharp wit that frequently turned venomous after a couple of drinks. His bass guitar had been known to fly towards the object of his frustration, but musically he was right on the money. A superbly melodic bassist with an inventive style which roamed genres and octaves, his playing possessed the kind of personality, presence and intuition which someone as adventurous and eclectic as Elvis needed.

The auditions took place in June at a small rehearsal space in Putney. Pete Thomas was not yet ready to take up his seat behind the drums, and instead Elvis used the rhythm section from The Rumour: Steve Goulding and Andrew Bodnar.

A veteran of the myriad tricks of the audition process, Bruce Thomas had bought and learned the early Costello singles to maximise his initial impact, but came a little unstuck when the rehearsal band started playing newly penned numbers such as 'No Action' and 'Watching The Detectives'. All in all, though, he found the songs easier to get to grips with than the man who had written them. 'Elvis was intense,' he recalls. 'Sweaty. Wouldn't make eye contact. Ungrounded. Very up in the air. All the energy was going up. Curt.'

It would often be a difficult relationship, but Elvis knew a great bass player when he heard one. It's probable that he was also swayed in his decision by the testimony of Pete Thomas, who had loved Bruce's earlier band Quiver and had been a frequent visitor backstage after their shows.

'Pete had his drum kit set up exactly like the Quiver drummer,' says Bruce Thomas. 'He once told me he saw me getting out of a taxi in west London with a guitar case, going into a takeaway to get some food and getting back into the cab. He thought that was the coolest thing he had ever seen. That was the defining moment when he decided he wanted to be a musician! So Pete kind of said, "I want to play with this guy", which is probably what got me in.'

The final piece in the jigsaw came in the eccentric form of Stephen Nason, a nineteen-year-old, classically trained piano player from the Royal College of Music who had absolutely no experience playing rock or pop music. Born in the suburbs of London in early 1958, Nason proudly boasted of his love for Alice Cooper and little else, and initally thought he was auditioning for an Elvis Presley tribute group. According to legend, he got the job because he drank a bottle of sherry at the audition and fell asleep on the floor. 'Steve was a fucking nutter,' sighs Dave Robinson. 'You could tell he would fit in perfectly.'

Elvis now had his band, but they needed bedding in. Typically, he couldn't wait. Straight after the auditions, he cut two new songs – 'Watching

The Detectives' and 'No Action' – with the rehearsal group of Bodnar and Goulding, with Nick Lowe producing.

'Watching The Detectives' had been written after prolonged, caffeine-fuelled exposure to The Clash's eponymous debut album, listening to it again and again until this menacing confection appeared. Recorded quickly in Pathway with just drums, bass and echoing, reverbed guitar, Steve Nason – or Steve Nieve, as he had by then been christened – would later add piano and organ overdubs before its release as an autumn single.

The song was a departure – or perhaps more accurately, a new starting point – for Elvis, owing more than a little of its rhythmic structure to reggae. He later claimed it was his 'first real record,'[2] an assessment which may have been unduly tough on Clover and My Aim Is True, but accurately captured the shift away from the derivative, Anglo-American country-rock peddled by the likes of Brinsley Schwarz and Graham Parker, towards a more contemporary, British style of urban paranoia. The latter came much closer to matching the ever-present sense of threat in Elvis's lyrics, not to mention the sound constantly swirling around in his head.

* * *

By June, Elvis was beginning to attract considerable interest. Partly, this was down to Stiff's unprecedented promotional zeal. Riviera and Robinson weren't exactly shy about pushing their new prodigy, but then they weren't exactly shy about anything.

'Elvis happened because of his own impetus,' says Dave Robinson. 'But we did a great marketing job on him.' Their guerilla tactics ran from scratching 'Elvis Is King' on run-out grooves to 'pre-planned deletions' of singles; from eye-catching picture sleeves for 'Less Than Zero' and 'Alison' to rampant sloganeering such as 'Help Us Hype Elvis' and 'Larger Than Life And More Fun Than People'. There was also an extravagant advertising campaign in the media: posters showing different portions of Elvis were printed in each of the main music publications, ensuring readers had to buy all the magazines to get the full picture. This didn't necessarily mean that people were buying the singles, but it did ensure that people became more and more aware of Elvis Costello.

Nevertheless, it would all have been so much hollow hype if the music wasn't beginning to make a few waves. 'Less Than Zero' had been described as 'a great record' by eminent rock writer Charles Shaar Murray in the NME back in March, adding: 'It doesn't have a snowball's chance in hell.' Accurate assessments on both counts, although Murray further buried the song's chances by calling the song 'Half Past Zero'. *Sounds'* John Ingham had been less impressed, describing it as 'a cross between Graham Parker and Brinsley Schwarz. The B-side is a little more palatable, but why bother when there's Brinsley Schwarz albums that do it far better?'

Other prominent journalists such as Allan Jones and Nick Kent were soon tripping over themselves to lavish praise on Elvis. Jones had reviewed the gig at the Nashville Rooms in May and in late June – a full month before *My Aim Is True* hit the shops – *Melody Maker* ran a gushing feature. Along with the more famous 'revenge and guilt' interview with the *NME*'s Nick Kent which came eight weeks later, the interview with Jones firmly established the abrasive, bitter, fuck-you-all Costello persona in the minds of both the media and music-buying public.

He went to ridiculous lengths to emphasise that his past was not just another country, it was another life, and one he had no intention of raking over. 'I don't see any point in talking about the past,' he said. 'Nobody showed any interest in me then.' Even one-time Stag Lane hero Bruce Springsteen got it in the neck. Convinced he was already in a position to bite back against the people who ran the record industry – who had apparently bequeathed him a lifetime's worth of bitterness – Elvis was wasting little time in making up for years of slights, both real and perceived. 'You just have to look at them to tell they're fucking idiots,' he said. 'They just don't know anything. They're not worth my time.'

The legendary little black book in which he noted down the names of all those who had crossed him in the past also began to make an appearance. 'He was enjoying being the nasty,' says Dave Robinson. '"I'm the real thing and I'll push it up your nose".' That was all natural. He needed scant encouragement when he found he could be unpleasant to people and get away with it.'

Whether or not he *needed* any encouragement, he was getting plenty of it all the same. Behind the snarl was Jake, who instinctively recognised Elvis's guarded, suspicious nature and his intrinsic – and often unintentional – ability for creating tension and unease. The logical extension of these natural characteristics was to create an appropriately aggressive and hostile façade, to 'burn some earth around me: don't come into this circle'.3

The press were given snippets of biographical detail, but no meat. When *Sounds'* scribe Chas De Whalley came calling, Elvis refused to play the game. 'No pictures,' he snapped. 'I want to keep my own face. I don't want people to know what I look like.' It was disingenuous, ridiculous even, considering his face was one of the major selling points used by Stiff, but it worked. The press were intrigued.

The mystique surrounding Elvis early on was very different from that of the young Bob Dylan, say, who jettisoned his middle-class upbringing in favour of a romantic invention of a misspent youth playing the harmonica on the railroads. On the contrary, the prosaic reality of Elvis's circumstances suited Jake just fine: a bitter computer operator, trapped in the suburbs with a young family, becoming steadily more incensed with the world was a perfect image. It had a modern – if not strictly poetic – appeal, one that fitted neatly with the image, the sense of impotence and rage of the music.

Computer geek to pop star was a nice story, but the idea of Elvis toiling for years in whimsical acoustic duos and second-rate pub-rock bands was less evocative. Rusty and Flip City were not names Jake wanted people to hear. Declan MacManus had been a failure as a musician, largely ignored by those who had stumbled across his wares, and Elvis had grown ashamed of him. As far as he and Jake were concerned, Elvis Costello's biography stretched back no further than 1977. Before that, he didn't exist.

As if to emphasise the point, he quit Elizabeth Arden on 5 July, 1977. It was not a decision Elvis made lightly. Like Ross, he took his family responsibilties seriously, even though he frequently found them stifling, and he demanded that he was paid as much as he was already earning at Elizabeth Arden. 'If I'd been on my own, I'd have taken the risk, but I couldn't for my family,'[4] he said. In any case, it was far from being a fortune, something in the region of £100 a week doled out in lieu of future royalties. *My Aim Is True* was at last being readied for release and there was promotional work and gigs to be considered. Finally, he was ready to begin.

* * *

Elvis and his new band rehearsed a little in London before heading west to a disused RAF base near the village of Davidstow in Cornwall for an intense week of rehearsals. Away from the glare of the capital, they would play their first shows and begin to take stock of each other. 'With Elvis, you never knew whether he was copping an attitude, doing an act or adopting a stance,' says Bruce Thomas. 'I remember driving halfway down to Cornwall and he was muttering, "Too many fucking trees, too many fucking trees!".'

The other three members of the band were equally idiosyncratic. Pete was a drummer, through and through, with all that that implies. Bruce was slightly world weary and cynical, but still possessed the ability to thoroughly enjoy himself. Steve was the baby of the band, a little quiet, eccentric and impossibly eager to lose his innocence.

From the outset, it was clear that this would never be a group with an unbreakable bond or a shared sense of identity. When it came to making music, they relished the collective sense of us-against-the-world antagonism which flowed directly from Elvis, but the reality of the personal relationships within the band was rather different. They got on well enough, and leaned on each other over the years during the molten pressures of constant touring, but Elvis never lost his remoteness. This was his career, they were his songs, and he was the leader of the band. It would always be one-plus-three.

Musically they gelled quickly, hitting on a style which Elvis, easily and unashamedly the least technically accomplished of the quartet, adapted to by very often staying out of the way. 'Bruce is a very melodic bass player and Pete is a very rhythmic drummer,' he said later. 'That meant we could almost get away with being a trio, because an awful lot of the time I didn't play. Rather than making a bad job of trying to play well, I was quite happy to exploit the simple things I could do.'5 The wild card was Steve, whose combination of technical ability and lack of schooling in conventional pop nuances meant that they had a truly unique twist. 'We had a thing nobody else had,' said Elvis. 'We had a *really* good piano player.'6

What emerged was a lean, muscular outfit, able to complement both the '60s classicism of Elvis's songwriting and the pushy, punkish energy of his attitude. It was almost immediately apparent Elvis had found, virtually by chance, through the lottery of auditions, a truly great *band*. They hung together as a unit, boasting a rare blend of virtuosity stripped of any extravagant tendencies. It was never really apparent whether he sufficiently appreciated his good fortune.

It may have been the overall sound of the band that really captured the imagination, but their input made an appreciable difference to the structure of the songs as well. Elvis favoured the 'immaculate conception' approach to songwriting. He didn't like to reveal or share his working process, almost always bringing his songs to the group fully formed. But although there was precious little jamming or consultation involved in the actual writing, there was often plenty of give in the style and the arrangements, and the band relished the process of claiming as their own both the songs from *My Aim Is True* and the newer songs he was writing.

The fruits of their creative process can be heard in the evolution of '(I Don't Want To Go To) Chelsea', a pointed dig at the shallow charms of swinging London. Many of Elvis's early songs were explicitly modelled on others, and in the case of 'Chelsea' it was The Kinks' 'All Day And All Of The Night'. Originally acoustic and played much slower, the song really took shape in the hands of the new rhythm section: the churning, arpeggiated bass riff and the choppy drums transformed it into something up-beat, distinctive and effortlessly modish. A hit, in other words.

They had a set together in a week, but took longer to find a name: the three low-key gigs at the Penzance Winter Gardens on Thursday, 14 July, Plymouth Woods on the fifteenth and Davidstow village hall on the sixteenth were simply billed as Elvis Costello. Even in this far flung corner of England, there was already sufficient media interest in Elvis for *Record Mirror* to send their reviewer Chris Rushton down to the Plymouth show. He returned impressed by the 'slightly stroppy creep of a school prefect' and his backing band. 'It's difficult to label Costello,' he wrote, before praising the 'tight lyrics, smooth aggression and power' of the performance. Jake also watched the shows and was typically forthright: 'You're a world-class band,' he told them at the end of the week. For once he wasn't exaggerating.

Filled with confidence, they dropped briefly into London before heading north, making their big city debut at Manchester's Rafters Club on 21 July, the eve of the release of *My Aim Is True*. Earlier in the day, Elvis performed a solo version of 'Alison' for Granada's regional programme *What's On*, his first-ever television appearance. That night, he played the entire album in the twenty-one song set, plus an additional eight numbers which were brand-new to the audience. Then it was back to London to watch and wait as the album finally hit the shops.

Despite the spontaneous, piecemeal nature of its making, *My Aim Is True* held together with a cohesion which belied its hesitant inception. It was lovingly put together, with a striking, iconic image of a knock-kneed Elvis clutching his Fender Jazzmaster on the cover, and the running order was carefully selected. Stiff and Elvis already had one eye firmly on their market: the new wave weathervane dictated that strong, country-esque songs like 'Radio Sweetheart' and 'Stranger In The House', which would have added texture to the record were deliberately dropped for fear of scaring away portions of the audience. The selectiveness also extended to the sleeve credits: there was no mention of Clover anywhere on the record.

In 'Alison', 'Red Shoes' and 'Less Than Zero', the record contained at least three enduring classics, but many of the other nine songs – 'Miracle Man', 'Blame It On Cain', 'Sneaky Feelings' and 'Waiting For The End Of The World' – were equally strong. The few weaker tracks were the ones that sounded the most derivative (the kitschy 'Leader Of The Pack' rhythms of 'No Dancing', the easy-going pub-rock of 'Pay It Back', the excessive guitar workouts on 'I'm Not Angry'), but the bulk of the record sounded extraordinarily fresh.

The sense of emotional intensity and self-laceration in the writing was only slightly curbed by the backing of Clover, which was discreet, but a little polite, embellishing the songs rather than sharpening them. While Elvis would struggle to ever match the pained tenderness of the recorded version of 'Alison', it was the exception that proved the rule: later live incarnations of the *My Aim Is True* material only served to give a glimpse of what a stunning record it might have been had The Attractions played on it. As it was, the album was an accurate and compelling marker of where Elvis had come from, rather than a statement of intent of where he was now heading. It made him a contender.

Reviews were of the rave variety. *Melody Maker's* Allan Jones – already hopelessly embroiled in a critical love affair with Elvis which would last the best part of two decades – noted the preoccupation with 'emotional violence' and 'sexual inadequacy' in passing, but was primarily overjoyed at the fact that the album contained 'enough potential hit singles to stock a bloody juke-box. I can think of only a few albums released this year that rival its general excellence. Buy, buy!'

Roy Carr's *NME* review was similarly positive, but more perceptive. 'Costello must have taken a lot of emotional knocks to come up with such a powerful album. To the extent that one is reticent to guess to what lengths he may have to go to enact a second instalment.' The answer? As far as necessary.

* * *

With *My Aim Is True* shifting a reported 11,000 copies in its first three days in the shops, Elvis hit overdrive. He and the band cut a Radio One session for John Peel on 25 July, playing 'Less Than Zero', 'Blame It On Cain', 'Mystery Dance' and 'Red Shoes'. Their London debut came the next night.

True to form, the gig at Dingwalls didn't go ahead without some Jake-inspired tomfoolery. On the day of the show, Elvis and a placard-carrying Stiff ensemble led by Riviera marched on a CBS Records convention being held at the Hilton Hotel in Mayfair's exclusive Park Lane. Setting up on the pavement outside the hotel, Elvis plugged into his battery-powered amp and began performing. It was all another harmless exercise in hype, with the added incentive of attempting to drum up some interest in Elvis from Columbia executives. He was still only licensed in the United Kingdom, and both Jake and Elvis knew that a US deal was the big prize.

Although the CBS execs who popped out at lunchtime to see what was happening seemed to be enjoying themselves, the combined effect of Elvis's typically bug-eyed, full-throated performance and the rowdy Stiff party worried the Hilton's management sufficiently for them to call the police. When they arrived, the lawmen accused Elvis of busking, which by definition means performing illegally for money. Ever the rebel in the three-button suit jacket, Elvis body-swerved all attempts to get him to stop playing and was eventually arrested for his impertinence and taken to the nearest police station, only to be rescued by his solicitor just as he was heading for the cells. 'I don't know what was said, but suddenly I was given a cup of tea, they completed the paperwork, and [I] was released,' he said. 'It was no big deal.'7

But the stunt worked. Elvis's pavement performance brought him to the attention of CBS boss Walter Yetnikoff and made an impression on A&R man Greg Geller, who was instrumental in signing him to Columbia Records in the US three months later. The legend told only part of the story, however: a combination of the frantic machinations of Jake Riviera and the fact that Elvis's profile in the UK was sky-high by the autumn of 1977 ensured that he would almost certainly have secured a US deal whether he had flirted with criminal noteriety or not.

Having escaped incarceration, the gig at Dingwalls that night should have been a cause for celebration. Elvis wasn't in the mood, however, and later called the set a 'disaster'. Indeed, it was not lost on observers that he was becoming increasingly difficult. At Dingwalls, the audience filled the space between the bar on one side and a restaurant area on the other. This did not go down well.

'People were eating,' recalls Ken Smith, who was at the show. 'Elvis said: "I can't play while people are fucking eating." That rather annoyed the management. He hadn't *quite* cracked it at that point.' All this did nothing to dampen the fervour of the crowd who greeted the show with 'hysterical enthusiasm', according to *Melody Maker*. Nonetheless, he wouldn't play Dingwalls again for six years.

Elvis dutifully arrived in court the following morning to take his punishment like a man,* and that night he was back at the Hope and Anchor, a last familiar stop before he embarked on his first steps into the madness of leading a professional touring band around the country. The Nag's Head in High Wycombe may not have been the epicentre of rock 'n' roll, but it was a start.

* * *

* He was fined £5 by the magistrate for the incorrect charge of 'selling records in the street'. Not having enough money with him, Elvis asked for time to pay, which he was granted.

The tour was a disjointed affair. A five-week-long Sunday night residency at the Nashville Rooms meant that they had to be back in London at least once a week, but between 28 July and 4 September they also played in provincial towns and major cities all over Britain, as well as to a couple of continental festivals. By now the group had been christened The Attractions, having initially and understandably resisted Elvis's idea to call them The Sticky Valentines, a line from 'Alison' which most assuredly did not translate into global superstardom.

By and large, the setlist remained the same throughout the tour: most of *My Aim Is True* reworked with The Attractions, plus at least half-a-dozen new songs. Towards the end 'You Belong To Me' was added and 'Radio, Radio' made its debut as an Elvis Costello rather than a Flip City song. Another oldie, the atypically quirky 'Hoover Factory', also made the odd appearance.

After the concert at Huddersfield Polytechnic on 29 July, Elvis and the band were drinking together at the hotel, and started chatting about what they aspired to achieve from their musical careers. 'I remember asking Elvis, "What do you want from all this?", says Bruce Thomas. 'And he just looked at me – he could be very arch – and said, "I want to be able to buy people".' The tour highlight was a memorable 'hometown' gig with Nick Lowe and Dave Edmunds at Eric's in Liverpool on 2 August. At the soundcheck Elvis caught up with his old Rusty sidekick Allan Mayes, who accompanied him back to Lilian's house for a cup of tea and a chat. The two had kept in contact sporadically, and were still on good terms. Indeed, Elvis had made sure Mayes heard *My Aim Is True* by sending him an advance copy of the album.

'I don't remember him changing,' he says. 'I don't remember any obnoxiousness, I don't remember any animosity.' There was one problem, however. His old friend didn't know what to call him, left flat-footed and a little embarrassed by the game of media cat-and-mouse which surrounded Elvis at the time. 'That was a nightmare for me, because nobody was supposed to know his real name,' he admits.

The local paper's review of that night's gig at Eric's was telling. Already, the praise came with a caveat. 'Enough has appeared in print on this gawky wonder for the time being,' cautioned the reviewer, before succumbing: 'The lad is great, and so is the band.'

And so they were, an explosive, ferocious live spectacle. Those who came to the shows expecting a reproduction of the chugging pleasantries of *My Aim Is True* were knocked backwards by the sheer violence, energy and electricity of Elvis and The Attractions. This was something quite different from the record, a wild, furious unleashing of frustration, unsettling in its intensity. It was irresistible.

Halfway through the tour, while Elvis was spending a couple of days in London en route to Marseilles, the news broke that Elvis Presley had died in Memphis. It was 16 August, 1977. Ken Smith and some friends were visiting Mary at the flat in Cypress Avenue when Elvis arrived home. 'I remember being in the front room when he came in,' Smith recalls. 'Very quiet. White faced.'

It wouldn't be too harsh to conclude that Elvis was not simply grieving the death of The King. The news could easily have been a hammer blow for his fledgling career, and indeed two of the more conservative national newspapers – the *Daily Mail* and *Daily Express* – dropped their planned features on Elvis immediately after Presley's death. However, for a label as confrontational as Stiff it was a matter of honour to seize the day. 'The King Is Dead, Long Live The King' ran the new slogan. The *NME* also saw an opportunity to further establish the battle lines between Us and Them, contemplating running the cover line 'Elvis & Elvis: Which One Is A Stiff Artist?', a masterpiece of bad taste which was quietly dropped pre-publication. Far from being damaging, Presley's death only helped to secure Elvis's growing status as a homegrown darling of the music press, as if somehow the mere presence of this skinny, acidic, seething young man had helped kill off the bloated, embarrassing, Las Vegas circus act that Presley had become.

If anyone at Stiff had any remaining concerns, they were quickly dispelled. Just four days after Presley's demise, Elvis and The Attractions played their usual Sunday night show in London. With *My Aim Is True* enjoying the third of its twelve-week run in the UK album charts, where it would eventually peak at No. 14, the 400-capacity Nashville Rooms was crammed with over a thousand people, eight of whom were arrested by police summoned to ease the chaos.

The same week, Elvis recorded a live version of 'Red Shoes' for inclusion on the BBC's flagship pop show *Top Of The Pops,* and on 10 September they played an ill-advised set supporting Santana at the Crystal Palace Garden Party. Elvis and The Attractions were second on the bill, and although the crowd was hostile – naturally, Elvis was suitably hostile back – and their music unsuited to the vast expanses of an open-air venue, it was a tangible sign of how quickly things were moving.

'When the record was totally done, Clover went back to the States to tour,' recalls John Ciambotti. 'And after we got back to London, Elvis was already famous. It was fast! It was *really* fast. It was astounding.' 'The King Is Dead, Long Live The King,' indeed.

'Love? I dunno what it means, really,'[8] Elvis had told Nick Kent in the summer, a strange public admission for a man with a wife and young child. Admittedly, he was drunk and drumming up press coverage at the time, but the footprints of domestic dissatisfaction were stamped all over his songs.

Aged twenty-three, Elvis had never really cut loose. He had been an awkward, chubby adolescent who'd had little luck with girls. He had been with Mary since his late teens, with parental and spousal responsibilities following soon after. He had never indulged himself in the illicit pleasures of excessive drink and drugs. Now, as his potentially successful career dictated that his absences from home would become more and more protracted, he felt duty bound to explore the new opportunities that were placed in front of him. Whether Elvis had been faithful to his wife up until this point in their marriage is impossible to say, but soon he was straying.

Mary maintained good relations with many of Elvis's friends; she had kept in touch with Ken Smith and Steve Hazelhurst from Flip City, and she quickly established a friendship with Bruce Thomas as well. Elvis would sometimes stay over at Bruce's if there had been a domestic row, and Mary would often call Bruce the next day to bend his ear.

'Mary rang me quite a lot,' he says. 'A couple of times I was the one who dropped Elvis in it. I'd say, "Oh well, I know he shouldn't have done this, that and the other." And she'd say, "I didn't know he'd done *that*!". At one of the first gigs we did at the Nashville Rooms, I said to Elvis: "Look, I think I've just blown it, I've just told her about that girl from Scotland." And he'd just say: "Oh, don't worry, where do you think all the songs come from?".'

Other people were beginning to ask themselves the same question. In the late summer of 1977, a Liverpool reporter had recognised that Elvis Costello was in fact ex-folk troubadour Declan MacManus, and contacted Allan Mayes about doing a story. Mayes called Stiff, leaving a message with the secretary that somebody wanted to go into print about the very early years. Within twenty-four hours he got a call from Elvis: 'Look, I don't have time for this. I've just got one thing to tell you, Allan. If these people print anything, Jake says legs will be broken.'

His tone was deadly serious, although the threat certainly wasn't. 'We all know it was only talk,' says Mayes. 'But I told this reporter I wouldn't do it. If they wanted to play the mysterious game, fine.' The aura of paranoia, the scare tactics and the secrecy surrounding his past would come to characterise – indeed define – the Costello-Riviera partnership in the coming months and years. 'Jake had a lot of charisma and he was a bit of a strongman,' says Dave Robinson. 'The pair of them got off on that.'

There were bigger problems brewing. Stiff were planning a '60s-style package tour for the beginning of October, a rotating revue featuring Elvis and The Attractions, Wreckless Eric, Ian Dury and The Blockheads, Larry Wallis and Nick Lowe. However, with the tour already booked, it became clear that the relationship between Jake Riviera and Dave Robinson wasn't going to last the distance. The reasons appeared vague even then, but it was Jake who wanted out, apparently driven to distraction by the business headaches of keeping a small label going.

'To this day, I do not know [why],' says Robinson. 'I'd spent ages in and out to America, we had this big deal with Sony which was really going to fund us if not into the big time then into the next stage. And just on the cusp of this Jake decided he couldn't go on with it. So I said, "You should take Elvis".'

When Elvis signed to Stiff, he had also signed a management deal with Robinson and Riviera. A secondary consequence of the split, therefore, was that Jake alone was left in the capacity of Elvis's manager, a position he would hold for almost twenty years. In truth, it was merely a formalisation of an emotional and intellectual partnership that had already been forged. Although in theory Robinson and Riviera shared everything, Elvis was Jake's guy.

It was agreed that not only should the Stiff tour go ahead, but that the forthcoming single, 'Watching The Detectives' b/w live versions of 'Blame It On Cain' and 'Miracle Man' would also be released on Stiff. Then Elvis would officially leave the label. It was cold comfort for Robinson, who also lost Nick Lowe and The Yachts with Jake's departure and was left to mop up a plethora of residual problems at Stiff, including significant debts which the label had accrued over the previous eighteen months. 'It was a dangerous time,' he admits today.

The Live Stiffs tour began on 3 October, 1977 at High Wycombe Town Hall, and became legendary for its swift, headlong descent into chaos and disorder. By all accounts, Elvis tried to keep his head while all around him were losing theirs, but his resistance could only hold firm for so long.

At first, however, it was all about the music. Never keen on pandering to the tastes of the audience, especially one that wasn't there exclusively to see him, on the opening night at High Wycombe he played a set featuring virtually nothing from *My Aim Is True* save for 'Less Than Zero'. Mostly, he played new songs and covers.

'The crowd was shouting for stuff off the album,' recalls Wreckless Eric. 'And Elvis said, "If you want to hear the album you can listen to it at home." Just incredibly arrogant.' Stiff publicist Glen Colson also remembers the gig: 'Elvis deliberately cut his own throat. He was just a perverse sort of guy and he did that sort of thing.'9*

It wouldn't be the first or last time there were traces of self-sabotage evident in the choices Elvis made in the guise of artistic integrity. It was as though he strove to make it as difficult as possible for both himself and the audience by choosing the least accessible route. Already, he felt a deep-rooted unease at meekly offering up what people wanted, doing what was expected of him. Partly, this was a genuine desire to keep things fresh for himself – after all, most of the songs on *My Aim Is True* were already a year old – but it was also indicative of a long-standing cussedness towards his audience and towards success which bordered on contempt.

It was a dangerous game to play so early on, and indeed Elvis swiftly backtracked on the tour to include several more *My Aim Is True* songs in his set. At High Wycombe, the reviewer from *Sounds*, Vivien Goldman, berated Elvis for his 'self-absorption' and 'lecturing' pose. Goldman's review went on to praise Eric's set and especially Ian Dury and The Blockheads, sparking an intense rivalry between Dury and Elvis which dominated the entire tour.

The antipathy was exaggerated by the general demeanour of both men, insecure at heart, with highly charged emotions held below the surface. The rivalry was rarely explicit, usually characterised by a tight-lipped tension when the two met and fuelled by the tacit acknowledgement that each man had a degree of professional admiration for the other: both Elvis and Ian were gifted songwriters heading for big things, and both took pride in the fact that they had excellent bands.

The stand-off was probably a little lop-sided. 'Ian hated Elvis, I'm afraid, he just hated him, but Ian absolutely hated everybody until he knew them,' says Wreckless Eric. 'He was terribly competitive. Elvis was a rival and it was like some war.'

Dury was still displaying traces of hostility not long before his premature death in 2000. 'It was not a relaxed, happy tour,' he said. 'It was geared towards launching Elvis, I didn't need it as much as he did. There was a certain amount of paranoia flying about because [my] band often upstaged Costello.'10 For his part, Elvis feigned indifference. 'It was anti-boring, stab-you-in-the-back stuff,' he later shrugged, before adding

* His clothes may not have helped. 'Elvis was wearing this kind of biker outfit,' says Wreckless Eric. 'It got described in one of the reviews as a "poofy biker outfit", some sort of leather jacket and trousers combination. He only wore that once!'

pointedly, 'There was lots of human chemistry but lots of it was just down to basic negativity. [The tour] was principally down to pushing Ian's album.'[11]

The fraught atmosphere was exacerbated by the fact that all the acts on the tour were alternating as the headliners each night, which ensured that it swiftly became a competition. In such circumstances, Elvis's insistence on playing songs by other Stiff acts on the tour was no accident. Dury's 'Roadette's Song', by his old band Kilburn and The High Roads; Wreckless Eric's 'Whole Wide World'; and The Damned's 'Neat Neat Neat' were all excellent additions to Elvis's set, but one suspected they were played more in the spirit of one-upmanship and anything-you-can-do bravado than sincere tribute or comradeship.*

Under the circumstances, writing a song for Dury seemed a rather perverse kind of provocation. An inveterate news junkie, Elvis was killing time on tour by flicking through the *News Of The World* in the hotel when Wreckless Eric pointed out all the strange little adverts, singing the praises of support shoes, commode chairs and special gadgets to squeeze spots. 'I said, "Look, 'stylish slacks to suit your pocket.' It's a line in a song, isn't it?" And he said, "Yeah! Let's have a race to see who can get it into a song first." I thought, "Oh God, we're off to work again!"'

Later that day on the coach, Elvis unveiled his new song, featuring the line from the paper. Called 'Sunday's Best', it was a sleazy litany of Middle England's tabloid pre-occupations, written with Dury in mind and debuted the same night – 31 October – at Guildford Civic Hall, where Elvis sauntered on stage with the words: 'I see we've got some cunts in the audience tonight.' Dury never did use the song, although the version that Elvis and The Attractions eventually cut for the *Armed Forces* album retained some of The Blockhead's swirling, vaudevillian flavour. Part grudging tribute, part V-sign.

Elvis set himself apart on the tour, preferring to avoid the schoolboy antics of 'this coachful of lunatics', to borrow Steve Nieve's description.[12]** While capable of enjoying himself when the mood took him, Elvis was not the kind of man who welcomed being cajoled into 'having fun'. So

---

* Elvis and The Attractions also played versions of Bacharach and David's 'I Just Don't Know What To Do With Myself'; Richard Hell's 'Love Comes In Spurts'; and The Lovin' Spoonful's 'Six O'Clock' on the Stiff tour.
** The tour provided Steve Nason with his enduring stage name, after he wondered aloud what a groupie was. 'The first few tours we did, I was just out of school and looking for a wild time,' he said. 'I can't really recall much about them.'[13] He didn't stay naive for long, but he would be 'Nieve' from then on.

while Larry Wallis was cavorting through a hotel foyer wearing a policeman's helmet, Elvis could be found rooting round Woolworths looking for rare EMI copies of 'God Save The Queen' in the remainder rack.

Such reluctance to throw himself full tilt into 'The 24-Hour Club' led to resentment from some quarters. One night when he was sleeping – and snoring – heavily on the bus, a prank ended with him having his shoelaces tied together and a full ashtray emptied into his mouth. He was understandably furious.

Nevertheless, it was impossible to stay straight for long. 'I did go strange towards the end,' he admitted. 'I'd blank out and just see red.'[14] Elvis had never been a drug taker; he had never dabbled with marajuana, nor did he smoke cigarettes, and he had rarely been a big drinker. As late as July 1977, he was adamant on the subject. 'I don't take drugs,' he stated. 'I can't even be in the same room as people doing cocaine.'[15] However, touring with a rock band – never mind *five* rock bands – has a way of making such clear-cut stances disappear into the ether.

'The excess started pretty much from when there was any money about, or from the first time people realised it was a happening band,' says Bruce Thomas. 'Once people realise that, people appear from everywhere offering you this and that. Nothing succeeds like perceived success.'

Women, drink and drugs played a big part on the Stiffs tour. Alcohol would always be a core constituent of The Attractions' touring antics, but the drug use would soon escalate. This time around it was primarily amphetamines, the quintessential punk drug.

Perhaps more damaging was the convoluted sexual affair which unwound as the tour went on. An American girl fond of calling herself Farrah Fuck-it-Minor – a pointed reference to *Charlie's Angels* star Farrah Fawcett-Majors – was travelling on the Stiff bus, ostensibly as the companion of Steve, whom she would go on to live with for many years and with whom she also has two children.

During the tour, Farrah had flings with both Elvis and Bruce Thomas, both of whom reportedly fell for her quite hard. The mess culminated in Newcastle on 4 November. Following the gig at the Polytechnic, Elvis wrote 'Pump It Up' on the hotel fire escape of the Swallow Hotel, scrawling pages and pages detailing his love-hate relationship with rock 'n' roll excess, viewed from both the outside and the inside. At the heart of the song is his barely concealed disgust at how easily he has been seduced by the lifestyle. 'It was getting so ugly I was compelled to write 'Pump It Up',' he later said. 'Well, just how much can you fuck, how many drugs can you do before you get so numb you can't really feel anything?'[16]

Among other things, 'Pump It Up' can be interpreted as a thinly-veiled account of the escapades involving Farrah Fuck-It-Minor, the 'bad girl' who is 'like a narcotic'. He ends with the resigned acceptance that he can do little else but succumb: 'No use wishing for any other sin.' True to form, the song underwent drastic editing the following day and was unveiled that evening – Bonfire Night – at Lancaster University, the tour's final calling point. From there, all concerned crawled home. It had only been four weeks, but it felt like a lifetime. And it was only the beginning.

Within a matter of days Elvis and The Attractions were heading off on their first trip to the United States. Starting on 15 November, the four-week Stateside trek took in shows in most of the major cities, beginning in San Francisco and ending at the semi-legendary Stone Pony at Asbury Park, New Jersey, the club where Bruce Springsteen had made his name.

If Elvis's rise to fame in the UK had been swift, his ascendence in the US was supersonic, when taking into account the vastness of the country and the fact that less than five months previously he had still been working at Elizabeth Arden. As the tour went on, he attracted the kind of attention usually reserved for genuine rock stars: *Time* and *Newsweek* magazines were tailing him, and he was approached to appear on NBC's flagship TV show *Saturday Night Live*.

My Aim Is True had initially been available only on import, but the newly minted deal that Jake had secured with Columbia ensured the record gained a full release to coincide with Elvis's shows; indeed, it had sold a remarkable 100,000 copies by the middle of the tour, helped by strong reviews from every organ that mattered: *Rolling Stone*, the *Village Voice*, the *LA Times*, the *New York Times* and the *Washington Post*. 'I can hum them all, but I don't understand any of them,' mused the *Post's* Mark Kernis wryly.

The paper's reviewer Tom Zito was already marking 'that special moment when the cult figure reaches the brink of fame's jettison', as he watched Elvis perform with 'unbelievable fury and rage and angst' in front of 600 screaming kids in Philadelphia on 7 December. The set at the Hot Club was broadly representative of the tour as a whole. The band kicked off with 'Welcome To The Working Week'. Elvis – for the time being – was seemingly amenable to the idea of plugging 'the product' on this side of the Atlantic, and played another fifteen songs: eight from *My Aim Is True*,* one cover – Ian Dury's 'Roadette Song' – and seven from the yet-to-be recorded next album.

* The US version included 'Watching The Detectives'.

85

Although the *New York Times* remained ambivalent about this thrift-shop rocker and his band, few shared its reservations. The shows at The Bottom Line in New York were sold out, the crowd clamouring for standing room. There was just something about Elvis and The Attractions that clicked. He could really *sing*, which has always been important in America, his tight, forceful voice crackling and snapping through the music. He could obviously write, too. '*My Aim Is True* got me listening to rock 'n' roll again,' says country-rock star Steve Earle, who first heard the record in late 1977. 'It was just that level of songwriting on a rock record was kind of a revelation until then. He was one of the handful of songwriters who from day one could knock down the facadium and never be a slave to any particular song form.'

And The Attractions were becoming an extraordinary group, locked down tight on a superbly solid but flexible rhythmic base, another major part of the reason America took to them so readily. After the let-down of the Sex Pistols and the thin, sexless, four-square monotony of most of punk, here was a band – and they really *were* a band, they effortlessly transcended the sum of their parts – who truly packed a punch.

In short, Elvis and The Attractions were made for America: different but not too different; a little punky, but firmly grounded in an accepted historical lineage which incorporated Dylan, The Beatles, Van Morrison and Springsteen. It was the latter's name which kept springing up most often, not so much in terms of the style of the music, but in the genuine, something-is-happening-here excitement Elvis was generating. It was hard to comprehend. But then so was America. Like most artists visiting the United States for the first time, Elvis found the country an endlessly fascinating source of confusion, inspiration and alienation. He was soaking it all up, filling notebooks that would go on to provide the lyrics for future albums.

Band relations were companionable, but edgy. On the road and away from home, they were thrown into each other's lives and became something like a gang, albeit one with a recognised leader who would pull rank whenever necessary. One of the early concerns was over billing, with The Attractions often being consigned to anonymous backing band on the publicity for the US dates. There were spirited discussions between the group and Elvis and Jake: 'Is it Elvis Costello and The Attractions doing these gigs or is it Elvis Costello?', they asked. 'Are we going to be clear about how this is going to be billed?' The situation was soon resolved, but it did little to foster inter-band harmony. Often, Elvis would simply retreat behind his headphones and stare out of the window of the bus, lost in his own thoughts. This was his show after all.

It was a strangely schizophrenic tour. Reactions ranged from ecstatic in the hipper cities like San Francisco, Boston, Philadelphia and New York to the surly indifference of New Orleans and Atlanta, where they shared a bill with Talking Heads. At the final show in Asbury on 16 December, Elvis treated the audience to one-off versions of The Everly Brothers' 'The Price Of Love' and Nick Lowe's 'Heart Of The City', before introducing Bruce Thomas as 'The Real Future of Rock 'n' Roll', a pointed reference to that 'other' Bruce from those parts. The cocky Englishman's jibe apparently went down so badly that they had to lock themselves in their dressing room to escape vengeful 'Boss' fans after the gig. At least he now knew not to try a similar stunt in Memphis.

The following night they were back in New York. Elvis and The Attractions had been booked to make their US television debut on *Saturday Night Live* as a replacement for the Sex Pistols, who had pulled out at the last moment, which at least explained Pete Thomas's 'Thanks Malc' T-shirt. Having performed 'Watching The Detectives' at the start of the show, they were midway through the original version of 'Less Than Zero' when – in some conjoined spirit of perversity and mischievousness – Elvis called an unscheduled halt to the proceedings.

'Stop! Stop!' he shouted to the band, cutting the song short by slicing his hand through the air. 'I'm sorry ladies and gentlemen, there's no reason to do this song here,' he said, before counting The Attractions into the unreleased 'Radio, Radio', with its 'I wanna bite the hand that feeds me' refrain. *Saturday Night Live* producer Lorne Michaels was far from happy, both with the unannounced change of plan – which threw the floor crew into a panic – and also with the song's sentiments. As the show was live there was little option but to let him finish the song. Elvis had made his point. 'Evidently it's not *that* live,'[17] he later sneered, admitting that he was sick of being 'bullied' into playing tracks from *My Aim Is True*. He wouldn't appear on live US televison again until the '80s.

* * *

By the time Elvis returned from the States for Christmas, he had signed with Radar Records, a new independent company financed by Warner Brothers. Jake had an amicable and long-standing relationship with Andrew Lauder, previously of United Artists and a man who had dealt with both Jake and Stiff in the past. Lauder had decided to leave United Artists and form Radar Records at around the same time as Jake decided to take Elvis and Nick Lowe away from Stiff.

'[Radar] was set up without Elvis Costello and without Nick Lowe,' says Lauder. 'It was only when I sat down with Jake to say we're leaving United Artists and starting another record company, that he said "Do you want Elvis and Nick?".' At the end of their conversation in a Greek restaurant in Shepherd's Bush, there was a gentleman's agreement that Nick Lowe and Elvis Costello would be joining Radar. And being a gentleman of a particular kind, Jake stuck to it.

Elvis's parting shot for Stiff had at least provided both artist and label with their first hit. 'Watching The Detectives' had climbed to No. 15 in the UK charts in November 1977, the only one of Stiff's first twenty-two singles to reach the Top 40. It was hailed by the *NME* as 'one of the most important singles of the '70s', and it certainly did much to fulfill the commerical promise of Elvis Costello. Until now, he had been a name to casually drop in hip circles. Now he had a hit record.

The recording of *This Year's Model* was squeezed in between the end of the first US tour and the beginning of the next one, booked to begin towards the end of January. There were also three dates at the Nashville Rooms immediately before Christmas. It was a punishing schedule, but Roger Bechirian – who engineered the album sessions at Eden Studios in London – recalls Elvis coming off the tour radiating energy. 'He was a star almost overnight, and I think he was quite bemused by it all, swept up with the excitement. I have a great laughing image of him being fairly fresh-faced, like a little boy in a sweet shop.'

During the recording, Elvis stayed at Bruce Thomas's new flat in Shepherd's Bush much of the time. Mary was by no means oblivious to what he was getting up to on the road, and life at Cypress Avenue was increasingly volatile. Indeed, the couple would soon separate. Nonetheless, Elvis was focused and the album came together easily. The songs had been thoroughly road tested and required little in the way of studio embellishment. The Clash's Mick Jones sat in on one session, playing guitar on 'Pump It Up' and 'Big Tears', but even his contributions were deemed surplus to requirements for the final cut.

Nobody was looking for a polished record. The blueprint was mid-'60s Stones – specifically, *Aftermath* – early Who and The Kinks. An accurate singer in the studio, it was not unusual for Elvis's live guide vocals to end up on the finished track, and there was very little in the way of additional over-dubbing: the odd keyboard part, the occasional guitar, percussion and some harmony vocals. 'We literally did the best tracks on the album – 'Pump It Up', 'Chelsea' – in one afternoon,' recalls Bruce Thomas. 'It was like Motown. We'd just go in, play them, and that was it.'

Nick Lowe was again an essential element in the creative process. He enjoyed playing the mad professor, pushing energy levels up to the max to extract the very best performances from the band. Lowe had an impeccable ear for recognising when the band had nailed that special take with all the excitement and energy in it; no matter how much was added, it would still retain that elemental thrill for the listener. He could be persuasive, and usually got his way. As the man who according to Elvis 'had the task of making a sonic reality out of Nick Lowe's directions, such as "turn the drums into one big maraca",'[18] Roger Bechirian played the straightman, often taking charge when things became too technical.

There was a firm distinction drawn between the touring antics and the more restrained behaviour in the studio. It was a sober and industrious working environment. The lights were always full up, they would start at about 10.30 or 11 a.m. and finish around 9 p.m.; all going well, they would be in the pub by 9.30. 'The whole thing was really good, it was really friendly, very positive,' says Bechirian. 'Everyone was really excited because they were the stars of the moment.'

Taking a short break over the New Year, they reconvened in early January to complete the record. Elvis even found the time to put down rough demos of some new songs, including 'Green Shirt' and 'Big Boys'. It took eleven days in all. Still a relative tyro in the recording process, Elvis didn't tend to be around much during the mix. He might stroll in at some point during the day to hear what had been done and make a few comments, but at this stage he was still happy to defer the bulk of the responsibility to Lowe.

With *This Year's Model* completed and scheduled for release in mid-March, Elvis and The Attractions warmed up for the US tour in January with a free concert at London's Roundhouse, where an 'aggressive' Elvis traded insults with members of the front row. They also fulfilled a long-standing commitment to play at a wedding in Davidstow in Cornwall, a thank you for the rehearsal space they had used back in July of the previous year. Then came a true assault on America and then the world, not to mention the collective sensibilties of Elvis and the band.

Chapter Five
1978–79

THE NEXT EIGHTEEN MONTHS WERE MIND-NUMBING. A non-stop, alcohol-and-chemical-fuelled trek around the globe which took a huge toll on Elvis and The Attractions. It was the American tours that really damaged the psyche. In Europe, they were usually away for a little more than a month at a time and much of that was in Britain, where the landscape and customs were familiar. But in America it was very different. The journeys between gigs were gargantuan, the cultural and geographical changes immense, the sense of isolation and loneliness limitless. 'You're sitting on a bus, looking out the window at a country you've never been to but have only read about, listened to and absorbed through your imagination,' said Elvis. 'Suddenly, it's out there, and it's somewhat different to what you thought. You get strange people offering you this, that and the other. It all gets mixed up.'[1]

There was growing professional pressure. By the end of January 1978, *My Aim Is True* had climbed to No. 32 on the Billboard chart, a hit record in anyone's book. Elvis was a wanted man, promoting the record through radio interviews rather than the print media, which he already felt was painting him into a one-dimensional corner. He may even have helped them. His newspaper and magazine silence would – with a few very notable exceptions – last until the early '80s, helping to build a certain mystique, yes, but also an intrinsic mistrust and misunderstanding between artist and media.

But there's no denying that America was new and largely fun, for the time being at least. The Attractions were like a particularly debauched incarnation of The Monkees, grabbing any opportunity to get up to mischief, getting drunk and following any whim. Pete and Steve roomed under the names of Vince Posh and Norman Wisdom, and legendary drinking would go on between them. At a CBS convention in New Orleans, the first order that went down to room service was eight quart bottles of vodka. On another occasion in Dallas, one member of the touring party had to be 'sprung' from jail.

'He got hold of a load of "leapers" [speed],' alleges Bruce Thomas. 'He stole them off some girl and ended up getting arrested. I got the police report: "Mr So-and-so attempted to fondle Miss Simpson's derrière." He got put in the detox tent; he had to swallow a load of stuff just as he was getting thrown in the hold, and we had to bribe a judge $20,000 to get him out.'

The shows themselves were a standard sixty-minute mix of *My Aim Is True* material and *This Year's Model*, with the odd cover and B-side thrown in. Elvis was writing all the time: 'Chemistry Class' and 'Moods For Moderns' were the first to show up, quickly slotted into the set towards the end of the tour following soundcheck renditions.

By the beginning of March, Elvis and The Attractions had become a truly awesome spectacle, both in concert and on record. The *NME* caught up with Elvis's final show of the North American tour at El Mocambo club in Toronto on 7 March, and witnessed scenes of utter rapture. One besotted female fan mopped Elvis's brow as he sweated out his demons on stage. The audience punched their fists and sang along to almost every word. Charles Shaar Murray watched this 'exportable proto-superstar' and reported the madness with an exhilaration which still leaps off the page today. 'Something's happening. I don't care what else goes down this year: Elvis Costello and The Attractions are the band to watch. Everybody else is so far behind that they'd have to double their speed just to choke on his dust.'

In Britain, '(I Don't Want To Go To) Chelsea' b/w 'You Belong To Me' was released to huge acclaim, the first, swaggering taster for *This Year's Model*. 'The single's so good, the very act of releasing it amounts to bragging on a colossal scale,' said the *NME*. 'Chelsea' quickly hit the Top 20. The following week, on 17 March, *This Year's Model* was released, the first 50,000 copies coming with a free single of 'Stranger In The House' and The Damned's 'Neat Neat Neat,' a little 45 rpm slice of country and punk bookending the classic, updated beat-pop of the album.

It is always tempting to view landmark records through the benevolent lens of nostalgia, but *This Year's Model* effortlessly stands up to scrutiny today. The tunes are tight and instantly memorable (although the appeal of 'The Beat' has always proved elusive), probably because Elvis was confident enough in his writing and his band to let his influences not so much peek through as strip off and run around naked. 'You Belong To Me' sparked off the riff from The Rolling Stones' 'The Last Time,' 'Pump It Up' took Dylan's 'Subterranean Homesick Blues' and bludgeoned it to death, while the bridge to 'This Year's Girl' was a shameless steal from

The Beatles' 'You Won't See Me'. No matter. Nick Lowe's production had given the songs a thick, powerful fuse on which to burn, and while Steve Nieve's organ danced and jabbed around the songs like a boxer, the rhythmic invention reached an exhilarating crescendo on the breathless bass and drum swordfight at the centre of 'Lipstick Vogue'. Elvis sang it all with 100 times the depth and range that he had shown on *My Aim Is True*.

The album title was knowing and the cover image, once again, iconic: Elvis hunched behind a camera and tripod, expressionless, both observed and observing. The reviews were superlative, and rightly so. The *NME* and *Melody Maker* brought out their Elvis big hitters – Nick Kent and Allan Jones respectively – to try to articulate the sheer breadth of the achievement. Kent claimed that 'there's simply no one within spitting distance of him,' calling the record 'too dazzling, too powerful, to be ignored'. Jones covered the same waterfront again. *This Year's Model*, he claimed, 'promotes its author to the foremost ranks of contemporary rock writers. Clear out of sight of most of his rivals and comparisons (so long, Bruce, baby).'

Few critics in Britain dwelled too long on the lyrics, but as time went on *This Year's Model* would be a record that regularly attracted accusations of misogyny. In the US, Jon Pareles's review in *Crawdaddy* judged the record 'so wrong-headed, so full of hatred, so convinced of its moral superiority' in regards to its view of women. It is true that Elvis almost always assumed the moral high ground in these songs: 'I am right and you are wrong, therefore my response – no matter what it is – is justified,' an attitude which was beginning to spill out from the grooves of his records and into his personal life.

But cries of blanket misogyny were oversimplistic. An easy confusion can be made between misogyny and somebody who has an extremely vehement position on the battle of the sexes in terms of specific relationships. Being hostile or angry or vengeful towards one woman in a song is not the same as being contemptuous towards all women. It was also a misreading based on mistaking the attitude of the *performances* on the record for the true sentiment of the words as written rather than sung, as well as a general reaction to the way Elvis looked and presented himself to the public: the bitter geek, the guy who never got the girl. 'If you're a laddish sort of singer, you can get away with all sorts of stuff and people think you're great,' he later said. 'The Stones wrote 'Stupid Girl' and they're heroes. I wrote 'This Year's Girl', saying that fashion is a trap, a much more compassionate song, and everyone said I was a misogynist.'[2]

Rolling Stone made the record its lead review, and the considered praise of the magnificent music came with a more astute ear for the lyrical nuances.

'For all his surface cockiness,' recognised reviewer Kit Rachlis, 'Costello is a man who's trembling underneath.' From the opening 'No Action', taking in the masochistic rough and tumble of 'The Beat', 'Living In Paradise', 'Lipstick Vogue' and 'Little Triggers', the album is littered with Elvis's 'trembling'.

The record's searing disgust comes from a colossal disappointment at what passes for real emotion. Or to put it another way, 'Sometimes I almost feel/Just like a human being'. The desperate double-bluffs of male and female interaction are dealt with in bluntly honest fashion; insecurity and duplicity exist on both sides, but clearly what the singer is searching for throughout is something approximating genuine feeling rather than a pale imitation of the real thing. 'A lot of the songs early on were more disappointed that anybody could fall for that cliché of romance or fashion or a cheap version of love,'[3] he later said. 'That's a constant theme. I see right through imaginary gutter romance.'[4]

He might have seen through it, but he was not immune to its appeal. Rachlis's review uses '(I Don't Want To Go To) Chelsea' as the prime example of the attraction-revulsion dynamic which exists in many of the songs. 'Costello can describe Chelsea with such precision because he knows its splendours. If the disdain in his voice appears a little too measured it's because it takes all of the singer's resolve to resist Chelsea's temptations.'

* * *

The UK and Irish tour began in Dublin on the eve of the album's release. For most of March the band tore through roughly the same set as had been making America weak at the knees, before introducing slivers of the next record, already forming in Elvis's mind. After Dublin came Belfast. This was Elvis's first visit to the trouble-torn city, where he saw 'mere boys, these children, walking around in battle fatigues carrying machine guns, knowing that the lads who got the least marks in the exam usually joined the army'.[5] On the plane back to London, Elvis began working on his ideas for 'Oliver's Army', using Oliver Cromwell's brutal occupation of Ireland in the seventeenth century as a historical stepping stone which allowed him to examine England's more recent imperialist past and Ireland's continuing woes. Elvis later admitted to *Time Out* magazine that Cromwell had been portrayed as 'the devil incarnate' during his Catholic school-days, and his legacy had obviously made a lasting impression. By the end of the tour he would be playing a tentative version of the song live.

The tour was beset by problems, mainly due to the fact that Bruce Thomas had cut his hand while demonstrating – not very well, presumably

– the correct 'bar-room method' of smashing a bottle following a gig at Rafter's in Manchester on 6 April. 'That was just me being pissed,' he says. 'Getting hold of a bottle and breaking it and finding it wasn't made of sugar glass, it was made of extremely thick glass and it was sticking out.' He needed eighteen stitches, although with the pain came the happy consequence of two weeks' leave from their gruelling schedule.

The constant travel and attention wasn't necessarily doing Elvis much good either. His moods were becoming increasingly dark. Ken Smith recalls visiting Cypress Avenue and finding Elvis watching a documentary on the Third Reich, listening to heavy dub reggae with a guitar on his lap, controlling the volume with his foot. The trickle-down effect was obvious in the new songs he was writing: 'Two Little Hitlers', 'Goon Squad', 'Chemistry Class', 'Oliver's Army'. Already, he was toying with calling the new record *Emotional Fascism*.

Nick Lowe deputised on bass for the remainder of the tour dates, with the result that the shows were understandably erratic. At Portsmouth's Guildhall on 12 April, Lowe was delayed getting to the venue, and Elvis came on an hour late and played the first six songs solo with just electric guitar. He seized the opportunity to perform some new numbers, opening with a salvo of 'Chemistry Class', 'Sunday's Best', 'Big Boys' and 'Green Shirt'. By the final shows at London's Roundhouse on 15 and 16 April, he was showcasing embryonic versions of two of his most significant new compositions: 'Accident's Will Happen' and 'Oliver's Army', accompanied only by Steve Nieve.

With another US tour kicking off on 19 April – a mere three days after the end of the UK tour and only six weeks on from the end of the last American trip – Elvis was left without a bass player for the opening dates of his most important tour to date. The Attractions were no longer merely a backing band. With Elvis at the front, this was now a four-piece group with its own unique chemistry, and to remove one component part left a gaping hole.

To fill it, Jake called John Ciambotti, Clover's bassist, and asked him to help out for a few dates, starting with the opening show at Minneapolis State Theater on 19 April. 'I had one day's rehearsal,' he says. 'I had these charts plastered to the side of my amp, and Elvis saw me looking at the stuff during rehearsal and he said, "What's this, then?" And I said, "Those are my charts." And he just took them off the amp and threw them away. "Don't worry about the notes, just throw the shapes." We had a ball. The band was so loud and the crowd was so loud that nobody cared.'

By now the Costello camp had gained a reputation for some seriously wild behaviour. 'I think I slept about four or five hours in the whole time

I was with them,' says Ciambotti. 'You couldn't sleep because there was always something happening. I was *wasted* when I got home. I laid on the beach for about a week just recovering.'

With no one in any doubt anymore that they were going to make it, Elvis and The Attractions found they could pretty much help themselves to whatever they wanted. There were increasing amounts of cocaine flying around, a somewhat guilty secret at the time. Cocaine represented the bloated excess that punk supposedly despised; it was the Fleetwood Mac and the Eagles drug, not the British punk drug. What they should have been doing was drinking cider and taking speed – and certainly, they all used amphetamine – but they also had a more sophisticated palate. 'We did have standards,' says Bruce Thomas, who rejoined the tour before the end of April. 'Expensive tastes. And all of a sudden, it's more a problem of how much you can bear to take.'

As well as the excess, a sense of collective schizophrenia soon took hold. There developed a distinct sense of an American Elvis and The Attractions and a British Elvis and The Attractions, and moving from one to the other took a couple of days to adjust. In the States, they were treated with the type of peculiarly American regard for celebrity which was very much at odds with the traditional British method of keeping people 'in their place'. 'We had a whole different persona,' says Thomas. 'You know what the Americans are like: the glossiness, it's a presentational thing. You had to be a bit more humble in England and a bit more flash in America.'

Jake was an integral factor in making sure Elvis played up to his designated role. He certainly encouraged the mood of intimidation, paranoia and anti-Americanism which began to surround the Costello camp, the 'creeping threat' which Elvis was documenting so vividly in his new songs. 'Jake was a bit of a cartoon character, the classic bully thing,' says Bruce Thomas. If there were reporters around he could be especially antagonistic. 'There were just a lot of people wanting a piece of the action,' recalls John Ciambotti. 'Jake would do his Jake thing and everybody would sit back and watch the show. It was very funny, actually.'

Not everybody thought so. Some of the tactics were shockingly heavy-handed. At the show in Milwaukee, contemporaneous press reports alleged that the road crew beat up a photographer during the performance and *Creem's* Patrick Goldstein was later subjected to an attempted physical assault from Jake and a successful verbal one from Elvis. Goldstein labelled Riviera 'a serious candidate for most despicable character of the decade'.

It was all leading them towards the outer limits of acceptable behaviour. They found they could get away with pretty much anything at all.

Aside from the violence, there were plenty of women. The relentless nature of the touring and the countless opportunities which fame was putting in the way of these four young men – albeit, two of whom were married – meant that yielding to temptation was virtually inevitable. On the second US tour, Charles Shaar Murray had observed that Steve Nieve was 'knocking down enough pussy these last six weeks to make Warren Beatty and Phil Lynott feel inadequate',[6] and the standard cliché of promiscuous, sometimes loutish rock star behaviour had enveloped them all.

'Some horrible things went on,' admits Bruce Thomas. 'One of the members of the band – not me or Elvis – after having his way with a young lady, cut all her hair off, left her naked in a hotel corridor with a business card stuck between the cheeks of her bottom. I mean, that's pretty hard. That's Led Zeppelin.'

Almost pathologically immune to clichés in song, in reality Elvis was as susceptible as the next man, and he embraced what life had to offer with equal enthusiasm in every department. A short way into the tour he wrote 'Party Girl', a romantic, considered ode to an American art student who had sparked Elvis's curiousity on-the-road, perhaps because it was one extremely rare occasion where the promise of desire hadn't been fulfilled*. He previewed the song in Boston on 4 May. 'Goon Squad', 'Two Little Hitlers' and 'Accidents Will Happen' were also making appearances.

All the new material was to a certain extent a reflection of life on the road. 'Even on the bus while we were touring Elvis could write songs,' says John Ciambotti. 'He was so prolific, he could write a song while watching a movie. It was just an amazing thing to be around.' Nick Lowe, supporting on the tour with Rockpile, also recalls Elvis's ability to rise above the madness and create something memorable: 'I couldn't believe that in the midst of this mayhem – and it really was mayhem on these tours – he could come up with such wonderful, soulful songs. He just seemed to be getting better and better.'[7]

In May, a few of Elvis's off-the-cuff quotes appeared in a profile in *Newsweek* magazine, laying down his no-nonsense manifesto. 'I'm a menace. I'm up for a fight. I'm here to corrupt America's youth, but my visa will probably run out before I get to do it.' Despite his bravado, many of the halls were half empty. The venues were mostly 2000-capacity theatres and halls instead of the 600-seater clubs he had played on the previous tour, and it was only in the major cities that they were guaranteed anything close to a capacity crowd. By the end of the month the

* The real-life protgaonists of 'Party Girl' never had sex, apparently because the girl's skin lotion smelt of coconuts and Elvis's ardour was dimmed.

contradictory pressures exacted by the odd combination of adoration and indifference were beginning to show.

At the Civic Auditorium in Santa Monica on 30 May, the strain was all too apparent, as Elvis wielded his guitar like a weapon above his head and kicked over amps before storming off-stage. 'A lot of things were going on that left me confused,' he said. 'I began to worry that it was all too phoney, that people had just convinced themselves that we were the thing to see this week.'[8]

If Elvis was worried about being flavour of the month then the audience at the Hollywood High in Los Angeles on 4 June, 1978 would have done little to ease his concerns. The more he seemingly strove to discourage admiration, the more it descended upon him. Middle-of-the-road queen Linda Rondstadt was in attendance, and so was Bebe Buell.

Buell was almost twenty-five when she first saw Elvis Costello. A glamourous American model and *Playboy* centrefold, Buell was also gaining a well-deserved reputation as a companion to rock 'n' roll royalty, who had enjoyed intimate relationships and flings with Steve Tyler – the father of her baby daughter, Liv, a little under twelve months old at the time – as well as Todd Rundgren, Jimmy Page, Mick Jagger and most recently Rod Stewart. At the Hollywood High, Buell watched a band at the peak of its powers, although her interest was focused entirely upon Elvis: 'I thought he was absolutely beautiful,' she says. 'But that's my Arthur Miller complex.'

The show opened with just Elvis and Steve, previewing an emotionally rich, open-throated 'Accidents Will Happen', capturing perhaps the most enduringly affecting version of the song in this earliest incarnation. Then the Thomas's joined the party, crashing into a high-octane 'Mystery Dance'. Already, the mixture of intensity and musical sophistication on show clearly set Elvis and The Attractions apart from any of their new wave contemporaries. A tender rendition of 'Alison' alerted the watching Rondstadt to the potential of Elvis's songs to cross over to a more mainstream market, although she was probably less sure of the razor-backed gallop through 'Lipstick Vogue' which the band cooked up immediately afterwards. The beautiful 'Party Girl' was also performed, debunking later suggestions that it had been written with Bebe Buell in mind.

After the show, Elvis was introduced to Bebe at the Whisky-A-Go-Go club, and was dazzled. The old MacManus trait of flirting with the prettiest girl, of taking on a challenge, seemed to kick into gear. The two immediately hit it off, arranging to rendezvous the following day. They kept the date, and Buell persuaded Elvis to smoke pot, a drug which he had never used before, 'and we just drove around all day laughing'.[9]

The couple met again before Elvis and the band flew to San Francisco for the final date of the tour on 7 June. The surly anti-pop star and the model-groupie actually had far more in common than their one-dimensional public images might have suggested. They were both obsessed with music, and had recently spilt from their respective long-term partners, Mary and Todd Rundgren. Furthermore, they both had small children, and enjoyed a good time. When Bebe asked Elvis if he was married, he 'swore up and down that they were legally separated,' she says. 'He even used the word "legally".'

For two people with extremely active sex lives, the early stages of their relationship were surprisingly demure. They didn't sleep together, and kissed only once before Elvis had to go back to the UK. Nonetheless, Bebe Buell claims she was already smitten. 'It was an immediate, head-over-heels slam dunk,' she says today. She already believed that she was in love, but Elvis, it seems, had simply decided that he did want to go to Chelsea after all.

* * *

He returned to Britain to find himself a pop star. *This Year's Model* had peaked at No. 4 in the album charts, while the current single, 'Pump It Up', would reach No. 24, ensuring another *Top Of The Pops* performance. However, his marriage was in disarray. 'I had left the family home and was living a totally wilful life with little sense of gravity,' he later admitted. 'I destroyed any possibility of trust and reconciliation in my marriage.'[10]

Elvis moved into Steve Nieve's fifth-floor flat at 48 Queen's Gate Terrace in Kensington while Mary and Matthew remained in Whitton. The couple were separated but not entirely estranged, and there was still a certain amount of rather fraught to-ing and fro-ing involved. 'It was very stormy,' recalls Steve Hazelhurst, who remained on friendly terms with Mary. 'She went through quite a bad period. All the stories about him were coming out.'

In mitigation for his almost continual absences, Elvis's utterly backbreaking schedule showed no signs of letting up. The European tour kicked off on 12 June, a mere four days after the end of the US tour. Hitting the continent for the first time, Elvis and The Attractions took in dates in France, Switzerland, Holland, Germany and Scandinavia. The shows followed the same template as the recent American tour, sprints through *My Aim Is True* and *This Year's Model* with a handful of new songs thrown in.

At the Roskilde Festival appearance in Denmark on 2 July, Elvis and The Attractions debuted the first full band rendition of 'Oliver's Army'. At the time, no one had any inkling of the song's future stature. 'I wasn't particularly aware that that was going to be our anthemic song,' says Bruce Thomas. 'Some of them I thought were pretty good songs, like 'Big Tears', were never big songs. It's hard to tell.' At this stage, Elvis had 'Oliver's Army' pencilled in as a potential B-side, nothing more.

For the remainder of July, The Attractions took a short and well-deserved rest to reconnect with their nervous systems. Elvis was restless and had little inclination to settle, and after a brief attempt at reconciliation in Bermuda with Mary, he flew on to America to indulge in a little country music vacation at Columbia's expense.

His first stop was New York's Lone Star Café on 25 July, guesting with Delbert McLinton on three songs, including a version of Tampa Red's 'Don't You Lie To Me,' an old Flip City cover learned from Chuck Berry. From New York he flew on to Nashville, ostensibly to record a version of 'Stranger In The House' with his hero George Jones. Jones was making a duets album for CBS and had been persuaded by the label to extend an invitation to his 'new wave' labelmate in order to drag a few new fans into the country section of the record shops.

'George Jones didn't show, which was a bit disappointing,'[11] said Elvis, although his reputation as a heavy drinker and his nickname of 'No Show' ensured that the singer's non-appearance wasn't a huge surprise to anyone. The session – recorded under the auspices of legendary country producer Billy Sherill – was rescheduled for another time, but Elvis did get the chance to meet Bruce Springsteen, another icon from the old days. 'Elvis said that Bruce had been trying to get the sound of *My Aim Is True* on his records,' recalls Ken Smith. '"How d'you get the sound on that?" You know, Pathway Studios! Elvis found that quite funny.'

Throughout this period, Elvis had been keeping in touch with Bebe Buell via letter and telephone. Less than two weeks after returning from the American tour in June, he had re-established contact, sending a letter to a mutual acquaintance at Columbia, who passed it on to Bebe. He claimed she was 'haunting' him. Then came a deluge. 'We had hours and hours and hours of telephone conversations,' says Buell. 'He wrote me in excess of twenty letters. The man was the master letter-writer, pages and pages of his passion. He swept me off my feet, he was very good at his seduction.' As their connection and rapport developed, Elvis invited Bebe to come to London, preferably to coincide with his twenty-fourth birthday on 25 August. With a week to spare, and a ticket in her pocket paid for by Elvis, she duly set off to be with her suitor.

Despite his later protestations to the contrary, Elvis seemed happy to have her around. Bebe Buell moved into 48 Queen's Gate Terrace during the sessions for the new album, being made under the provisional titles of *Cornered On Plastic* and *Emotional Fascism*. The team at Eden studios were the same as *This Year's Model*: Nick Lowe in the producer's chair, with Roger Bechirian handling the technical side as engineer. Six weeks had been set aside over the late summer and autumn of 1978, the extended recording time a sure sign of the desire to exert a little more craft and sophistication in the studio.

Again, the discipline was strong. 'Elvis wasn't the kind of guy who slept all day,' says Buell. 'He got up and went to the studio to record and rehearse. He was a working boy, not a loller.'[12] Elvis's work ethic extended to his clothes: he almost always arrived at Eden wearing a suit and often a tie. 'I'd have this mad hippy hair and there was Nick looking like the pub rocker and Elvis would always be in his suit with his Doc Martens,' says Roger Bechirian. 'And he would always come in with a carton of orange juice, because he believed it would keep colds away.'

The sessions were not without their tensions, primarily due to Elvis's attitude. It had only been a year since the release of *My Aim Is True*, and in that time he had become perhaps the most feted of all his peers. He took the praise as his due, primarily because he agreed with it: there was no one around who could touch him.

'By the third [album] I thought I was God's gift,' he later admitted. 'I was totally convinced. I had no doubts.'[13] At work, this manifested itself in a desire to assert himself a little more in the studio. 'Elvis had the final say,' said Nick Lowe. 'All the way down the line.'[14] This was new territory. Previously, the lion's share of the production and mixing decisions had been left to Lowe and Bechirian, and the new developments caused a little unease.

Regardless, Lowe remained a vital cog in orchestrating the record and drumming up enthusiasm on a daily basis, as well incorporating some of the modernist sounds Elvis wanted on the record without diluting the essence of the songs or The Attractions. 'The whole way those things were directed and put together was very much down to Nick,' says Bechirian. 'Nick had a real pop sensibility about him.' And make no mistake, this would be the record where Elvis went 'pop', in more ways than one.

Steve Nieve, in particular, really came to the fore. The scale of the songs was grander, and Steve was involved a great deal in the arrangements. He'd moved away from the edgy sound of the Farfisa organ, and now the piano became the central feature of his playing.

This shift was never more apparent than on 'Oliver's Army', which was transformed from a potential B-side into a sure-fire classic when Steve added a piano part in the style of Abba's 'Dancing Queen'. The Beach Boys' 'Don't Worry Baby' had provided the initial inspiration for the song, but once Steve's euphoric, chiming piano runs were added, it took on an entirely different feel. 'Nick and I were like, "This is a fucking hit!",' says Roger Bechirian. 'You could smell it from the first note. They were cutting the basic track intro and we were just in hysterics, thinking this is just so good. We couldn't wait to get it finished.'

Abba had become an unlikely but major influence on the clean, refined pop sound that Elvis was searching for. If *This Year's Model* had been an approximation of a mid-'60s British beat album, the new approach was self-consciously modernist, drawing on more diverse and current sources. 'We borrowed sounds from some records that we listened to constantly, almost obsessively,'[15] admitted Elvis. David Bowie's classic *Station To Station/Low/Heroes* trilogy had been a constant soundtrack in the tour bus in America (Bowie's 'Rebel, Rebel' riff was also lifted wholesale for 'Two Little Hitlers', while the melody had ghosts of 'TVC-15' in its bones), along with Iggy Pop, Kraftwerk and the late period Beatles of *Abbey Road* and *Yellow Submarine*.

These were all artists as interested in the sound as the song, and their influence could be heard most obviously on the production tricks and keyboard effects which were smeared all over the record, such as Nieve's skewed riff shadowing the title refrain on 'Moods For Moderns'. But despite the attention to detail in the studio and hints of a concept, ultimately what drove the sessions forward was Elvis's continuing acceleration as a songwriter. Songs such as 'Accidents Will Happen', 'Chemistry Class' and 'Party Girl' simply demanded a wider, grander stage to perform upon, and their demands were met.

It was hardly ELO, though. There was still plenty of room for the archetypal Attractions method of simply going in and nailing the basic track live. 'Party Girl', for example, had changed little from the imperious live version that had been knocked into shape on the last US tour. The new-found slickness and subtleties in the performances could not simply be attributed to studio trickery; above all, they were the inevitable by-product of a year of non-stop touring. As the sessions wore on, there was a real sense that this going to be the record which really made the big, bold moves for Elvis's career. 'It was incredibly exciting,' says Roger Bechirian. 'When you make an album that in general is great to listen to and you know that there are three or four hits on there, it's great fun to do.'

The album was almost wrapped up by the last week of September. The band warmed up for their slot at the Rock Against Racism concert in Brixton on the twenty-fourth with a gig at the Grand Hotel in Brighton. A meddling journalist at the scene ended up with his wrist broken and requiring five stitches to a head wound, emphasising the fact that Elvis's self-enforced media blackout was not going to be breached without a fight.

Then it was back to London, where Elvis and The Attractions provided the high point of a day of varied entertainment organised by the Anti-Nazi League, playing to an audience of 150,000 people in Brockwell Park. Opening with an ominous 'Night Rally' and ending with a fitting '(What's So Funny 'Bout) Peace, Love & Understanding', they played a sixteen-song set featuring only one song from the new sessions: 'Oliver's Army'. Here to stay.

* * *

Living together in London, there was no question that Bebe and Elvis had fallen for the each other fast and hard. At first, it was a lot of fun. 'There was a very sweet, generous, romantic person in there,' says Buell. 'A very good present giver, very creative. He had a very endearing side. He was a movie buff, and we spent hours watching movies, like [Truffaut's] *L'Histoire d'Adele H.* I turned him onto *Mean Streets* and *Animal House*.'

The relationship remained a secret outside of the inner circle. Although there was definitely a happy synchronicity about the romance which plugged neatly into the theme of *This Year's Model*, Jake Riviera worried what the attentions of a media hungry American model who hung out with everyone from the Sex Pistols to Billy Idol would do for Elvis's image. Lowe – perhaps more mindful of Elvis's core insecurities and vulnerability – had more personal concerns. 'If you hurt Elvis, if you do anything to hurt him, you're going to answer to me,'[16] he reportedly told Bebe.

On 22 October, the affair become public property when the couple attended a recital by 'punk poet' John Cooper Clarke at Speaker's Corner in Hyde Park. Elvis made a very poor attempt at passing off incognito, with a pork pie hat jammed over his head and shades over his eyes, and he and Bebe were soon spotted by journalists and photographed, as they surely realised they would be. Indeed, the next morning an excited Elvis was the first down at the newsagents to check out the papers. The story duly appeared – with pictures – of this 'surly superstar escorting bountiful American model Bebe Buell' around London, commenting acidly that 'Costello is – of course – happily married with one child.'

The reality was – of course – somewhat different. Elvis was still living in Steve's flat, and relations remained highly fraught on the domestic front.

Ken Smith recalls accompanying Mary Costello to an after-show party for ex-New York Doll David Johansen at the Lyceum Theatre on the Strand: 'I was escorting Mary for the evening, and out of the blue in walks Elvis with Bebe Buell. I thought, "Oh no, this is not going to be good!". There was no way the two of them were going to ignore each other. I was expecting the worst, I thought it was just a matter of who she went for first. But she kept her cool, although she was getting vexed, I can assure you. Elvis – as I remember – was quite flippant.' Elvis wasn't so much flippant as delighted, happy that Mary had spotted him at first-hand with his new squeeze. After the party, Elvis and Bebe decamped to an Indian restaurant to reflect on the meeting. 'I remember him being elated like a little schoolboy,' Buell recalls. 'He got some kind of ghastly pleasure out of that. He was giggling all night about it.' The affair reportedly left Mary seeking a divorce.

In such circumstances, November's 'Wake Up Canada' tour came as something of a relief. While everyone in the Costello camp was excited at the prospect of the new album and its commercial potential, 'Radio, Radio' was released as a stand-alone single in favour of any new material. Designed to bridge the gap between *This Year's Model* and the new album, still provisionally entitled *Emotional Fascism* and scheduled for an release early in 1979, it scraped into the Top 30 in October, affording Elvis the opportunity to shake his fists at Tony Blackburn – the somewhat asinine Radio One DJ – on *Top Of The Pops*.

On tour also, Elvis and The Attractions decided to keep their powder dry, holding back on the new material in order that it would have maximum impact upon release. Instead, they performed a variation of the set they had been playing for almost a year, along with a few surprises: two superior songs which would be left off the album – probably because they were too reminiscent of the style of *This Year's Model* – were aired on the first night, 3 November, at Toronto's O'Keefe Centre 'Tiny Steps' and 'Girls Talk', the latter a blatant hit given away by Elvis to Dave Edmunds in a moment of drunken generosity. During the short tour, Elvis also added a new cover to their repertoire, The Merseybeat's 'I Stand Accused', which would later be recorded for *Get Happy!!*. The final date in Vancouver on 17 November included 'Accidents Will Happen' and the first tour outing for 'Alison'.

From Canada it was off to conquer more uncharted territory in Japan and Australia, but first there was a detour. In Hawaii, director Chuck Slatter recorded a video promo for 'Oliver's Army', already ear-marked as the first single from the new record.

Elvis and The Attractions would never be anyone's idea of photogenic icons for the pre-MTV generation, and their early videos were a slapstick montage of drunken revelry, live performances and some of the most inept dance steps ever captured on film. The clip for 'Oliver's Army' was filmed in a local strip club at 4 a.m. after the band had been out all night recceing for locations, and the dishevelled quartet were about as sober as they looked in the finished film.

Filming continued in this haphazard manner when they reached Japan, where they assembled footage for the fall-down-drunken clip for '(What's So Funny 'Bout) Peace, Love & Understanding'. 'We're jumping up and down in the hotel corridor, we'd had eighteen bottles of saki each,' says Bruce Thomas, who was still rooming with Elvis on tour at that time. 'I remember waking Elvis up at three in the morning and saying, "Hey! Guess what?" "What?" "I am indestructible!" "You fucking won't be if you don't get off this bed".'

The Japanese tour opened in Osaka on 23 November. Aside from a minor tantrum from Elvis on the opening night when some technical problems hampered the sound, it passed off a little too peacefully until they reached Tokyo. Overall, the Japanese media hadn't been especially impressed with Elvis and the band and as a result they took promotion into their own hands, playing a short set from the back of a truck daubed with a banner proclaiming: 'Elvis Costello Is Now Touring Japan'. They were fined ¥4000 by the police for the accurate if unsympathetic charge of 'making a noise in the street'.

The trip to Australia was an even less rewarding experience. The opening concert at Sydney's Regent Theatre on 3 December ended in chaos after Elvis played a fifty-minute set and then refused to give an encore, even following an increasingly ill-tempered eight-minute standing ovation. According to local press reports, 'the crowd threw bottles, lightbulbs and even seats onto the stage. No one was hurt.' Elvis later received some half-hearted death threats live on the Double Jay radio show, and was stampeded at Sydney Airport as he attempted to make his escape.

By the time the last gig of the tour rolled around in Adelaide on 12 December, everyone was ready to go home. But to paraphrase a later Elvis song, home wasn't where it used to be. Instead, it had come to constitute little more than a hotel, a stage, a bus, or an aeroplane. Jake had never been an advocate of the less-means-more policy, and he had booked a thirty-date British tour to promote the release of the new record, beginning with a seven-day residency at the Dominion Theatre in London running from 18 December to Christmas Eve.

Riviera had at least granted them Christmas Day off, and Elvis joined Mary and Matthew for the day. Bebe Buell had stayed on in London while

Elvis had been on tour, remaining at Queen's Gate Terrace at his behest. He often called 'collect' from the road, running up enormous phone bills which Jake was often left to pay. When he returned, he had wanted Buell to bring her daughter Liv over to London to spend Christmas with them, but instead she returned to the States to spend the holiday with her family in Maine.

The band reunited on the twenty-seventh for a tour which would take them up to the end of January, before – once again – heading on to America. It was a bruising schedule, and it was hardly surprising that the week-long festive extravaganza at the Dominion proved to be something of an anti-climax. Despite the inclusion of many songs from the forth-coming album and guest appearances by the likes of Nick Lowe and The Rumour's Martin Belmont, Elvis and The Attractions couldn't help but sound tired and a little lacklustre; the shows were duly met with deliber-ations as to whether the wunderkind was finally beginning to run out of steam. 'We were all fried,' admits Bruce Thomas. 'It wasn't just the drink and all the rest of it, we just didn't get a break. I know what Jake was doing, but I think he pushed it too hard, I think he really did.'

* * *

The new album was released on 5 January. Now called *Armed Forces* after CBS flinched at the idea of trying to sell a record called *Emotional Fascism* to Middle America, the record was an audacious upping of the stakes. From Barney Bubbles' garish, complicated fold-out sleeve to the smoother sounds within, it was clearly a declaration of a vaulting ambi-tion. It also revealed Elvis as both master and maniac of the word game, throwing puns, double entendres, double-bluffs and non sequiturs into the air like confetti, almost like a form of textual Tourette's.

There was an element of the emperor's new clothes in all of this: the dense, encoded language and scattergun wordplay was dazzling on a surface level, but a closer inspection revealed little to grasp onto; the technique became an end in itself. It certainly *felt* like there were some deeply felt personal pre-occupations being exorcised, but what were they exactly? 'Either he doesn't want anyone to know what he's talking about, or he doesn't know what he's talking about himself,' concluded Bruce Thomas, and he had a point.

The impact of the self-lacerating 'Big Boys' and 'Busy Bodies' – side swipes at Elvis's own promiscuity – and the desperate tour postcards of 'Accidents Will Happen' and 'Goon Squad' ('Mother, Father/I'm here in the zoo') was partially dulled by the military imagery, not to mention the feverish switching from first to second person mid-song and often mid-verse;

but then disorientation and obscurity was precisely the intention.

'I got fascinated with words and playing games and disguising things, and I've written some really good songs that are not about literal things, because they're not trying to be,' he later said. 'The big lie is that everything has to make sense.'[17]

Some were disturbed by this lack of clarity. The material drew a sometimes haphazard line connecting individual acts of emotional violence and deceit to global and military atrocities, a conceit which Elvis later admitted was wildly flawed: 'Betrayal and murder are not the same thing.'[18] In particular, 'Oliver's Army' and 'Sunday's Best' came in for criticism, partly for using such incendiary terms as 'nigger' and 'darkies' amidst such emotionally charged material. 'At best it's feeble, at worst it's offensive,' reprimanded *Melody Maker's* Tony Rayns, although it was a mere blip in a broadly positive review. Elsewhere, Rayns commented accurately that Elvis's voice and phrasing had improved considerably, while singling out Steve Nieve for special mention. '[His] keyboards have a range and bite unique in contemporary rock. It falls to him to introduce most of the gorgeous cross-melodies that distinguish many of the songs, and he brings it off every time with terrific finesse.' In the same issue, *This Year's Model* was voted 'Album of the Year' for 1978.

In the *NME*, Nick Kent declared *Armed Forces* 'Costello's most fervent declaration of intention yet for the title of great '70s pop subversive. The only comparisons even worth making are with The Beatles and Bowie, and they scarcely scratch the surface.' This was a little too much. The record was bursting with brashness and confidence, and sounded unlike anything Elvis had done before, but perhaps that was half the problem. Beneath the gimmicky touches and lyrical gymnastics, *Armed Forces* was only half the towering pop masterpiece it proclaimed itself to be. Aside from 'Oliver's Army' and 'Accidents Will Happen', only another four tracks – 'Green Shirt', 'Party Girl', 'Chemistry Class', 'Two Little Hitlers' – were truly great pop songs. The remaining half-dozen were inventive, lyrically mesmerising at times, beautifully performed and sung, but the nagging sense remained that they were more reliant on a varied palette of sounds and textures than might have been advisable. The end result was often brilliant but contrived, and date-stamped in a way which *This Year's Model* has managed to escape. In the *NME*, Charles Shaar Murray concluded with the warning that Elvis may simply be trying too hard to fulfill a role others had mapped out for him. He would soon come to a similar conclusion himself.

* * *

Armed Forces hit the album charts at No. 2, promoted by a poster campaign of Elvis with a shotgun in his mouth. It would stay in the charts for a further six months. Although happy enough to make a somewhat incongruous appearance as a 'pop star' on the children's TV show *Tiswas* and turn up on local radio, the print media blackout was still in full effect, as Nick Kent discovered when he caught up with Elvis at Sheffield City Hall on 18 January, midway through his most extensive British tour to date. Kent found the band in 'magnificent' form after the damp squib of the Dominion shows, but his exaltation of 'the real return of the prodigal' didn't help him get any nearer to an interview.

The inter-band chemistry was as volatile as ever. Increasingly, violence seemed to surround the band, and when nerves and tempers frayed things often got physical. Elvis in particular was susceptible to blacking out and punching blindly when he was drunk, but they were all involved in fist fights with each other at some point. On this occasion, matters reached a head after the show in Cardiff on 27 January. Pete was good friends with Welsh singer and guitarist Andy Fairweather-Low, and they set up in the hotel room with amps and a little drum kit and started having a jam session through the night. 'I wasn't having this,' recalls Bruce Thomas. 'So I knocked on the door and Pete said, "Oh, have you come to join us?" and smack! I bruised his ribs. The next morning Elvis found out. Pete was sitting there with a bottle of claret, red wine with his cornflakes, and Elvis dived over the breakfast table and whacked him again. "You're fired".' As ever, Pete was re-instated before the next gig.

By the end of the tour they were all exhausted. Jake had hastily arranged a final date at the Hammersmith Palais on 30 January, a sentimental return to his father's old work place for Elvis and an attempt to atone for the Dominion shows a month earlier. Although Elvis was trying hard to meet the expectations of being both a critically acclaimed artist and a genuine pop star – a tightrope act which meant playing the singles as well as throwing new songs like 'Opportunity', Steve Nieve's tender 'Sad About Girls' and rare live renditions of 'Chemistry Class' and 'Two Little Hitlers' into the set – there was no disguising the fact that both he and The Attractions were feeling the pace and the pressure. 'Elvis and his boys are completely dead on their feet,' fretted the *NME's* Charles Shaar Murray. 'Wiped out, drained. Trying to be dynamic but the starter won't start.'

Furthermore, the fatigue and the fame were beginning to make Elvis question himself and the motivations of his audience. 'I saw people responding without any kind of understanding or consideration,' he later said. 'We'd play a set where we'd play brilliantly all night and then we'd do our hit single and people would go crazy. Yet they would be bewildered by the rest of what we were doing.'[19]

Much of this was attributable to the unprecedented success of 'Oliver's Army'. Gaining radio exposure throughout January, the single was released in early February and climbed to No. 2 in the chart in March. 'Oliver's Army' marked the pinnacle of Elvis's ability to be all things to all people: a subversive, challenging songwriter who melded serious lyrics to insanely catchy pop hits and sold almost 500,000 singles in the process. It was reminiscent of nothing so much as Dylan in the mid-'60s.

In his rather disheartened frame of mind, however, Elvis was aware that it was a Pyrrhic victory. He was able to take some solace from the fact that 'we managed to get a pop record about militarism to No. 2,'[20] but he was also aware that to this day, most people have no idea what the song is saying. 'Of course, you could sing along with the chorus without ever thinking what it was about,' [21] he admitted, sadly. Such things were beginning to trouble him.

Chapter Six
1979–80

THE TOUR OF AMERICA WAS THEIR FOURTH in a little over a year: by its end, in mid-April, Elvis and The Attractions would have spent almost exactly half of the previous eighteen months in the States and Canada, criss-crossing the continent with an increasing sense of dislocation.

Armed Forces had been well received in America. 'Sunday's Best' was taken off the record and substituted with '(What's So Funny 'Bout) Peace, Love & Understanding', a fair swap, and the momentum created with *My Aim Is True* and *This Year's Model* was still gathering pace. *Rolling Stone* weighed in with a glowing review, while the *Washington Post's* Eve Zibart concluded that 'his third and most polished album, stakes out New Wave's first major fiefdom in the United States'.

Nonetheless, Elvis flew off to his newly-conquered territory to face the fifty-seven shows in sixty-eight days with some ambivalence, to say the least. He spent some time with Bebe Buell in Maine in the days before the opening show of the 'Armed Funk' tour in Seattle on 6 February, and she then accompanied him to California for a few days. When the tour set off into the hinterlands, Elvis arranged for Bebe to rejoin the convoy in New York at the end of March.

Perhaps it was just as well that she didn't follow the whole tour. She was not always the most popular member of the entourage, and her liasion with Elvis was often a topic which amused the band. 'She was a super-groupie, obviously, a bit of an airhead,' says Bruce Thomas. 'Steve's girl-friend once said, "You know what I really hate about you, Bebe, you're blah blah blah," this long tirade. Bebe turned around and said, "You know, I like you because you're so frank." She was just indestructible.'

Buell required a pretty thick skin. Not only was she subjected to the barbs of the band and the increasing hostility of Elvis's management – who by now simply hated the relationship and delighted in spreading rumour and gossip about her, some of which she undoubtedly encouraged – but she was often on the receiving end of Elvis's mood swings. No stranger to infidelity himself, he was less able to deal with suggestions that Buell may not have been entirely faithful, and the relationship fell prey to his dark moods. 'He was pretty mean to her,' says Bruce Thomas. 'There was lots of power play involved, humiliating people just to make them feel bad. Pretty dysfunctional. Whatever else went on, I think she genuinely had something for him, probably more than he did.'

Buell admits that the tour was 'drug-fuelled, alcohol-fuelled and violent. Things got crazy'. During their increasingly frequent, high-octane arguments, she would disparagingly call him 'Uncle Elvis' or a little 'Napoleon Coward', much to his fury. 'I've protected Elvis quite a bit and there are many things about him I will never reveal, but it was pretty horrible,' she says. 'He would wake me up at three in the morning from a sound sleep and accuse me of dreaming about somebody else. He became suspicious, paranoid, inquisitive. For example, I could always tell when he'd been going through my diaries. I could never find a hiding place which he couldn't discover.'

There were unprecedented amounts of alcohol and cocaine on the tour, and the mood in the camp was dark and jittery. Jake and Elvis seemed hell-bent on conquering America entirely on their own terms, and all the least pleasant aspects of the Riviera style of man management combined to create an atmosphere which wound up everyone, from journalists and photographers to the audience, the band and the crew.

As if keen to remind America that it needed Elvis Costello more than he needed it, the antics were inflammatory from the start. The road crew wore army fatigues and the tour bus flaunted the legend: DESTINATION CAMP LEJEUNE, NC, home of the Marine Corps, the US crack military regiment. Anyone inclined to write this off as a humorous extension of the album title were swiftly set right. Tour manager Des Brown executed a fairly brutal reading of Jake's desire to keep photographers and bootleggers out of gigs, while the press were treated with utter disdain by Riviera, alienating most of the writers who had been championing Elvis since he had first appeared in the States.

None of this would have mattered too much if Elvis was producing the goods on stage. Instead, he seemed intent on extending the policy of non-co-operation to include his concerts. With homegrown hero Bruce Springsteen regularly playing sets clocking in at three hours, American audiences expected value for money. What they got on the opening night of the tour in Seattle was a monosyllabic Elvis playing a slight fifty-minute set and no encore, followed by ear-piercing feedback which sent the crowd scurrying from the hall.

Outside, posters of Elvis were torn down and set alight. And it got worse. *Rolling Stone* writer Fred Schruers and *New West's* Greil Marcus were in attendance for the show at Berkeley's Community Theatre on the ninth: 'Costello barely played forty minutes before lock-stepping offstage with no intention to return,'[1] wrote Schruers, while Marcus commented that 'the show was meant as an insult and performed as such, and people caught on.'[2]

The audience were justifiably hostile, ripping seats out of the venue and later breaking windows in the tour bus. 'They were jumping up and down in the balconies,' said Marcus. 'An hour later they were trying to break into the box office.'[3] Backstage, Jake threatened to attack the writer if he went into print about the incident. 'Jake's just a little thug,'[4] Marcus concluded. At the Fox Theatre in San Diego on the 13 February, Elvis played a mere eight songs before leaving the stage. *Armed Forces* may have been beginning to climb towards the Top 10 in the Billboard charts, but all was clearly not well.

He was still managing to write through the chaos. At the Long Beach Arena on 14 February, Elvis previewed the beautiful country-soul ballad 'Motel Matches', and as the tour moved on he would add 'Idle Hands' – an early version of 'Temptation' – 'Secondary Modern', 'B-Movie' and a slow, lumbering version of 'High Fidelity' to the set.

The show at the country-based Palomino Club in Los Angeles on 16 February also provided a welcome diversion, Elvis adding John McFee on pedal steel to take the chance to play some country songs. Elvis would finally record his duet of 'Stranger In The House' with George Jones in Nashville later in the tour, and at the Palamino the song made a rare appearance, alongside standards such as Jim Reeves' 'He'll Have To Go' and Jones' own 'If I Put Them All Together (I'd Have You)'. This time Elvis relented and played an encore, although he resisted repeated calls for a second one.

But it wasn't long before the clouds scudded overhead again. In St Louis on 6 March, Elvis proved once again how effective he had grown at not just biting but amputating the hand that was attempting to feed him. Local radio station KSHE had been cherry-picked by Columbia to sponsor the show, but Elvis had heard through the grapevine that KSHE's local rival – KADI – were playing *Armed Forces* more frequently. During the concert, he dedicated 'Accidents Will Happen' to 'all the boys at KADI' before playing a splenetic 'Radio, Radio' in honour of 'all the local bastard radio stations that don't play our songs – and to KSHE'.

Armed Forces was dropped from KSHE's playlist with a resounding thud. 'I am upset and shocked that a performer would behave in such an unprofessional manner,' KSHE's executive vice-president Sheely Grafman told the local press, as Columbia engineered frantic diplomatic manouevres to smooth things over. As *Rolling Stone*'s Fred Schruers later remarked, Elvis seemed 'bound to make doubters and enemies out of his strongest American partisans'.5 Then the wheels really came off.

On 15 March, the 'Armed Funk' roadshow pulled into The Agora Club in Columbus, Ohio, half way between Cleveland and Cincinatti. The short, fifteen-song set had been unremarkable, a distressingly routine feature of the tour. Afterwards, they returned to the Holiday Inn to discover that Stephen Stills and his band were also staying after playing a gig at another venue in the city.

'I remember seeing this other bus in the driveway of the hotel and the general feeling on our bus was – another group! Right!', recalled Pete Thomas. 'It would be like if sailors had come into harbour and found another boat there, and they knew they were having a night off. "Oh, we're bound to end up having a punch up with them." And then finding out who it was. Whoooah! It's Stephen Stills! The old school.'6

Stills was the kind of musical 'dinosaur' who 'just seemed to typify a lot of the things I thought were wrong with American music',7 according to Elvis. He had been a member of Buffalo Springfield and, of course, Crobsy, Stills and Nash (and occasionally Young), one of Elvis's favourite groups back in the early '70s. But times had changed, for both Elvis and Stills. Post-punk, his career had faltered and he was regarded by Elvis and the band as a burnt-out relic of a bygone age, ripe for abuse.

Stills was with his manager Jim Lindersmith, percussionist Jim Lala, backing singer Bonnie Bramlett and other members of his party in the bar of the Holiday Inn when the Costello contingent joined them. Pete and Steve didn't stay long and it was left to Elvis and Bruce to continue the conversation with their fellow musicians. What had started as reasonably good-natured joshing soon grew much nastier as the alcohol flowed.

'I think we started it,' says Bruce Thomas. 'Steve Stills was being quite friendly, but we would just take exception to anybody. That was the way we did it.' As Bruce and Elvis trotted out their usual routine of anti-Amercian jibes that had been a feature of their US tours since the very beginning, Stills' camp began to get agitated.

'Stills said, "If you hate us so much, what are you doing in our country?",' recalls Thomas. 'And Elvis said something like, "We've come to take your money and your women." Then it just got worse. "What about our music?" "You haven't got any good music." "What about James Brown?" "James Brown?" Bang! That's pretty much how that one started. It was just us being obnoxious bastards.'

In this instance, being obnoxious bastards culminated in Elvis describing James Brown as 'a jive-ass nigger' and Ray Charles as 'nothing but a blind, ignorant nigger'. Before his final descent into these drunken bar-room taunts, Elvis had already responded to inquiries about his feelings on Buddy Holly, Elvis Presley and other white artists with a volley of obscenities. He would probably have said the same about Mozart, or Caruso, or John Lennon, had their names come up. It was not a considered argument.

Nevertheless, Stills was outraged and left the bar, but other members of his party stuck around, including Bonnie Bramlett. At some point during the ensuing squabble, in which Bramlett reportedly told Elvis 'that anybody that mean and hateful had to have a little bitty dick', the argument became physical and Elvis dislocated his shoulder. He was so drunk he barely noticed. 'I only remembered that the thing had even taken place when I got back to my hotel room and discovered that my arm hurt somewhat,'[8] he later said.

The fracas was later described by the bartender as 'just a lot of shoving', and certainly it was a minor bout. The Attractions often had more physical bust-ups between themselves, and there was no question of the following night's show in Detroit not going ahead. As the tour moved on and the Elvis camp celebrated *Armed Forces* hitting the Billboard Top Ten in America, the only remaining legacy of the incident appeared to be the fact that for a few days Elvis was wearing his arm in a sling when he wasn't playing.

However, Bonnie Bramlett had other ideas, and once she decided to leak the story to the media it spread like bush-fire. Elvis opened the show at Rochester Auditorium on 24 March with 'I Stand Accused', his only tacit acknowledgement that something might be amiss, but soon everyone could see that he was in real trouble. 'By then it's on the news and in the papers,' remembers Bruce Thomas. 'They've gone public with it and there's death threats.'

By the time they hit New York a few days later, the death threats were being taken very seriously. Jake drafted in two armed policemen to look after Elvis around the clock as fears for his safety grew. Something clearly had to be done. The emergency press conference called at CBS headquarters in New York on 30 March was seen as a last chance to salvage something from the mess. Whether he was a racist or not – and once the dust had settled it was generally accepted that he was not – wasn't really the issue, merely the catalyst. In reality, Elvis was dragged in front of the press not to atone for his comments about Ray Charles and James Brown, but to atone for his behaviour towards the press themselves, to be contrite and charming; to repent. Had he done so, he would have been let off the hook, and CBS would have been soothed.

But typically, Elvis couldn't allow himself to back down. He badly misjudged his approach, simply adding more confusion and resentment where there was already plenty.

The fall-out was immense. Even as the press conference was taking place, in the same building executives from CBS were discussing how best to proceed with Elvis's career. Reportedly, they even discussed dropping him from the label, but ultimately decided against it. However, neither did they opt to stand up and fight on behalf of their embattled artist, unprepared to endure the bad press and escalating costs of trying to get Elvis's image back on track in America. Nor – on the strength of his performance with the press – were they convinced that Elvis would comply with the need for greater accessibility and charm required to win the media back over.

The simplest option seemed to be to let him wither on the vine. *Armed Forces* had risen to No. 10 at the time of the incident and further progress was confidently expected, but by the end of April the album had left the Top 30 and was fading fast. Columbia declined to release a follow-up single to 'Accidents Will Happen', which had stalled at No. 101 in the singles charts. When Jake had suggested that CBS book New York's Shea Stadium for Elvis after an estimated 250,000 people responded to a draw for free Costello tickets on the radio, the label hadn't been interested. Days later, Riviera sent a truckload of shovels to CBS executives, with a caustic note attached: 'If you *really* want to bury my act, I thought you could do with some more help.'

There were still shows to do, and the band played on: 1 April was to have been the triumphant pinnacle of the tour, with Elvis playing three club dates in New York on the same day in an 'April Fool's Day Marathon'. Specially printed singles of 'Talking In The Dark' b/w 'Wednesday Week' were given to each audience member, all 1200 of whom had won tickets via a radio promotion.

It was another of Jake's bright ideas which merely became a considerable security headache under the prevailing circumstances. Again, Elvis didn't make any specific allusion to the incident or its fall-out, but those reading between the lines found some clues. At the opening gig at the tiny Lone Star Club, he joked, 'This playing three clubs in one night is someone's idea of an April Fool, and I think I know who the fool is,' before pointing to himself. Then again, he seemed more relaxed than he had been for some time, imbued, perhaps, with a sense of relief that the bubble had finally burst.

The second gig at the Bottom Line was attended by Mick Jagger and Jerry Hall, not to mention a gaggle of Rock Against Racism protesters, disappointed Elvis fans by any other name, sending a message to their man with placards reading 'Kick Him Again, Bonn!' and 'Send Elvis Back To Computer School'. He started the show with 'I Stand Accused'.

There was no let up in security. Indeed, with death threats flying around, the sense of menace and paranoia had only increased. At the final show at Great Gildersleeves two extra bodyguards prowled the side of the stage, while Hells Angels were drafted in to back up tour manager Des Brown. Ever-present *Rolling Stone* scribe Fred Schruers reported that one badly beaten young fan was led bleeding onto the pavement, apparently having been set upon by about eleven members of the Costello entourage. The day ended at 3.30 a.m., and not a minute too soon.

The tour finally limped to a close on 14 April at Rhode Island College in Providence, and all concerned were left to survey the wreckage. It was almost unfathomable. 'We never really recovered from that tour,' admits Bruce Thomas. 'Every time Elvis is doing something well, he kind of sabotages it. Even then that mechanism was at work, subconsciously sabotaging the possibility of being a really big, A-League band. We were probably poised to be like Elton John or Bruce Springsteen.'

Elvis, it seems, had taken a look over to the other side and decided he didn't want to go there after all.

* * *

In early May, as the aptly titled 'Accidents Will Happen' was released as the second UK single from *Armed Forces*, Elvis took stock of his life and his music. He was twenty-four, flirting with divorce and deeply unsatisfied with the way his career was panning out. 'I decided, "That's it! I've got to get a grip,"' he recalled. 'There's something wrong. The mission has gone wrong somewhere.'9

He had reluctantly parted from Bebe Buell at the end of the US tour, and wouldn't see her again for over four years. Following the incident in Columbus, Elvis had been 'driven deeper into cocaine and alcohol and despair',10 according to Buell, and she had caught the brunt of it when the tour arrived in New York. She had arranged to meet up with Mick Jagger and Jerry Hall at Elvis's show at the Bottom Line on 1 April, but had remained in her hotel room following a bitter row with Elvis in the bar of the Mayflower Hotel the previous night. He was suspicious of her persona and her lifestyle, and swung between helpless desire of her beauty and unpleasant contempt at what she supposedly represented. Consumed by guilt and self-loathing at the way he was behaving, Elvis was also convinced that some terrible harm was going to befall them both.

Meanwhile, Bebe had fallen pregnant to Elvis three times in the previous six months, and each time had suffered a miscarriage. It was a mess, and one that both of them finally seemed resigned to walking away from.

Breaking off all contact with Bebe Buell had been a prerequisite for his return to Mary, Matthew and the family home. By now, the Costellos had moved from Whitton to a small but infinitely more upmarket terraced property in St James Cottages in Richmond, just over the river from Twickenham. It had been bought largely on the proceeds of Linda Rondstadt's recording of 'Alison' on her latest album, *Living In The USA*, for which Elvis had reportedly received around £30,000. As he later admitted, he was sniffy about Rondstadt's syrupy treatment of his song, but he wasn't too sniffy about the money.

Early signs of Elvis and Mary's marriage reconciliation included a short trip to France and the couple's attendance at shows by the J. Geils Band in both Paris and London in mid-May. Later that month, Elvis, Mary and Matthew all took the train up to Liverpool for a trip home to see Lilian, taking the chance to play a little music at the same time. It had been a month without any live action, and it was a somewhat bruised and battered Attractions who made an impromptu appearance at a Radar Records party on 22 May, held on the Royal Iris ferry which travelled between Liverpool and Birkenhead.

The headline acts were Clive Langer and The Boxes and The Yachts, both of whom were managed by Jake Riviera and signed to Radar. According to the *NME*, Elvis and the band looked 'anaemic and unhealthy' as they opened the proceedings with a six-song set which – aside from an opening 'I Stand Accused' – was all singles, but Elvis seemed in good humour and at ease with the small crowd.

Following the nerves and neuroses of the 'Armed Funk' tour everything seemed slightly lacklustre, probably pleasantly so. The rising balloon of Elvis's career had been pricked and the sense of urgency and momentum slowly leaked out. He needed time to recover, both physically and emotion-ally. It was the longest – indeed only – sustained break that Elvis and The Attractions had had from touring for almost exactly two years, and over the summer they all took time to regroup and recover from the largely self-inflicted mental and physical batterings that had been meted out in America.

Occasionally, they would meet up to rehearse and demo new songs, slotting in a one-off recording session at Abbey Road in late May designed to yield a 'stand-alone' single before work began on the new album in the autumn. Elvis chose an obscure cover of 'So Young' by the Australian band Jo Jo Zep and The Falcons, backed with The Merseybeats' 'I Stand

Accused'. However, the session at Abbey Road with Nick Lowe at the helm was 'blighted by flying coffee cups and overwhelming blueness',[11] and the plan for a single was quietly shelved.

There was the occasional festival appearance in Europe and five Scandinavian dates in late summer, but everyone had other things to do: The Attractions recorded a surprisingly poor 'solo' record with Roger Bechirian, a forgettable affair released as *Mad About The Wrong Boy* in September 1980, while Elvis produced the debut album by British ska group The Specials at TW Studios throughout June.

He kept it simple, using what he had learned from Nick Lowe: trying not to get in the way of a great live band, while at the same time doing all he could to get the best performances down on tape. He also brought the more specialised Attractions recording 'method' to the project. 'The main thing I remember is him sitting behind the desk and falling off his chair,' said chief-Special Jerry Dammers. 'Everyone was pissed. We spent most of the time in the pub over the road and then we used to work during closing time, which was between four and six in the afternoon.'[12]

When not in the pub with The Specials, Elvis was demo-ing fleshed-out versions of his own new material. Usually, he would bring his songs to the band and play them through on the guitar, letting the arrangement develop organically between the four of them. However, for many of the new demos he went into tiny eight-track studios like Archipelago in Pimlico and played all the instruments himself, producing sometimes eccentric versions of 'Black And White World', 'Riot Act', 'Five Gears In Reverse', 'Love For Tender', 'King Horse', 'New Amsterdam' and 'Men Called Uncle'.

He had grown to hate *Armed Forces*, the slickness, the preconception, and was casting around for a solution. However, the answer didn't lie in the solo demos. Although he enjoyed the process, and the tender 'New Amsterdam' would eventually make the final cut, they were a little too idiosyncratic to be seen as potential tracks for a new album.

When The Attractions joined Elvis in September and October to rehearse and begin taping the new songs in trial sessions at Eden Studios, his frustration grew. Most of the new record was written, but both he and band were well aware that the material was not coming together the way they wanted it to. Having had little time or energy on the US tour to do anything to the new songs except learn them and play them in a similar style to *Armed Forces*, when Elvis brought the tracks back home and played them live and in the studio, he found they sounded thin, lacklustre, and derivative.

'We sounded like The Jags,' recalls Bruce Thomas. 'Bad Elvis and The

Attractions impersonators, basically, who played everything fast and in eights.' Elvis was equally unhappy with the 'wretched'[13] performances. The classic Attractions sound had been worked to death, with the organ pushing to the front and lots of tremolo guitar. Their initial attempt at 'B-Movie' sounded like a desperate attempt to rewrite 'Oliver's Army'. They were becoming a parody of themselves.

The solution presented itself one afternoon over a few post-rehearsal drinks. 'We went to the pub and said, "What are we gonna do?",' recalled Elvis. 'Why don't we try playing some of these songs slower, and use more rhythmic accompaniment, instead of these tricky, nervy kind of backings.'[14]

He had always been up-front about the way in which he used other songs as launchpads for his own material; by the time he had mixed in his own ideas and added The Attractions, it was normally nigh on impossible to trace a link back to his original inspiration. This time, Elvis moved away from the clean, European line of the Bowie and Abba records which had previously dominated his turntable, and instead immersed himself in the soul music he had loved as a teenager. Perhaps the answer to his troubles lay in the grooves of the classic songs of Stax, Atlantic and Motown?

Elvis raided his own record collection and spent a further £50 on classic soul singles from Rock On record shop in Camden Town. Then he distributed tapes to the band, making sure everyone was getting into the same feel and musical frame of mind. 'Elvis dug out *Motown Chartbusters: Volume III* and said, "Listen to this, get this dynamic in your head, this is where we're going this time,"' recalls Bruce Thomas.

It was probably not meant as an overt apology to the black acts he had bad-mouthed in Columbus, but subconsciously it seemed to acknowledge that there was room for a little more warmth and emotion, a little more vulnerability in his music. Nor was it meant to be a direct case of adopting a wholesale genre or sound – that would just be flirting with another kind of parody – rather it was an attempt to tap into the freshness and vitality at the heart of '60s soul music to bring the new songs, and probably Elvis as well, alive again.

In the studio, this working method rapidly refined itself until the band were playing each new Elvis song in the style of a soul classic, using it as a template for the mood and rhythm before letting the new song burst through. 'I was literally taking the songs and saying, "OK, what song are we going to play this like?",' said Elvis. 'Each song I could go through and tell you which band we were being: Al Green on one, The Four Tops on another.'[15] To which he might have added The Supremes, Martha and The Vandellas, Booker T and The MG's, Garnet Mimms, Eddie Floyd, Marvin Gaye, Betty Everett, Curtis Mayfield and – on 'Human Touch' –

(Above left) Ross MacManus in 1960, leading the Joe Loss Orchestra from the front. *(Right)* Embarking on a solo career in 1968.

Credit: Liverpool Daily Post and Echo.

(Below) Nos. 15 and 16 Beaulieu Close, Twickenham Park. No. 16 *(the top right flat)* was home to Ross, Lilian and Declan from 1961-1970, and Ross continued living there after the break up of his marriage. No. 15 *(the bottom right flat)* was home to Declan, Mary and Matthew between 1975-76.

Declan during his time at St Edmunds RC school in Whitton, circa 1962. *(Above, centre)*
Already displaying a talent for stealing the limelight.

Courtesy of Brian Burke

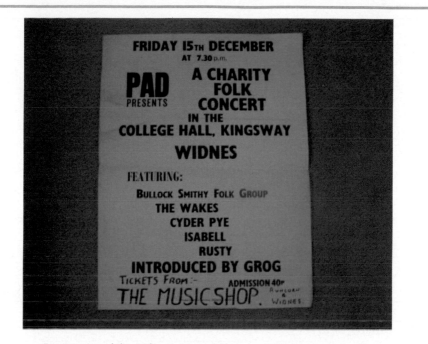

Rusty memorabilia. *(Above)* A poster from 1972 illustrating the band's typical place in the pecking order.

(Below) A detail of the handwritten lyrics for one of Declan's earliest original compositions, 'Sunflower Lancers' Courtesy of Allan Mayes.

Dull Echoes

My mandolin picks out of tune
And at of tune as well
A simple song I learnt a while ago
When you were sleeping

One more time I do without
I'll play ~~for~~ you on my broken fiddle
I have a waterfall over my window

~~Dull~~ Though they are dull echoes
And they will not last a single
minute
Though they are not worthy
May I sing them to you slowly
And maybe ~~I~~ will find a rhy.
Which you ~~will~~ will find most pleas.

Go down to the river
Lay down at the water's edge
Don't you lean over
'Cos you start to be falling
I think of days I've spent [...
they really are to few
My waterfall is endless
But I also have a fantan[...

Now I'm standing on a [...
Watching everything arou[...
Hearing every sound
Or at least it will see[...
We will take them in the [...
and write them in our [...
And open them on days wh[...
Find it hard to see

A detail in Declan's own handwriting of his original composition, 'Dull Echoes', written circa 1972.
Courtesy of Allan Mayes.

Scenes from Flip City: *(Above)* Declan in trademark dungarees
at an open-air festival in Stepney, 1975.

(Below) Dickie Faulkner, Ian Powling, Steve Hazelhurst, Declan MacManus,
Mich Kent. **Courtesy of Ken Smith and Steve Hazelhurst**

(Above) Playing at the Fitzrovia Festival, 1975

(Below) Trying their very best to be The Band.
Snapped in Nonsuch Park, Surrey, 1975.

Courtesy of Ken Smith and Steve Hazelhurst

(Above) Palgrave House, Cypress Avenue, Whitton.
Declan and Mary's marital home between 1976 and 1978, where he wrote
many of his most enduring songs, including 'Alison'.

(Below) Declan marries Mary Burgoyne, 9 November 1974.
Mich Kent is best man.

Credit: Peter Brown

Unleashed. Elvis leads The Attractions on their first tour of the UK
in the summer of 1977.
Credit: Starfile/Ian Dickson

Elvis Costello
Credit: Pennie Smith

Pete Thomas
Credit: Pennie Smith

Bruce Thomas
Credit: Pennie Smith

Steve Nieve
Credit: Pennie Smith

LIVE STIFFS LIVE *(l–r in all but top picture)*: Elvis, Nick Lowe, Wreckless Eric, Larry Wallis and Ian Dury prepare to do battle in the autumn of 1977.

(Above) Bruce Thomas and Elvis: Lost in America. Credit: Roberta Bayley

(Below left) Bebe Buell in classic pose, and (right) spending time with Elvis in Portland, Maine, immediately prior to the 'Armed Funk' tour, February 1979.
Credit: Bob Gruen/Courtesy of Bebe Buell

An accident waiting to happen: Sheffield, January 1979.
Credit: Pennie Smith

his more recent collaborators, The Specials. 'We were actually listening to those records to get us in the mood before we put a track down,' says Bechirian. 'And suddenly the whole feel of it changed.'

This approach met head on with the traditional Attractions wallop to make some wildly exciting music, with the loose punch and swagger that Elvis was searching for. On some songs – such as 'Love For Tender', 'High Fidelity', 'Secondary Modern', 'Temptation' and 'Clowntime Is Over' – the debt was more overt than on others, but each and every song felt the benefit in approach if not always directly in style.

By this point in the proceedings they had tired of Eden Studios in London and decamped to Phonogram's studio complex in Wisseloord, in Holland. Situated in the forest, away from the traumas and temptations of working in the middle of a city, the change of scenery was initially refreshing, but it soon became apparent that the hard personal lessons of the 'Armed Funk' tour hadn't been learned.

For the first time they began drinking in the studio, and soon the sessions took on an edge of frantic desperation. 'It was pretty wild,' admitted Nick Lowe. 'It was just like you had your foot flat down on the accelerator. Swallowing life down, guzzling it down.'[16] Literally. At one point Jake flew over to Holland to confront Elvis and the group after they had run up a bar bill worth thousands of pounds, whilst, according to Roger Bechirian, 'everything was a cocaine haze'.

Matters swiftly reached the point of emotional meltdown, particularly for Steve Nieve. 'You would have him slamming the piano lid down: "I'm not playing any more of this goddamn monkey music",' says Bruce Thomas. The general pace of life and the increasing excess was a major contributing factor in the organist's unhappiness. He was still only twenty-one, a little more introverted than the rest of the band, and creatively had pushed himself hardest to explore the outer limits of his capabilities. At one point he broke down, sobbing over the piano, simply burnt out.

There were also musical problems. On Elvis's first two records with The Attractions, the tracks had been played-in on tour and most of the arrangements set in stone by the time they went into the studio. This time around, the songs were being pushed and pulled into different shapes with the tape running and very little time for reflection. This was exactly what Elvis wanted: disillusioned with the studied smoothness of *Armed Forces*, he was trying to capture the music as it spilled out, with as little forethought as possible. So having written 'Possession' in a Dutch taxi after drunkenly 'falling in love' with a waitress in a bar in Hilversum, it seemed logical that The Attractions should learn and record it the same night. It was the kind of 'method' which could yield sometimes stunning results, but it was a stress-filled way of working for everybody.

There were other issues. Pete Thomas was unhappy about his drum sound, while Bruce Thomas 'hated' his bass sound. 'The whole thing was just an endless catalogue of "I don't like this", "I don't like that",' says Bechirian. 'It wasn't pleasant at all. You could see the seams coming apart at that point.' The band argued over the merits of recording the Sam and Dave ballad 'I Can't Stand Up For Falling Down', Bruce Thomas insisting it was one of the worst songs Sam and Dave ever did and it would never be a hit in a million years. He was proved quite spectacularly wrong.

Meanwhile, behind the producer's console and in as bad shape as Elvis and the band, Nick Lowe was obsessed with prising a 1950's-style reverb sound out of Phonogram's state-of-the-art studio, often putting Elvis in the booth designed for recording string instruments to keep his vocals raw. '[The studio] was extremely Euro,' Lowe recalled. 'It was like trying to make a record as the Eurovision song contest was going on all around you.'[17]

Despite – or perhaps because of – the excess, the fraught atmosphere and the musical struggles, the songs were infused with a compelling emotional intensity which was light years ahead of the versions the group had cut in Eden Studios. Somehow, the record was finished through the fog, but it was painstaking and emotionally exhausting work. In the end, the title of the record seemed more a desperate hope than a playful instruction.

With the record wrapped up, Elvis was left kicking his heels. There were legal problems surrounding the release of *Get Happy!!*. Jake and Andrew Lauder had left Radar in late 1979 and formed a new independent record company called F-Beat. However, because Radar had been financed by Warner Brothers in the UK, any act signed to Radar was also technically signed to Warners as well. As such, Warners weren't particulary keen to simply let Elvis and Nick Lowe walk away from under their noses to join F-Beat without any recompense.

The situation was further complicated by the fact that Elvis had never put pen to paper on a contract with Radar. 'It was difficult,' says Lauder. 'The deal between Radar and Elvis [and Nick Lowe] was never actually signed. So it ended up potentially getting a bit messy.' Jake and Andrew negotiated the possibility of F-Beat forming a new relationship with Warners, but talks broke down and Warners took the matter to court. The release of any new Elvis product was hamstrung until the matter was resolved.

In early January 1980 a very limited edition of the single of 'I Can't

Stand Up For Falling Down' came out on the Two Tone label, home of The Specials. 'It was a bit of a flanker, really,' says Lauder. 'Because we thought that was the last thing anyone would expect.' With the ownership of Elvis's recorded work under legal dispute, the single was swiftly removed from sale following an injunction from Warners, and was later given away free at The Rainbow in September 1980, and at other Elvis concerts.

Just as the stand-off was poised to go to a potentially long and financially draining trial, in February F-Beat and Warners finally came to an edgy compromise. 'We were faced with very large bills,' says Lauder. 'We'd already started manufacturing *Get Happy!!* and there were singles and everything else. In the end we did end up doing a deal with Warners for pressing and distribution. It was against their wishes, but as a way of resolving it that was what was done. Effectively [Elvis and Nick] were still within the Warners fold, but it was now F-Beat instead of Radar.'

Get Happy!! – originally scheduled for an early January release – wouldn't hit the shops until mid-February. In retrospect, Elvis felt the dispute damaged the support his subsequent records got from Warners. 'That's when things started to go wrong for us in this country in a business sense,' he claimed. 'I think we've paid dearly for that dispute.'[18]

As all this was unfolding, Elvis did his best to keep relatively busy. He was already writing and demo-ing new songs at Nick Lowe's Am-Pro Studio in Shepherd's Bush, putting down embryonic versions of 'New Lace Sleeves', 'Watch Your Step', 'From A Whisper To A Scream' and 'Just A Memory', which were in various stages of completion. He also met Johnny Cash at Nick Lowe's house on Boxing Day 1979. At that time, Lowe was married to Cash's stepdaughter Carlene Carter, and Elvis was part of a high-spirited session band which cut Lowe's 'Without Love' and a duet of George Jones' 'We Ought To Be Ashamed', which apparently proved an accurate assessment of the day's proceedings.

Since their return from America, live appearances had been few and far between. There had been a smattering of dates in France and Spain in mid-December and an appearance at the Rock For Kampuchea benefit concert at the Hammersmith Odeon on 29 December, alongside Wings, Rockpile and comedian Billy Connolly. In the New Year, Elvis and The Attractions played for *NME* prize-winners at The Clarendon in London, before making a one-show-only trip to New Zealand to play the Sweetwater Festival on 27 January. The festival appearance was the first known occasion of Elvis playing Elvis, as he and The Attractions ripped through Presley's 'Little Sister', which would become a feature of their live set that year.

Taking advantage of the lull in proceedings, the trip to the Antipodes turned into an excuse for a brief, hedonistic break in the sun. 'We were getting £70,000 for the gig,' remembers Bruce Thomas. 'Elvis said, "OK, we'll share it all out. We'll just have a good time and whatever's left when we get back we'll share it all out." Out of £70,000, we got just over £1100 each! We did about £15,000 apiece in two weeks, which would have bought a house back then.' At least it bought a good time.

* * *

Get Happy!! was released on F-Beat on 15 February, 1980. It was the anti-*Armed Forces*, crammed with twenty songs, a quarter of which were under two minutes long and barely hung together. And it was a masterpiece.

The record showcased The Attractions at their rawest and roughest, with little of the sophistication of the previous album. This was not a record of stand-out individual cameos; rather, it was the sound of a band sticking close together for protection, flying on instinct and intuition, feeding off their singer's desperation and turning it into something remarkable. Up front, Elvis's voice ran the gamut from wracked hysteria on 'Human Touch' to a whispered soul croon on 'Secondary Modern', finally reduced to a ragged bark on 'Beaten To The Punch'.

Many of the songs were half-formed and empty-sounding, betraying the frenzied nature of the recording process, but the sense of drama and energy spilling out swept away any misgivings. The up-tempo numbers were absurdly fast, the opening 'Love For Tender' shooting by in a blur of pilfered Motown bass riffs and frantic word association, while the few subdued tracks were stripped painfully bare and laced with a new-found sadness. 'New Amsterdam' was the one oddity, culled from the solo demos Elvis had cut over the summer at Archipelago studios in Pimlico, its quiet reflection and acoustic strum setting it apart from the manic mood of the rest of the record.

Lyrically, there were nods to the 'Columbus Incident' and the many small, sour betrayals and temptations of life on the road, but often *Get Happy!!* was so dense as to be almost indecipherable. Elvis devoured books, specifically biography, happily scrutinising the minutiae of someone else's life, and among his most significant recent reading matter was a work on the hidden meanings of Picasso's paintings. The book explained the various devices that the artist employed to squirrel codes and secret messages in his work, usually to his lovers. As was normal with any idea he liked, Elvis had decided to try it for himself, with the result that his relationship with Bebe Buell was heavily – if obscurely – documented on

Get Happy!!: 'Beaten To The Punch', 'Riot Act' and the slow-burning regret of 'Motel Matches' were all reflections on the theme of that doomed romance, while 'Men Called Uncle' specifically referenced a furious argument towards the end of their relationship, where a desperate Elvis had found himself grabbing onto Buell's ankles in a darkened hotel room.

It was a brave, berserk record, less artless than it sounded but as emotionally open and as musically joyous as anything Elvis had recorded. He has always regarded it fondly, declaring it five times the record *Armed Forces* was. The *NME* cottoned on immediately. 'Twenty tracks, fifty minutes, with the single first, just like Motown,' gushed Paul Rambali, who appeared to have fallen foul of Elvis's deliberately ambiguous labelling on the original album. The CD re-issue later revealed 'Love For Tender' as the album's opener. Praising the pared-down sound of The Attractions and the more expressive, less polished vocals, he concluded: 'It's a record you didn't expect. Elvis has gotten off the treadmill. Get it.' *Melody Maker* was less sure, griping about the 'uneven' material and the retro '6os-style production, which only proved that some people found it harder to get happy than others.

In the US, there was little hint of any hubris hanging over from the previous year's antics. Robert Palmer in the *New York Times* was positively brimming with positivity. 'The stylistic range, emotional depth, melodic richness and verbal invention displayed on *Get Happy!!* make it Mr Costello's most satisfying album,' he wrote, with that odd formality that some American critics insist upon.

In *Creem*, Jeff Nesin simply concluded, 'If you care at all about rock 'n' roll you must have this album.' Eve Zibart's review in the *Washington Post* was one of the few that commented on the haphazard production, which she felt let the record down. 'Where Phil Spector painstakingly built a wall of sound, producer Nick Lowe has constructed a chain-link fence. It works to the advantage of several numbers, but Lowe overdoes it.' But then Nick Lowe always did.

Following the release of *Get Happy!!*, Elvis and The Attractions hit the road for the first time in almost a year at the end of February. It was a UK tour with a difference, loosely hung around the theme of playing seaside towns and places lying outside the normal concert circuit. They soon found out why. Taking in such pop-starved outposts as Cromer, Matlock, Fishguard, St Austell, West Calder and Dunfermline rather than London, Leeds, Liverpool, Cardiff and Glasgow, it was an exercise in eccentricity which – although performed in good faith – probably did little to aid the commercial progress of the new record.

Support was provided by Clive Langer and The Boxes. As well as 'opening' for the band in May on the Royal Iris ferry, Elvis had recently produced their cover of the '60s hit 'If Paradise Was Half As Nice' for their debut album *Splash!* and now wanted to introduce them to a wider audience.

Touring with The Attractions was not for the faint-hearted, although at least one member had pulled back from the abyss. Bruce Thomas had come to his senses upon his return from Holland, when his wife saw him lying on the floor, pale and listless, and had screamed because she thought he was dead. 'It was after the *Get Happy!!* sessions that I thought I'd better just cut back to six bottles of wine a day, rather than two bottles of vodka,' he says. 'I stopped taking drugs at that point, too.'

The shows were strong, taking in the full sweep of Elvis's four records but focusing primarily on *This Year's Model* and *Get Happy!!*. Despite their extended absence from the road, The Attractions soon revved up to full speed. 'I was amazed by them live,' says Langer. 'The power. They would just come out of the dressing room and attack.'

As if to punch home the renewed heart in his music, Elvis introduced a smattering of soul and R&B covers into the set, including 'Help Me', Sly Stone's 'Dance To The Music' and Smokey Robinson's 'One More Heartache', which he hadn't performed since the penultimate Flip City gig in November 1975. 'Watch Your Step' also made its live debut during the tour.

However, for the first time Elvis's excesses on the road were beginning to directly interfere with his ability to perform. 'Whatever enthusiasm he'd started out with had dissipated after three or four numbers and reached its nadir when he came to a grinding mental halt at the start of 'Alison',' reported a review of the show at Hastings Pier Pavillion on 4 March. 'He stopped and started blankly, scratched his head again. The band carried on through the verse and a roadie stepped up to Elvis and after a short consultation removed his guitar and led him out.'

'I Can't Stand Up For Falling Down' had recently been released as a single, and by the time the tour hit Hastings it was well on its way to its chart peak of No. 4. The attendant celebrations throughout the day had got severely out of hand, and left Elvis in an advanced state of disrepair. He eventually returned to finish the show, but he was in poor voice, forgetting lyrics and looking mentally disorientated all the way through to the end.

It all ended in Nottingham on 1 April, on the surface a long way down the road from the madness and malice of the previous year's 'April Fool's Day Marathon' in New York. Even so, Elvis was feeling perhaps even more dejected than he had twelve months earlier. It seems clear that his use of drugs and alcohol had escalated to the point where the arrogance and certainty of old had been replaced with self-doubt and a weariness about the whole business. Disillusioned, he made the decision to quit.

Elvis frequently told members of the band that he was throwing his hand in, usually a short-lived impulse brought on by fatigue and a self-confessed taste for melodrama. However, this time he was more adamant, despite the fact that he had a European tour scheduled to begin a mere two weeks later.

Steve Nieve didn't need a second bidding: he took a holiday in America, where as a passenger he was almost immediately involved in a serious car accident in Los Angeles which laid him low for some time. By the time Elvis had eventually and somewhat inevitably come to his senses and decided to press on, he found himself without a keyboard player. It would be June before Steve was well enough to rejoin The Attractions.

The initial Plan B had been to adapt to Steve Nieve's absence by playing as a trio. This was overly optimistic, considering Elvis's considerable short-comings as a lead guitarist, and was swifly jettisoned after the opening two warm-up gigs on the Channel Islands of Guernsey and Jersey proved to be catastrophic, the songs badly battered by layers of ill-used guitar effects.

Before the European tour moved to Holland, Germany and Belgium in mid-April, Elvis decided to augment the remaining two Attractions with The Rumour's guitarist Martin Belmont. The setlist was adapted by neccessity. Without Steve's warm organ sound, only a handful of songs from *Get Happy!!* made the cut. 'High Fidelity' was usually included, having been released as a single in April, alongside covers of Jim Reeves' 'He'll Have To Go', Smokey Robinson's 'Don't Look Back' and Presley's 'Little Sister'. The concerts were ragged, and those members of the audience coming to the shows before deciding whether to buy *Get Happy!!* were unlikely to have been persuaded to storm their local record shop.

Such pitfalls were not helping the promotion of the record. *Get Happy!!* had proved a considered commercial success, but those expecting the carefully sculpted pop music of *Armed Forces* were inevitably disappointed. The record climbed to peaks of No. 2 in the UK and No. 11 in the US – both highly creditable chart placings – but it didn't sell anywhere near as many copies as its predecessor. 'Jake actually laughed about having a *Get Happy!!* house in his garden made with all the unsold records,' recalls Roger Bechirian.

It's likely that the 'Columbus Incident' had something to do with the disappointing sales, if not directly. Vast numbers of people hadn't suddenly stopped buying Elvis Costello records on the strength of that one moment of madness, but the events of March 1979 undeniably had a knock-on effect. CBS were unwilling to market the record with any great fanfare; indeed, according to Roger Bechirian, 'they were horrified with *Get Happy!!*'. On top of it all, Elvis had decided not to tour America this time around, unquestionably a reaction to the madness of the 'Armed Funk' tour.

However, the story wasn't that simple. The legal dispute with Warners had muffled a little of the record's initial punch, but the drop in sales was primarily attributable to Elvis's rough-and-ready, radical switch in musical direction. In the States especially, a country that has always liked its music neatly labelled and pigeonholed, this was clearly not the polished new wave sounds of *Armed Forces*, and radio stations were unsure what to do with it.

The net result was not promising. 'F-Beat was running into financial struggles at that time,' admits Andrew Lauder. 'We had overpressed on the album based on the sales of *Armed Forces*, which was a platinum album. We had a situation where we were shipping out lots of records and they were all coming back. Having paid for all the advertising and all the publicity, financially it was a tough one to make work.' With a promotional campaign which included 100,000 free posters, over 500 record shop window displays, double-page magazine adverts and radio and television exposure, the cost of failure was high.

Chapter Seven
1980–81

ELVIS HAD RELEASED FOUR FULL-LENGTH ALBUMS in the space of two-and-a-half years; had toured the world almost constantly, and become one of the foremost musical figures of his generation. Throughout it all, he had been under no illusion that playing to the hilt the 'Elvis Costello' character established in the opening months of his career would provide the quickest route to success. He had stuck to it, cutting his musical cloth as simply and efficiently as he could, adhering to the somewhat one-dimensional template that the public recognised. It wasn't really artifice, it was simply that he restricted himself to displaying only a certain side of his personality: the vengeful, cocksure, embittered side, which undoubtedly existed. But he was finding the parameters frustrating.

Get Happy!! had marked the first step away from that persona, and now he felt the urge to add even more of himself to the music. 'There was really the need in me to reflect something else: a bit more tenderness, a bit more regret, because you make mistakes in your life and you have to sing about those as well as the things you're very confident or cocky about.'[1]

He was looking back to move forwards. Earlier in the year he had cut eccentric versions of old D.P. Costello songs 'Ghost Train', 'Hoover Factory' and 'Dr Luther's Assistant'* at Am-Pro and TW studios in Fulham. They were beguiling doodles, floating around without a beat, not songs that could easily be played with The Attractions. He was also picking up on threads of songs and lyrics he had written in the mid-'70s. 'Different Finger', 'New Lace Sleeves', 'Luxembourg', even a short instrumental piece called 'Weeper's Dream' were all dusted down and re-arranged, a sure sign that he was beginning to change direction, focusing on the wider musical ambitions he had set aside in 1977.

* Two of the songs would end up on the *New Amsterdam* EP in June 1980, while 'Hoover Factory' would appear on the B-side of the 'Clubland' maxi-single in December 1980.

Elvis's musical frame of reference had always been immense, but only a fraction of it had been suggested in his musical output to date. This was set to change. He had bought a baby grand piano at the beginning of the year, which had an almost immediate impact on his songwriting process. Although it would be a full year before he began to feel his way around the instrument with enough confidence for it to become his principal compositional tool, he quickly wrote 'Shot With His Own Gun', a restrained, almost formal piano piece which would later become a live *tour de force*.

His mind was already on the next record. He envisaged it combining the melodic lushness of *Armed Forces* with the rhythmic drive of *Get Happy!!*, and throughout the summer he stockpiled songs with this template in mind: 'You'll Never Be A Man', 'Lovers Walk', 'Clubland', 'New Lace Sleeves', 'Watch Your Step' and 'From A Whisper To A Scream' were already written and demo-ed, although some of them would change dramatically during the album sessions: at this point, 'Watch Your Step' was a raucous rocker and 'New Lace Sleeves' a swaying, reggae-tinged number laced with melodica.

Elvis showcased some of the new material in festival appearances in Orange, France and at the Montreux Jazz Festival in Switzerland, in July. Steve was back in the swing after his LA car-crash, and paid his professional respects to Squeeze's keyboard whizz Jools Holland in three concerts at the Albany Theatre in London on 12–14 August. Holland was leaving the band for pastures new, and Elvis and The Attractions, cunningly disguised as Otis Westinghouse and The Lifts, supported Squeeze each night and joined them on a few of their own songs as well.

The two bands' paths had crossed before on *Top Of The Pops* and other television shows, but they had become firm friends earlier in the year after stumbling upon each other in a hotel bar in Buxton in the north of England while on tour. 'We stayed up until the sun came up,' recalls the band's guitarist, singer and lyricist Chris Difford. 'Talking about country music, old music, management, record deals and God-knows-what.'

The result of the meeting was significant in many ways. Squeeze were having problems with their manager Miles Copeland, and Jake – ever the knight in shining armour – stepped into the breach. Soon his managerial responsibilities were being shared between Elvis and Squeeze, the beginning of a working relationship which would span the next few years.

Festival appearances were dotted around the summer. A performance at the Edinburgh Festival in August – a greatest hits set with a live debut for 'Shot With His Own Gun' thrown in for good measure – was followed by an appearance at the Heatwave Festival in Toronto on 23 August, the one and only trip to North America the band made in the twenty months following the 'Armed Funk' tour.

The trip to Canada coincided with the release of *Taking Liberties*, a record specifically designed for the US market, mopping up stray B-sides, UK album tracks and unreleased out-takes. *Taking Liberties* was only intended to be available on cassette in Britain, with a slightly altered track listing and under the name *Ten Bloody Marys & Ten How's Your Fathers*, but vinyl imports soon made their way across the Atlantic.

At twenty songs, it was an impressive – if incoherent – collection of material which was by no means second-rate: 'Radio Sweetheart', 'Stranger In The House', 'Night Rally', 'Chelsea', 'Girls Talk', 'Hoover Factory' and covers of 'My Funny Valentine' and 'Getting Mighty Crowded' were all on offer. A minor addition to the canon, more than anything *Taking Liberties* was a useful document in tracking Elvis's changing musical obsessions over three years of enormous creativity. 'The harried Costello fan can pause and actually weigh up the pros and cons of the man's work to date,' wrote Nick Kent in the *NME*, before concluding: 'I'm glad I've got this record.'

* * *

Elvis and The Attractions demo-ed material for the next album at Eden Studios throughout September, and work began in earnest at DJM studios in Holborn in central London the following month, with the old team of Nick Lowe and Roger Bechirian still in place. Working practices had changed somewhat. Lowe would produce for two or three days at a time on his own and then Roger Bechirian would take charge for a few sessions.

The difference in the two men's techniques and the lack of consistency didn't help the album's progress. Relations within the band were also beginning to fall apart. They arrived in the studio following several days spent rehearsing in the country, which had soon collapsed into an exercise in alcoholic futility. 'By that point, I think everybody was just fed up with seeing each other,' says Bechirian. 'There was a real sense of animosity, a cloud over the project. It was just a real struggle, because nobody seemed to care about it.'

In this mood of extreme disillusionment and disenchantment, the songs Elvis was writing were mired in 'sour and rotten doings,'[2] detailing a very English pre-occupation with sleaze, cheap assignations and corruption when the lights are dimmed. The Conservative Party had recently come back to power, and the looming shadow of Thatcherism infiltrated the songs and contaminated the mood in the studio. In addition, Elvis was at a personal low. His marriage to Mary had once again reached a point where it was approaching 'terminal fracture' and he was 'close to nervous collapse on a diet of cider, gin and tonic, various powders, Seconal and Johnnie Walker Black Label.'[3]

The atmosphere at DJM was predictably dire. The sound was dry and lifeless, ill-suited to the more expansive music that Elvis wanted to make. The band were drinking their way through the sessions and generally the prevailing mood was that they were getting nowhere fast. As with *Get Happy!*, it was swiftly decided that a change of scene would help. This time, the familiarity of Eden Studios seemed attractive, and once there, the record began to take shape.

Elvis had tired of playing up to the angry, aggressive stereotype, and he and The Attractions finally located the heart of the record in the wiped-out, resigned lushness which characterised the mood of the strongest tracks. Much of the credit for this fell to Steve Nieve, who – having come close to quitting after *Get Happy!!* – was determined to exert more influence this time around. His piano and organ work dominated the songs, lending a sense of poise and calm restraint which belied the miserable mood of the sessions. In many ways he held the record together.

The previously frantic demo's of 'Watch Your Step' and 'New Lace Sleeves', slowed down and performed with a new, held-back power, benefited most from Steve's attentions, but 'Shot With His Own Gun', 'You'll Never Be A Man' and 'Black Sails In The Sunset' were all enriched by Nieve's 'lead' piano playing. Vocally, Elvis experimented with a low, quiet croon, first utilised on 'Secondary Modern' on *Get Happy!!* and now developed into a silky, lascivious moan, at once amused and disgusted. It was very effective.

The on-going friendship with Squeeze further energized the record. With both acts now managed by Jake, Elvis had already agreed to produce the band's new record upon finishing his own album, and vocalist Glenn Tilbrook was happy to return the favour. During the sessions, Elvis's voice was often suffering from the cumulative effects of a little too much hard living, and on one such occasion Tilbrook offered to sing a guide vocal for 'From A Whisper To A Scream' to enable The Attractions to cut the backing track. 'The effect was so impressive that we decided to cut the song as a duet when I recovered,'[4] said Elvis.

By early November the record was finished, and right until the end the atmosphere was fraught. 'I remember when we were mixing there were fights,' says Roger Bechirian. 'Bruce Thomas walking out of the control room, leaving the band and Jake chasing after him. The whole thing was mental.' In the end, the darkly ironic title of *Trust* was considerably more apt than the original title: *Looking Italian.*

On his return from a short tour of Sweden and Norway, which mixed songs from *Trust* and *Get Happy!!* with only a selection of old favourites, Elvis was back in the studio to co-produce Squeeze's *East Side Story* with Roger Bechirian. Initially Jake had planned for Squeeze to make a double album with Paul McCartney, Nick Lowe, Dave Edmunds and Elvis producing a side each, but although all parties were willing, logistically it proved impossible for everybody to find the time.

It was left to Elvis and Roger to spend the six weeks preceding Christmas 1980 producing the entire record, which was eventually scaled down to a single album. Loosely speaking, Elvis filled the Nick Lowe role as all-round creative inspiration while Roger Bechirian covered the technical aspects, although Bechirian articulates the distribution of talents a little differently. 'Elvis sat there and pontificated a lot about this, that and the other and I got on with getting the stuff down and rallying the band. I mean, Elvis did have an influence to some extent, but it wasn't that great.'

Thankfully, the band were a little happier to have Elvis in the studio. For Chris Difford and vocalist Glenn Tilbrook in particular, sparring with him was an experience that was both slightly terrifying and wildly inspiring at the same time. 'I was in complete awe of working with him,' admits Difford. 'It was a great challenge to come in every day with a lyric that would be better than the one that he might come up with. I worked diligently and furiously to get the lyrics in such a shape that he would be pleased with them – and me too. I mean, I wasn't just doing it for him! But it really raised the bar. I could tell which were the weak ones just by looking at his face.'

A shrewd judge at spotting an apt cover version when it came to his own career, Elvis proved particularly adept at seeing the potential in material that the band were disenchanted with. Later becoming a hit single for the band, 'Labelled With Love' was destined for the scrap heap until Elvis heard it and immediately recognised a hit. He bullied and cajoled the band into having a second stab at it until they succumbed, in a way that a conventional producer might not have been able to.

Halfway through the recording, John Lennon was shot dead in New York, on 8 December 1980, and work on the album ground to a halt. 'We went into the studio and a dozen or so musicians just dropped in,' recalls Difford. 'We cracked some beers and just played John Lennon songs the whole day. It was highly emotional. We'd lost somebody that we looked up to, a father figure, and one way that we knew how to demonstrate how loved he was was to play his songs in the studio.'

Elvis's immediate response to Lennon's murder was to write 'Kid About It', which name-checked the traditional song 'The Leaving Of Liverpool' and in its original version contained the line: 'Someone got killed/And he cried.' He later changed it, but the sense of sadness and loss remained in the finished song.

Upon its release, *East Side Story* was hailed as a classic and remains arguably the best record the band ever made. 'I think the sound they got was amazing on that record,' says Roger Bechirian. 'I'm really, really pleased with it. I think it's one of the best works that I've been involved in.' Difford agrees, arguing that Squeeze made two great albums 'and that's one of them. Working with Elvis was obviously the major reason why'.

* * *

In a craft shop in Washington DC, they were selling stuffed-cloth Christmas tree decorations of Elvis, complete with skinny tie, dark glasses and a curling forelock, for a bargain price of $6. The slightly more valuable genuine article landed less than two weeks later, riding into town on the back of another Jake-inspired masterplan: The English Mugs Tour. Six weeks in all, west to east, with Squeeze supporting Elvis and The Attractions throughout.

He arrived back in America with the knowledge that 'Clubland', the opening single from *Trust*, had stiffed at No. 60 in the UK charts. It broke a run of nine straight Top 40 singles, and effectively marked the end of Elvis and The Attractions' flirtation with pop stardom. For the time being at least, he appeared unconcerned.

From the start of the tour in Vancouver on 4 January, the legacy of the 'Columbus Incident' was discreet but strong. There was tight security, with two guards on the bus most of the time. 'I just remember his feet hardly touching the ground when he walked through the lobby,' recalls Chris Difford.

That aside, the contrast to the last time Elvis played North America was vast. The shows were often twice as long as they had been in 1979 – up to thirty songs a night, never less than twenty – and evenly paced, with far more light and shade than before. During the tour he played over sixty songs, spanning his entire career, but almost every date opened the same way – quietly, with 'Shot With His Own Gun' or 'Just A Memory', featuring just Elvis and Steve on piano, usually followed by the band crashing into 'Accidents Will Happen' and 'Strict Time', or occasionally 'Hand In Hand'.

One notable exception was Elvis and The Attractions' first-ever Nashville show on 20 January, where they opened with revved-up versions of three Hank Williams songs: 'Move It On Over', 'Honky Tonkin'' and 'Mind Your Own Business', which did little to impress a young Tennessee crowd who dismissed country as the music of their parents, and were still seeking their new wave kicks in 1981.

Tellingly, there were several other country songs aired on the tour, including Billy Sherill's 'Too Far Gone', Loretta Lynn's '(S)He's Got You', and Elvis's own 'Stranger In The House'. While in Nashville, Elvis took the opportunity to record two songs at the legendary CBS Studio B, where he had sung his duet with George Jones two years earlier. He and The Attractions cut 'He's Got You' and 'Too Far Gone' in a day, with Pete Drake sitting in on pedal steel and Billy Sherill producing. The session was significant: it would turn out to be a deceptively smooth dry-run for the *Almost Blue* album later in the year.

Throughout the tour, Elvis's on-stage demeanour was generally amiable; he at last seemed pleased to be there. Cameo appearances from Squeeze's Glenn Tilbrook and also Martin Belmont during many of the shows also added a bit of spark and sparring which was a million miles away from the surly, arrogant demeanour of old.

At his trio of concerts at the Palladium in New York in early February, Elvis even cracked a few weak jokes, responding to the crowd's exuberance by ramping up the energy levels, tearing into the new songs. Praising the tightness of the band and the contribution of Steve Nieve in particular, veteran Costello-watcher Robert Palmer of the *New York Times* concluded that 'there isn't another singer-songwriter today who can match Costello's range, depth, richness of language or sheer productivity. It can only be hoped that he won't wait two more years to tour this country again.'

At the final show at the Palladium, Elvis had opened with a solo guitar version of Reszo Seress's melancholic ballad 'Gloomy Sunday', a tune so bleak it was also known as the 'Hungarian Suicide Song'. Made famous by Billie Holliday in 1941, it was a wilfully contrary choice, and one that was virtually ignored by a restless crowd eager for something easier to digest. But it was another sure sign that Elvis was moving away from current pop conventions – and perhaps his core audience – towards the deeper, lasting values of jazz and country.

There was a focused power, a new-found elegance in the music. Elvis himself did his best to match up, sporting a mean line in Al Capone chic: smart suits, shades, waistcoats, silk tie and polished Italian shoes, a slightly more dapper version of his normal attire. He even agreed to be interviewed on the Tom Snyder talk show, his first appearance on live television in the US since the heady days of the *Saturday Night Live* stand-off in late 1977. The self-imposed media blackout still extended to all print mediums, but it was further evidence of a slight thaw in the air.

In any case, Snyder was an easy ride, a lightweight talk show host who wasn't going to delve too deep. He didn't even allude to the events in Columbus, and in general Elvis was free to exert the easy, if guarded, charm which could come naturally when he was so inclined. He dropped Cole Porter and Lorenz Hart into the short conversation, little hints of where his heart now lay.

Despite the poise, the touring antics were often far from refined. With the exception of Bruce – who was merely drinking a lot – Elvis and The Attractions were still running wild on a diet of alcohol, drugs and adrenalin. To cut costs, Jake had put Squeeze on the same bus, which only intensified the activities.

'The first week or so was fantastic,' says Chris Difford. 'There were so many of us it was just like being men on a submarine, and we were all playing cards and getting on really well. By the end of it we had to have security in the middle of the bus to keep us apart. There were a few occasions when bass guitars were flying around.' There were other jittery moments: following the show at New Orleans, the English Mugs gained a unique insight into some of the more arcane traditions in the American south, when the tour bus was stopped by the Ku Klux Klan. 'It was ten o'clock in the morning, and they had guns,' recalls Difford. 'Most of us were asleep and the bus driver just told us to keep our heads. The guy got off the bus, he realised we were an English rock band and he let us through.' First Rock Against Racism, now the Ku Klux Klan. Just what was it with Elvis and America?

According to press reports, Jake conformed to type by sparring with journalist Charley Crespo after the show at Providence on 4 February, but Elvis seemed more relaxed. He had put on weight and appeared less up-tight, more intent on enjoying America than he had been previously. Always interested in good food and expensive wine, he ensured that the culinary standards were higher than the normal roadside café culture of most touring bands. He even took a *Good Food* guide book. 'It would be Japanese meals all the time, we'd take a cab sixty miles to go off to lunch together,' recalls Bruce Thomas. 'And we polished off some good wine. I remember having a waiter literally weeping on the table because Elvis and I ordered the last bottle of '61 Haut Brion, whilst having very erudite conversations about social reform, Jeremy Bentham and William Blake. We weren't idiots.'

By the time the tour ended in Toronto on 9 February, *Trust* was in the charts on both sides of the Atlantic. The American reviews had been strong: *Newsweek*'s Jim Miller proclaimed it an 'extraordinary' record, while Ken Tucker of *Rolling Stone* was frequently bowled over by the technical brilliance of Costello's phrasing and wordplay, although he added as a caveat that '[*Trust*] contains some of his very best work and some of his very worst – none of it readily comprehensible, all of it shot through with surprising images and strikingly lovely music'.

Elvis would eventually be unhappy with the record, but *Trust* was a dazzlingly brilliant album in places, full of beautifully crafted, intelligent pop music. Although often latterly viewed as little more than a bridging point between the young, angry Elvis and the more sophisticated, humane incarnation of the mid-to-late '80s, *Trust* had enough strong songs and outstanding lyrical invention to ensure it stood upright all on its own.

The first side in particular was full of magnificent group performances: 'Lovers Walk', 'Pretty Words', 'Strict Time', and 'You'll Never Be A Man' all swung on teak-tough rhythmic hinges, as supple and sure as the up-beat *Get Happy!!* numbers had been hyperactive and confused. In striking contrast, Elvis sounded less certain of himself, more intimate, older.

However, after the back-to-back, miniature masterpieces of 'Watch Your Step' and 'New Lace Sleeves' that formed the emotional heart and musical peak of the record, things began to tail off: the ill-chosen single 'From A Whisper To A Scream', the oddly studied 'Shot With His Own Gun', the C&W pastiche of 'Different Finger', all smacked of a man skipping genres in an desperate attempt to keep himself interested, and the coherency of the album had all but evaporated by the ominous finale of 'Big Sister's Clothes'.

In many ways, *Trust* marked the end of something. It would be the last stand for the production team of Nick Lowe and Roger Bechirian, while the traditional Attractions stomp of songs like 'Luxembourg' and 'Fish 'N' Chip Paper' was beginning to sound gauche and forced amid the more sophisticated material on show.

Nonetheless, at its best *Trust* showcased Elvis at his most darkly dramatic and The Attractions at their most restrained yet widescreen. The *NME* noted that Elvis now possessed a 'highly compassionate, personally political voice', concluding that 'he is performing a vital task – the resuscitation of words, ideas, meanings that are in danger of being neglected or crushed by either cultural poverty or general boredom.'

In *Melody Maker*, Allan Jones also acknowledged the change in tone.

'Costello's vision is as fierce as ever, but the malice has gone; he can still rage but he no longer scolds.' Comparing the album favourably to the 'glib' and 'flippant wisecracks' of *Armed Forces*, Jones said approvingly: 'The points here are harder won, the observations more touching, tinged with a bruised humour, more human.'

Nevertheless, *Trust* ensured that the commercial decline hinted at with *Get Happy!!* continued apace. Without the aid of anything even approaching a hit single, the album scraped into the Top Ten in Britain at No. 9 and stalled at No. 28 on the Billboard charts in the States. The relative lack of success made Elvis stand back and question what he might have been doing wrong to encourage the decimation of his audience numbers. In particular, he had become increasingly disillusioned with his songwriting, and specifically his ability to express his current sense of disaffection and sadness through his own words and music. 'I just wanted to sing other people's songs,'[5] he admitted, sensing they could articulate certain fundamentals he was struggling to grasp.

In the previous few months, Elvis had cut acoustic demo versions of several standards, including Cole Porter's 'Love For Sale' and 'Gloomy Sunday'. He had in mind an album of cover versions, to test himself as a singer and an interpreter of songs, a modern Sinatra or George Jones who could express universal emotions with his voice, rather than a writer of very personal and often obscurely coded preoccupations. Having already proved himself to be the finest songwriter among his peers, he now wanted to prove – to himself, as much as anybody – that he could be artlessly soulful as well as consciously clever.

Initially, the record was designed as 'a collection of melancholy songs of many styles',[6] but Elvis soon found himself drawn to country ballads, the saddest of the sad. He had become obsessed with the genre: *Trust* had featured 'Different Finger', the most overt and traditional country song Elvis had ever written and recorded, and although the tour of the United Kingdom in March featured two new songs – 'Human Hands' and 'Little Goody Two Shoes', an early incarnation of what later became 'Inch By Inch', – far more significant were the number of country songs on show, as Elvis and The Attractions began playing-in some of the material short-listed for the record. The setlist was constantly refined and expanded to include old and new favourites.

Several songs were road-tested, some only once: 'Colour Of The Blues', Gram Parsons' 'How Much I Lied', Loretta Lynn's 'He's Got You', Hank Williams' 'Why Don't You Love Me Like You Used To Do?', Patsy Cline's 'Sweet Dreams', Merle Haggard's 'Tonight The Bottle Let Me Down'. When they came off the tour at the beginning of April, the sifting process began, Elvis and the band rummaging through hundreds of records to find the songs they could make their own.

Rehearsals at Nick Lowe's Am-Pro Studios were hindered by the fact that Bruce Thomas had fallen ill with chicken pox. Lowe had taken Thomas's place on 28 April for a TV special with George Jones in Los Angeles, where Elvis – looking pasty and slightly eccentric with a scarf tied around his neck, a wide-brimmed hat and shades – got to sing 'Tonight The Bottle Let Me Down', 'He's Got You' and 'Stranger In The House' live on stage with his country hero. Pete Thomas's old Chilli Willi partner Paul 'Bassman' Riley took up bass duties for rehearsals, and right up until the beginning of the Nashville sessions with Billy Sherill on 18 May, Bruce's participation was in doubt. As a result, he wasn't as fully prepared as he would have liked.

'I had two huge vitamin shots, got on the plane and went to Nashville,' he says. 'I had difficulty remembering the songs, because there was the same bloody three chords in them only in a slightly different order. They were actually harder to remember than a complex song which had some personality.'

Bruce would never be convinced of the allure of country music, and from the start there seemed to be a number of people at cross purposes. Elvis had tried whittling down the songs he wanted to record before he went to America, but John McFee – now one of the Doobie Brothers, and who had been asked to play pedal steel and extra guitar to help bring a genuine country flavour to the sessions – recalls arriving in Nashville without a firm idea of what they were going to be doing.

'We rehearsed quite a batch of songs, and I remember saying to Elvis, "Man, do we have this arrangement together enough?". And the consensus was: when we get to Nashville, Billy Sherill – this great, classic country producer – will help us sort it out. He'll be going, "Let's see, in the first verse, Steve you do the piano fills, and then I guess the chorus will have John on the pedal steel . . .", the type of things you do with country arrangements. Ironically, when we got to Nashville it turned out Billy Sherill was not a lot of help at all.'

Furthermore, Studio B – the legendary CBS studio where dozens of country classics like 'Stand By Your Man', 'Behind Closed Doors', as well as Bob Dylan's *Blonde On Blonde* were cut – was being renovated, meaning that they had to record in Studio A, which 'could have been anywhere'.[7]

To add to the fraught atmosphere, a camera crew were recording the events for *The South Bank Show*, the British TV arts programme. Their presence leant a slightly schizophrenic air to the proceedings. 'As soon as the cameras stopped rolling, it was, "Right – more drugs, where's the fucking drinks?",'[8] recalled Elvis, who had been seduced by the allure of the music he was singing, letting the mythology of country iconography get to him. 'I had to pull Elvis back and say, "Look, you're going to be dead in six months and nobody's going to tell you except me",' recalls Bruce Thomas. '"You'd better fucking calm down. You're losing the plot big time".' He looked terrible – overweight, his face pale and bloated and permanently hidden behind shades – and could often be heard eulogising Gram Parsons and Hank Williams, who had both died sad, drink-and-drug induced deaths in their twenties.

'There's an element of self-destruction evident in the sound of the voice,' Elvis said of the songs they were recording. 'I don't actually believe in the dying young thing, but at the same time I am inexorably drawn towards that, and certainly the songs that come from that area. I can't work out whether I'm flirting with it or whether it's starting to take me over.'9

More than once he talked about the need to drink alcohol in order to get under the skin of the songs – a classic piece of self-delusion if ever there was one – and he looked tired and unhappy, utterly drained of any enthusiasm for maintaining a pop career. 'I think this business sucks you in eventually,' he concluded sadly. 'I've had the disturbing feeling that what I do is more based around the perversion of truth for quite a while.'10

If Elvis was seeking the truth from Billy Sherill, he was to be sorely disappointed. Sherill's involvement had been the result of much arm twisting by CBS, who were allowing Elvis to record an album which many – including Sherill – viewed as an Englishman's indulgence, a cultural holiday in music he didn't really understand. Few people seemed to grasp the simple concept that Elvis merely wanted to sing some of his favourite country songs and put them on a record. *Almost Blue* was the fulfilment of a long, sincere and fondly held ambition, as well as being something of a gift – or perhaps an apology – to Mary, a huge country fan who was, according to Ken Smith, an even bigger George Jones nut than Elvis.

Instead, Billy Sherill seemed amused, suspicious and dismissive that an English 'punk' singer would want to come to Nashville and record faithful versions of songs which he considered old and unable to yield any new surprises. 'I entered into the thing totally in the dark,' he admitted. 'I really wasn't into him that much. I didn't know what I could contribute.'11 One day in the control room, Sherill wheeled around and asked John McFee, 'What the hell does this guy think he wants to make a country record for?' 'I kinda went, "Huh?! Well, actually he really loves country music",' says McFee. '"He's totally sincere, I think he's a great singer, and he wants to make a real country record".' But I thought that was kinda rude!'

It was almost immediately clear that what Elvis wanted to do was the direct opposite of what the producer was expecting, or willing to deliver. He had produced and written some of Nashville's most enduring songs, among them Tammy Wynette's 'Stand By Your Man' and Charlie Rich's 'The Most Beautiful Girl In The World'. As such, he was a man who had a tried and tested – and wildly successful – formula for producing hit records. In the eyes of The Attractions, however, his artistic sensibilities didn't seem to stretch far beyond dollar signs and buying a new speedboat.

If Sherill was not particularly interested in Elvis and The Attractions' crumpled cloth, neither were the band particularly enamoured with him. Although both Pete and Steve enjoyed country music, and Steve in particular relished the genre-style piano parts he was asked to bring to each song, Sherill's manner was a marked departure from the genial enthusiasm of Nick Lowe. In general, the producer was distant and uncommunicative. He didn't always make it into work every day and when he did he was inscrutable.

He became more animated when Elvis and The Attractions tore through an 100-mph trashing of Hank Williams's 'Why Don't You Love Me Like You Used To Do?', after which he suggested that the band played the song again, exactly mirroring the first take, to give a full double-tracked performance. It was a novelty which amused both Sherill and The Attractions, but which did nothing for the music, as a disgruntled Elvis noted. 'I think Billy Sherill double-bluffed us on that one,' he said after the session. 'He realised we were setting out to outrage him and so he deliberately went over the top.'[12]

Ironically, it was the one track that fitted into the producer's preconceived idea of what he thought Elvis wanted. 'I loved it,' laughed Sherill, who seemed to be intent on simply making things fresh for himself. 'I've heard that song since I was eight weeks old and it's the only time I've ever heard it done that way. In fact, it's what I *thought* he was going to do with all the songs.'[13]

The many frustrations and disappointments on both sides were exemplified in the attempt to get one of Elvis's own recent compositions – 'Tears Before Bedtime' – up and running. The song was half-formed, the playing poor and the singing slack, and Sherill had little inclination to try and work any magic with it. Instead, he left the studio, insinuating – correctly, as it transpired – that it was not a country song and didn't fit the mood of the record. Elvis was stymied. Reluctant to admit defeat or come down too hard on Sherill, he was caught between frustration at how badly things were turning out and a genuine and touching desire to 'impress' Sherill out of his nonchalance. He never did.

* * *

The sessions for *Almost Blue* ended on 29 May, after which it was a relatively quiet summer. The band played the festival circuit in Europe, with concerts in Ireland, Belgium and Sweden. At the end of July they played a one-off gig at the Metro Hotel in Aberdeen, intended to show-case Elvis and The Attractions' country excursion in a true country environment. John McFee came along for the ride. The other concerts were more business-like. Elvis slipped some of the country material into the sets, but it was primarily the 'traditional' Attractions music which took precedence.

Come August, it was abundantly clear that Elvis's self-imposed song-writing hiatus hadn't lasted too long. He had started using the baby grand piano as his principal writing tool, searching for new melodic structures, relishing the fact that he was a comparative learner on the instrument and therefore by neccesity had to avoid the tried-and-tested compositional tricks and licks so easy to fall into on the guitar.

Now, he was taking the music he had been exposed to as a child – jazz, the popular standards of the '30s and '40s, even classical music – as inspiration for many of the new songs: Billie Holliday, Frank Sinatra's midnight albums *Only The Lonely* and *In The Wee Small Hours*, Miles Davis, Erik Satie and Debussy were key touchstones. The results were melodically ambitious pieces that included 'The Long Honeymoon' and 'Boy With A Problem', both of which he felt he was unable – or unwilling – to write lyrics for.

'The Long Honeymoon' had started as an abstract piano piece, which Elvis had demo-ed in the spring as an instrumental. With typical fear-lessness, he had sent the somewhat rambling demo to the legendary Sinatra lyricist Sammy Cahn in the hope of interesting him in a collaboration. A bewildered Cahn eventually responded but politely declined, unable to find a suitably coherent melodic structure to work on, so Elvis tightened the song's structure himself and added his own pointed words, about a decaying marriage and an absent husband.

For 'Boy With A Problem', Elvis looked closer to home for help, borrowing the talents of Squeeze lyricist Chris Difford, who took Elvis's unfinished draft lyric and rewrote the bulk of the song. 'He accepted it, just changed one or two lines,' says Difford. 'There was one line I had which he threw out: "I won't bore you with the problem/I've got all the snow but no toboggan." He thought it was a reference to cocaine.' Elvis's sensitivity to the line may have been down to the fact that he was cleaning up his own act at the time, and at some point between the summer of 1981 and the spring of 1982 he would stop taking drugs, apparently for good. Still, Difford denies that there was anything personal or knowing in the lyric. 'It was about a boy who had snow and no toboggan!'

On 21 and 22 August Elvis crept into Pathway Studios to cut full demos of some other new songs: 'Shabby Doll', 'You Little Fool', 'Town Cryer' and 'Man Out Of Time'. The chorus line of the latter had come to Elvis as a rhetorical question on a suitably dramatic moonlit night on the tour bus in Sweden. The remainder of the song had been written in a Scottish country house hotel outside Aberdeen, where he had been staying in preparation for the gig at the Metro Hotel and which reminded him of 'a scene for a scandal in fiction or in the newspapers. A picture of decay, corruption and betrayal.'[14]

Elvis had clearly got the thirst for interpretation out of his system with the recording of *Almost Blue*. At least many critics hoped so. His country record was released in October 1981 and received by far the harshest critiques of his career. Not all of them were justified, but it was true that *Almost Blue* was a mis-step; above all, The Attractions were ill-used, neutered almost throughout, a crackling A-league band reduced to second-rate country session men. It sounded like they were sleepwalking through most of the material, so palpable was the confusion and lack of enthusiasm. Only the closing 'How Much I Lied', laced with Steve's distinctive piano motif, hinted at the riches that a great beat group playing classic country songs in their own style could unearth.

Meanwhile, after the rich, multi-faceted vocal expressions of *Trust*, Elvis often sounded one-dimensional, melodramatic and shrill, his voice overwhelmed by the material. Sometimes, such as on 'I'm Your Toy', the record's stand-out ballad, he succeeded in pulling the genuine torment of both song and singer out into the open, but it was a rare jewel.

There was little invention in the arrangements. Billy Sherill had added his requisite Nashville fairy dust to proceedings: harps, strings and the Nashville Edition vocal group sugared 'Sweet Dreams', 'Good Year For The Roses' and several other tracks, papering the cracks of some ragged performances, but even at a little over half an hour, *Almost Blue* dragged. The melancholy that Elvis was searching for proved elusive, and instead the album merely sounded funereal and oppressive. Even the up-tempo numbers like 'Honey Hush' and 'Why Don't You Love Me Like You Used To Do?' were lumbering rather than fleet of foot.

Almost Blue was a difficult record to love. Nonetheless, it provided Elvis with one of his best-loved and widely known songs: 'Good Year For The Roses' became an unlikely UK hit single in November, rising to No. 6 in the charts. Billy Sherill proved that – whatever else – he still knew how to produce a Top 10 country song. The success of 'Good Year For The Roses' also provided an interesting statistic: for all his undoubted and celebrated prowess as one of Britain's finest songwriters, two of Elvis's three Top Ten UK hit singles to date have been achieved with cover versions, while a disproportionately high number of his other Top 40 singles – 'I Wanna Be Loved', 'Don't Let Me Be Misunderstood', and 'She', his first Top 20 hit for over fifteen years – were also covers. His initial and brief spurt of singles success notwithstanding, it seemed there was something inherently and stubbornly obtuse in Elvis's music which prevented enduring commercial returns, at least in the ever-fickle singles market.

In Britain, where country music was something of a novelty and the songs were fresh to most listeners, *Almost Blue* got a reasonably positive hearing. In *Melody Maker*, the ever loyal Allan Jones predictably gave it the thumbs up, concluding that 'it's a relief to know that passion isn't completely out of fashion'. Paul Du Noyer's *NME* review was also on-side. 'Costello and company cut through the layers of smart prejudice to find the music's enduring values: its sly humour, its lyrical craftmanship, its melancholic dignity. The tunes are lovely as well.' On the back of the single success and the *South Bank Show* documentary, which was aired on LWT in early November, the album reached No. 7, a respectable showing considering the nature of the material and that there was no real tour to support it.

It was a very different story across the Atlantic, however. The American notices were caustic, the record regarded with a mixture of incomprehension, suspicion, venom and dismay. Negative reviews in the *Village Voice*, *Trouser Press* and a decidedly mixed one in *Rolling Stone* reached a crescendo in *Creem*. 'Time after time he comes off like some hack lounge singer coming to fingertip grips with heartbreak,' wrote Craig Zeller. 'Only thing is, the heartbreak is drowning in a sea of clicked saphead, angst-vocal mechanisms.'

Boo Browning in the *Washington Post* was even more troubled. Raising the spectre of the 'Columbus Incident' in the opening lines of his review, he misread *Almost Blue* as some kind of extension of a perceived assault on traditional American values, or at best an attempt to win back record buyers. It was clearly neither. 'Costello has invaded the trusting soul of country music and made a mean-spirited mess of it,' he claimed. 'I don't expect him to have any shame about this; I just want him to go home.'

Even the less jingoistic reviews tended to agree that Elvis was not an accomplished enough vocalist to take on many of these songs and win the fight. The release of *Almost Blue* marked a career low in America, selling a mere 50,000 copies and crawling to only No. 50 in the charts, while also proving that the events in Columbus had not been entirely forgiven. 'They didn't understand the motives behind it and they sort of resented us playing their music,' said Elvis. 'Maybe it was the aftermath of 1979, maybe that was the final exorcism of all the unhappiness.'[15] And not before time.

Chapter Eight
1981–83

THE 'MASTERPIECE' WAS ORIGINALLY CALLED *Music To Stop Clocks*. Then it changed to *This Is A Revolution Of The Mind*, taken from James Brown's 'King Heroin'. Finally, Elvis settled on *Imperial Bedroom*, the title of a new song which was eventually left off the record.

Setting aside an unprecedented twelve weeks to pull together all his disparate influences and make an ambitious, melodic record which paid little heed to current pop trends, Elvis booked AIR Studios in London to record with Geoff Emerick in late October and November. Although initially he wanted to record most of the album live with only minimal overdubs, after *Trust* Elvis realised that the tried and tested methodology of Nick Lowe and Roger Bechirian had reached the end of the road. 'I remember feeling a bit hurt by the fact that we weren't going to be involved in it,' admits Bechirian. 'It was something I really wanted to do. I know [Nick] wasn't terribly happy.'

As an engineer at Abbey Road, Emerick was a veteran of almost all The Beatles' recording sessions post-1965, a genuine pioneer in terms of manipulating sounds in the studio. Making all the principal creative decisions himself, Elvis was effectively producing the record, relying on Emerick to make his scattershot ideas a reality. 'He was used to being thrown an incomprehensible garble of sounds and musical directions and making some sense of it,' said Elvis. 'After working with The Beatles at the height of their psychedelic era, he was used to innovation.'[1]

Emerick's inclination was to let the musicians find their own way into the music, letting Elvis use the expanded studio time to find whatever it was he wanted from the songs. 'I wouldn't say a lot on the sessions, on purpose really,' Emerick later said. '[I wanted] to draw Elvis out of himself. Knowing that this man had the talent and I didn't, rather than me interject with something, he [had] to think a little bit more. That's my idea of producing: to draw things out of the artist.'[2]

Initally, this approach proved a spectacular failure. The first two weeks in the studio were especially non-productive, the band driving into the songs with little subtlety, the results sounding like a pale imitation of *Trust*. Then they began to experiment. 'The thing about *Imperial Bedroom* was that we went away and rehearsed all the songs and then didn't do the arrangements when we got in the studio,' says Bruce Thomas. 'We just improvised totally new versions, changed the lyrics, changed the melody, changed the arrangement, so it's like we learned the structure of the songs then just deconstructed them and played completely different versions. [They] were changing all the time.'

It was easily the least unified record Elvis and The Attractions had made, partially because Elvis was producing, and thus found himself concentrating more on the sound of the recordings than anything else. The melodies and lyrics were in a constant state of flux, and he was often searching for the right words or meter well after the backing track had been cut. 'Beyond Belief' was a case in point, the final lyric and melody boiled down from the more frantic 'The Land Of Give And Take'. Other times, the backing track might be completed without Elvis, who wasn't always able to get to the studio due to increasing tensions at home.

His marriage to Mary was going through familiar problems: it remained faithless, and the lack of trust and reconciliation was a constant thorn in both their sides. The family had moved from the house in Richmond to a larger, detached property in Chiswick, but Elvis's affair with Bebe Buell – although long over – was neither forgotten nor forgiven, and it remained the source of numerous rows. In particular, Mary was suspicious – rightly, as it later transpired – of the sentiments of one of Elvis's new songs, 'Human Hands'. With its 'Oh darling, how I miss you' sentiments, it seemed to pine for a lost love. In response to Mary's suspicions, Elvis penned 'Tears Before Bedtime', goading his wife that he knew 'the name on the tip of [her] tongue'.

On the days when he couldn't make it to the studio, Elvis would post demos to the studio. 'Pidgin English', 'Boy With A Problem', we pretty much recorded on our own,' says Bruce Thomas. 'Then he'd come in and say, "Don't like that, don't like that," and we'd say, "Well, you weren't here!".'

This idiosyncratic, piecemeal approach meant that it was often a particular instrument or sound which defined each track, rather than the full force of the band as a unit. In 'Shabby Doll' it was the piano and the bass flourishes which stood out; in 'Beyond Belief' the rhythm section, especially Pete Thomas's brooding drums, which had sprung directly from the drummer's brutal hangover.

'I staggered into the studio and it was one of those days when you've just got to own up,' Pete recalled. 'But you see, Elvis is clever: ninety-nine per cent of people would fire you or send you home. He didn't. He said: "Have a drink, get yourself happy. I've got this song . . ." So we went into the studio and literally just jammed 'Beyond Belief', and that was it. One take. Then he said, "All right Pete, you can go home now!".'3

The freewheeling nature of the sessions allowed them any eccentricity they wanted, adding unusual instruments like mellotrons, accordions, twelve-string guitar, marimbas, as well as strings and trumpets to the songs. Each track was treated individually and exhaustively, until virtually all the possibilities and permutations had been explored. When he was satisfied that Elvis knew the direction he wanted the record to take, Geoff Emerick began using his vast experience and expertise try to make sense of it all. 'He had a wonderful ear for the crucial performance,' said Elvis. 'I realized that it was Geoff who really pulled all the best musical ideas into focus.'4 Slowly, things began to come together.

Steve Nieve was again vital, and the piano was an over-riding presence. It was most prominent on 'Almost Blue', a new track which confusingly took its title from his last album, even though the song itself couldn't have been further removed from country music. Perhaps his most beautiful and tender composition to that point, it was based explicitly on Chet Baker's recording of 'The Thrill Is Gone', and a clear and mesmerising indication that Elvis had all but mastered the art of the classic piano torch song. Elsewhere, '. . . And In Every Home' was transformed by Steve's eccentric string and brass score, while his accordion playing and arrangement for three French horns added colour to the already distinctive mood piece of 'The Long Honeymoon'.

There were also some classic band performances on show, nowhere more monumentally than on 'Man Out Of Time'. The first recorded version – snippets of which book-end the final album track – was a tuneless thrash, stamping all the intrigue and mystery at the song's heart into the ground. In the later, more considered studio sessions it was transformed into an epic, flowing masterpiece, Elvis's own 'Like A Rolling Stone'. All the classic Attractions elements were in place: the octave-skipping piano, the warm organ stabs, the inventive rhythm section, the evocative wordplay, but the sum was a masterful display of both majesty and malice which transcended virtually every other recorded performance Elvis and The Attractions had cut, the ensemble sounding somehow weightier, more expansive and more affecting than ever before.

The basic tracks for *Imperial Bedroom* were recorded in November, but only after the raw material had been assembled did much of the real work begin. It would be well into 1982 before Elvis had an album he was happy to release.

* * *

If the records weren't selling as well as Elvis would have liked, there was no disputing his enduring pulling power as a live act. Following warm-up shows at Guildford Civic Hall on 21 December and two pre-Christmas shows on the twenty-third and twenty-fourth at London's Rainbow, he fitted in three shows in the States.

The concert at the LA Arena on 29 December attracted a capacity 18,000 crowd, while on New Year's Eve in New York he sold out two sets at the Palladium. Elvis looked slimmer, happier and healthier than he had for some time. In New York, he played over forty-five songs with The Attractions, ranging from country covers to new numbers like 'Pidgin English'; from old crowd pleasers like 'Red Shoes' and 'Oliver's Army' to superior album cuts like 'Secondary Modern' and 'New Lace Sleeves'. It was a stunning *tour de force*, almost a summation of the breadth and diversity of his career in two-and-a-half hours. The new songs in particular shone. 'Some of them have the harmonic and melodic sophistication of pop standards from the 1930s and 1940s,' said Robert Palmer from the *New York Times*. 'As Costello matures, he seems intent on becoming a kind of latter-day Jerome Kern, and one suspects he has the talent to pull it off.'

But he didn't just want to be Jerome Kern. The final stop was Nashville's legendary Grand Ole Opry on 3 January, where most of *Almost Blue* got an enthusiastic reception at the home of country music. The Attractions – always so much more than a one-trick pony – powered through the likes of 'Lipstick Vogue' and 'Radio, Radio' for good measure. Then it was back to the Royal Albert Hall in London on 7 January for the most ambitious concert of his career.

This – truly – was Elvis's final goodbye to any pretence of still being the gnashing aggressor of stereotype. The fifteen-song first set focused largely on *Almost Blue* material and the new *Imperial Bedroom* songs, before Elvis came out for the second set dressed in a bow-tie, singing over a voodoo combination of The Attractions, John McFee and the Royal Philharmonic Orchestra. There were more country covers, re-interpretations of oldies like 'Watching The Detectives', 'Accidents Will Happen', 'Alison' and a monumental, slowed-down Philly soul version of 'I Can't Stand Up For Falling Down'.

It was a somewhat unclassifiable experiment, and one that got off to an inauspicious start when an under-rehearsed and clearly nervous Elvis fluffed the opening verse of the first song with the orchestra. Although later he called it 'a disaster', he was being hard on himself. Who else among his peers would have taken such a risk? And while the arrangements didn't always work, Elvis was in absolutely staggering voice throughout.

The concert was filmed and recorded in its entirety. It's an indication of Elvis's opinion of the performance that no footage has ever been generally released, except a live version of 'I'm Your Toy' in April 1982. More than anything, the concert was a further indication of his ceaseless desire to keep things interesting and stimulating for himself. It didn't always have to work.

Elvis continued tinkering with *Imperial Bedroom* in the early months of 1982, working alone for several weeks, experimenting with different vocalisations and textures on the likes of 'Kid About It', 'Human Hands' and 'Pidgin English.' He was trying to get away from having one feel throughout, a characteristic which had blighted the performances on *Almost Blue*. 'I went completely the other way and used overlapping vocals and conflicting styles to suggest there was more than one attitude going on inside the songs,'[5] he said.

While he did so, he took the band into Matrix Studios in London in February to bash out a hatful of cover songs, primarily intended as B-sides. Steve Nieve was 'out of town' for the sessions, so they played as a trio with Elvis producing. The songs were light, a million miles away from the dark preoccupations of *Imperial Bedroom*. The stand-out track was a version of Smokey Robinson's 'From Head To Toe', a breezy, good-natured rendition which kept jumping key and featured The Attractions on bawdy call-and-response backing vocals. It was a sign of how much Elvis's original music was flying against the prevailing commercial winds that when 'From Head To Toe' was released as a stand-alone single in September 1982, it became a bigger hit than the two cuts released from *Imperial Bedroom*: 'You Little Fool' and 'Man Out Of Time'. Tellingly, neither of the three troubled the Top 40.

Work on the new album finally finished in March, but its release would be held up until July due 'to contractual things in America',[6] according to Elvis, which in reality meant financial problems between F-Beat and Columbia. According to Andrew Lauder, Elvis had been extremely helpful and understanding regarding the sometimes haphazard cash flow problems that F-Beat were experiencing. His reward was to be appointed co-owner of Demon Records and Edsel, both offshoots of F-Beat. While Demon had started as a hobby, releasing independent singles in the frequent gaps between F-Beat releases, Edsel soon expanded into a reissue label, buying up the rights to deleted albums or old material, repackaging them and putting them back into the shops.

To fill the gap between the completion and release of *Imperial Bedroom*, Elvis and The Attractions went back on the road: a short, six-date tour of Holland in late April, followed by more dates in Australia and New Zealand throughout May and June.

When Elvis returned from the Antipodes in mid-June, he was in possession of a new song. It was called 'Shipbuilding'. A co-composition, its genesis lay in the music Clive Langer had written for Robert Wyatt, having been influenced by Wyatt's aching version of the Billie Holliday song, 'Strange Fruit'. Langer recorded a basic demo of the song, but was struggling with the lyrics until he played the backing track and a sketched-out melody to Elvis at a party at Nick Lowe's house one evening in the spring of 1982.

'I said, "Do you want to write the words, and write them for Robert Wyatt?",' Langer recalls. 'Then I went to America to produce a band and he went off to tour Australia, and he called me at my hotel in New York and said: "I've written the best words I've ever written".'

Elvis's lyrics were inspired by the harsh mood of the times. Enduring the opening spell of a decade of gross national mismanagement under Conservative Prime Minister Margaret Thatcher, Britain was 'at war' with Argentina over the Falkland Islands, a tiny colonial outpost in the South Atlantic. While touring Australia in June, Elvis watched the tabloids salivating over every last detail of the tawdry affair, and for once put aside his customary splenetic rage and mined a deeper seam of reflective, resigned sadness.

'I was trying to think from the point of view of a father,' he later explained. 'The kid's gone away [to war] on a ship that he's built. He got his job back, he got his way of life back, only to send his own child to go and get killed.'7 Evoking both the numb waste of war and the destruction of traditional British industries under Thatcher's Government, the words were a stark warning call which perfectly matched Langer's poignant melody.

Lyrics in hand, Elvis's arrival back from Australia pre-empted Langer's return from America, and he took the opportunity to put down a guide vocal, before going into the studio to record Robert Wyatt's vocal over the original backing track. When Langer returned, they all got together and mixed it. The result was 'Shipbuilding', the Wyatt version – the original. 'When I heard the final mix I just left the studio and burst into tears,' says Langer. 'It was the most amazing thing. The whole track was beyond my dreams.' Robert Wyatt's 'Shipbuilding' reached No. 36 in May, 1983, by which time it was being re-visited by Elvis both in concert and on record.

* * *

Imperial Bedroom arrived on the back of a promotional campaign consisting of one simple word: 'Masterpiece?' It may have flirted with the truth but probably riled as many people as it attracted. Elvis stared from the back cover of the record wearing half-moon spectacles and a straw boater, looking both bored and a little mischievous, all traces of malevolence wiped away.

To complete the sober, grown-up image, he began talking to the press again. 'In the beginning [of my career] I did a few interviews, and I didn't feel they went very well, so I just stopped doing them,' he explained. 'Why be a conspirator in this nonsense they're writing? Then when the time went by, and I felt there were some things that were perhaps necessary to explain, I changed my mind.'[8]

There were other, more practical concerns. Giving interviews was an almost essential part of publicising any new album release. The lack of cooperation on Elvis's behalf hadn't helped flagging sales, and his consent to giving interviews was part of a sustained charm offensive designed to run parallel with the US tour. But primarily it felt like he wanted to clear the air, specifically regarding the Columbus incident, about which he had remained silent since that combative press conference in New York in 1979.

The most significant of all the interviews he gave was with Greil Marcus in the July 1982 issue of *Rolling Stone*, which served as both an apology and an explanation for that drunken brawl in the bar of the Holiday Inn. 'It's become this terrible thing, hanging over my head,' he admitted. 'It's horrible to work hard for a long time and find that what you're best known for is something as idiotic as this.'

He was even more candid in the *New York Times*. 'A lot of people were very angry, and rightfully so. If you make a career out of contriving anger up on stage, whether you're feeling angry or not, sooner or later you'll find yourself saying things, using words you don't mean. But I don't want to sound like I'm making excuses. There aren't any excuses for saying things like that.' He repeated the apologies in the *LA Times* and in *Newsweek*. It must have been hard medicine to swallow for a man as proud and wary of press hypocrisy as Elvis, but he surely must also have realised that if he had said those simple, heartfelt words three years earlier, he would have spared himself a lot of heartache.

In any case, the critics were already in a forgiving mood. *Imperial Bedroom* was lauded almost universally. In *Rolling Stone*, Parke Puterbaugh awarded it four-and-a-half stars out of five, praising Elvis's imaginative use of his voice and the crisp production. The *Village Voice* cared less for The Beatles touches but loved the songs, applauding the new humanity in the writing by concluding: 'The Elvis Costello we know may have made his last record. Could that radiant entity have been merely the chrysalis of an emerging Declan MacManus?' Robert Palmer evoked Cole Porter and Rodgers and Hart in the *New York Times*, concluding that 'the album seems to be a concious attempt to get away from rock entirely, to write pop songs worthy of a Sinatra or Ella Fitzgerald'.

Perhaps the comparisons to the great songwriters and singers of the '30s and '40s were taken too far. After all, only a handful of the songs on *Imperial Bedroom* – 'Long Honeymoon', 'Almost Blue', perhaps 'Kid About It' and 'Town Cryer' – could legitimately be said to have been composed or performed in anything approximating that style.

The pre-rock influence was more overt in terms of the instrumentation, the restraint and detail in the music, and the compassion in the voice which coloured most of the record. For despite its myriad influences and restless insistence on shunning all the easy options, *Imperial Bedroom* was ultimately an album of fantastic, richly drawn pop music. Crafted, instantaneously beguiling and bewildering at the same time, it endlessly rewarded repeated listens in a way that *Armed Forces* or *Trust* simply couldn't. There was nothing that bore comparison with the angry swagger of *This Year's Model* or the bare-knuckled punch of *Get Happy!!*. This was something new. Brighter than *Trust*, frequently humourous, grown-up without being dour or unadventurous, it was a coherent, audacious fulfilling of much of Elvis's immense potential.

The *NME*'s Richard Cook observed that 'the obsessive little misanthrope has been displaced by a cooler commentator', and noted astutely that 'Costello has finally achieved a synthesis of words and music'. *Melody Maker* was a rare dissenting voice, yearning for a little less cleverness and a little more 'raw passion' and songs which really stick. 'Frankly Elvis,' concluded Adam Sweeting, 'I expected more.'

* * *

The US tour kicked off in Santa Cruz on 14 July, and it was clear that Elvis's new-found charm had not deserted him on stage. His high spirits, apparent throughout the tour, peaked at the Merriweather Post Pavilion, Columbia on 25 August. It was his twenty-eighth birthday, and before the final encore, Jake came on stage and announced to the audience that 'a dangerous animal has escaped from the zoo'. The Attractions then returned to the stage followed by Elvis wearing a full gorilla suit, jamming the microphone inside the gorilla head to sing a jazzy R&B cover of Percy Mayfield's 'Danger Zone'.

A funky, R&B flavour was evident throughout the tour: regular covers included James Brown's 'I Got You', The O'Jays' 'Backstabbers' and The Youngbloods' 'Pontiac Blues', a Flip City live staple from way back in '73 and '74. Elvis played somewhere between thirty and forty songs a night, primarily focused around *Get Happy!!, Trust* and *Imperial Bedroom* material, but finding room for everything from the country material to 'This Year's Girl' and 'Waiting For The End Of The World', both of which made a rare appearance during the first of two nights at Los Angeles' Greek Theatre on 20 July. 'Shipbuilding' was the only 'new' song on display.

With a larger body of work to draw on, catering for all aspects of the audience's tastes proved problematic. In San Diego on 24 July, *Newsweek's* Jim Miller found that 'most of Costello's new material seemed to sail right past the restive young crowd. What grabbed the fans was the jackhammer beat of 'Pump It Up' – one of those angry songs out of Costello's past.' Elvis admitted that pleasing everyone as well as himself was becoming something of a conundrum. Previously, he would have played whatever he wanted.

But representing all the extra nuances and textures of his most recent recorded work on stage was the greatest challenge. As he stretched himself in the studio, trying to reproduce *Imperial Bedroom's* subtleties of voice, instrumentation and style in an hour-and-a-half was nigh on impossible. He had fewer options in concert, both with his vocal stylings and The Attraction's arrangements. The shows were often powerful, but the power came at a price: '. . . And In Every Home', 'Beyond Belief' and 'Man Out Of Time' in particular were proving tricky to pull off live.

The tour ended on 6 September, and Elvis and The Attractions immediately flew home to do it all again in Britain. There had been no hit singles in the UK, and although the album reached No. 6 – but only No. 30 in the States – it quickly dropped. '*Imperial Bedroom* got some of the greatest reviews imaginable, [but] it didn't sell more than any other record,' said Elvis later. 'The record company couldn't find any obvious hit singles on it, though I thought it had several.'[9]

He had legitimate cause for complaint. In America in particular, Columbia still hankered after the golden age of *Armed Forces*. They had little appetite for the new, cultured Costello, at least not musically, and Elvis felt they were shamefully timid in promoting the record. However, the stuttering sales of *Imperial Bedroom* also marked the beginning of a dedicated Costello campaign, devoted to blaming the record company for any number of woes. Largely through his own appetites, Elvis had become an artist with a loyal core audience, but his career now operated on the fringes of commercial viability. With only a few exceptions, the music he made from this point on was too varied, too challenging and often too downright bloody-minded to attract huge audience numbers or score hit singles. He couldn't have it both ways.

Nonetheless, Elvis appeared relaxed and amiable throughout 'The Bedroom Of Britain' tour, letting fans backstage to meet and talk to the band, signing autographs, posing for photographs and handing out kisses. As one observer noted, 'no angry words, no sneers, just smiles and jokes'.

On the opening night in Southampton, he played for well over two hours, cramming in nearly forty songs. Aside from his own interpretation of 'Shipbuilding', the only other new song unveiled during the four-week tour was 'Everyday I Write The Book', written quickly in a Derby hotel room on 23 September as a Merseybeat spoof, and performed the following evening at Leicester De Montfort Hall. Just like the old days.

Elvis spent part of the time following the end of the tour on 6 October in the studio, producing six tracks for The Bluebells,* who had provided support on the tour. He was writing new material, wrestling with a way of putting on a more sophisticated live show that could cope with the complexities of his most recent songs.

Having watched *Imperial Bedroom* die something akin to a commercial death despite a keen promotional campaign, rave reviews and a successful tour, he was eager to change direction once again with the next record. With The Attractions in tow, he road-tested some of the songs for what would become *Punch The Clock* in late 1982 with a single show at the Royal Court Theatre in Liverpool on 21 December and two shows at London's Royal Albert Hall on the twenty-fourth and twenty-seventh.

Each night, as the shows reached their conclusion, The Attractions were augmented by the Imperial Horns, the brass section from Dexy's Midnight Runners: Big Jim Paterson on trombone, Paul Speare on tenor sax, Jeff Blythe on alto sax, plus newcomer Dave Plews on trumpet. 'I had the idea of getting some horn guys in and they were available,' he said later. 'So we [rehearsed] songs going back over the last two or three albums and did arrangements for those. It worked out so well that I was keen to have them come in and play on the new album.'[10]

He had already used a 'thrown together' brass section on the November single 'Party Party', a dreadfully jaunty number written and recorded

* These can be found on the *Sisters* album, released in 1982. The Bluebells later had a No. 1 single with 'Young At Heart'.

quickly to accompany a truly forgettable film of the same name. Now Elvis planned to make horns an integral feature of his new sound.

The handful of new songs on show at the Christmas concerts – among them 'Mouth Almighty', 'Everyday I Write The Book', 'The Comedians', and 'The World And His Wife' – bore scant relation to the versions that would eventually appear on the next record. The early, storming live version of 'Everyday I Write The Book', for example, showcased the song in the traditional, bustling Attractions mould, while 'The World And His Wife' was originally played solo as an acoustic ballad.

However, it became clear that everything was open to change, similar in a sense to the spirit that Elvis and the band had harnessed during the *Get Happy!!* sessions. While that record had been a breakneck, drug-fuelled sprint through every rough-and-ready soul styling in the book, *Punch The Clock* was to be a slicker, more calculated take on the pop-soul sound.

It would not be a record where critical plaudits were high on the list of priorities. For all his belief that success wasn't measured in terms of shifting units, Elvis badly wanted a hit single. Rather like a film actor who deigns to star in the occasional Hollywood blockbuster in order to fund his more heartfelt independent efforts, from this point on he would always insist upon trying to pick up the threads of his pop career after spells of single-minded experimentation; partly to show that he could, and partly because he understood how the realities of the business worked. 'Counting *Trust*, we'd gone three records without any substantial hit apart from 'Good Year For The Roses',' he later admitted. 'You have to consider if you allow that contact with the mainstream audience to be severed for too long, you may lose the freedom to do what you want to do.'[11]

From the very start, *Punch The Clock* was a conscious attempt to reconnect, and Elvis needed a production style to match his ambitions. Having satisfied his more sprawling, cerebral cravings under the tolerant gaze of Geoff Emerick, he sought out the services of Clive Langer and Alan Winstanley. They were undisputably the hottest pop producers of the day, and had recently scored a US No. 1 single with 'Our House' by the quintessentially English pop group Madness. The fact that Elvis's old friend Langer was the dominant partner in the axis was an added incentive, but the duo's Midas touch in the charts accounted for the major part of their appeal. 'I think he accepted that that's what we did as producers: [have] hits,' says Langer. 'He always reacts against what he's done before, so we went for it. We tried to get singles.'

As soon as rehearsals began in early 1983, it became obvious that the new production team would have a more active role in the creative process than had been usual in the past. While Emerick had largely left Elvis to his own devices, Langer and Winstanley demanded a far greater degree of discipline.

They shaped the songs, applying a jerky, rhythmic logic to them, structuring each one in a way that left little room for improvisation. Langer was ruthless about getting The Attractions to play the same things over and over again, and much time and attention was taken over the contribution each instrument made to each song. It was a way of working that was alien to the traditional happy spontaneity of Elvis and The Attractions. 'Langer and Winstanley favoured the building block method of recording,' Elvis recalled. 'Retaining very little from the original live take and tailoring each instrumental overdub to best serve the arrangement.'[12]

In rehearsal, these methods teased out an arrangement of 'Everyday I Write The Book' that was unlike anything they had ever recorded. 'It's like a Beatles song, but Elvis would come in and say, "I'm listening to Marvin Gaye, can we go in this direction?",' says Langer. 'I was really excited by the idea that Elvis Costello could make a calculated pop record. I wasn't very interested in recording the band, you know, as just a *band*. I was interested in the whole idea that Elvis could make incredible pop music.'

The challenge of making a gung-ho pop album with contemporary rhythms and lots of instrumental hooks affected the way Elvis wrote. Having used the piano to compose the bulk of the *Imperial Bedroom* material, he had initially continued in this vein for the new songs, picking out soft melodies and melancholy ballads. Although Elvis later claimed that *Punch The Clock* was an upbeat, outward looking record, it was clear to Langer that the familiar woes weren't far away from the surface. 'I thought there was a lot [of issues] from his first marriage when I worked with him,' he confirms. ''TKO' and things like that, I thought they were based on domestic issues. We did talk about it at times.'

Langer cajoled him into picking up a guitar to write some more lively material. 'The Element Within Her', 'The Greatest Thing' and 'Let Them All Talk' were all written to fulfill this criteria, bold slices of bright pop which complemented the preordained sound they were after. In some instances, Elvis even wrote with the new horn section in mind. 'I wrote at least three songs on the album leaving the gaps,' he said. 'I used to go "ba baba, ba baba!" when I sang.'[13]

This process was not without calculation. The perky 'Love Went Mad' was an example of a slight song that was included on the final record at the behest of Langer, even though its author had serious reservations about it. Such were the compromises in creating a record with one eye on current trends and the other on the pop charts. However, Clive Langer stresses that making the record was a mutually creative process. 'Elvis was up for it. At certain times I would have control, other times I'd just let him do it, but if he really didn't like something it wouldn't go on, it was as simple as that.'

The producers brought many of their own 'house' musicians and trademark musical reference points into the mix: backing vocalists Caron Wheeler and Claudia Fontaine, known as Afrodiziak, had worked with them several times, and became a central part of the *Punch The Clock* sound. Dave Plews apart, all of the horn section – now dubbed the TKO Horns – had been involved with Langer and Winstanley on the last Dexy's Midnight Runners album; string arranger Dave Belford had also worked with Madness.

For the first time in the studio, the fiercely independent Attractions were sharing musical space with a number of session musicians. 'I think the band enjoyed the process of that album,' says Langer. 'The more difficult it was, the more of a challenge it was. There was a discipline, because I had a certain amount of control which they weren't used to. Normally Elvis had control.' Nevertheless, neither Elvis nor the band were ever completely convinced of the merits of their producer's highly calculated approach to making the record. 'Those trendy production values,' recalls Bruce Thomas with a shudder. 'Everything gated together, very bright and shiny. It wasn't our thing, but it worked on a couple of tracks.'

Ironically, the two stand-out tracks on the record were the sparsest, the ones that mostly steered clear of sonic gimmicks. 'Pills And Soap' was a stark, stabbing piano track based on Grandmaster Flash's 'The Message', rush-released as a single in May on Elvis's own IMP label and then supposedly deleted – in actual fact, it never was – on the eve of the 1983 general election. Loosely inspired by a film about the abuse of animals which had made Elvis turn vegetarian, it hid a scabarous – if obscure – political viewpoint beneath the surface.

Meanwhile, 'Shipbuilding' stood up against the very best of his recorded output. While always conceding that Robert Wyatt's version was the original, Elvis liked the song so much he wanted it to be heard by the widest number of people possible. To make his version even more distinctive, he visualised a trumpet solo on the track.

Chet Baker wasn't the first choice. Langer recalls that Wynton Marsalis was discussed but wasn't in the country, while a typically undaunted Elvis had Miles Davis as his original first pick, but it so happened that Baker was in London in May playing a residency at The Canteen. His melancholy, melodic trumpet sound and remarkable good looks had made him a 1950's poster boy, but he had since descended into a grim cycle of cocaine and heroin addiction which gripped him until his death in 1988.

By his own admission, Baker had never heard of Elvis Costello, but when Elvis sounded him out at The Canteen, he quickly agreed to play for scale. 'It was a cash deal,' recalled Elvis. 'He just came in; it may well have been the next day.'[14] Elvis offered to double the jazzman's standard union fee, and few could doubt he was worth every penny.

'One of the best things we ever did was 'Shipbuilding',' recalls Bruce Thomas, still moved by the experience many years on. 'That was probably one of the musical high points. Chet Baker, this wizened corpse on death's door, strung out, just *played*. He followed this bass line and played his solo, so simple, with so much soul in it. It really touched me. It was one of those things that really made me think about how you judge people.'

While Langer concurs that Baker's final contribution as heard on the record was inspirational, he remembers the session being a tough one. 'We recorded the track live, but he kept blowing bum notes when we got to his solo. He was going, "This isn't jazz!" so he couldn't quite get it. That solo is three whole takes – the band as well – edited together, to get it to work. He was pretty spaced out.'

* * *

Elvis and The Attractions embarked on a short and rather hastily arranged tour of Ireland and England in June. During the album sessions, Elvis had found time to participate in a couple of shows at London's Dominion Theatre in March as a guest of Madness, and a few days later had popped over to Sweden with The Attractions to showcase three new songs – 'Invisible Man', 'Charm School' and 'Shipbuilding' – on a TV show. But that was the sum total of his live work until the summer.

The aim of the low-key tour was to play in the new material and get tight with the TKO Horns, who joined each gig midway through and held on until the end. It was a rather ragged affair, and most concerts were far from sold out. It ended on 28 June with an appearance at Dingwalls' tenth birthday charity bash, where Elvis and The Attractions joined a stellar pub-rock line up which included Nick Lowe, Paul Carrack and a for-one-night-only reunion of Chilli Willi and The Red Hot Peppers, with Pete Thomas back behind the drum stool.

Revisiting one of their earliest haunts, Elvis resisted the temptation to wallow in nostalgia, both on- and off-stage. 'Oliver's Army' was the only pre-1980 song aired, and Ken Smith recalls a brief, cool meeting with his old Flip City friend. 'I went up to him and he sort of said, "Hello mate", and shook my hand, but that was it,' he says. 'I had a chat with Mary, but he wasn't bothered.'

Following the end of the tour, Elvis took the chance to add to the IMP repertoire. Having started the independent label because he couldn't get 'Pills And Soap' out in desired time span through the regular channels, Elvis recognised an opportunity for releasing other interesting works that lacked an obvious mainstream outlet.

Former Radiators From Space man and future Pogues guitarist Philip Chevron was working in Rock On in Camden, the same record store where Elvis had stocked up on his Stax and Motown records prior to recording *Get Happy!!* Elvis remained a regular customer, and as the two chatted one day Chevron outlined an idea he had for a version of 'The Captains And The Kings', from Brendan Behan's play *The Hostage*. 'Everybody I knew in the business were saying, "You can't approach Elvis that way, you have to talk to Jake, you gotta go through the usual channels",' remembers Chevron. 'I thought, "Fuck that, I'll just ask the guy!".'

Elvis liked both Philip's approach and his demo, and devised an 'Elgar-meets-Palm Springs Orchestra' arrangement of the song. Moving quickly before the US tour kicked off in early August, he and Chevron recorded the song at Jam Studios in north London, with Colin Fairley as engineer. 'I loved his attitude in the studio, which was: nothing but the best,' says Chevron. 'He got in Dave Bedford [who had arranged strings on 'Shipbuilding'] to orchestrate it, we got the best studio possible for the sound he wanted for the orchestra, and then like an old-fashioned independent label in America, we skimped on the B-side! It's Elvis playing everything and me singing, and we did that in an hour including all his ad-hoc overdubs. That's a great way to work.'

'The Captains And The Kings' was released on IMP in October and gained a little media attention and even a degree of airplay. It also cemented a friendship and working relationship between Elvis and Philip Chevron which would continue for a few years. From that point on, Chevron effectively became the de facto A&R man and sometime producer for the IMP label.

* * *

Punch The Clock was released in the first week of August. Elvis had been uneasy about the record even as he was making it, unsure whether he actually liked it or not. 'He was a bit freaked out when we mixed it and he heard it back,' admits Clive Langer. '"Fucking hell, what have we done? Created this pop album".' He had to go on *Top Of The Pops* and buy a Gucci jumper.'

It was, of course, exactly what he had set out to do, but by the time of the album's release, Elvis's unease had grown into significant reservations. *Punch The Clock* became one of the few records that he publicly and categorically stated his dislike for: he bemoaned its lack of heart, its misplaced arrangements, acknowledging that it was not a record which was necessarily designed with longevity in mind. 'A lot of the planning, the imaginary production of the record relates to pop music of the moment,'[15] he conceded, as good as admitting it wouldn't stand the test of time. Later, he would be more unforgiving, lambasting the 'passionless fads of that charmless time: the early '80s.'[16]

Many of his criticisms held water. The record had a clear identity and a unified sound throughout, but it was thin and contrived. The Attractions were stripped of much of their personality, while Afrodiziak and the TKO Horns were filtered into the mix with very little subtlety. But it was not all down to the production. These were self-evidently not the greatest batch of songs Elvis had ever written. The rambling 'King Of Thieves', the insipid, forced jollity of 'The World And His Wife', and the worryingly high number of mediocre tunes jarringly welded onto their choruses ('Love Went Mad', 'Mouth Almighty', 'TKO') all lacked the craft and melody of the vast majority of Elvis's previous output.

It wasn't all gloom, however. Aside from the peaks of 'Shipbuilding' and 'Pills And Soap', the slinky 'Charm School' retained its sultry slouch in the face of the unsympathetic production, while 'Invisible Man', 'Let Them All Talk' and 'The Greatest Thing' were all fine pop songs. And 'Everyday I Write The Book' was a fantastic song in any guise, perhaps the closest Elvis ever came to matching the witty word-play and universal melodic reach of Smokey Robinson. But even then, both the song's initial live incarantion with a full-pelt Attractions, and its later acoustic transformation, outstripped the poppy recorded version.

The reviews were generally strong, if a little cautious. The *NME* heard 'a hit, but not quite a knockout', before astutely wondering 'whether Elvis hasn't sacrificed a degree of emotional resonance in his bid for pop acceptability'. The *New York Times* praised the record for its 'surprising textural contrasts that sound commercial but not cliched'.

Having made a consciously populist record, Elvis made sure he was more accessible than ever before. An unprecedented amount of promotion was conducted for the new record in Europe and America. He gave over 100 interviews in total, and became a virtual fixture on radio and television. Throughout May, June and July, Elvis would pop out at unsuspecting viewers, finding his way on to everything from *Top Of The Pops* to BBC 1's *Breakfast Time*, where he reviewed the morning papers with a typically acerbic eye.

It all paid off. Despite its flaws, *Punch The Clock* achieved its goals. It arrested the commercial slump, attaining gold status on both sides of the Atlantic, becoming Elvis's best-selling album since *Get Happy!!*. In addition, 'Everyday I Write The Book' gave him his biggest US single yet, climbing to No. 32 in the autumn of 1983. In America in particular, the accessibilty of *Punch The Clock* – coupled with the previous year's round of polite, contrite press interviews – finally laid the one-dimensional truculent persona of old to rest. In a country that positively revels in *mea culpa* and the subsequent happy ending, however contrived, Elvis was firmly back in the good books. Now his problems were to be found closer to home.

Chapter Nine
1983–86

AS MARY COSTELLO APPEARED TO KNOW only too well, Elvis had never quite succeeded in extricating Bebe Buell from his mind – or his heart. 'He had written me a couple of letters between 1979 and 1982, basically apologising for not "being able to promise me anything", but that he wanted me to know that he loved me,' claims Buell. 'He left me dangling.' In the summer of 1982, with his marriage in a familiar state of disarray, and with Mary already suspicious, Elvis sent Buell another letter, this time more romantically forthcoming. He probably felt that he might as well commit the crime he was being punished for. Buell was still very much in love with Elvis, and responded to his initial letter by bombarding him with notes sent to his office. 'I completely forgot he was back with his wife and child,' she said. 'I acted as if he were mine and mine alone.'[1]

However, it was a full year before they saw each other again. Contact via letter and telephone continued for some time, with Elvis torn between doing the right thing as a father and husband on the one hand, and surrendering to his desire and the avalanche of attention and affection from Bebe on the other. Physically, at least, he seemed resolved to keeping Buell at arm's length, and the game of emotional cat-and-mouse continued for months until a four-hour telephone conversation in March 1983, when Elvis told her that he 'needed' to see her again. 'It was all at his instigation,' says Buell. 'He was trying to resolve his feelings, revisiting me to see if there were any possibilities of a reconciliation. I don't think he was strong enough to deny me. Of course, I played along. I adored him.'

The meeting finally occurred in July in New York, where they had parted over four years earlier. Elvis was rehearsing for the US tour, as well as meeting with Yoko Ono to discuss cutting one of her songs, 'Walking On Thin Ice'. As arranged, Buell came to his suite at the Parker Meridien Hotel, and within twenty-four hours they had reconsummated their affair.

Before Elvis flew back to London, they made plans to meet up again during the 'Clocking Across America' tour the following month. It would eventually prove to be the knockout blow for his marriage.

* * *

The new live show leaned heavily on *Get Happy!!*, *Imperial Bedroom* and *Punch The Clock*, but the songs spanned the entirety of Elvis's six-year recording career. He had put together a lengthy set which was more ambitious and more structured than anything he'd previously attempted. The equation was simple: there were more people on stage, thus less room for spontaneity. Afrodiziak hadn't made the trip to the States, but the TKO Horns appeared on the opening six-song salvo, which on almost every night consisted of 'Let Them All Talk', 'Possession', 'Watching The Detectives', 'Secondary Modern', 'The Greatest Thing' and 'Man Out Of Time'. They then departed, before returning for the climax of the show, usually ending in a combination of 'Pump It Up', 'Alison' and 'I Can't Stand Up For Falling Down'.

The horns added drama to some of the songs and gave them a solid, clearer outline, but Elvis experienced vocal problems throughout the tour. His singing voice was never the most pampered of instruments – indeed, The Attractions sometimes called him 'The Barking Cabbage' – and throughout the 'Clocking Across America' tour it often sounded forced or flat, and his words unclear. The rigours of being heard over a brass section – as well as the typically bruising Attractions – every night were taking their toll.

There was no hiding place on 8 August, when Elvis took the unmissable opportunity to sing a duet with Tony Bennett as part of a television special in the Red Parrot club in New York. His voice was shot to pieces, and he only just survived the humiliation of croaking his way through 'Lil' Darlin'' and 'It Don't Mean A Thing If It Ain't Got That Swing' with the Count Basie Orchestra and the man Frank Sinatra regarded as the greatest singer of all time. 'Mr Bennett was patient, sympathetic and paternal,' Elvis recalled. 'By the looks on their faces, the same could not be said for some of the saxophone section.'[2]

The show at Columbia's Merriweather Post Pavillion on 16 August found Elvis in better voice and in a congenial mood, something to do with the imminent arrival of Bebe Buell that night, perhaps. Geoffrey Himes of the *Washington Post* watched a twenty-nine song set 'ranging broadly from whispered jazz reflections to punchy soul shouts', and praised a performer who was 'more generous, more subtle and more satisfying [than ever before]'. Towards the end of the tour, the recently composed 'Great Unknown' was thrown into the set, while the 22 September show at Irvine Meadows Amphitheatre opened with a rare and welcome flash of crowd-pleasing nostalgia, six back-to-back surges of crackling electricity, played nowhere else on the tour: 'Radio, Radio', 'Waiting For The End Of The World', 'Chelsea', 'This Year's Girl', 'Miracle Man' and 'Lipstick Vogue'.

Bebe and Elvis kept in touch after he and The Attractions flew home to resume touring in Europe and the UK at the end of September. Though there had been frequent telephone contact throughout the US tour, the couple had met only twice. Bebe hadn't been the only woman Elvis had slept with in America, but the intensity of her feelings remained undiminished. Elvis, on the other hand, seemed to be trying to work out what exactly it was that he felt, in order to resolve old, unfinished business once and for all.

Back in Britain, backing vocalists Afrodiziak were added to the mix on-stage, but the shows never strayed far from the US prototype. Many of the concerts were dogged by very poor sound, and Elvis's voice remained patchy. Nonetheless, the shows were a hit with reviewers and audiences alike. Fans in Bristol on 29 October were treated to a rare 'Big Tears' and a thankfully even rarer stab at Gary Glitter's 'Leader Of The Gang', while in Liverpool, Elvis received a standing ovation, led by his son Matthew. From there, the tour rumbled through Europe until the end of November, whereupon everyone – with one exception – took a break.

Elvis spent most of the time up until Christmas writing songs for a new record. He moved an electric piano and a couple of guitars into a disused F-Beat office above a hairdresser's salon in Acton, north London, and worked a business day, Brill Building-style. The relocation was an indication of deteriorating relations at home, but it was also Elvis's attempt to apply more craft and focus to his writing, a reaction to Clive Langer's disciplined approach and the retrospective belief that the songs on *Punch The Clock* were not as strong as they could or should have been.

There was a reflective, narrative thread to the new songs, many of which Elvis demo-ed at Eden Studios in December. They included 'The Great Unknown', 'Worthless Thing,' and 'Peace In Our Time', a ballad first performed at The Big One, an anti-cruise missile benefit at the London Apollo on 18 December, where Elvis had ended his brief appearance by duetting with Paul Weller on a vamped version of The Style Council's 'My Ever Changing Moods'.

By early February, Elvis had enough new material to be able to take The Attractions – shorn of both horns and harmonies – on a short tour of the south of France. Between 13 and 19 February, they road-tested nine of the thirteen songs that would end up on the next record. The gigs were loud, ragged and short, and it was neither a happy nor a particularly sober experience.

'We were staying at this place in Cap de Ferrat where David Niven used to go,' recalls Bruce Thomas. 'I remember Pete Thomas lining up four brandies at one end of the pool and four brandies at the other. He drank one, swam to the other end, drank another, swam to the other end, drank another, swam to the other end. There was a different drink all the time.'

This kind of behaviour was largely born of boredom and disaffection rather than hi-jinks. There had been a lot of tension on the *Punch The Clock* tour. The strain of having six extra people on the tour bus and on-stage didn't help, and when it got too much Elvis had occasionally pulled rank and bailed out, popping on a plane instead. Having already found themselves set up behind two backing vocalists and a horn section on stage, this wasn't perhaps the best way to foster inter-band harmony amongst The Attractions.

By the time they returned from France to record the new album, relations between Elvis and the band were on the contemptuous side of familiar. Elvis was full of doubt and unsure about the continuing validity of what they were doing musically; personally, he was at a severely low ebb, recognising that his affair with Bebe Buell had finally made his marriage irreconcilable.

In a state of flux, and unbeknown to the band, he decided privately that his union with The Attractions had probably reached the end of the road. 'He said to me on the sly, "I think this is going to be our last album",' recalls Clive Langer. With tar-black humour, it was to be called *Goodbye Cruel World*.

Despite substantial artistic misgivings, the satisfying commercial returns of *Punch The Clock* had been sufficient for Elvis to allow Langer and Winstanley a second bite of the cherry. However, when they entered Sarm West Studios in London in early March, the relatively happy compromise between art and commerce which had proved partially successful on *Punch The Clock* quickly evaporated.

Elvis believed many of the new songs were strong, and he had in mind a ragged, folk-rock sound. This, however, didn't appeal to Langer and Winstanley, and artist and producers soon found themselves at loggerheads.

'He would have been better off going back to Nick Lowe,' says Clive Langer. 'I wanted to carry on from where we had got to with 'Everyday I Write The Book', but Elvis was saying he wanted it really rough. I didn't think it was his greatest bunch of songs, anyway, and we did say, "It would be great if you could write some more pop songs." But he never did.'

After a couple of stress-filled weeks, where Elvis and The Attractions grappled unsuccessfully with live takes of the songs, things reached meltdown in the studio. Langer felt he was being sidelined, and eventually sat down and confronted Elvis. 'At one point I did say, "Thanks a lot for inviting me along to listen to you make your record!" He drank a bottle of gin and I drank a bottle of vodka and we had a good talk and made up, but there was quite a bit of friction.'

The real problem was that Elvis had no firm idea what he wanted. Keen not to relinquish too much of the commercial ground he had gained, he felt bullied into continuing with a production style he had little affection for. But the sound he was seeking proved elusive. As a consequence, he was changing his mind frequently about the best way to present the songs, alienating the band and generally driving everybody to distraction. Eventually, a truce was called. 'I agreed to let them work their magic on a few cuts and give the record company some commercial focus,' said Elvis. 'The rest of the tunes went fairly unadorned.'[3]

Langer and Winstanley were let loose on 'The Only Flame In Town' and a cover of an obscure Teacher's Edition B-side called 'I Wanna Be Loved'. Both were unashamedly calculated stabs at scoring another hit, utilising all the duo's pop tools in an attempt to scrape a single or two together. Scritti Politti's Green added barely audible backing vocals to 'I Wanna Be Loved', while Daryl Hall harmonised with Elvis on 'The Only Flame In Town'. Big Jim Paterson was back with his trombone, while Gary Barnacle provided less-than-subtle saxophone adornments – The Italian Traffic Jam, as Elvis witheringly put it – to a few of the tracks. It was pretty desperate stuff.

The addition of guest vocalists and session players did little to rally the spirits of The Attractions. 'They were just there to inject an extra element that meant we weren't stuck with each other all the time,' admits Bruce Thomas. 'The same four guys who were probably not on a creative high at the time.'

As a further perceived slight on the band, Elvis had booked his first-ever solo tour to begin in the States in April, with a European trip to follow later in the year. The omens were clear, and it all added up to a tense, difficult few weeks. 'It was like going to the dentist every day,' said Pete Thomas. 'It was the sort of thing where, if you started having fun you felt guilty. The whole feeling was so down.'[4] Elvis wasn't any happier than the band. 'I was having a miserable time,' he admitted. 'I basically ran away to sea.'[5]

* * *

Coming straight after the completion of *Goodbye Cruel World* in April, Elvis's solo tour of the US initially stuck closely to the kind of set he would normally play with The Attractions, opening with the same six songs almost every night: 'Accidents Will Happen', 'Stranger In The House', 'Men Called Uncle', 'The Only Flame In Town', 'Mouth Almighty' and 'Kid About It'. He played like a man released from chains: the *Washington Post*'s reviewer caught the opening show at the University of Virginia on 10 April, 1984 and found it 'emotionally devastating'.

American singer-songwriter John Henry (T-Bone) Burnett was his support act, and almost immediately the two men hit it off both personally and artistically. Burnett was a tall Texan, a born-again Christian who had toured with Delaney and Bonnie (one half of whom was Elvis's one-woman downfall, Bonnie Bramlett) and Bob Dylan's Rolling Thunder Revue in the mid-'70s. He then made several albums with The Alpha Band, before embarking on a solo career in the '80s. In possession of a light, pleasant voice, Burnett favoured a rootsy, acoustic style of music which sometimes bordered on the anonymous. More significantly, he was also becoming a sought-after producer, having recently finished work on the acclaimed Los Lobos album *How Will The Wolf Survive?*.

Shortly into the tour, Burnett and Elvis formed a duo of mock-warring siblings called The Coward Brothers – loosely based on The Everly Brothers – who had supposedly reunited for one final fling. It was a simple conceit which allowed them to have some fun: each night T-Bone would join Elvis and they became Henry and Howard Coward, playing guitar and harmonising on a number of classic covers: George Jones's 'Ragged But Right' and 'She Thinks I Still Care'; The Beatles' 'Baby's In Black'; The Byrds' 'So You Want To Be A Rock & Roll Star'; Scott MacKenzie's 'San Francisco (Be Sure To Wear Some Flowers In Your Hair)'; and Bobby Charles' 'Tennessee Blues'. It was light-hearted escapism, a world away from the stresses and strains of London, and Elvis was clearly energised by the experience.

His rapport with the audience had changed enormously: he was funny, frequently a little silly, warmer, more vulnerable. There was a strong emotional current running through the shows, much of it gaining its energy from Elvis's voice, which in the more intimate environment was allowed to display far more of its range and colour. With just a guitar for accompaniment, he could let himself swoop, or croon, or whisper, or sob at the end of 'Alison', where he frequently stopped playing completely and just let himself go.

It was a timely reminder of what a fearless, versatile singer Elvis could be, and as the tour went on, he began to stretch himself even further. The gigs grew longer and less predictable, Elvis throwing more and more covers into the sets, searching for the songs and words which best summed up his mood on any particular night: June Tabor's 'Smiling Shore'; James Carr's 'The Dark End Of The Street'; The Beatles' 'Yes It Is'; Bob Dylan's

'I Threw It All Away'; numerous country songs, even The Band's 'Stagefright' and Brendan Behan's 'The Captains And The Kings'. 'I had a ball,' he said. 'I did songs one night and then never again. And the thing with T-Bone also balanced out the sombreness of some of the songs.'[6]

Bebe Buell remained in the picture. She had stayed with Elvis in Detroit on 22 April, and the couple spent more time together in San Francisco as April turned into May. At the Warfield Theatre on 28 April, Elvis responded to Buell's presence in the audience by changing the opening three songs in his set to 'You Little Fool', 'Human Hands' and 'Somebody's Back In Town', pointed selections played nowhere else on the tour. No one was supposed to know about Bebe, and the couple enjoyed the cloak-and-dagger nature of their affair. After the San Francisco show, Elvis expressed how 'thrilled' and 'amazed' he was that Bebe had been in the audience without anyone knowing.

They called each other Henry and Jane; occasionally Buell was Candy. In San Francisco, she spent much of her time sequestered in Elvis's suite at the Miyako Hotel to prevent anyone finding out about their relationship. In truth, despite the strength of feeling on both sides, it was hardly a conventional relationship at all. Elvis saw Bebe on perhaps five or six separate occasions between July 1983 and May 1984, and he seemed determined not to put Mary through the same old heartache. 'Elvis is a very honest man,' said Buell. 'He was obviously participating in something he felt was wrong.'[7]

At the end of the solo tour, Elvis left America and hooked up with The Attractions for dates in New Zealand, Australia and Japan. In early June, while in Japan, he watched from afar as both his marriage and his relationship with Bebe finally fell apart.

In a bizarre set of circumstances which were almost farcical but far from funny, Mary Costello had found out that Buell was pregnant. Having read a misdirected letter which Bebe had sent to Elvis in London, Mary phoned Buell and the two participated in a two-hour conversation which ranged from a shouting match to sisterly empathy. 'She was just as puzzled as I was as to what our roles were in this man's psyche,' claims Buell. Afterwards, Mary called Elvis in Japan; then Elvis called Bebe.

According to Buell, Elvis reacted angrily to the news that she was pregnant, allegedly refusing to have anything to do with the baby. 'I don't believe in abortion, but I will not help you with the child,' he reportedly told her. 'I will not be involved with this pregnancy.'[8] Everything unravelled. The two didn't speak again for over a year, until a brief phone conversation in Los Angeles in September 1985, while Elvis was making *King*

Of America. He asked what had happened to the baby and Buell lied, telling him she had had a miscarriage. In fact, she had had a termination. It was the last time they spoke.

* * *

However much he didn't want his marriage to break up, it had now become inevitable. Elvis finally succumbed to the fact following his return from the tour of the Far East in June 1984. Mary filed for divorce, and he moved out of the family home in Chiswick and was soon ensconsed in a two-bedroomed flat in Holland Park, west London.

Almost immediately, his love life took an even more tumultuous turn. Keen to keep an eye on the prevailing trends in London, Elvis asked Philip Chevron to act as his musical guide. Chevron took him along to gigs by The Men They Couldn't Hang and *outre* German cabaret act Agnes Burnelle, both of whom would soon become IMP acts. But there was one band in particular that he was adamant Elvis should check out. 'I said, "You gotta see The Pogues",' recalls Chevron. '"They are *the* happening band in London at the moment".'

On 22 June, Elvis dutifully went along to the Diorama in Euston to see the rag-bag group of Anglo-Irishmen and women who melded traditional Irish folk music to punk, with chaotic but often electrifying results. He loved them straight away. 'But what I didn't quite realise until a bit later when the penny dropped, was that he kept talking about the bass player,' says Chevron. '"She's sensational, isn't she? Look at her! Look at her!" Next thing I knew, Elvis had booked The Pogues to support him on tour.'

Elvis had inadvertently stumbled upon his next, life-changing romantic encounter. Over ten years younger than him, Cait O'Riordan – pronounced Cot – was nineteen at the time Elvis first saw her. Born in Nigeria on 4 January 1965, her father was from Lahinch, County Clare, Ireland and her mother from Musselburgh, near Edinburgh, in Scotland. She had grown up near Heathrow airport in west London, not that far from Elvis's old stamping ground, and later lived amongst the Irish diaspora in Camden and Kilburn.

In her teens Cait bought a bass guitar. Although she didn't learn to play it for some time, a chance meeting with The Pogues' maverick singer-songwriter Shane MacGowan in Rocks Off record shop – the sister shop to Rock On in Camden Town – led to her joining the band in 1983, probably more on the strength of her look and her Irish heritage than for her musical ability.

Elvis was smitten with both the band and its tall, skinny, black-clad bassist, and The Pogues were invited to support Elvis and The Attractions on their upcoming UK tour, which would begin at the end of September.

First, there was the pressing matter of *Goodbye Cruel World*. Having played many of the songs from the record on his solo US tour, finally unearthing the kind of naked intensity he had been searching for all along, Elvis had little enthusiasm for his new album by the time of its release in June. 'I hated the record,' he admitted. 'I knew we'd got most of it wrong.'[9] Clive Langer received his finished copy and shared similar thoughts: 'I remember listening to it and saying, "Oh fuck, it's no good." It's a crap album.'

Allan Jones in *Melody Maker* begged to differ. 'From where I'm sitting, it sounds like the most approachable Costello LP since *Trust*,' he wrote, concluding that it 'isn't just a great album, it's a great Elvis Costello album'. Everyone else had less enthusiasm for the record. And with good reason.

Some albums that meet with critical dismay upon their release are later hailed as lost, overlooked gems, but *Goodbye Cruel World* will never be one of them. It opened with 'The Only Flame In Town', a mediocre, pun-laden number made almost excruciating by its thin saxophone and anaemic rhythm, and it got little better.

The handful of decent songs – 'Home Truth', 'Worthless Thing', 'Peace In Our Time', 'The Comedians', 'Inch By Inch' and 'Deportee Club' – would later be redeemed and reborn in stripped down, acoustic solo versions in concert, or in sympathetic cover versions. The lifeless 'I Wanna Be Loved' was also transformed in concert in 2002. On record, however, the incoherent production left the songs shapeless and muffled, drifting off into inconsequence.

The remainder of the tracks weren't as bad as the album made them out to be, but neither were they as strong as Elvis seemed to think. 'Room With No Number', 'Love Field', 'The Great Unknown', and 'Joe Porterhouse' were all hesitant and uncertain, virtually devoid of all feeling. It was a murky, depressing record, hamstrung by compromise and uncertainty, and whose tinny, Muzak-like frills made *Punch The Clock* sound like *Blood On The Tracks*.

By and large, the critics were disappointed and those who had caught Elvis's mesmerising solo shows in the States were especially confused. It was almost like watching two different artists. 'What the new album lacks is the sustained intensity of Costello's performance on his recent solo tour,' wrote Jim Miller in *Newsweek*. 'The recording of 'Peace In Our Time' sounds heavy-handed; but in concert, the song had the immediacy – and impact – of a broadside.'

If the title of *Goodbye Cruel World* was an apt summing-up of a career low, it almost proved to be more personally prophetic. Not long after its release, the student-run WTJU radio station in Virginia announced that Elvis had died in an aeroplane crash, before playing an hour-long tribute consisting solely of his records. The late-night DJ later admitted that he pulled the prank to check if anyone was listening to his show. They were, and distraught Elvis fans called other media outlets before they were finally convinced that the story was untrue.

The DJ was subsequently sacked, but his stunt did little to boost the fortunes of the record. It sold poorly, limping to No. 10 in the UK and No. 35 in the US. However, Clive Langer's pop touch did succeed in keeping Elvis in the UK singles charts. 'I Wanna Be Loved' reached No. 25 over the summer, aided by a peculiar video shot during the Australian tour in May, featuring a weary Elvis, slumped in a photo booth in Melbourne train station, whispering the lyrics to the song as dozens of unidentified men and women entered the shot to kiss him. It wasn't to everybody's taste. 'I was in the dressing room and said, "Sorry, I'm off",' recalls Bruce Thomas. 'The other guys – when there was still a bit of solidarity left – said, "We're not doing it either then", so he was left on his own.' As a sop to the stroppy Attractions, the next video, for 'The Only Flame In Town', was shot in New York and the band featured heavily, but nobody was quite sure what was happening in terms of their long-term future.

Elvis seemed equally confused as he and The Attractions set off on their US tour, beginning in Florida on 3 August and snaking around the States until 16 September. The shows made the fundamental mistake of trying to recreate the sound of the album: there was lots of thick, heavy synthesiser and a certain amount of instrumental showboating. The sets were weighted in favour of very recent, synthetic material and often sounded dull and lacking edge, while old songs were extended and rearranged. 'Costello's reworkings sometimes obscured his pointed associative lyrics and showed the limits of his abilities as a melodist,' wrote Jon Pareles in the *New York Times*, reviewing the show at Forest Hills, New York, on 18 August. 'There were also times when the band simply seemed to be doodling away.' There was a certain amount of wilfulness in Elvis's approach. He had tired of knocking out faithful versions of his songs after experimenting in his live shows with the TKO Horns and his solo ventures. He was also tiring of The Attractions, and – increasingly – they of him.

* * *

As The Attractions and The Pogues rattled through the UK and Ireland in September and October, Bruce Thomas encountered Cait O'Riordan for the first time. 'It was quite strange,' he remembers. 'She was very like Elvis. Intense, volatile, pretty cerebral. I went in the room and she was shaving her head, she had little razor nicks all over her scalp, and she carried a teddy bear all the time.'

It was to be an eventful tour in many ways, but musically it remained pedestrian. Most of *Goodbye Cruel World* was dutifully played in order to promote the record, although a more promising new song called 'I Hope You're Happy Now' featured throughout the tour. But Elvis was essentially treading water, going through the increasingly unsubtle motions with The Attractions when his heart lay in his more intimate solo performances, which were often the highlight. He would perform 'Peace In Our Time', 'High Fidelity' and 'Riot Act' alone, or revisit many of the covers he had played in the US and adding new ones, such as Richard Thompson's harrowing 'End Of The Rainbow'. At the penultimate show at London's Dominion on 2 November, he showcased a beautiful new song called 'Suffering Face'. The crowd, however, were loud and restless, and Elvis couldn't disguise his frustration. 'We just hit the 2000 people who were prepared to pay £6 to hate our guts,' he said. 'I tried everything. I tried being nice to them. I did the panic thing of playing a well-known number, but of course you just play it worse. We walked off.'[10]

The Pogues hadn't toured before, but they already had a well-deserved reputation for causing mayhem and a certain amount of antagonism wherever they roamed. Elvis stepped in early on when it appeared that a mixture of financial wrangles, missing equipment and deteriorating relations between the band and the Costello road crew would result in them leaving the tour. 'Elvis saved the day,' says Philip Chevron. 'I suppose he wanted Cait to stay.'

It was clear to everyone that Elvis had taken a real shine to the bass player, although initially it had seemed that the attraction might be one-sided. Elvis was well respected but something of a figure of fun to all The Pogues, including Cait. He was thirty, stalled in his career, and considered a little *passe* by the band. They saw him chasing Cait on tour and dubbed him 'Uncle Brian', a suitably seedy nickname in their eyes for an older man running after a younger woman.

Not to be outdone, The Attractions were a little amused by this young, intense woman whom they watched Elvis admire from a distance and then at increasingly close quarters, and they christened Cait 'Beryl', after the tomboy comic-book character Beryl The Peril. It was all good sport, until Cait and Elvis surprised everybody by embarking on a love affair. 'One night I got on the bus and there they were: very much an item,' recalls Bruce Thomas. 'We'd been joking about her and then all of a sudden it got serious. And Elvis gave me a look of absolute shit-eating defiance, as if to say: "Don't you make a joke, don't you even fucking *think* it, pal. This is no-go area".'

It was one of two blossoming relationships which would help hammer the final nail in the The Attractions' coffin. Although singer and band would stagger around in a fog of confusion and resentment for over two years, working together occasionally in a pretence of unity, it would never be the same again.

With a divorce already pending, Elvis wasn't sure if he could afford to keep a band who received royalties from the records on top of a yearly retainer which kept them on-call and permanently available to him. It was an expensive business. His disaffection with the group was also taking on an increasingly personal edge. Elvis now felt protective of his feelings for Cait and wary of The Attraction's response. He withdrew, severing the few remaining emotional and fraternal ties with the group in the process.

T-Bone Burnett became his closest musical ally. Almost as soon as The Pogues tour had finished, Elvis went back out with T-Bone in tow. They played all over Europe between 9 November and 9 December, finding time to write an Everly-esque tribute called 'The People's Limousine' together as they rode through Italy.

The concerts were becoming mammoth undertakings, ever-changing and veering wildly in mood and content from night to night and song to song. At London's Royal Festival Hall on 3 December, Elvis played over forty numbers, including a beautiful new piano ballad called 'Having It All', written for Julien Temple's film *Absolute Beginners* but never used. Mid-set, The Coward Brothers re-united – one last time, folks, until the next time – for a rag-bag of country covers and '60s classics. Many of the stronger songs from *Punch The Clock* and *Goodbye Cruel World* in particular were transformed in their simple guitar and piano arrangements, while Elvis's singing was deeper, more emotionally resonant than ever before.

Captivated by his friend's solo shows, T-Bone encouraged Elvis to record his next album using his voice and the acoustic guitar as the primary textures, allowing the tenderness in his music to shine through relatively unadorned. 'I [knew] how to write songs already,' said Elvis. 'What I learned from T-Bone was when to leave them alone.'[11] After the over-cooked debacle of *Goodbye Cruel World*, he needed little persuading.

Seeking a sound palette to complement the mood of the new songs, in January 1985 the two men flew to Hollywood to make some trial recordings. A veteran of the Los Angeles session scene, this was Burnett's patch, and Elvis allowed himself to be lead towards the A-list session men at Sound Factory: bassist David Miner and drummer Ron Tutt, previously of Elvis Presley's '70s band, known to all as the TCB Band – 'Taking Care of Business'.

The first item on the agenda was to cut The Coward Brothers' 'The People's Limousine', to be released as a one-off single later in the year. The sessions were quick, light-hearted, and recorded live, a world away from the laborious and fractious atmosphere of *Goodbye Cruel World*. As a B-side they knocked off Leon Payne's classic 'They'll Never Take Her Love From Me', with high, keening harmonies and twinkling mandolin. 'It was very cool, feel-good stuff,' Ron Tutt recalls, and it became the blueprint for the way the next record would come together.

While in Los Angeles, Elvis also took the opportunity to record some rough demos of his new songs with just voice and guitar at Sunset Sound. These included 'Poisoned Rose', 'Indoor Fireworks', 'American Without Tears' and 'Suffering Face'. The songs were musically straightforward but very strong, radically different in style and approach to those on the last two records, with the emphasis placed firmly on naked, emotional honesty. 'I started thinking more about the songs and much less about the records,' said Elvis. 'It became clear to me that I had to write very, very simple songs. It just seemed a lot easier for me to say something straight out.'[12]

Elvis drank a lot of whiskey during the session, and the next morning another new song – 'The Big Light' – popped out of the empty bottle, complaining of suffering 'a hangover with a personality'. However, despite the ragged nature of the demos, he returned to Britian convinced he had found a template that would give him an escape route from the cul-de-sac he and The Attractions had backed themselves into.

Satisfied, he turned his mind to more personal concerns. Following the autumn tour, Jake Riviera had informed Pogues manager Frank Murray that Elvis would be interested in producing the band. This was partly down to a genuine enthusiasm for the music, which dovetailed neatly with his regained enthusiasm for roots music, acoustic instruments and raw energy; it was also undoubtedly a way of spending more time with Cait.

Their relationship intensified in the studio. 'They'd come in together and leave together, that was on-going,' says The Pogues sound engineer, Paul Scully. Their blossoming and very tactile romance may have been the focus of a certain amount of ridicule – often affectionate, sometimes with a harder edge – from the band, but by and large it didn't get in the way of the recording process. 'Elvis was extremely professional and certainly commited to the project the whole time,' says the session engineer Nick

Robbins. '[Although] the occasional evening may have been spent chasing Cait around the studio!'

Initially, Elvis was only meant to be producing two songs: 'A Pair Of Brown Eyes' and 'Sally MacLennane', intended for a single. However, the sessions at Elephant Studios in Wapping, east London, stretched on through January and beyond as Elvis agreed to produce the whole album. He was hands-on, supplying equipment, adding acoustic guitar to the backing tracks, altering Cait's bass part, and suggesting changes in instrumentation and song structure. The Pogues were in many ways tyros in the recording process, and they were impressed by Elvis's ability to augment the songs without adding layers of production effects or tampering with the unique style and balance of the band.

It was clear, however, that the album wouldn't be completed in one sitting. The Pogues had dates booked throughout 1985 and Elvis was often hopping on to planes to hook up with them as they toured Europe throughout April and into May and June. 'He would just turn up in places,' says Philip Chevron, who had now joined The Pogues on banjo and guitar. 'We would play Kenmare in Ireland and he'd be there with rough mixes of the album. He and Cait were an item, so that kind of gave him licence to turn up anywhere. He became literally part of the entourage then.'

The record – now titled *Rum, Sodomy & The Lash* – was happily pieced together between the scattered tour dates. 'It was a great, sort of fresh time,' says Paul Scully. 'There were some great musical ideas going down, and I seem to remember Elvis having a big input.' Indeed, he even played some of the bass parts on the record, which some of the band construed as him showing off to Cait. Nobody seemed to mind.

While The Pogues were becoming Elvis's new gang, The Attractions had been busy twiddling their thumbs. 'He still hadn't decided whether he wanted to split the band up or not,' says Bruce Thomas. 'We were all on wages doing nothing.' Although Elvis seemed determined to break out of the age-old album-tour-album-tour cycle which he had rigidly and exhaustively adhered to since the middle of 1977, he was keeping his options open. He wasn't yet ready to completely sever his links with his old band.

Following the hard lessons of working with Clive Langer and Alan Winstanley, Elvis had brought back Nick Lowe for a one-off session with The Attractions at Eden Studios towards the end of 1984. They'd attempted versions of 'I Hope You're Happy Now' and Sam Cooke's smokey 'Get Yourself Another Fool', but while it was a distinct improvement on the *Goodbye Cruel World* material, the old spark proved difficult to locate.

It was some months before Elvis coralled the band again for a concert at Logan Hall in London on 9 March, a benefit for the miners involved in a long and bitter industrial dispute with the Conservative government. The set included pointed, politically motivated versions of 'Big Sister's Clothes', The Beat's 'Stand Down, Margaret', 'Oliver's Army', 'Shipbuilding', and 'All You Thought Of Was Betrayal' – a very early blueprint for 'Tramp The Dirt Down'.

It would be the last Attractions concert appearance for well over a year. When the call came for Elvis to play at Live Aid on 13 July, he performed alone, stepping on stage at Wembley Stadium with just an acoustic guitar and a scraggy beard for company. Introducing an 'old northern English folk song', he played a sing-along rendition of one of the most famous songs in the world. 'I remember beforehand saying to him, "Fine, do anything",' recalls Live Aid organiser Bob Geldof. 'And then when he did 'All You Need Is Love', it was fucking great. He has such great taste, it was a really wonderful moment.' With lyrical prompts scribbled on his hand, Elvis's pared down version of The Beatles' classic was a deliberately ironic choice. 'I thought it was entirely appropriate,' said Elvis. 'Because [love] is transparently *not* all we need.'¹³

Nobody had to tell that to The Attractions. A few days earlier, at T-Bone Burnett's solo show at the Duke of York Theatre on 7 July, a member of Elvis's road crew finally let slip to the band that they were pencilled in to play on only a section of the new record. Steve Nieve in particular was extremely upset at the news, not to mention the manner in which it had been delivered. He had always seen Elvis and The Attractions less as a singer-plus-hired-help, and more as a unit, like The Rolling Stones. The insensitive and somewhat underhand way in which they were now being sidelined hurt him badly, and at the Duke of York he drunkenly and publicly harangued Elvis about the plans. It looked increasingly like a band entering its death throes.

* * *

Recording for *King Of America* began in Los Angeles in July, 1985 immediately after Live Aid. It was a piecemeal affair, spread out through the summer and autumn; Elvis wasn't using the same band for all the sessions, and anyway, he was reluctant to spend large amounts of concentrated time in Los Angeles, a city he remained far from fond of.

The identity of the record had formed during Elvis's solo tour of Australia, New Zealand and Japan in June and early July. Again, T-Bone Burnett was supporting, in every sense. 'There was a tremendous amount of planning that went into that record,' said Burnett. 'We had pages and pages of production notes.'[14] On the long flights to and from the Far East, he and Elvis had started scheduling sessions for the album, drawing up lists of musicians, tailoring the musical line-up to suit the specific needs of each song.

Elvis had already demo-ed most of the new material, and the tour was a chance to play-in the songs and settle on their arrangements. Nine of *King Of America*'s thirteen original songs featured, and each one indicated beyond any dissent that Elvis had found a new lease of life in his writing. Lyrically, Cait was proving an inspiration. 'Jack Of All Parades' and 'I'll Wear It Proudly', in particular, were unabashed declarations of love for his new girlfriend. Elvis was a romantic at heart, and having spent so long looking for the real thing, he was finally allowing himself to admit in his songs that he might just have found it. Always an incessant chatterer on the telephone, he reportedly spent a total of almost $5000 on daily telephone calls to Cait while he was in Australia. On one occasion, they co-wrote 'Lovable'.

The first session for the album took place at Ocean Way studios, with T-Bone Burnett and Larry Hirsch co-producing with Elvis. They started with what became the core band on the record: Ron Tutt on drums, Jerry Scheff on bass and James Burton on guitar, all of whom had been members of Elvis Presley's TCB Band in the '70s. Burton had also worked with Gram Parsons, a particularly seductive addition to his CV.

If he was initially nervous and probably a little sceptical about playing with a band consisting entirely of session men with such mainstream – if stellar – pedigrees, the laid-back virtuosity of the musicians soon put Elvis at ease. The four-piece quickly settled in, cutting finished versions of 'Our Little Angel', 'The Big Light' and 'American Without Tears' in the first few hours of recording.

The musicians were quick to pick up on the song's needs and generous in putting aside any tendencies to show off their musical prowess, instead simply and selflessly serving the nuances of each number. 'He told me that when we first got together on *King Of America* he was sort of waiting for us to have an attitude about it,' admits Jerry Scheff. 'And none of us did, although he did say that there was one thing that got him: when we got through playing the first really high intensity song ['The Big Light'] he was really out of breath when he finished, and I told him, "Yeah, well even the ballads were like that with Elvis Presley!".'

In response, Elvis was eager to be as inclusive as possible. In direct contrast to his method of working with The Attractions, he took time to explain what each song meant and to play them through on the guitar for each of the musicians, in order that they could gain a real feel for what he was singing about and the intimacy he was searching for.

Nonetheless, Elvis was still in charge. He had learned the folly of compromise on *Goodbye Cruel World*, and despite initial nerves and a few misgivings, his natural self-assurance and controlling streak came to the fore. 'In the studio he kept control of everything,' says Scheff. 'It was very much his deal and his visions.' By the second day 'Glitter Gulch' and 'Shoes Without Heels' were finished, while they had knocked together strong rehearsal arrangements of a handful of the other tracks as well. Almost half the album was recorded in the first three days.

T-Bone Burnett played a vital role in the production of the record, guiding, directing and experimenting with sounds and styles, participating in a very musical way without actually playing a note. He also picked the band: aside from the TCB group, the other principal players on *King Of America* were drummer Mickey Curry, bassist T-Bone Wolk, pianist Tom Canning and organ and piano player Mitchell Froom. 'T-Bone is one of the best at putting the right people together,' says Ron Tutt, and the casting was indeed immaculate throughout. Burnett saved his *coup de grace* for the jazz-country torch song 'Poisoned Rose', for which he had hand-picked a majestic rhythm section: Earl Palmer on drums, a stalwart of the early Little Richard and Fats Domino singles, and Ray Brown on string bass, who had been married to Ella Fitzgerald and played in her band, as well as with Louis Armstrong, Duke Ellington, Dizzy Gillespie and Charlie Parker.

Elvis wasn't easily scared, but he later admitted that it took the opening – and drinking – of a bottle of Glenlivet whisky halfway through the session to calm his nervous voice and find the sound he was searching for. 'We started, and it really wasn't very good, because I found out later that Elvis was intimidated by Ray Brown's presence, in particular,' recalls Mitchell Froom. 'Then finally, Ray took the lead and everybody fell in after him. When we finished that track he sort of gave his nod of approval and we felt we were OK.' Once 'Poisoned Rose' was through, the well-refreshed ensemble then cut 'Eisenhower Blues', a loose R&B jam and the only other song recorded with that stellar line-up.

Over the next few sessions, Elvis captured much of the rest of the record with James Burton, Jerry Scheff, Mitchell Froom and Jim Keltner, the line-up who would later tour as The Confederates. Each of them added their own personal, subtle additions to the songs: Burton's tender, picked guitar lines on 'Indoor Fireworks'; Scheff's shimmering, impossibly high bass intro on 'I'll Wear It Proudly'; Froom's ghostly organ floating through 'Sleep Of The Just'; and Keltner's mean, slap-happy drumming on 'Lovable', where Los Lobos's David Hidalgo joined in on harmonies for good measure.

The Attractions burst into this companionable creative hive in mid-August, about two-thirds of the way through the *King Of America* sessions. Originally, the plan had been for Elvis to record half the record with the US musicians, then ship in The Attractions to complete the rest of the album, playing on the tracks most suited to their style.

However, it became clear that the reality would be somewhat different. The band arrived to find that Elvis had some new playmates. Cait was present on many occasions, and Elvis and T-Bone were thick as thieves: having bonded on the road and in the studio, they now enjoyed the shared sense of humour and musical repartee that Elvis and the band had lost. It immediately became something of an Us vs Them scenario. Always protective when it came to sharing the spotlight with other musicians, The Attractions were wary, tense and very probably dismissive of what looked like a Californian mutual appreciation society, far removed from the raucous sessions of old in London.

Meanwhile, Elvis felt personally renewed by his relationship with Cait and creatively excited by the music he was making. He swiftly came to the conclusion that the resentful presence of his old group was casting a dark cloud over proceedings, and that the classic 'Attractions sound' would simply unbalance the reflective tenor of the rest of the record. 'The Attractions had got to a point that many bands get to: they get the chords, they start to work out what they're going to do and they're almost over-familiar with the way someone writes,' says Mitchell Froom. 'The American musicians were much more subtle in general. Which was the idea.'

Eventually, The Attractions got the call to go to the studio on 21 August. Unsure of their role and mightily pissed off with Elvis, they were 'jumpy and paranoid and generally edgy',[15] and their initial attempts at 'Brilliant Mistake' – a song Elvis had set aside specifically for The Attractions to open the album with – were particularly lame. Eventually, they got acceptable versions of 'Suit Of Lights' and the throwaway out-take 'Baby's Got A Brand New Hairdo', but the mood was irreconcilably grim. 'I think [the situation] put them on edge and made them defensive and hostile,' Elvis said. 'Which made me defensive and hostile. The sessions were a disaster.'[16]

Disappointed with the standard of the performances, Elvis scrapped any plans to use the band again, but neglected to inform them. The Attractions spent the rest of their time in Los Angeles sitting in the hotel at Elvis's expense, quietly fuming, waiting for an invitation that never came. 'I was furious about it, absolutely furious,' said Pete Thomas. 'He should just have said, "I'm going to make a solo album, don't worry about it." The worst thing about it was that we were all there, day after day, not getting the call to go to the studio.'[17]

The fiasco killed the already shaky morale of the band. 'I thought, "If you're going to fire us, fire us",' says Bruce Thomas. 'It was like being sacked by instalments.' Elvis, they felt, had become distant and arrogant, treating them like little more than faceless session men after eight years of close, constant collaboration and companionship. 'We had more or less been alienated,' admits Thomas, who for one detected a growing sense of eccentricity in Elvis's behaviour. 'I remember going into his room at the hotel and he'd just had all the album sleeves done; there were all these pictures of him with a crown on dotted around the room, big three-foot squared photos. I thought, "You're basically having your psychosis now, aren't you? Your identity crisis." I stuck a Burger King crown on my copy.'

* * *

Elvis had always been high profile, putting out at least one album a year and touring relentlessly. Throughout 1985, his relative reclusiveness – and his dishevelled appearance on the odd occasion when he was sighted, such as Live Aid – provided the perfect fodder for gossip. Heavily bearded, usually wearing a hat and shades and sometimes a shawl, rumours had been circulating in the press for some time: he was an alcoholic, he was suffering divorce trauma or writer's block, he was a heroin addict.

Elvis has always been fanatical about keeping abreast of what the media are saying about him, as both Bebe Buell and Bruce Thomas can testify. 'He reads every review,' says Thomas. 'He was always the first one down at the news-stand every morning.' Pogues engineer Nick Robbins recalls Elvis keeping close tabs on the gossip when they were recording *Rum, Sodomy & The Lash*. 'Every day in the studio he'd come in with all his newspapers and the first thing he'd do is hunt through to see whether he'd been mentioned. He'd get quite upset if he had and quite upset if he hadn't!'

Media talk of a personality crisis was given passing credence by the fact that Elvis had made the decision to revert back to his real name. Since as early as 1982 he had occasionally raised the subject in interviews. 'I was tired of the way people saw Elvis Costello,' he said. 'They saw this funny pair of glasses and a load of mannerisms.'[18] Now, he legally made the swap back to Declan MacManus. There were other factors in the reversal: he was involved in divorce proceedings with Mary and probably felt it was easier to use the name he was married under, while the relationship with

Cait and his tightness with The Pogues seemed to be teasing some of the latent Irishness out of him. Although Elvis often cited professional reasons for changing his name, ultimately it seemed to be a private decision, marking a return to some kind of personal contentment. He has never released a record as Declan MacManus,* merely changing his publishing credits to D.P.A. MacManus. The 'A' is for Aloysius, added as a light-hearted tribute to comedian Tony Hancock, or Anthony Aloysius St John Hancock, as he was known in *Hancock's Half Hour*.

Tales of Elvis's growing eccentricity and creative impasse would be conclusively killed off in 1986 by the strength of *King Of America*, but the record was still many months away from its release date. He had completed the album with further combinations of the American session musicians, finishing in the autumn of 1985 with an aborted take on 'I Hope You're Happy Now' and an aggressive, hoarse-voiced cover of The Animals – and Nina Simone's – 'Don't Let Me Be Misunderstood', with Tom Waits percussionist Michael Blair on marimba. The latter song was a late addition to the running order, added as a last-minute sop to Columbia who, with their predictable set of priorities, didn't hear any singles on the record.

With the record done, Elvis had time to take stock and work out what he wanted to do, and how he wanted to do it. He needed time to recharge the engine. The Pogues were touring heavily, capitalising on the success of *Rum, Sodomy & The Lash* – released to much acclaim in August 1985 – and throughout October, November and December, Elvis trailed the band through Europe.

He was enjoying the opportunity to indulge in the kind of extended break he hadn't experienced since the release of *My Aim Is True*. Spending time away from home, falling deeper in love with Cait, was the perfect antidote to the previous year's personal and professional pressures. 'I think it's fair to say that people in his office clearly thought he'd lost the plot,' says Philip Chevron. 'They could never get hold of him. He was off in fjords of Norway with The Pogues, giving no account of his actions, living a sort of belated youth. He was having a great time.'

On his travels as an unofficial Pogue, Elvis was happy to take on any duties that were required of him. He might stand in for the guitar roadie when he fell sick; in Freiburg in Germany he took the place of drummer Andrew Ranken, who had a septic hand. On 6 November in Malmo, Sweden, he even agreed to be Shane MacGowan. The singer had gone

---

* Only his work on the Various Artists soundtrack for *The Courier* has ever been credited to his real name, although a one-off single was credited to The MacManus Gang in 1987.

down with a serious bout of pneumonia, and Elvis filled in, singing 'A Pair Of Brown Eyes', 'Old Main Drag', 'The Band Played Waltzing Matilda', 'Dirty Old Town' and 'Boys From The County Hell'. It was – predictably – a drunken, shambolic set.

Elvis was generally well-liked by the band, and his presence on tour was accepted for a variety of reasons. 'He was always good for a tenner,' admits Chevron. 'Certain people shamelessly touched him for money.' He didn't try to steal their thunder, mostly content to stay firmly in the background as they made tentative inroads into the big time. However, it was not all sweetness and light. There was a degree of professional needle, primarily from Shane MacGowan. As the principal songwriter and visionary of The Pogues, MacGowan regarded himself as Elvis's peer and equal in a way that the others did not. Already sensitive, volatile and quick to attack, MacGowan felt threatened and a little patronised by Elvis's adoption of the band, and began to retrospectively criticise the job he had done producing *Rum, Sodomy & The Lash*.

Furthermore, The Pogues were a band of merciless mickey-takers, and the humour became increasingly cruel and crude as Elvis's relationship with Cait developed and deepened. The couple had started dressing the same way, reading the same books, and they became a ripe source of amusement to the band. There was nothing underhand in The Pogues' behaviour. Elvis knew what people thought about him. 'It was very often [to his face] or Cait's face,' recalls Philip Chevron. 'He became the whipping boy for a number of people in the band. Not just the guy you pushed for money but the guy you took the piss out of, the guy that you bullied almost. There were times when I felt the cruelty went too far.'

It was a strange turnaround. Elvis had often been a figure of fun to The Attractions, especially as time wore on, but he paid the wages and called the shots, and was always regarded as the boss. This time, he was an outsider – a guest – among a large group of complex and fiercely individual characters. As a man who had plenty of experience travelling the world being nasty to people from within the cocoon of a rock band, it was an interesting process to be on the receiving end of the same kind of behaviour. 'Groups like The Pogues, groups that are in a class of their own, can be very cruel,' Elvis rationalised. 'When I'm about, the cruelty just transfers to me.'[19]

He tolerated the barbs because of his relationship with Cait, but it also fed into the deep-rooted sense of being apart – even of victimisation – that had spurred him from an early age. There had always been a whiff of masochism in Elvis's music and motivations, and ultimately the jibes brought him and Cait closer together. They were a very tactile, demonstrative couple, and all the sweetness started to become a little too sugary for many of the band. 'Occasionally, it got just a bit nauseating,' admits Philip Chevron. 'Canoodling at the back of the studio while you're trying to do some work.'

The growing ill-feeling reached a head when Elvis agreed to produce the *Poguetry In Motion* EP at Elephant Studios in January 1986. Matters combusted over the recording of 'A Rainy Night In Soho', The Pogues most ambitious song to date. By this point, Shane MacGowan hated even being in the same room as Elvis, and had taken to not showing up in the studio when he wasn't needed. He felt that Elvis's production ideas were limiting the vision of the band – and his own artistic vision in particular – while infringing too much on the personal politics of The Pogues. 'Essentially Elvis got sacked from *Poguetry In Motion*,' says Chevron. 'He was questioning the structure of the band. There was a groundswell of anti-Elvis feeling.'

The problems soon affected Cait. The taunts and abuses heaped upon Elvis continued even in his absence, and when The Pogues arrived in America in February 1986 she was feeling increasingly isolated. By the time the tour reached New York in late February, she had tired of the relentlessly masculine atmosphere in the band, and was feeling increasingly overwhelmed by the first real rush of fame. The Pogues were taking New York by storm, feted by the critics and meeting the likes of Matt Dillon and Robert De Niro, who loved the band. Twenty-one-year-old Cait was swept up and almost away in the excitement. Taking a lot of cocaine and drinking 'for twelve hours straight'[20] in the VIP lounge of the Limelight Club, she eventually broke down. 'Cait was going way off the rails, she was just like a kid in a sweet shop,' recalls Mat Snow, the *NME* journalist who accompanied The Pogues on that tour. 'Wasn't sleeping, was just getting a little bit psychotic.'

Back in Britain, Elvis was concerned by the reports coming back to him. He arranged for Bill Flanagan, a New York-based journalist and MTV supremo whom he'd been friends with for many years, to visit Cait at the hotel, take her to JFK Airport and put her on the next flight back to London. The first The Pogues knew about it was waking up the next day and finding that their bass player was nowhere to be found. They were far from pleased.

Cait returned to America in early March to complete the tour, having reportedly slept for two days straight. She clearly needed the break, but the covert manner in which it was taken would prove to be the beginning of the end of her involvement in the band.

Chapter Ten
1986–87

BY THE TIME *KING OF AMERICA* was climbing the nursery slopes of the charts in the spring of 1986, Elvis was back making a row with The Attractions. It would ultimately prove to be a valedictory reunion, but in truth the band hadn't really been missed on the new record. Their sole contribution on 'Suit Of Lights' was sober and dignified, but it would be difficult to imagine them improving on the finished album.

Finally released in February 1986, *King Of America* showed a bearded Elvis on the cover, decked in a gaudy, brocade jacket and wearing a crown. He wore almost-round, wire-rimmed spectacles and looked both older than his years and slightly bemused, daring the audience to laugh at his world-weariness. The name Elvis Costello didn't appear anywhere on the record, which must have delighted Columbia. Instead, it was lumberingly credited to 'The Costello Show featuring The Attractions and The Confederates', co-produced by Declan Patrick Aloysius MacManus. The sleeve dedication was to all four of his grandparents.

It was a beautiful record, restrained, sad and personal, featuring some of Elvis's very best writing and monochrome, Dylan-esque shifts in the music. The smart word games and hedged bets had all but vanished, replaced with a compelling honesty. The bitter-sweet 'Indoor Fireworks' was a book-end to the domestic pain of 'Home Truth', and a fittingly tender goodbye to Mary, while 'I'll Wear It Proudly' was a defiant declaration of his love for Cait, with a dig at The Pogues buried in its centre.* In between, there were break-neck country canters, minor-key folk songs and heartbreaking ballads, while lyrically it spanned the lacerating social side-swipe of 'Little Palaces' to the laugh-along 'Glitter Gulch', all played with impeccable style and grace by the disparate band of musicians.

Not everything worked. The most unrepresentative and least alluring

---

* The line, 'If you'll wear it proudly through the snakepits and the cat-calls' seems to draw on Elvis and Cait's on-tour experiences with the band.

cut from the record had been released as a single in January. A clumpy, footsore complaint, 'Don't Let Me Be Misunderstood' reached No. 33 in the UK, backed with the third-rate Attractions tear-up 'Baby's Got A Brand New Hairdo'. Elsewhere, the callow R&B of 'Eisenhower Blues' was simply uneccesary, while the bouncy, puppy-like charms of 'Lovable' wore thin.

But overall *King Of America* was a triumphant return to the fray, fighting it out with *Get Happy!!* and *Imperial Bedroom* as Elvis's finest record. In *Melody Maker*, Nick Kent (who had crossed the floor from the *NME)* heralded him as 'still this blighted isle's finest songwriter, a force who, at his best, is simply beyond peer'. The *NME* seconded the motion. Both reviews placed perhaps undue significance on the name change, reading 'Suit Of Lights' in particular as the burial of Elvis Costello and the rebirth of Declan MacManus. In the US, *Creem* astutely praised Elvis's musicianship, rightly placing his austere, undulating rhythm guitar-playing at the heart of the album. Elsewhere, the majority of the critics were pleasantly surprised at the warmth and compassion on show, the all-encompassing excellence of the songs and the playing.

But it was the same old story: rave reviews, poor sales. *King Of America* reached No. 11 in the UK and No. 39 in the US, and Elvis was becoming increasingly disillusioned with what he perceived to be Columbia's growing indifference to his career. Believing that the record company still regarded *This Year's Model* and *Armed Forces* as the commercial template for the kind of music he should still be making, Elvis decided to tackle them head-on. The new songs he was writing suited the particularly no-nonsense recording approach of his initial records with The Attractions. He already had 'Blue Chair', 'I Hope You're Happy Now' and 'Next Time 'Round' left over from the *King Of America* sessions, and he wrote several more songs quickly on guitar.

The generic style of the new tracks was brutally simple and rhythmically primal, often featuring little more than two or three chords. 'Uncomplicated' – something of a theme tune for the record – was written in the middle of the night by Elvis banging his hands on his kitchen table and singing into a tape player, dispensing with any musical accompaniment at all. Under such circumstances, who else could he call but Nick Lowe and The Attractions?

The tentative rapprochement began with a one-off session at Eden Studios, cutting a hastily co-written song called 'Seven Day Weekend' with reggae legend Jimmy Cliff for a film called *Club Paradise*. The presence of Cliff probably kept everyone on their best behaviour, but it was always going to be an uneasy truce.

The 'air of suspicion and resentment still lingered',[1] according to Elvis, when they went into Olympic Studio One in Barnes, London, in March to begin work on the album. 'It was a much more uptight situation,' said Nick Lowe. 'It wasn't a gang feeling. I never really knew what their internal arguments were, but they had plenty of that, Lord knows.'[2]

The idea was to get the songs down on tape before the personal chemistry became so negative that they would have to abandon the whole project. Taking the 'uncomplicated' maxim as far as they could, Elvis and the band played the songs loud and live through a stage PA with no separation, ensuring lots of spillage in the sound. It was a unique approach, essentially like recording a live concert in a cavernous studio with a few microphones dotted around the room. Subsequently, the denser songs like 'Tokyo Storm Warning', 'Honey, Are You Straight Or Are You Blind?', 'Home Is Anywhere You Hang Your Head' and 'Uncomplicated' became thick, dark blocks of noise, each part virtually inseparable from the other.

'It was a total mess,' says Bruce Thomas. 'There were no screens, no separation on the drums, the bass, nothing. It was a soup.' They often captured a track in a single take, usually taking no more than three stabs at each song before moving on. There was little deliberation. The few overdubs that were required were usually completed straight after the best take had been decided upon. The album's title, *Blood & Chocolate*, seemed to perfectly sum up the texture of the music.

These techniques might have created the kind of claustrophobic effect that Elvis was looking for, but it was not a particularly rewarding experience for the band, and did little to ease personal tensions. 'I thought it all added to it, the fact that there was a little bit of bile in there,' admitted Nick Lowe. 'In fact, I used to rather encourage it.'[3] Elvis, too, was rarely happy if the atmosphere was too easy-going in the studio, although he sometimes had trouble recognising when to let go of the compulsion to create tension. In Olympic, he stirred up the sour atmosphere to accentuate the primitive, violent music they were making. 'He created situations where you just basically wanted to strangle the bastard,' says Bruce Thomas. 'You'd be just about to walk out and he'd say, "What's the problem? What's wrong?". So you'd stay and do the take and he'd get the angst that he wanted, but then you'd go away for two days thinking: "Fucking bastard". I suppose it was an artistic device, and maybe now I can see it a lot more than I did at the time.'

It was astonishingly effective on 'I Want You'. Perhaps Elvis's darkest, bravest song, it was immeasurably enhanced by the uptight, quietly furious Attractions burning a slow fuse behind six minutes of Elvis's increasingly unhinged cravings. The primal studio technique added to the sense of drama, and in the final minute everything the listener hears is coming through the vocal mike, the band bleeding onto the backing track to create a ghostly echo behind the choked voice. 'The vocal performance sent shivers down my spine,' admitted Colin Fairley, engineer on the sessions. 'The mix used on the album is the original monitor mix thirty minutes after we cut the track, warts and all. I'm convinced this performance from the whole band was achieved because of this unusual studio set-up.'[4]

As the highly-strung sessions continued throughout March, April and May, The Attractions eventually succeeded in conjuring up a rolling pop sound on some of the more melodic songs: Steve Nieve's chiming keys turned 'Blue Chair' into a thing of considerable beauty, while Elvis did a passable John Lennon impersonation at the end of the bridge. Bruce Thomas's 'Taxman' bass line finally nailed 'I Hope You're Happy Now', while 'Next Time 'Round' seemed to take 'La Bamba' as its lift-off point. Elvis often undercut the songs with a degree of malevolent humour and – when it worked – it made for some exhilarating music.

Cait was around, naturally. She provided backing vocals on 'Poor Napoleon' and 'Crimes Of Paris' and co-wrote the sweeping global nightmare of 'Tokyo Storm Warning' with Elvis. Some of The Attractions were rather chauvinistically sceptical of this creeping 'Yoko Ono' factor, but her contributions to Elvis's songs throughout their relationship consisted of much more than suggesting the odd word here or there over breakfast. 'It is a huge pity Cait wrote so little in those years,' says Philip Chevron. 'But it would be a mistake to underestimate the work she did do. Cait was very much an equal partner on those co-compositions. She genuinely is a great writer.'

Immediately after the sessions concluded, Elvis and Cait were 'married' on 17 May, 1986, the day of Self Aid, a well-intentioned if politically dubious attempt to provide charity for Ireland's unemployed, featuring U2, Van Morrison, The Pogues and Elvis and The Attractions. In true rock 'n' roll fashion, the ceremony – such as it was – was romantically squeezed in between the afternoon soundcheck and the evening performance at the RDS Showground in Dublin.

In fact, the marriage was not a legally recognised union at all. Elvis was still married to Mary, and although her initial petition for divorce was decreed on 17 November 1986, the decree absolute did not take place until much later: 3 February 1988. As such, Elvis and Cait's union was in name only. 'It was a spiritual wedding,' Cait later said. 'Dec's been married before so we didn't get married in church, and a registry office would have been too cold.'[5] The fact that neither of these options were legally available to the couple mattered little. They were very much in love, and instead of a formal ceremony, they held hands in St Stephen's Green in the centre of Dublin and exchanged rings by the duck pond, as firm and genuine a commitment as either of them required. They never would officially be man and wife.

That night, Elvis and The Attractions opened with 'Leave My Kitten Alone,' Little Willie John's dynamic blues, recorded for *Blood & Chocolate* but left off the final album. He dedicated the song to, 'Cait, my kitten from Clare'. The rest of their short set was enthusiastic, but a little rusty. Having played just one gig prior to Self Aid, there were definitely a couple more gear changes to be made. In Dublin, 'Uncomplicated' and 'I Hope You're Happy Now' fought it out on stage with 'Pump It Up' and a rough, misguided cover of Jimmy Cliff's 'Many Rivers To Cross', but Elvis was in fine form throughout, teasing and working the 30,000 crowd like an old hand. As if to herald the fact that he was making classically recognisable 'Elvis Costello' music again, he was clean-shaven, back in his trademark black horn-rims and dark suit.

Blood & Chocolate had been finished in May with everybody just about still on speaking terms, and although the mood within the camp was frosty, European festival dates had been booked throughout early July. The relatively short sets featured only a handful of the new tracks, usually 'Honey, Are You Straight Or Are You Blind?' and 'Uncomplicated'.

The album was scheduled for a September release and Elvis had the summer free of muscial responsiblities. He popped over to America to join Cait and The Pogues in Chicago on 12 July, getting rip-roaring drunk with Tom Waits and his band after-hours at Holsteins folk bar. Much of the rest of his time was spent making a film.

Elvis had done tiny pieces of acting before: he had appeared as Earl Manchester in *Americathon* as early as 1979, and had recently had speaking bit-parts as a family member in the TV series *Scully* and as bungling magician Rosco de Ville in *No Surrender*, both written by Liverpudlian Alan Bleasdale. But *Straight To Hell* was his first feature film.

The film had been conceived by British director Alex Cox, featuring The Pogues, Joe Strummer, Courtney Love and Elvis, as well as 'proper' actors such as Sy Richardson, Kathy Burke and Dick Rude. Cox had recently directed The Pogues in the video for 'A Pair Of Brown Eyes', and was fresh from the success of *Sid And Nancy*, his biopic of Sid Vicious and Nancy Spungeon.

A political animal to the bone, Cox had organised a benefit gig for Nicaragua at the Brixton Fridge in 1985, at which most of the musicans taking part in the film had played. Initially, he had planned to get all the acts to play a similar concert in Nicaragua in solidarity with the freedom movement there, before releasing the footage as a concert film. However, no one seemed willing to put up the funds for such a blatantly politically motivated venture, and eventually the project fell through, with the result that, according to Cox, 'there was an embarrassing hole in everybody's schedule which I was really responsible for'. To plug the gap, the director proposed *Straight To Hell* as an alternative, a homage to the Sergio Leone spaghetti westerns that he loved, to be filmed in searing heat in Almeria in Spain in August and September 1986.

The script for *Straight To Hell* had been knocked off in a matter of days and the filming wrapped up in about four weeks. The speed of both the film's conception and execution was glaringly apparent. 'I should have worked harder on the script and not just dashed it off,' admits Cox. The film was an extravagant exercise in pastiche which capitalised on the fame of its main participants (there were also cameos from Grace Jones and Dennis Hopper) while making little impact beyond that.

Elvis played Hives, the obsequious butler. Cox was impressed with his ability and clearly saw something in his performance which most people missed. 'He really stands up next to Kathy Burke, next to real professional actors,' he says. 'He was very studied, and very thoughtful and serious about it. He thought what his character would do and came up with improvisations for extra scenes. He took it very seriously.'

For Elvis, *Straight To Hell* was fun for a short while and then became a drag. His presence in Spain was essentially as a companion to Cait, and despite Cox's comments, his role as the subservient butler appeared to have been loosely thrown together as a dramatic extension of his real-life role as the most put-upon member of The Pogues entourage. 'It was quite interesting actually, the way things were played out as a sort of parallel to real life,' says The Pogues' multi-instrumentalist Jem Finer. 'There was a scene where Elvis was tortured which was cut out, and he was a sort of bullied character, a loser. In a sense it was almost like Alex Cox and maybe everyone else – in some sort of collective consciousness – played out the things that they would like to do in real life.'

The most significant fall-out from the shoot in Spain was Cait's departure from The Pogues. It had been coming for some time, spreading slowly through the year. When Elvis flew to Los Angeles in late September to prepare for the start of his tour with The Attractions, Cait posted AWOL and accompanied him, instead of meeting The Pogues at Eezihire Studios in London to rehearse for their imminent tour. Eventually, she showed up for rehearsals a week late and stayed for a day, before taking her bass home. Two days later she was back with Elvis in Los Angeles, and phoned the band to say she was leaving, this time for good.

The increasing strain in her relationship with The Pogues, not to mention the difficulty of maintaining a personal relationship in which both parties were successful musicians touring the world had proved too much. Cait chose to bail out and support Elvis, and for the next decade and a half she was his almost constant companion on tour, and occasionally on stage and on record. 'She actually faced up to the choice of being with the man she wanted to be with or being with the band,' said Pogues banjo player Terry Woods. 'When decisions get down to personal levels like that then I think personal life takes precedent.'[6]

* * *

Following the making of the twin polarities of *King Of America* and *Blood & Chocolate* within a few months of each other, Elvis constructed a stage show designed to reconcile all the disparate elements of his career over the past two years: solo balladeer, roots revivalist, and spitting mad Attraction. He also wanted to have a little fun. He planned extended residencies with both The Attractions and The Confederates in fifteen cities in the US and Europe, playing between two and five nights in each city, attempting to make each night in each town a markedly different spectacle from the other.

This unprecedented and ambitious tour came on the back of *Blood & Chocolate,* released on 15 September. With a bizarre cover painting by Elvis's transparent alter-ego Eamnon Singer and a back photo featuring him as Napoleon Dynamite, those looking for an identity crisis could find plenty to shout about. But the sleeve attributed the record simply to Elvis Costello and The Attractions, and the searing music held within left no one in any doubt.

Many listeners welcomed it as his most musically straightforward record since before *Get Happy!!*. Robert Hilburn in the *LA Times* made copious – if erroneous – *Armed Forces* comparisons, opining that it was the record fans had 'been waiting seven years for him to deliver'. But a closer inspection revealed that this was something new. Although *Blood & Chocolate* featured The Attractions at full volume and fundamentally unadorned, it was darker, less harmonically ambitious, and lyrically much more personal than anything Elvis had done in the late '70s. This was a subterranean record, with little emphasis on subtlety or melody. Most of the time, the band were recorded as though they were a single instrument, as brutal, blunt and effective as a club.

The record was roughly split in two, between the repetitive, mono-rhythmic nightmares of 'Uncomplicated', 'Honey, Are You Straight Or Are You Blind?', 'Home Is Anywhere You Hang Your Head', 'I Want You' and 'Tokyo Storm Warning'; and the brighter pop of 'Blue Chair', 'I Hope You're Happy Now', 'Crimes Of Paris', and 'Next Time 'Round'. Only the dreary, disjointed 'Battered Old Bird' and the atonal 'Poor Napoleon' failed to quicken the pulse.

As an extended mood piece it worked brilliantly, but *Blood & Chocolate* required an element of faith from the listener. This was not easy listening, and reviews were mixed. In the *NME*, Adrian Thrills celebrated the 'welcome resurrection of a tough, uncompromising streak that has been underplayed since the turn of the decade', but *The Times* was less impressed with the 'maudlin songs peopled with morose, cobwebbed characters', concluding that the record sounded as though it were conceived in a 'bout of musical agoraphobia'. *Rolling Stone* occupied the middle ground, singling out 'I Want You' as a career highlight, but viewing much of the rest of the record as 'too often glib and sketchy'.

It was easily the starkest record Elvis had made, and perhaps his truest, but the density and idiosyncracies of *Blood & Chocolate* ensured that he was increasingly destined to make his big splashes in a small pond. Columbia viewed the record with some distaste, the long, murderous songs and murky production a world away from the clean, crisp pop of *Armed Forces* which they still coveted. 'They hated it and subsequently just fucking buried it,'7 said Elvis, although he did little to aid his own cause.

With pop songs of the calibre of 'Blue Chair' and 'I Hope You're Happy Now' at his disposal, to release the doggedly uncommercial 'I Want You' and 'Tokyo Storm Warning' – both over six minutes long – as the first two UK singles was a wilfully perverse move on Elvis and F-Beat's part. Elvis always expressed surprise that 'Tokyo Storm Warning' wasn't a hit, clearly crediting the record-buying public with more adventurous tastes than they merited. It made No. 73. Little wonder that *Blood & Chocolate* would be the last record Elvis would make with Columbia, and his least commercially successful, limping to a pretty disastrous No. 16 in the UK and a truly awful No. 84 in the US. With typically contrary timing, Elvis saw this as the perfect moment to embark on the most creatively ambitious and financially draining tour of his career.

Beginning on 1 October 1986, at the Beverly Theater in Beverly Hills, California, the concerts were intended to showcase the full span of Elvis's abilities and enthusiasms. The opening night was a loosely based 'Greatest Hits' – or rather, best-loved – set with The Attractions, including a request slot and three tracks from *King Of America*: 'Lovable', 'Jack Of All Parades' and 'I'll Wear It Proudly'. 'The music itself was stirring,' said Robert Hilburn of the *LA Times*, which was on 'Costello-watch' and reviewing all five nights at the Beverly Theater. 'Terrific songs sung with passion and played by The Attractions with captivating force.' However, the much-vaunted request slot was a mess and inherently unspontaneous, as Elvis rather comically rifled through the crumpled notes thrown on to the stage, before choosing the one he wanted to play. It all ended – predictably enough – with 'Pump It Up'.

The next night, Elvis performed mostly alone, featuring only a handful of songs that had been played the previous evening. Highlights included a tongue-in-cheek cover of the Psychedelic Furs' 'Pretty In Pink', a live debut for *Blood & Chocolate* out-take 'Forgive Her Anything', a beautifully rewritten 'Deportees Club' and a stunning solo 'I Want You', which reduced the audience to silent awe.

After fifteen solo songs the mood changed, as T-Bone Burnett jumped on-stage and The Coward Brothers rifled through five songs, including The Beatles' 'Twist And Shout'. The Confederates, consisting of *King Of America* stalwarts James Burton, Jerry Scheff, Jim Keltner and Mitchell Froom, joined in for the final ten songs, and the next night they had the whole show to themselves.

The emphasis was on rootsy, good-time rock 'n' roll and country. Most of *King Of America* received an airing, as well as well-worn R&B covers such as 'Sally Sue Brown', 'It Tears Me Up' and 'That's How You Got Killed Before'. The original songs worked well in concert, but the handfuls of covers tended to drag. Despite an increasing insistence on playing blues music, Elvis would never be particularly convincing handling such stodgy material, often sounding puffy and uninspired. However, mid-set he slipped five gems into his solo spot: 'Green Shirt', 'Party Girl', 'Heathen Town', 'Little Palaces' and 'American Without Tears', the latter with a brand-new lyric.

If night three was a gently swinging, somewhat middle-aged affair, then the following evening's show was where the real fun erupted. Saturday, 4 October marked the debut of the Spectacular Spinning Songbook, the dramatic centrepiece of the tour. The Songbook was a twelve-foot-high carnival wheel plastered with thirty-eight different song titles, from Elvis favourites to obscure or bizarre covers like Prince's 'Pop Life' and Abba's 'Knowing Me, Knowing You'.

Like a cheap TV game show, members of the audience were taken on-stage to spin the wheel, overseen by Elvis in the guise of MC Napoleon Dynamite, as well as any passing celebrity who happened to be in the area. As the band played their chosen selection, the audience member could listen to the song in a section of the stage named The Society Lounge, or they could dance along in the go-go cage. 'It started as a flip suggestion for solving the problem of which songs to sing,' said Elvis. '[But] it made for an interestingly random evening.'[8]

Having strolled down the aisle towards the stage as Napoleon Dynamite, Elvis led The Attractions into a lashing 'Tokyo Storm Warning' before the interactive festivities commenced. Elvis's personal assistant Paddy Callahan – to be known as Xavier Valentine for the evening – picked members of the audience to come up on stage to spin the wheel. They were greeted by the two guest MCs, X's John Doe and the exemplary Tom Waits. Replete with bowler hat, the gruff Waits in particular was a masterstroke, hollering out the evening's entertainment with an intrinsic understanding of the ringmaster's art. He set an impossibly high standard for the rest of the tour.

In Beverly Hills, the wheel threw up a few nice surprises: 'Strict Time', 'Miracle Man', 'Motel Matches' and 'Temptation' among others, but in truth, Elvis's long-standing predilection for changing his sets around on a nightly basis, throwing in rare old songs and brand-new ones, rendered the Spinning Songbook largely superfluous. It was primarily there for Elvis and the audience's amusement rather than to conjure any genuine musical oddities.

Elsewhere during the evening's entertainments, John Doe joined in on The Troggs' 'Wild Thing', Waits duetted with Elvis on a cover of 'I Forgot More Than You'll Ever Know', and three-quarters of The Bangles replaced The Attractions mid-set, adding backing vocals on The Beatles' 'Yes It Is', their own 'If She Knew What She Wants' and Elvis's 'Next Time 'Round'. Then The Attractions roared into the second half with 'You Belong To Me', before closing on the irresistible one-two of 'Everyday I Write The Book' and 'Pump It Up'. In the *LA Times*, Chris Willman called the hugely entertaining proceedings a 'spectacle akin to a meeting of PT Barnum, any slick TV game show host you want to name and The Troggs. It was all warm, witty and wonderful.'

It was also difficult to top, but that wouldn't stop him trying. The final night's performance at the Beverly Theater was designed to showcase the *Blood & Chocolate* material. Elvis and The Attractions played nine songs from the record, but there were other delights: 'The Beat', 'Man Out Of Time', 'Clubland', 'Suit Of Lights', 'Kid About It' and a medley of 'Ferry 'Cross The Mersey' and the ultra-rare 'Tiny Steps' to name a few. The encore featured Tom Petty on '(What's So Funny 'Bout) Peace, Love & Understanding', 'American Girl' and 'So You Want To Be A Rock & Roll Star'.

The shows were an undoubted triumph, but it wasn't all sweetness. Elvis was having a fractious time with the media. First, he had banned news photographers from the concerts, attracting widespread criticism. Jake Riviera claimed that photographers would 'ruin the show for the 1300 people who bought tickets', adding with typical forthrightness that 'most newspapers and magazines in this country aren't worth reading'.[9] Instead, one photographer was hired to distribute syndicated photos to all the papers.

Then there was a one-sided spat with Robert Hilburn from the *LA Times*, whose review of the opening night's show – though largely positive – had attracted Elvis's ire for its charges of the 'predictability' of the setlist. In response, Elvis had taken a few over-sensitive pot-shots at Hilburn from the stage during the five-night run. Clearly not a man to hold a grudge, Hilburn was brave enough to review the final show, and declared the entire five nights 'one of the most memorable engagements ever in Los Angeles rock'.

It was a tall claim, but true. The diversity of Elvis's shows defied the predictability of standard rock convention, leaving virtually every other live act around looking tired and unadventurous. But then only an artist with an enormous repertoire of quality material and a loyal and willing audience could have pulled it off: over the entirety of the US tour, Elvis would play over 125 different songs in wildly differing formats.

No matter how artistically fulfilling it would prove to be, however, Columbia had finally come to the conclusion that their new wave goose was not going to deliver any more gold records. They were also tired of throwing good money after bad in what they perceived as bizarre and commercially suicidal moves, like releasing two six-minute singles or playing five nights with two bands in tiny theatres. Elvis's Spinning Songbook may have sown the seeds for the infinitely more hi-tech but equally chaotic, ironic and inventive rock shows of the '90s, such as U2's 'Zooropa' tour, but it was the end of the road for his record company.

* * *

After the highs of Los Angeles, everything else risked becoming anti-climatic. They played only three nights in San Francisco, Chicago, Boston and Philadelphia, and the sets were compressed and adapted accordingly. There was also a dearth of musical celebrities. Huey Lewis was a solid MC in San Francisco, but in Chicago it was left to members of the Chicago Bears NFL football team to spin the wheel. In New York, magician-cum-comedians Penn and Teller were co-MCs, and the show at the Broadway Theatre ended with Penn riling Elvis by shouting for Bruce Springsteen songs, calling Bruce 'the greatest rock 'n' roller the world has ever seen'. Elvis kicked him off stage and played 'Pump It Up' instead.

However, there were numerous musical highlights: Cait played bass on 'Poor Napoleon' and added backing vocals to 'Crimes Of Paris'; in Chicago, the Spinning Songbook threw up a nostalgic cover of 'I Just Don't Know What To Do With Myself', while Elvis dedicated a new piano ballad called 'The Last Time You Were Leaving' to Cait; in Boston, there were solo versions of 'Shipbuilding' and 'Tokyo Storm Warning' and a rare outing for the superior *King Of America* out-take 'Shoes Without Heels'.

In New York, there were solo versions of 'Party Girl' and 'You Little Fool', covers of Bob Dylan's 'I Threw It All Away' and Buddy Holly's 'True Love Ways' – dedicated to Columbia and Cait respectively, with very different motivations. The final three dates in Philadelphia saw Mitchell Froom depart and Benmont Tench take over keyboard duties in The Confederates. 'King Horse' got a one-off airing with The Attractions, while Elvis performed 'Hoover Factory' solo and 'Shot With His Own Gun' with Steve, neither of which were played anywhere else on tour.

The budget didn't stretch to bringing The Confederates over to Europe and anyway, their contribution was probably the least inventive of all the creative elements of the tour. It was just Elvis and The Attractions again, and left alone they finally began to fall apart. 'My relationship with the band had now soured almost beyond repair,'[10] Elvis admitted.

At Dublin's Olympia Theatre on 2 December, Elvis opened his solo set with a short story, called 'How Joe Soap Got Into Everyone'. This followed on from the set in London on 28 November, where he had begun with a short story entitled 'Getting Into Showbiz'. Both were pointed responses to the fact that Bruce Thomas had begun writing about his life on the road, extracts of which were being published in instalments in London's *Time Out* magazine. These loose memoirs would eventually become a book called *The Big Wheel*, and the portayal of Elvis was not necessarily flattering. Thomas disparagingly called him 'The Pod' while also referring to a certain lack of thoroughness in aspects of his personal hygiene. 'I knew what corns to tread on,' he admits.

When the tour ended in Liverpool on 9 December, Elvis quickly followed through on the decision he had made back in 1984. He took The Attractions out to dinner over Christmas and essentially told them their time was up, that he could no longer afford to keep them on salary and that he wanted a break from the responsibilities of being a band leader to do new things.

In future, he envisaged occasional *ad hoc* projects, essentially using them as session musicians.

It was delivered with all the coolness of a straightforward business decision. 'We were never particularly friendly,' Elvis later explained. 'We didn't spend lots of time together when we weren't on the road. We were thrown together so much because we were touring, so you assumed there was a very strong bond. But what it really was was me *and* a really great group. It had to be my decision the way we went, because I was the mug out front.'[11]

After almost ten years, the band took it very badly. 'It did hurt,' said Pete Thomas. 'It *really* hurt, and I'm sure he knew it would.'[12] Steve Nieve was the worst affected. Always the least bouyant member of the group, Steve had been badly hurt by the deterioration of the group's spirit, and the fact that, musically, he had been made to feel superfluous to requirements for some time. The most innovative and often inspired member of The Attractions – and certainly the most instantly identifiable contributor – his sidelined role on *Blood & Chocolate* and the subsequent manner in which The Attractions were jettisoned was a hammer blow. 'It was a shock,' he later admitted. 'It resulted in a depression that eventually caused me to take a long, hard look at myself and make some difficult changes.'[13]

In the circumstances, The Attractions' three-night last stand at the Royal Albert Hall between the 22–24 January was the last thing the pianist needed. Both Steve and Bruce felt strongly that Elvis was less than supportive in the way he responded to Nieve's depression, a belief which played a significant part in the resentment that lingered over the ensuing years. Little wonder that the Albert Hall shows were some way short of peak performances. The Attractions knew their time was up and the manner in which the parting of the ways had been conducted left them playing with pent-up bitterness rather than the euphoria of a final fling.

Thankfully, there was a chance for one final goodbye later in the year, a long-standing contractual obligation to play at the Glastonbury Festival on 20 June 1987. Elvis played the longer opening set solo, as if to delay the final showdown as long as possible. Los Lobos's David Hidalgo came in on backing vocals on 'American Without Tears', while Elvis added a beatbox to a raucous 'Pump It Up', which also took in Prince's 'Sign 'O' The Times' and Bob Dylan's 'Subterranean Homesick Blues'.

Then The Attractions appeared, bursting into 'I Hope You're Happy Now', and this time they blazed. It was a short eleven-song set, savage in its intensity. Elvis seemed happy to veer off at tangents, morphing 'Less Than Zero' into 'Twist And Shout', while 'You Belong To Me' explicitly acknowledged its debt to 'The Last Time'. It all ended with 'Poor Napoleon' sidestepping into a violent, improvised 'Instant Karma': 'I'm sure it was suppposed to mean something at the time,'[14] said Elvis, ruefully. And that was that. It would be their last concert together for over seven years. It was time to move on.

PART THREE
Having It All

Chapter Eleven
1987–89

IN AN ATTEMPT TO ALLEVIATE THE TENSION and pressure of almost continual touring during the early years of his career, Elvis had visited a masseuse. 'You're all wound up, just relax,' he was told. 'It's my *job* to get wound up,' replied Elvis. Throughout the '70s and first half of the '80s there was a real sense that this was a man who was rarely happy within his own skin. But now, freed from the responsibilities of being a band leader and settling into domesticity with Cait, the idea of living a life filled with tension and upheavals, and putting everybody else through the wringer in the process, seemed to have lost a substantial amount of its appeal. 'He became really friendly and a completely different man, almost,' says Bob Geldof. 'I suppose it's a function of age. We all change. But he became really *overtly* friendly and chatty and helpful. I [started to] like him as a person a lot.'

As his ten-year relationships with both Columbia and The Attractions reached acrimonious ends, Elvis felt unfettered, free to write, record and perform in any style he wanted. It was the perfect opportunity to explore all the options before committing himself to making a record, and throughout the spring and summer of 1987, he continued playing and composing instinctively, with little agenda. Having released two magnificent records in the previous twelve months, he was in no hurry to return to the fray just yet.

He was spending much of his time in Dublin. Cait had a part in an Irish film called *The Courier*, and Elvis had allowed his arm to be twisted into writing much of the incidental music. Over the summer, the couple spent a few months in the Gresham Hotel on O'Connell Street, and the first batch of new songs began to take shape.

Elvis had performed 'Any King's Shilling' throughout both The Confederates' first UK tour in January and early February, and the short solo tour of American university halls he undertook with Nick Lowe in

April.* The song was a restrained, sincere narrative detailing his grandfather Pat's experiences as an Irish-blooded British soldier in Ireland. 'He fell in with a couple of brothers who – shortly before the 1916 Rising – warned him to keep his head down,' Elvis recalled. 'They were aware of what was gonna go down and didn't want to see one of their own getting their head shot off.'[1]

Following his return from the solo US tour in early May, Elvis went into Windmill Lane Studios in Dublin to make vocal, guitar and piano demos of more new material: 'Let Him Dangle' and 'Tramp The Dirt Down' were two furious, Dylan-esque political broadsides; 'Veronica' and 'Pads, Paws And Claws', on the other hand, were playful pop songs, and the product of a significant new songwriting partnership.

Paul McCartney was emerging from a period of serious under-achievement and looking to both tighten up and simplify his song-writing again when he made contact with Elvis in early 1987. Loosely acquainted with each other in the manner of many musicians who become friendly through the occasional meeting in the studio or at gigs, the two were by no means close. McCartney's need was unarguably the greater. He was readying to begin work on a new record, and looking for a collaborator who would push him further than he had recently been pushing himself. A rabid Beatles fan for more than twenty years and always keen to test himself against the best, Elvis wasn't slow to accept the offer.

News of the collaboration didn't begin to filter out until July, but work began some months before that, kept under wraps in case the whole thing proved to be a disaster. Initially, the pair made no attempt at writing anything from scratch. Instead, they each played songs that they felt needed some work, letting the other make suggestions and criticisms. 'There may not be too many people who say to him, "That's boring, Elvis",'[2] said McCartney. Or, indeed, vice versa.

In this manner, Paul finished up 'Veronica' and 'Pads, Paws And Claws' for Elvis, adding a couple of lyrical phrases and tightening the bridges. In the case of the latter, the notoriously disciplined ex-Beatle felt that Elvis hadn't adequately explained the punning title, and so he helped pin down the song's bridge. Elvis returned the favour by helping out with the words to McCartney's 'Back On My Feet', before work began on their first genuine co-compositions: 'Lovers That Never Were', 'So Like Candy', 'You Want Her Too' and 'My Brave Face'.

* The US tour between 15 April and 2 May again involved the Spectacular Spinning Songbook. In Washington, Elvis rigged the wheel: 'If you can't cheat in Washington, D.C. where can you cheat?', he joked.

It was a craftsman-like process, the two men throwing musical references at each other, trying to resist falling back on their usual compositional tricks and methodologies. In all, around eight original co-compositions came out of the opening pair of two or three-day writing sessions, and they continued to write sporadically through 1987 and beyond.* 'It was a workshop situation,' said Elvis. 'We would sit around with a couple of guitars, a piano and a tape recorder and throw ideas around, improvising until we got a structure. We worked very quickly, bouncing a lot of ideas off each other.'3

The work was done 'nose-to-nose', in the manner of the early Lennon and McCartney compositions. And although Elvis repeatedly insisted in no uncertain terms that those who viewed him as a Lennon substitute – providing the bitter bite to balance McCartney's notoriously sweet tooth – were being wildly over-simplistic, even McCartney acknowledged the similarities: 'I can tell in Elvis's whole stance, his whole attitude, his whole singing style,' he said. 'It's all there, it's all sort of John-ish.'4

Elvis must have allowed himself to be just a little flattered. He wasn't too old or experienced to be occasionally daunted by the reality of working with a real, live Beatle, but his natural self-possession ensured he more than held his own in the partnership. In the end, it was McCartney who reigned in their initial collaboration, fearing that Elvis's typically head-on style might threaten to overpower him. 'At one point, we were thinking, "Well, this might be the way to go, to do the whole album together",' he said. 'But I started to feel that would be too much of Elvis. And I thought the critics would say, "Oh, they're getting Elvis to prop up his ailing career", you know?'5

The songs were generally strong, but more might reasonably have been expected. Only a couple of tracks came anywhere near the best of either musician's previous output. 'That Day Is Done' was a gorgeous, gospel-flavoured track with a moving lyric which detailed the funeral of Elvis's much-loved grandmother, while 'So Like Candy' was a moody, minor-key rummage through the everyday detritus left by a departed lover, who just happened to share the name of Bebe Buell's *nom de plume*. Of the rest, 'You Want Her Too' was a clever, somewhat Beatles-esque angel-and-devil duet, while 'My Brave Face' and 'Veronica' were the most commercial things either had written for some time.

---

* They came up with at least a dozen new songs in all: 'My Brave Face', 'You Want Her Too', 'Don't Be Careless Love', 'That Day Is Done', 'Mistress And Maid' and 'Lovers That Never Were' appear on McCartney's *Flowers In The Dirt* and *Off The Ground*. 'Playboy To A Man', 'So Like Candy' and 'Shallow Grave' made it onto Elvis's *Mighty Like A Rose* and *All This Useless Beauty*. In addition, 'I Don't Want To Confess', '25 Fingers', 'Tommy's Coming Home' and, in all probability, several more exist, but have never been officially released.

The collaboration later came unstuck, however, when Elvis and McCartney took the songs into the studio in 1988 to attempt a co-production for McCartney's *Flowers In The Dirt* album. The two men had profoundly differing ideas about how the songs should be produced: Elvis wanted their recordings of 'So Like Candy', 'My Brave Face', 'You Want Her Too', 'Don't Be Careless Love' and 'That Day Is Done' to remain raw and edgy, while McCartney insisted on a terribly over-produced, consciously 'modern' sound.

It was an uneasy combination, and Mitchell Froom – increasingly in demand as a producer – was parachuted in to find some common ground. 'I think they had had a falling out,' he says, although that's probably over-stating the case a little. However, there were clearly strong disagreements on either side. 'Paul has a clever way of side-stepping confrontation by making jokes, like "Well, you can never trust anything he says because he hates effects!",' said Elvis. 'Rather than disagreeing with you, your argument is devalued before it's started. After a while that made the production rather redundant.'6

Much of what Elvis contributed in the studio was scrubbed when *Flowers In The Dirt* finally appeared in July 1989. His vocals remained on the duet of 'You Want Her Too' and his background vocals and keyboards could be heard on 'My Brave Face' and 'That Day Is Done', but he was quite justifiably disappointed at the way some of the tracks ended up sounding, especially the latter, which all but ruined a terrific song by miring it in a preposterous, lurching production: '[Paul] sort of gave them a more highly polished sound which obviously was what he heard in them,'7 said Elvis, with uncharacteristic diplomacy. Those who heard the unvarnished *joie de vivre* of Elvis and Paul's widely bootlegged acoustic demos reduced to formulaic mediocrity on *Flowers In The Dirt* could be forgiven for being a little less charitable.

* * *

Elvis lay low over the summer of 1987. He briefly broke cover for The Attractions' belated swan song at Glastonbury on 20 June, but just as quickly vanished again. His time was taken up with writing in Dublin, as well as embarking on a cruise ship holiday with Cait to Greenland, where the vast Arctic expanses inspired a new song called 'God's Comic'. 'Thoughts occur to you out there about the comedy of what we call civilization,' he said. 'It reminds you how puny we are.'8

It was a good time to disappear. In early July, the disastrous *Straight To Hell* was released to generally savage reviews. 'The film "began as a joke" and was written in three days,' ran *The Times'* review. 'It is hard to see how they used even that much time on it.' In the US, *The Record* simply called it 'an abysmally bad B-movie', and there was little disagreement from the rest of the critics, or indeed the public. It quickly sank without a trace.

In his retreat, Elvis was increasingly growing into the role of accepted elder statesman, welcomed into the pantheon of A-list rock stars. Now aged thirty-three, he had grown friendly with U2, while back in January Van Morrison had slipped on stage with The Confederates in London, duetting with Elvis on 'Jackie Wilson Said', 'Help Me' and Ray Charles' 'What Would I Do'.

On 30 September, it was the charms of Roy Orbison which tempted Elvis back on stage. T-Bone Burnett had organised a televised tribute to The Big O entitled 'A Black And White Night', to be filmed at the Cocoanut Grove Club at the Ambassador Hotel in Los Angeles. For the occasion, Elvis tailored 'The Comedians' into a dramatic ballad specifically for Orbison, and played guitar, keyboards and harmonica as part of a backing band which included Bruce Springsteen, Tom Waits, Jackson Browne, Bonnie Raitt and k.d. lang.

Despite the talent on show, the concert was all about Orbison. 'You could imagine Springsteen and Costello – seated near each other and playing their guitars – in a schoolroom somewhere, trying to please their favourite teacher as they nervously followed their notes,' wrote Robert Hilburn in the *LA Times*. It was a stop-start affair, constantly interrupted by the demands of the TV cameras, and didn't really explode until the show-stopping finale of 'Oh, Pretty Woman', but it was a memorable piece of fantasy fulfilment for all concerned.

A few weeks later, *Out Of Our Idiot* slipped out almost unnoticed. Over the summer, Elvis had signed to Warner Brothers, the label that had funded both Radar and F-Beat in Britain, and which now owned his signature worldwide. It was a contract which gave him much more financial support and creative independence than he had enjoyed in his latter years with CBS. Fulfilling his final contractual obligation to Columbia, *Out Of Our Idiot* was essentially Volume II of *Taking Liberties*, a round-up of out-takes, B-sides and rarities from the years between 1979 and 1987.

Notable for finding a suitable resting place for such gems as 'Black Sails In The Sunset', 'The People's Limousine', 'From Head To Toe', 'Shoes Without Heels' and 'So Young', it was inevitably a hit-and-miss affair. '*Out of Our Idiot* is a remarkable testament to how bloody unremarkable Elvis Costello can be when he puts his mind to it,' wrote Jon Wilde in *Melody Maker*. '[But] it is not without its gold foil moments.' It may have failed to chart on either side of the Atlantic, but it did give Elvis the chance to confuse and confound with his ever-expanding list of aliases: the spine credited the album to 'Various Artists', while the pop-art cover heralded the likes of Napoleon Dynamite and The Royal Guard, The Emotional Toothpaste, The Confederates and The Coward Brothers. He even found room for Elvis Costello and The Attractions.

His old band were busy earning an honest living after ten years' service,* but Elvis wasn't especially inclined to look back. He had lined up a short tour of the southern states of America, Japan and Australia with The Confederates, kicking off on 5 November in Atlanta. He opened each show solo with 'Red Shoes' and played many of the subsequent songs alone, The Confederates joining him on the *King Of America* material and the numerous, often indistinguishable R&B covers.

Over the course of the tour the new songs began to surface, mainly in the solo sections. 'Tramp The Dirt Down' was a regular from the beginning, but by the time the tour reached Japan in mid-November, many more were dotted throughout the set. 'God's Comic' arrived in Tokyo, alongside 'Pads, Paws And Claws', 'Veronica' and 'Last Boat Leaving'. In Osaka on 24 November, 'Miss MacBeth' was also aired. In addition, the tour featured band versions of 'Let Him Dangle' and a reclaimed 'That Day Is Done'.

* * *

Work finally began on *Spike* in Dublin in the spring of 1988, and would continue through much of the year. Even with a fistful of new songs played-in, Elvis deliberately hadn't rushed into recording. He had continued writing into the new year, and in January and February of '88 he had entered Eden Studios in London to lay down precise demos of most of the songs. Approaching the material with more care than ever before, a number of the tunes' distinctive instrumental riffs and motifs were already established.

Aside from the tracks already played live, he now had 'Baby Plays Around', 'This Town', 'Deep Dark Truthful Mirror', 'Satellite', 'Coal Train Robberies' and 'Put Your Big Toe In The Milk Of Human Kindness', a sweet little song originally written for an unidentified Disney project but never used, and which Elvis had been playing in concert for a couple of

* Steve Nieve and Pete Thomas became part of the house band on Jonathan Ross's weekly TV show *The Last Resort*, while all three Attractions were involved in session work with the reformed Madness and Andy White, among others.

years. One of Elvis's most delightful sidesteps, it would eventually turn up on Rob Wasserman's *Trios* record.

Just before work on the album began in earnest, Elvis found the time for a quick diversion. Returning from his holiday to Greenland the previous year, the cruise liner had stopped off at the Shetland Islands, and Elvis escaped into the Thule Bar in Lerwick for a Guinness. He found a couple of his own songs on the jukebox and – suitably smitten – asked if he could make an appearance at the annual folk festival the following year.

Following a predictably positive response, Elvis returned to play Whiteness County Hall on 28 April, Lerwick Garrison Theatre on the 29th and Whalsay Public Hall on the 30th as well as a handful of twenty-minute spots around Lerwick on 1 May. Most of the halls held a maximum of 200 people, and Elvis relished the intense atmosphere, performing solo sets which had little to do with traditional folk music, but which undeniably provided the highlights of the festival.

It was in Shetland that Elvis realised beyond question that 'Tramp The Dirt Down' was going to have a substantial and lasting impact. Loosely tugging on the hem of Bob Dylan's 'Masters Of War' (compare: 'And I'll stand o'er your grave 'til I'm sure that you're dead', with 'I'll stand on your grave and tramp the dirt down') the song explicitly wished the demise of the current Prime Minister Margaret Thatcher. It was bound to raise emotions. 'I sang it in one place that was very brightly lit and I could see the audience quite clearly,' Elvis recalled. 'And all the way through there was one guy nodding away, applauding every line, and on the other side, there was another guy being physically restrained from getting up on stage and hitting me. He just fused, you could see it in his face. And I thought, "Well, I've really got a winner now!".'9

At the other end of the spectrum, the light-hearted hangover song 'The Big Light' became a kind of unofficial theme tune for the majority of the drink-happy festival-goers, while at the Children's Concert on 1 May, Elvis played 'Put Your Big Toe In The Milk Of Human Kindness', 'Leave My Kitten Alone' – coaxing high-pitched miaows from the youngsters – and an unidentified new song which ran: 'Saw an iceberg go past my window/ Saw a whale on the starboard bow/Summer time above the Arctic circle/ And all the huskies go bow wow wow!' It wouldn't make the new album.

Back in Dublin, Elvis and T-Bone Burnett adopted the same approach for *Spike* as they had with *King Of America*, but this time the landscape was much broader and the pre-production much more involved. Elvis's music was becoming harmonically quite complex, and with a bigger budget to work with following his deal with Warners, he felt less inhibited, sensing a greater deal of freedom than he had at Columbia. 'I had the blueprint of five albums in my head,' he later admitted. 'I seem to have elected to make all five at once.'[10]

Tom Waits had become a big influence, and although nothing on the final record sounded much like Waits, the air of strangeness, rootsiness and lack of musical boundaries that had inhabited his recent records was clearly in the air when *Spike* was being made. Elvis imagined the songs as scenes from a film, each one requiring a different sense of location and lighting. The narrative for 'Any King's Shilling', for instance, was set in the early 1900s, and Elvis consciously tailored the measured words and the 'drawing room' music to conjure up a turn-of-the-century idiom.

Drawing up a wish-list of the best possible musicians, instruments and textures to suit this kind of approach was time-consuming, and the foundations for *Spike* took several weeks to build, with endless phone calls and scheduling problems. Elvis had also wanted to use The Attractions on some of the songs, an idea hampered by the fact that two-thirds of the band were effectively not speaking to him. He tried establishing contact but it came to nothing. 'Elvis rang me up on Christmas Day, the time you reconcile with people, and I just said, "No, tell him I'm busy",' says Bruce Thomas. 'I was still angry about the way he had been with Steve.' Steve was indeed still hurt, and also refused to get involved in a project where he was going to be just another session piano player. Pete Thomas, however, remained on better terms with Elvis, and would play on one track on the record.

Having worked out what he wanted for each song, Elvis laid down most of the basic tracks in Windmill Lane with just a guitar and a sparse drum machine, often eschewing any kind of recognisable beat. On such a fluid base, he was then free to add, subtract, and potter with each song as he pooled the resources of top-class musicians the world over.

Back in May 1987, Elvis had recorded an Irish television broadcast with an assembled group of Irish folk musicians, which planted the seed of perhaps using traditional instruments on the new record. A year on at Windmill Lane, he recorded some of the few live ensemble performances on *Spike*, using local legends such as Christy Moore, Derek Bell, Davy Spillane, Donal Lunny and Steve Wickham on 'Any King's Shilling', 'Miss MacBeth' and 'Tramp The Dirt Down'.

The sessions then moved to Southlake Studios in New Orleans for a week's work. Having already messed around with a computer-generated gumbo rhythm for 'Chewing Gum', Elvis flew to Louisiana to record the real thing. The Dirty Dozen Brass Band added their deep Southern bottom-line not only to 'Chewing Gum', but also to 'Deep Dark Truthful Mirror', 'Stalin Malone' and 'Miss MacBeth'. It was intensive work. 'We worked twelve- to fifteen-hour days for about six or seven days,' said band leader Gregory Davis. 'He knew what he wanted to do.'[11] While in New Orleans, Elvis also coaxed celebrated arranger Allen Toussaint into adding a towering piano part to 'Deep Dark Truthful Mirror'. In this considered way, the intial song sketches began turning into full-blown paintings.

Much of the leg-work was done over the summer in Ocean Way Studios in Hollywood. It was here that most of the basic component instruments of bass, drums and guitars were added by a core of musicians who had worked on *King Of America*: Jerry Scheff, T-Bone Wolk, Jim Keltner and Mitchell Froom, plus Confederates' Benmont Tench and Tom Waits's guitarist and percussionist, Marc Ribot and Michael Blair respectively.

Almost always, each musician worked alone to the existing backing track, adding their contributions in isolation. It was a world away from the live fireworks of *King Of America* and *Blood & Chocolate* and perhaps closer in technique – if not in feel – to the building-block method used five years earlier by Clive Langer and Alan Winstanley. 'I didn't see other musicians on that record,' says Mitchell Froom. 'Some of it was done with a drum machine to begin with and then the musicians played over.'

It was a strange way of working, and couldn't help but make for a somewhat stilted final product. But although many of the songs had been written with close attention to detail, each musician was given a degree of freedom to express themselves.

'Chewing Gum' – having already been roughed up by The Dirty Dozen Brass Band – was further shaped by Marc Ribot's distinctively skewed guitar playing. 'The basic technique would be that I would jump into it like it was a playpen or a sandbox and splash around and see what I could come up with,' says Ribot. What he came up with sounded like an iron bar in a tumble dryer. On 'Veronica', Mitchell Froom was given free reign with a keyboard-type instrument called the chamberlain, conjuring up the distinctive, Beatle-esque trumpet line which distinguished the final track. Elvis liked the results so much he encouraged Froom to add chamberlain parts to several other songs. It was a hive of creativity and exemplary musicianship. 'I was somewhat awed by the whole thing,' admits Ribot. 'T-Bone Burnett was hanging around and Roger McGuinn was putting down a guitar track and there was Elvis just looking like Elvis. I thought, "Wow!".' On one occasion, Elvis played a version of 'Satellite' to Burt Bacharach, who was working in the same studio complex.

Perhaps the heart of the record lay in Michael Blair's idiosyncratic contributions. Tom Waits' percussionist had been one of the first names on the list for the record, and his palette of weird textures and details were an essential part of the album's off-kilter sound. Sometimes it was a metal pipe, a 'Martian dog-bark' or an Oldsmobile hubcap, sometimes a parade drum or a simple glockenspiel, but Blair was hard to miss.

He also gifted the record its title. Originally called *Pantomime Evil*, the idea of calling it *Spike: The Beloved Entertainer* came to Elvis during the mixing stages as he listened to the eccentric percussive sounds that ran through the record. 'I listened to the whole album by homing in on Blair's percussion and it just jumped out,' said Elvis. 'I thought, Spike Jones! That's it.'[12]*

The record was almost finished by the time Elvis left Hollywood and flew back to London to add some final overdubs. Paul McCartney was in AIR Studios working on *Flowers In The Dirt* and added bass to 'Veronica' and 'This Town', while Chrissie Hynde sang harmony vocals on 'Satellite'. Elvis added his own contributions as he saw fit: sometimes just vocals, but also layers of guitars and occasionally piano or bass or more eccentric nuances like mandolin or melodica. *Spike* was then mixed carefully and attentively in Ocean Way in Hollywood, with close consideration given to the individual parts played by each of the thirty-two musicians involved.

Once the album was finished, Elvis popped into Wessex Studios in London for a quick, self-produced session with Pete Thomas and Nick Lowe, knocking off four covers for B-sides to the singles. Typically, they were the very antithesis of *Spike*: loud, crude and cut in a day.

* * *

Increasingly, Elvis was tiring of traditional forms of rock music. His instrumental work on *The Courier* had been largely either ignored or maligned, but it was an interesting and significant experiment. Its strings and saxophones marked the first staging post for ideas and approaches which bore fruit on *Spike* and several subsequent albums.

The broader sweeps of his most recent recordings and the array of musicians he had met and played with had opened Elvis's mind to the almost limitless possibilities of music and melody, and he became determined to explore the outer reaches of his creativity. His tastes were typically diverse: he was listening to a lot of jazz – Charlie Mingus, Sonny

* Spike Jones was a 'musical comedian' who worked in the '30s and '40s, assembling a group of fine musicians whom he trained to play toilet seats or tune gunshots to C-sharp. Mixing learned instrumental virtuosity with sonic hi-jinks, they blended comedy and music in a way that was unique, funny and sometimes slightly disquieting. Elvis seemingly recognised a similar quality in his own recent music.

Rollins, Henry Threadgill – the Bulgarian vocal group Balkana, Haitian guitar music, but increasingly in the late '80s it was classical music that demanded his attentions.

Elvis had had a passing interest in classical music since the early '80s, and had been known to drop Shostakovich, Sibeluis, Satie, Messian, Debussy, Bach and Stravinsky into interviews. Disillusioned with the routine predictability of rock concerts – excluding his own, naturally – he and Cait began attending classical concerts. The biggest eye-opener was a performance of Schoenberg's *Gurrelieder* by the City of Birmingham Symphony Orchestra conducted by Simon Rattle at the Royal Festival Hall in January 1989. The *Financial Times* called it 'one of the best perform-ances of anything I have seen anywhere', and Elvis was similarly capti-vated, given little option but to acknowledge the immense power of this music as a live, emotional entity, rather than something remote and schol-arly. 'I knew absolutely nothing about the piece,' he admitted, 'but I found it overwhelming. Very physical.'[13]

Later the same month, Elvis saw some of the Brodsky Quartet's series of five concerts at the South Bank and The Barbican in London, in which they performed all of the Shostakovich quartets. It was the beginning of a love affair with the Brodsky Quartet which took nearly three years to fully blossom. Viola player Paul Cassidy, cellist Jacqueline Thomas, and violinists Michael Thomas and Ian Belton had formed the group in 1972 as students in Manchester, naming themselves in honour of their mentor Rudolf Brodsky. They had a reputation for pioneering collaborations and taking on challenging commissions, spanning the fields of classical, jazz, pop and opera. And they tended to play standing up, a unique calling card for a classical quartet.

Between 1989 and 1991, Elvis would make several trips to see them. 'He [came to] something like twenty of our concerts,' says Paul Cassidy. 'He'd turn up in Paris, he'd turn up in Dublin, he'd turn up in Manchester, over a two-year period. So we knew that this was serious. Our friends would come backstage and say, "My God, I was sitting next to Elvis Costello", and we'd say, "Yeah, sure".'

Elvis would remain only a distant admirer of the Brodsky Quartet until late 1991, when a meeting between the two parties was finally engineered, but for those two years classical music became his primary fascination. Once he had developed a taste for it, Elvis began to submerge himself in the music, with the intention of finding out exactly how it hung together from the inside out.

* * *

Spike was released on Valentine's Day 1989, a warped little love letter. Elvis was determined to give the record all the help he could. With a new album on a new record label following a recording silence of two and a half years, there was an unprecedented media assualt. He was a fixture on television, radio and in magazines and newspapers throughout February and March, happily explaining the songs and often picking up his guitar to play a few selections: several radio studios throughout the land rang to the cheery 'String 'em up!' refrain of 'Let Him Dangle'. In general, Elvis was genial and charming, a world away from the surly and combative interviewee of old.

It was all in aid of a strange, oddly aloof record, easy to admire but difficult to love. It was only possible to be an 'angry young man' for so long without descending into self-parody, and Elvis had ensured that his music kept abreast of his life. He admitted with surprise that he was finally happy – he had reached an unprecedented degree of peace and stability in his private life, and his writing had changed accordingly. Almost every song on *Spike* was a third-person narrative, Elvis standing back and observing the sad, emotionally hamstrung protagonists in 'Chewing Gum' and 'Satellite', or playing an easily identifiable dramatic role in 'God's Comic' and 'Any King's Shilling': 'I'm more into observing illusions taking their toll on other people,'[14] he later said, rather than – as before – spending much of his time wrestling with the toll they took on himself.

As a result, there was a distance, a coolness at the heart of the record. The changing personas and lack of musical coherence from track to track meant that *Spike* was often more technically impressive than emotionally resonant, almost a sampler, rather than a unified album. And some of the tracks fell short. 'This Town' was over-cooked and melodically patchy, the lumpy 'Let Him Dangle' bordered on the banal, while 'Chewing Gum' and 'Stalin Malone' were rhythmically interesting but hardly worked as songs.

Elsewhere, some of the melodic structures were uncharacteristically static, to the extent that 'Satellite', 'Tramp The Dirt Down' and 'Any King's Shilling' tended to drag, while lyrically, songs like 'Deep Dark Truthful Mirror' plumbed depths of obscurity unusual even for Elvis. If ever an album needed detailed companion notes, it was *Spike*.

There probably weren't quite enough great songs to sweeten the pill. However, 'Deep Dark Truthful Mirror', 'God's Comic' and 'Baby Plays Around' – written by Cait on bass and finished off by Elvis – were beautifully realised, while the lyrics to 'Satellite' were an eerily prescient pre-internet premonition of the way technological advances would be used to fuel a globally interactive pornography industry.

'Tramp The Dirt Down', meanwhile, was a consciously crude and one-dimensional response to ten years of Tory misrule, which – by choosing to eschew a politically correct moral – hit its target with merciless precision. And 'Veronica' – the touching tribute to Ross's late mother Molly – may have divided loyalties with its crisp pop production, but it was a huge commercial success as a single, due in no small part to Evan English's memorable video. It eventually became Elvis's biggest-ever single in the US, hitting the Top 20 in the spring, as well as reaching No. 31 in Britain.

On the back of the single and a determined marketing campaign from Warners, *Spike* sold in numbers that Columbia must have once dreamt about, becoming the most successful record of Elvis's career. It reached No. 5 in Britain and No. 32 in the US, sticking around for some time, and the reviews were almost universally strong. *Melody Maker* noted the 'detached and objective' feel, but concluded that although perhaps too versatile, the record was 'thoughtful, furious, eloquent and witty'. The *NME* had no such reservations, awarding *Spike* ten out of ten, calling it 'an exciting, inspiring, bewildering and bloody frightening record which could well be regarded as his most accomplished yet'. Andy Gill in *The Independent* simply reckoned that 'it may well be his masterpiece'. The beloved entertainer had been missed.

It was always going to be a tricky record to replicate on stage. Rather than try, Elvis elected to go out on the road alone between 31 March and 24 April with just his guitar, an electric piano, and Nick Lowe – naturally – for company. Instead of the Spectacular Spinning Songbook, this time he brought along a red satin heart, cracked down the middle. It was marked with thirteen and a half deadly sins, the seven originals and six and a half new ones, including 'Awesomeness'; 'Girls, Girls, Girls'; 'Doing Lunch'; 'Getting Caught Again'; and 'Trump' – as in Donald, the current and seemingly randomly selected focus of Elvis's ire.

For the final encore, Elvis – as Monsignor Napoleon Dynamite – would emerge in a red velveteen jacket clutching a plastic pitchfork. Audience members, usually women, were dragged on-stage by a man in a wolf costume, blindfolded, and asked to drive the spike into the heart. They were then asked to pick a song that most represented whichever sin they pierced.

This somewhat laboured, time-consuming rigmarole was more fun in theory than in practice, and not particularly rewarding in terms of the music. Not everyone in Elvis's audience was adept at picking out a long-lost gem from his back catalogue. Most of them only knew the classics. In Kingston, Rhode Island on 1 April the red heart threw up 'Alison', 'Red Shoes' and 'Pump It Up'; on 5 April it was 'Pump It Up', 'Oliver's

Army' and 'Almost Blue'. By the time the tour reached Greenvale on 9 April, Elvis was forced to spring an ambush, undercutting the jollity of the proceedings with his own choice: 'I Want You'.

Spike had played well with the Americans. *Rolling Stone* called it 'an ambitious sampler of his astonishing musical creativity', but although the songs from the record seemed to open up and come alive in concert, Elvis often played less of the album than might have been expected, sometimes as few as four songs.

Nevertheless, it was a well-oiled solo act. There was little mention of The Attractions. Elvis had become something of a showman, who had mastered the tightrope walk between intensity and droll geniality, deftly reeling the audience in. The true dramatic centrepieces of many shows were medleys of 'Radio Sweetheart/Jackie Wilson Said' and 'New Amsterdam/You've Got To Hide Your Love Away', where Elvis would sometimes take up to ten minutes exploring musical links and crescendoes. The loose structure allowed him to take a few considered risks, throwing musical quotes from Dylan, Abba, The Beatles, Van Morrison, Buddy Holly and even *West Side Story* into his own songs and embarking on long, surrealistic monologues in 'God's Comic'. Nick Lowe would join him for a few numbers on the first encore, nodding to 'the other Elvis' on 'His Latest Flame' and sparring on the songs they stole from each other: 'Indoor Fireworks' and '(What's So Funny 'Bout) Peace, Love & Understanding'.

The British leg opened at the London Palladium on 7 May, the first night of a four-week-long 'Month of Sundays' residency in the capital. The sets were similar to the US shows, and perhaps a little comfortable and lacking in surprises for most fans. They could also be very long. Aware of the vagaries of the British public transport system, a sizeable portion of the audience had often gone home before Elvis had exhausted his repertoire.

As the tour moved on, he added only a few eyebrow-raisers to the set and no new songs. In Bristol on 9 June he opened with the McCartney duet 'You Want Her Too', spinning around the microphone to give the impression of two different voices, and also played another two McCartney collaborations, 'That Day Is Done' and 'So Like Candy'.

By the time the final show at London's Palladium had come around on 28 May, it seemed that Elvis was tiring of the acoustic format. For the final encore he was joined by Nick Lowe on bass and Pete Thomas on drums, and the three-piece clattered through raucous versions of 'Pads, Paws And Claws', 'Leave My Kitten Alone', 'Lovable' and '(What's So Funny 'Bout) Peace, Love & Understanding'. On his final night of three shows at the Royal Albert Hall on 2 June he once again 'went electric', adding Squeeze's Glenn Tilbrook and Chris Difford to the Lowe-Thomas rhythm section.

For some time, Elvis had been thinking about touring *Spike* with a band, and following festival dates in Europe throughout June and a smattering of dates in Japan in July, he assembled The Rude 5 for a five-week US tour beginning on 8 August in Clarkston, Michigan. The group were put together at speed. Elvis rented the Metro club in Chicago for a week prior to the tour and they learned the entire set in seven days, meaning that there was very little room for deviation from the setlist once the tour got under way.

Energised by his recent cameos with Elvis and always the Attraction with the least residual resentment, Pete Thomas came in on drums. The others were picked for their ability to cope with the nuances and musical subtleties of the material: Confederate Jerry Scheff on bass and tuba; Michael Blair on percussion; Larry Knetchel on keyboards; Steven Soles on various textural additions, including mandolin, acoustic guitar, vocals and trombone; and Marc Ribot on guitar and E-flat horn.

Simple arithmetic revealed that The Rude 5 were actually six, seven if you included Elvis, but that was the only gimmick this time: there were no spinning wheels or pierced hearts. They were looser than The Attractions, but Elvis surely knew that few bands could better his old group when it came to playing the majority of his back catalogue. On most nights, less than half a dozen pre-1986 numbers were played, and those that made the cut were often radically reworked. 'Some of the [old tracks] he was happy to rearrange, if people had a new idea,' says Marc Ribot. 'At that moment he really wanted to try a lot of new and different things and take it as out as far as he felt like taking it.'

The likes of 'Pump It Up' had little scope for wholesale reinterpretation, but the airy, slightly threatening take on 'Clubland' added layers of shade to the original. 'Watching The Detectives', on the other hand, managed the 'improbable fusion of walking bass line, a jazzy disonant breakdown and a heavy metal blitz', in the words of Jim Sullivan of the *Boston Globe*, reviewing the show in Great Woods, Massachusets on 18 August.

The results were mixed. Sometimes, as with 'Watching The Detectives' or an oompah version of 'Let Him Dangle', the rearrangements appeared wilfully obtuse, using experimentation for the sake of it, while the smaller sonic augmentations – the glockenspiel parts on 'Alison' and '(What's So Funny 'Bout) Peace, Love & Understanding', for example – grated. Furthermore, the sound mix at many of the concerts was so poor that the brass, extra guitars and more sophisticated arrangements were rendered virtually impenetrable.

In general, however, the *Spike* songs were improved by the fact that Jerry Scheff could recreate the tuba part on 'Miss Macbeth', and that the full, jazzy lushness of 'God's Comic' could be brought to life. The Rude 5 offered a much fuller palette of sounds than The Attractions;

Elvis just hadn't yet learned how to use them most effectively. It's debatable whether he ever would.

* * *

Elvis and Cait had made the decision to leave London for Ireland in 1988. They made good on their promise the following year, fitting the move around Elvis's touring schedule for *Spike*. Their new home was called Waymark, a house situated on the Ballyedmonduff Road in Stepaside, about ten miles outside Dublin at the foot of the Wicklow mountains, and a move away from the city which necessitated the need for Elvis to learn to drive. The white-walled, three-bedroomed bungalow was modest enough for a rock star, although the grounds stretched to almost four acres and featured both an ornamental lake and a tennis court, as well as spectacular views over Dublin Bay.

Elvis hung on to his small two-bedroom flat in London's Holland Park just the same. Matthew was now fourteen, living with his mother in Chiswick, and enjoyed a close relationship with his father. The two shared holidays together to Russia and elsewhere, and Matt was an avid music fan, even if Elvis took a dim view of his liking for Guns N' Roses and Public Enemy.

There were several reasons behind the move to Ireland. Cait had never made any secret of the fact that she wanted children and, according to press reports, she fell pregnant in 1989, although sadly it seems that her pregnancy never reached full term. The couple needed more room than they had in their somewhat cramped flat, and house prices in Dublin were eminently more affordable than in London. Cait was also a nature lover, fond of walks, solitude and peace away from the clamour of Elvis's 'other' life, and her influence had partially convinced her essentially urbanite partner of the joys of the countryside.

Although Ireland also offered favourable tax breaks for artists and a thriving creative community in Dublin, with friends such as U2 and Chrissie Hynde based nearby, Elvis had felt a push as well as a pull. 'I don't want to live in a country run by this government,' he said of Great Britain. 'They're doing their utmost to engineer a new society, and it's not one I want to live in.'15*

* In the mid-'80s, Elvis stated categorically that he 'wasn't Irish', but later changed his view to one of ambiguity. 'I talk about "we Irish",' he later said. 'I love to tease by virtue of my mixed nationality. I say that the problem with you English is that we're younger, smarter, better educated and eventually will be richer than you, because we're not insular like you are.'16 On 13 May, 2001 he played U2's 'Please' and his own 'Heart Shaped Bruise' at the Irish Festival at the John F Kennedy Center for the Performing Arts in Washington DC, introducing himself as an 'accidental Englishman'.

Following the end of the *Spike* tour on 16 September, from the rural calm of his new home Elvis could look back upon a creatively satisfying and commercially successful year, topped off with awards for Best Male Video from MTV for 'Veronica' and Male Artist of the Year at the New Music Awards. His only other public activity in the remaining months of 1989 was a genuinely impromptu appearance at the Olympia Theatre in Dublin on 10 December, at a concert for the Temple Street Children's Hospital. Elvis showed up backstage about an hour before the concert was due to start and asked if he could play, later singing 'Radio Sweetheart' and 'God's Comic' to a surprised and delighted audience.

At the Olympia, his appearance showed signs of change: he was sporting a beard and his hair was longer, and over the course of the winter the shagginess would become even more exaggerated. He was entering a period of enormous change and evolution, and not just on the outside.

Chapter Twelve
1990–91

THE DEEPER ELVIS IMMERSED HIMSELF in classical music, the more fascinated by its detail he became. It was like an entirely new language, with its own sub-genres: folk, country, blues, rock and pop, all had comparable corollaries in classical music.

Typically, Elvis found something to savour in almost every aspect, just as he did in almost all popular music, but preferences emerged. 'I tend to discover new composers by following a particular performer or conductor,' he said. 'You get certain passions. For me, it was Schubert for a while. I went to all the London concerts and was hearing about half the sonatas for the first time.'[1] He was also absorbed by woodwind arrangements of songs from the late eighteenth century; he loved lieder* recitals and string quartets; chamber music and solo piano pieces; he would often only go to opera if he was interested in the vocalist – such as Italian mezzo-soprano Cecilia Bartoli – rather than the entire spectacle.

Elvis had spent much of the early months of the year writing, planning to record over the summer with Mitchell Froom producing, and these new and diverse influences started impacting upon his aspirations for his next record.

Envisaging that the new songs would contain many more live ensemble performances than *Spike*, Elvis wanted The Attractions to be involved. This time it appeared that his old group might be more amenable to the reunion, so he organised a farewell busman's holiday for the group of American musicians he had been touring and recording with since 1985. It may have seemed like an oddly sentimental idea, but despite his abrasive image and his often tempestuous relationship with The Attractions, Elvis has a well-deserved reputation for the respect he accords fellow musicians. Virtually every individual or band who has ever worked with him – from Clover to Bill Frisell to the Brodsky Quartet – can do little but sing his praises. 'Maybe it's because his father was a musician and he's aware

* A form of ballad.

of the older traditions, but he was always very respectful and professional with the musicians,' says Marc Ribot. 'No bullshit. You see, Elvis isn't just a songwriter; he's a student of music in general, so he's actually heard at least half of [the other players'] discographies, and that's very flattering. It gives Elvis and the musicians a common language right off the bat, even if they've never met, because he can say: "Well, you remember that sound you got on such-and-such a song?" That's how he deal with musicians.'

This musical momento took the form of a two-week session at Blue Wave Studios in Barbados in April 1990, the band consisting of Jerry Scheff on bass, Jim Keltner on drums, Larry Knetchel on keyboards, and James Burton on guitar. As planned, Pete Thomas and Marc Ribot flew in for the second week of recording, replacing Keltner and Burton.

Elvis arrived looking as though he were preparing for an Arctic expedition rather than the Caribbean, sporting a shaggy beard and long, woolly hair. He had grown it over the cold winter in Ireland and kept it 'once I realised how it infuriated people',[2] a typically contrary motivation.

The album concept was as simple as 'some of my favourite songs performed with some of my favourite musicians',[3] which sounded like something Sinatra might have written as a sleeve note back in the mid-'50s. There were blues and R&B tracks ('Strange', 'Leave My Kitten Alone', 'Payday', 'Everybody's Crying Mercy', 'Bama Lama Bama Loo'); country ballads ('Must You Throw Dirt In My Face'); soulful numbers ('Remove This Doubt', 'Please Stay', 'Running Out Of Fools'); standards ('The Very Thought Of You'); and songs from the great pop singer-songwriters (Bob Dylan's 'I Threw It All Away', Randy Newman's 'I've Been Wrong Before', and Ray Davies's 'Days') on the record.*

With Kevin Killen producing, the band cut through the material quickly. Most of the tracks were played loud and live, befitting a record which was clearly an exercise in fun and self-fulfilment rather than anything particularly bold or exciting. Elvis had played most of the material during his solo gigs, or with The Confederates and The Rude 5 over the past few years, and it had rarely shone. More often than not, it was performed with a kind of sturdy, uninspired deference. It was musician's music, the kind that's often more fun to play than to listen to. 'We just went in and had a ball on that album,' admits Jerry Scheff. 'I don't think he ever expected it to sell a tremendous amount, it was just a labour of love.'

The recording in Barbados was completed in two weeks, whereupon backing vocals were added in London and the album was finished.

---

*Elvis also cut a version of the Grateful Dead's 'Ship Of Fools', which would be left off the final album, appearing instead on *Deadicated*, a tribute record released in 1991.

However, Warners apparently saw little commercial appeal in the often obscure cover material and in any case, with Elvis planning a 'proper' album release in the new year, they didn't want too many albums flooding the market in a short space of time. Over the next few years the record – eventually titled *Kojak Variety* – would become widely bootlegged before its release in 1995, but it was far from being a lost classic.

His thirst to be a singer in a bar band sated, work started on the new record at Ocean Way in Hollywood in the summer. The leaps in Elvis's interests and ambitions quickly made a mockery of Mitchell Froom's initial plan to make 'a record where almost nothing happens'. On *Mighty Like A Rose,* everything happened, often all at once.

As a direct result of his curiosity about classical music, Elvis had taken a radically different approach to his newer compositions, often writing several overlapping melodies for each piece of music. This, of course, was at the very core of orchestral music, but ran against the traditional, idiomatic rock or pop premise of a primary melody and perhaps a simple harmony and little else.

'He had bought a computer, and he started messing around with a lot of different melodic lines and counter melodies,' says Mitchell Froom. 'It was a new writing tool for him. You could have an unlimited number of different lines going on. It would be orchestral, almost, and there was this very dense, complicated music arising.'

It didn't necessarily mean that the songs were complicated in terms of their basic structure; they could all still be played on an acoustic guitar. But it did mean that Elvis wanted much more from the finished product. As with *Spike*, all the songs were written well before Elvis entered the studio, and the home demos for the album were more detailed than anything he had recorded before, his ideas illustrated with far greater precision.

The more harmonically involved numbers such as 'Harpies Bizarre', 'All Grown Up', 'Invasion Hit Parade' and 'The Other Side Of Summer' came to the studio with their instrumental parts already set in stone, while the string or brass arrangements had been worked out on a computer and played on keyboards. 'Sweet Pear' had a precise guitar solo that had been devised as part of the song, rather than as an improvisation.

Lyrically, his vision was equally individual. Elvis was drinking considerable amounts of alcohol around the time he wrote and recorded the album, and there was a certain bleakness in his world-view that filtered into the writing. 'The Other Side Of Summer', 'Hurry Down Doomsday', 'How To Be Dumb', 'After The Fall' and 'Invasion Hit Parade' were dense essays in personal or global decay, with more than a whiff of the apocalypse about them. They also stubbornly defied literal analysis. 'Invasion

Hit Parade', for instance, touched on members of the Underground movement left stranded at the end of the Cold War, someone on a train finding fake limbs, and The Sex-O-Lettes: all the great pop themes, in other words. Even after a twenty-five-minute conversation in which Elvis outlined the song's true meaning, Mitchell Froom was left none the wiser.

As a final pre-production flourish, Elvis had already sequenced the final running order of the record before he entered Ocean Way, an almost unheard of conceit. 'I think Elvis struggles with his music but the struggle is private one,' ponders Marc Ribot. 'When he comes into the studio he works.'

The idea of using The Attractions on the new record had quickly and somewhat predictably hit a brick wall. Elvis claimed their participation was 'scuppered by an unseemly legal squabble' which centred on an argument over whether the band should receive royalties for playing on the record rather than a straight session fee. For The Attractions it was less about greed and more about being properly valued, while for Elvis it was a straightforward business decision. 'It was a simple matter of I made an offer, the offer wasn't enough, and so I got some people who would do the job,'[4] he concluded.

In the end, the core band for what became *Mighty Like A Rose* was full of familiar faces. Having bade a fond farewell to his band of favoured American musicians in Barbados in April, in the absence of The Attractions Elvis found himself rounding them all up again. The group was much smaller than that used on *Spike*: Pete Thomas – firmly back in the fold – and Jim Keltner sharing drum duties, T-Bone Wolk and Jerry Scheff on bass, Larry Knetchel, Benmont Tench and Mitchell Froom on assorted keyboards, Marc Ribot and James Burton on guitar.

With Elvis asserting such close control over his music, recording was never likely to be an easy experience. Since *Goodbye Cruel World*, it had never been his custom to compromise or defer to a producer in the studio, and he was at his most assertive and ambitious on *Mighty Like A Rose*. He was always in charge, fiercely protective of his vision, and the musicians had far less room for improvisation and self-expression than there had been on *Spike*. 'Mighty Like A Rose was a more tightly controlled record,' admits Ribot. 'He was actively studying arranging ideas and he wanted to hear them back. I have to say that I was highly sceptical, but one can't and one shouldn't get in the way of that process.'

With very few exceptions, all the basic tracks on the record were cut live, no matter how ambitious the arrangement. On 'The Other Side Of Summer', for instance, there were eleven musicians playing simultaneously, before Elvis double-tracked the entire song – in the same way that had given Billy Sherill such a blast on *Almost Blue's* 'Why Don't You Love Me Like You Used To

Do?' back in 1981 – to achieve the dense, Spector-esque effect, everything threatening to topple over at any point. As if that wasn't enough, Elvis then added three separate vocal harmony lines over the basic melody, to the bemusement of Mitchell Froom and engineer Kevin Killen. 'We were saying, "We can't hear anything, there's too much singing, we can't pick out the words",' says Froom. 'And Elvis said, "Oh really? I hear all that very clearly." I think he hears music in such a way it's almost like a hyper-ear.'

The kitchen sink production style came to charcterise the whole record. 'Nothing,' claimed Elvis, 'seemed beyond the realm of the pop song.'[5] When it worked, such an approach could be very effective: 'So Like Candy' was crammed with little instrumental details and motifs, teasing the tension from a terrific band performance. But good ideas and even songs sometimes got lost in a maze of the heavy-handed production and wilfully obtuse renditions of often simple songs.

'How To Be Dumb' was perhaps the most straightforward and musically familiar track on the record. A big, melodic number with Hammond organ stabs and sweeping grand piano aping the classic Steve Nieve style, lyrically it was a none-too-subtle riposte to Bruce Thomas, or the 'funniest fucker in the world', as Elvis chose to call him.

The Big Wheel had been published in 1990 and Bruce had sent a copy to Elvis as 'a matter of courtesy'. He wasn't best pleased. 'I remember him singing 'How To Be Dumb',' says Mitchell Froom. 'It was a cathartic experience. He came into the control room covered in sweat, and all I remember is being very relieved that the song wasn't about me!'

Towards the end of the sessions, the Hollywood smog began messing with Elvis's throat, and after a brief hiatus – which included a performance with Neil Young in the San Fernando Valley – he returned to England to complete the record in Westside Studios in the winter of 1990. The Dirty Dozen Brass Band flew over from New Orleans to play on 'Sweet Pear' and 'Interlude', while Elvis finished off the vocals and added strings and brass overdubs to the tapes. Fiachra Trench orchestrated 'All Grown Up', 'Harpies Bizarre' and 'Georgie And Her Rival', and although he was one of the best in the business, Elvis ached at the frustration of handing his lovingly prepared arrangements over to someone else.

While in London, there was also time to fit in some other business. A songwriting session with Paul McCartney at the beginning of December produced 'three nice songs', according to McCartney, probably including 'Mistress And Maid'. Perhaps more significantly, on 8 December, Elvis and Cait saw the Swedish mezzo-soprano Anne Sofie Von Otter perform Brahms and a set of Scandinavian lieders at London's Wigmore Hall. Elvis had first seen Von Otter perform in 1989, but it was this concert that finally made him swoon. 'I was moved beyond words,' he said. 'I have haunting memories of that night.'[6] She would stay in his mind for many years to come.

* * *

By the time Elvis returned to Ocean Way in the New Year to mix *Mighty Like A Rose*, he was essentially working on two projects. The previous year, he had agreed to compose the soundtrack music for Alan Bleasdale's latest TV series, *GBH*, alongside avant-garde film composer Richard Harvey, scheduled for transmission on Channel Four in the summer of 1991. Elvis had acted for Bleasdale before, and the two shared similar, left-wing values. 'They have an enormous amount of respect for each other,' says Harvey. 'And Alan really rates Elvis's writing, which is a huge compliment.'

The idea for the collaboration had been made by the director, Robert Young, in 1990. Elvis was given scripts of the series and later rough-cut videos, developing character studies and working on mood pieces until he knew the raw material inside out. It was a bruising process, writing and recording music for eleven hours' worth of television drama, turning around each ninety-minute episode in approximately ten days. Essentially, it was like scoring a full-length movie every week and a half.

Mostly, these frantic undertakings were done apart. Elvis sketched out musical themes while he was mixing *Mighty Like A Rose*, making demos in the studio while Kevin Killen and Mitchell Froom were working in the control room. He was working extremely hard on what might be called musical literacy, struggling to put across his more sophisticated musical ideas without the aid of being able to read or write music. He would put his work onto cassettes or MIDI print-outs from his computer, trying as best he could to cut through his feelings of frustration to present the results as fluently as possible.

He would then send his work to Richard Harvey, or call him with outlines of what he wanted to do. 'He would leave answerphone messages in some insomnia-fuelled frenzy,' says Harvey. 'The phone would click and I would have between twenty minutes and half an hour's worth of ideas to work on; or we would have two-hour phone conversations. He almost drove me to a breakdown, it was eighteen to twenty-hour days.'

Among the musical ideas that Elvis sent to Harvey were *Mighty Like A Rose*'s 'Couldn't Call It Unexpected', which became part of the closing title theme of *GBH*, plus fragments that were later developed for *The Juliet Letters*. Harvey would pick the bones out of the music, then orchestrate it, often rearranging it substantially and adding textural material in the process.

Despite the long-distance working methods, it was a genuine collaboration and co-production. And although it was a fraught process for both men, recording the twenty-two instrumentals with a full orchestra in London between February and May 1991 made all the panic worth while. 'To stand there and have fifty people play one of your tunes and it not accompany anything except pictures is about the most exciting experience I've had in the studio in a long while,'[7] said Elvis.

He was rewarded in other ways. On 22 March 1992, Elvis and Richard Harvey won a BAFTA for Best Television Soundtrack for *GBH*. Elvis didn't attend the ceremony, but he did repeat the collaboration in 1995 on *Jake's Progress,* an eight-and-a-half-hour long TV drama written by Bleasdale for Channel Four. Elvis and Harvey again worked together on the score, although there was much more individual composition and less collaboration than there had been on *GBH*. Perhaps that was why it didn't quite scale the same heights.

* * *

'The Other Side Of Summer' was released as a single on 2 April 1991, heralding the arrival of *Mighty Like A Rose* three weeks later. A deliberately over-the-top Beach Boys pastiche, the single reached No. 43 in the UK charts, a faintly disappointing result for one of his most commercial songs for years. In retrospect, the video of Elvis looking like a busker on Brighton beach may not have helped.

The album was a more unified affair than *Spike*, with stronger songwriting, but it was a dense and difficult record, undeniably burdened by the bleakness of the mood which inspired it. Elvis's harsh, contrary singing in particular meant that many of the tenderest songs on the record – 'All Grown Up', 'Couldn't Call It Unexpected No. 4', 'So Like Candy' – failed to get the vocal performances that the richness of the music and melodies deserved.

This juxtaposition of grimness and beauty was deliberate, but the over-riding sensation was of melody and the song being sacrificed in a dizzying maze of vaulting and often misguided ambition. 'You hear the further outreaches of his musical mind on it,' admits Mitchell Froom. 'I thought a few things were successful; maybe a few things were overdone.' Just maybe. The opening five-song assault was amongst the most all-encompassing litany of social and cultural scepticism Elvis had ever recorded, but the production turned the songs into over-stuffed sofas, uncomfortable, misshapen, the springs poking out all over the place.

Elsewhere, 'After The Fall' was simply dreary and depressing, 'Georgie And Her Rival' was far too busy, its bright pop melody lost in an avalanche of detail, while it was a struggle to hear how songwriters of the calibre of Elvis and Paul McCartney could have spent more than a solitary lunch break on 'Playboy To A Man'. Fittingly, Elvis barked the vocal through a metal pipe.

Even when the album reached a kind of exhausted and very personal hopefulness on the trio of songs that ended the record, the gorgeous melody and genuine regret of 'Couldn't Call It Unexpected No. 4' was saddled with a circus-like arrangement which did the song few favours. All in all, there were far too many layers, too many curves. The end result wasn't dazzling, just heavy, difficult and misconceived. Not a record for the faint-hearted.

There were plenty of favourable reviews, but generally (aside from Almost Blue) Mighty Like A Rose attracted the worst notices of Elvis's career. The NME seemed to view the orchestral flourishes as a signal that this was some kind of follow-up to Imperial Bedroom, and measured it harshly against old glories. 'Even the "good" tracks – a lamentable four out of thirteen – would pant with shame if forced to socialise with the bulk of his back catalogue,' said Barbara Ellen. 'The music for the most part is self-indulgent and sour, or lazy and glutinously sweet. Worst of all, it's dull.' The Independent struggled to find 'crumbs of melodic comfort. It's a case of too many cooks cluttering up nearly every song.' The Times laced an utterly negative review with the preface that Elvis had swapped his 'wimpish geek look in favour of a more organic, got-1op-for-a-cup-of-tea-mate image'.

Many of the reviews in Britain made much of the dramatic change in Elvis's appearance, used as apparent evidence of a general loss of focus or a sign of rock star megalomania. 'I apparently let some people down who didn't want me to change my image,' mused Elvis. 'I'd successfully buried the geek guy for good. But it's my life and my body, and if I want to fuck myself up and have a beard and wear my hair long, that's my business. I have my own reasons for that change of image – some of them personal, some of them just damn wilful.'[8]

Even Warner Brothers, generally supportive in the early part of their working relationship, were somewhat dismayed by his change in his appearance. Executives from the record company began dismissing Mighty Like A Rose as the 'beard record'.

There was undoubtedly a degree of myth-breaking in the new image. 'Quite rightly, he invented a look [in the past] that a whole lot of people wanted to copy, but the problem is that the mask can turn on you and strangle you after a while,' says Marc Ribot. 'It's good to break it, and if it pisses people off, well, fuck 'em.' However, the fuss created over the new image was in reality something of a smokescreen. Elvis wasn't the first man in musical history with a very clear and identifiable image to have shunned the barber. Ask The Beatles. If people were having trouble relating to the man with the beard and the long hair, it was principally because Elvis had released an album that was almost impossible to warm to. Far from burying the 'geek guy', it was the long-haired Elvis incarnation who took on the status of an imposter – and eventually got buried instead.

He rehearsed in California through May in preparation for the 'Come Back In A Million Years' tour, breaking cover for a TV appearance on *Saturday Night Live* in New York on 18 May, where he performed 'So Like Candy' and 'The Other Side Of Summer'. Then it was on to the rest of America.

There was a rigidity about the shows, largely unanimated affairs focusing on material from *Spike* and *Mighty Like A Rose*, with a smattering of the 'Barbados' covers thrown in. Elvis usually opened with a contemplative take on 'Accidents Will Happen', backed by a truncated Rude 5 featuring Pete Thomas, Larry Knetchel, Jerry Scheff and Marc Ribot, but there was a limited and generally predictable display of old Attractions material. Only the occasional inclusion of 'Suit Of Lights', 'Watch Your Step', 'New Lace Sleeves', 'Temptation' and 'Home Is Anywhere You Hang Your Head' could have been considered surprises, while for some reason, 'The Other Side Of Summer' had been transformed into an uptempo waltz, sacrificing most of its melody in the process.

Yet there was a darkness and anger in the performances that hadn't been heard for some time. Ironically, despite the beard, the baggy suits and the dearth of old material, there was more here that bore comparison with the withering disgust of the younger Elvis Costello than might have met the eye. Only this time it was global, rather than personal.

Five dates into the tour Elvis was already apologising for the hoarseness of his voice, and when he came to tape a show for MTV's *Unplugged* programme on 3 June he was in even poorer vocal shape, with the result that a mere twenty-four minutes of the set was eventually broadcast. By the time he reached New York's Madison Square Gardens on 22 June, however, he seemed to be back-firing on something approaching all cylinders. Stephen Holden from the *New York Times* found the music 'richly fleshed out and at moments even operatic. If Costello's world view is still forbiddingly gloomy, his music has expanded into something much larger than post-punk minimalism.'

It was when the tour reached Europe in July that the battle really commenced. *Mighty Like A Rose* had managed a respectable No. 5 placing in the charts in Britain, but it had not sold terribly well and had already had something of a critical savaging. Following a near-fifteen-year run of critical adulation in his homeland, the time seemed ripe for some extra scores to be settled.

Even before it came to reviewing the music, there was already resentment in the air. It was the first time that The Rude 5 had performed in Britain, and there seemed to be some residual animosity about the fact that The Attractions weren't there, as if this new, classical-loving Costello was somehow looking down upon his past and the band that did so much to create it. This basic hostility may not have been helped by the relative paucity of old songs in the set, and fact that *GBH* – featuring Elvis and Richard Harvey's classical score – was airing on Channel Four as the tour progressed. Furthermore, Elvis's ragged appearance and weight gain were almost constantly referred to: 'Long-haired, bearded bum'; 'eccentric uncle'; and 'Elvis Costello these days resembles a continent' were just some of the jibes.

But these were only peripheral factors. The primary fact remained that the shows were often uninspired, and many critics and fans alike simply didn't have time for much of the new material Elvis was playing. On the first of six nights at the Hammersmith Odeon on 1 July, the response veered from lukewarm to openly hostile; the audiences were strangely undemonstrative, seemingly unsure of who it really was beneath the beard.

The headline above a stunningly critical review in *Melody Maker* simply read 'The Imposter', while another proclaimed: 'This Year's Muddle'. The next night at the Odeon, Elvis responded to a shout from the audience calling him a genius. 'Ah, not yet I'm not,' he replied. 'That's next week. And the week after that I'll be a fucking idiot again.'

The sets were merely solid rather than spectacular, similar in composition to the ones in the States, although 'Oliver's Army' and 'Watching The Detectives' were added to most concerts. There was a single rendition of 'Shipbuilding' in Glasgow and airings for 'Almost Blue' in London and Bristol. 'Tramp The Dirt Down' – virtually meaningless in America – also came into the British set, sung solo and complete with a post-Thatcher verse encompassing the 'glove puppet' Prime Minister John Major, calling for him to 'Kick the royal cuckoos out of the nest/And place the Queen Mother under arrest.'

On 16 July Elvis fulfilled a long-standing – and financially suicidal – commitment to return to the Shetland Isles with a band, playing the Clickimim Centre in Lerwick, where he seemed to get a kick out of playing for locals rather than sneering critics. From there it was on to the rest of Europe, where there were a handful of cancellations due to poor ticket sales.

The torrential 'Tokyo Storm Warning' became the new opening song on most of the remaining tour dates, first played at the Irish Feile festival on 3 August, and carried over into the second leg of their American tour a few days later. The derision was becoming contagious. 'Costello has the musical equivalent of Woody Allen Syndrome,' said Fred Schuster in the *Daily News*. 'He wants to be taken for a mature, serious artist; his public wants the funny songs.' Schuster then went on to rate Elvis's performance at the Universal Amphitheatre on 17 August as exuding 'all the passion and personality of a plate of cottage cheese. It hurts to say it: Elvis is dead.'

Chapter Thirteen
1991–93

THE NEXT DECADE SAW ELVIS COSTELLO moving even further away from the solid ground of being Britain's greatest, most incisive songwriter, into less certain, less convenient territory. Along the way, he effectively ceased to be anything remotely resembling a pop star.

He was thirty-seven years old and keen to test himself further by exploring the outer reaches of his fascinations. Far from being daunted by the negative press for *Mighty Like A Rose*, Elvis felt he was only beginning to touch the surface of his capabilities, and was as sure as ever of the intrinsic value of his artistic instincts. 'Critcism just makes him more determined in his own way to do whatever he wants to do,' says Mitchell Froom. 'And *Mighty Like A Rose* gave him the confidence to do anything.'

The logical conclusion of Elvis's obsession with classical music was to start working and writing squarely within that idiom. His on going enchantment with the Brodsky Quartet and his frequent attendance at their concerts had not gone unnoticed by Warner Brothers, who were also the Brodsky's record label. A meeting between the two parties was subsequently engineered following one of their lunchtime Shostakovich concerts at the South Bank Centre in London in November 1991; the get-together between the Quartet, Elvis and Cait in the Archduke Wine Bar, proved a spectacular success, each of them quickly establishing a bond which had little to do with high-brow classicism, but rather was founded on personal chemistry and wide-ranging musical enthusiasm. 'From the first afternoon we met, we were discussing the possibility of collaboration,' said Elvis. 'It was a very natural thing.'[1]

The lunch meeting dragged on happily until seven o'clock in the evening, when everyone suddenly remembered they had other places to be. As they drifted out to the street to say their goodbyes, the six began crossing the road back towards the Festival Hall. It transpired that they all had tickets for a performance of Mahler's *Seventh Symphony* that night. 'It was really weird,' says Cassidy. 'We went to the concert and then went back to the wine bar! That was a Thursday, and we started work on the Monday.'

Throughout November and December they would meet in the Quartet's rehearsal space at the Amadeus Centre in Maida Vale, north London, and quickly realised that musically they were all coming from the same place. They compiled tapes of their favourite songs and instrumental passages, played music to and for each other, and talked constantly, trying to formulate a musical language that they all understood.

Almost immediately, the Brodsky Quartet realised that Elvis was not some bored, dilettante rock star, dangling his toes in classical music for want of anything better to do. 'We thought that maybe he knew a wee bit about this and a wee bit about that, but the fact that he could talk about orchestral pieces or a Stravinsky ballet was the extraordinary thing,' says Paul Cassidy. 'It was fascinating for us to find that Elvis was not only aware of the music of Shostakovich, for instance, but knew it intimately and was able to say, "You know that bit in the *Fourteenth Symphony*, that's the sort of thing that turns me on".' According to violinist Michael Thomas, 'Elvis [knew] more about classical music than we did.'

Similarly, Elvis was excited and a little relieved to discover that the Quartet were not confined to the cloistered world of classical music. Not only did they know his own music well and had attended many of his concerts, but they also had a wider awareness of the more innovative artists in pop and rock. 'We were able to say to him, "Don't you think Brian Wilson is a genius?",' confirms Cassidy. 'We were aware of Tom Waits and Joni Mitchell and Meredith Monk and Bjork and he was aware of the sort of people we were building up.'

It proved to be an almost perfect mixture of personalities and interests. Before breaking up for a Christmas hiatus in December, they agreed to reconvene in January and February and begin writing together. Already, they had settled on a format. Cait had read a newspaper article about a professor in Verona who had taken it upon himself to reply to the thousands of letters that came addressed to Juliet Capulet, the heroine of Shakespeare's *Romeo and Juliet*. The professor started replying to each letter, until one day he was subjected to allegations of impropriety in the Italian press and subsequently dropped the project. As such, there was a vacancy, and an advert in the British newspapers requested applicants for the job of replying to Juliet's anonymous correspondents. Cait saw the story and showed it to Elvis, who in turn brought it to the attention of the Brodsky Quartet, and they all agreed that it provided a good starting point as a focus for the project: the letter form.

* * *

By his return in mid-January, Elvis had achieved two new personal landmarks: he had learned to read and write music; and – perhaps just a little less remarkably – he had written an entire album for Wendy James.

In the late '80s, British trash-pop band Transvision Vamp had launched a minor pop career based on James' overtly sexual pose and the ability to come up with a decent quote. At the Feile festival the previous August, James had watched Elvis from the wings with admiration and envy as the last seconds of her fifteen minutes of fame ebbed away. 'I could see that everything he was saying and doing were in my heart and mind as well,' she later said. 'People might take at face value the music of Transvision Vamp and the way I had behaved in the past and the way Elvis conducted himself and think we were poles apart, but we're not.'[2]

Having decided to leave the band, Wendy James put her rather optimistic theory to the test. When she bumped into Pete Thomas in America while on an autumn promotional tour, Pete had suggested – without any promises – that she contact Elvis if she was interested in his work. A little later, James claims she sat down in Washington and wrote Elvis a letter. 'It was a bit like a letter to an agony aunt,' she said. 'I wrote down all the reasons why I wasn't really a happy person – not with my emotional life, but with my musical life. I simply said, "I need to get better, and you're what I consider is better. So can something be done?".'[3]

Within two weeks, Pete Thomas called to tell Wendy James that Elvis and Cait had written her an entire album. It had been composed between Friday evening and Sunday night, a weekend diversion for their own amusement as much as anything else. With its echoes of The Stones writing for Marianne Faithfull, or Lee Hazelwood for Nancy Sinatra, it's likely that the Svengali-ish nature of the project also appealed to him. 'We did it as a kind of gag,' Elvis admitted. 'I just took some fragmentary things from the odd newspaper article which told me what she was supposed to represent and then invented a character for her which she could probably play.'[4]

The songs were short and simple, closest in feel to *This Year's Model* out-takes and a world away from anything Elvis had written recently. Lyrically, they referenced a litany of London landmarks, and baited James into conceding that her wildly ambitious, loud-mouthed public persona was something of a joke, and not a very good one at that. The first song was called 'This Is A Test'. Another, 'Puppet Girl'.

Elvis went into Pathway with Pete, and over two days they knocked the ten songs together in single takes, Elvis playing guitar and bass and a little piano, and Pete on drums. When James returned to Britain from the US in December there was a demo tape of an entire album's worth of material waiting for her at her flat. 'I thought I'd landed in heaven,' she said. 'It was only later it dawned on me that it was now down to me to do something with it.'5

Despite her public enthusiasm, James was reportedly a little reluctant to record all the songs as a piece, but Elvis's all-or-nothing ultimatum eventually forced her hand. When the album was finally released in March 1993, entitled *Now Ain't The Time For Your Tears*, it failed to have the impact that she desired. Her voice hadn't improved any, the songs sounded tinny and badly produced, and it would prove to be the last record she would make. As Elvis had had nothing to do with the making of the album other than writing the songs and letting James get on with it, he claimed not to care one way or the other.

Learning to write music, in contrast, was serious stuff, and the minimum commitment Elvis felt was required to make his work with the Brodskys an equal and enjoyable collaboration. He had resisted making the leap into notation for some time, wary that he might be disconnected from the impulse of simply creating music by instinct. 'I didn't want to lose sight of the other way of writing songs,' he admitted. 'Just picking up a guitar and making a noise and getting something out quick.'6

However, neither did he want the frustrations he felt when relying on Richard Harvey to orchestrate his ideas on *GBH*, or Fiachra Trench on *Mighty Like A Rose*, to compromise him on this project. So he taught himself – with the help of a tutor in Ireland – the basic craft of reading and writing music in about a month. Although Elvis was some way down the road to musical notation already, and initially he was only able to work painstakingly slowly, it was nevertheless an astonishing accomplishment. 'It's a very complicated process,' says Paul Cassidy. 'It's something I learnt over the years, gradually.'

Composition with the Brodsky Quartet began in earnest in the New Year of 1992. They were already tentatively thinking in terms of an album, but primarily the ensemble were simply playing for their own amusement. They approached it systematically. On any given day they would go home and write a love letter, the next it would be a begging letter, or a chain letter, or a postcard, a thank you or a suicide note, coming in the next morning with their homework from the night before. Then they would mesh all the ideas together into something that worked as a whole. 'One of the best ways to work was for one person, namely myself, to be the editor,' explained Elvis. 'Everybody would come with these things and I'd say, "That's great, that bit, that whole paragraph there is really the way his character speaks, and it can be juxtaposed with this". Little by little it came to make up a text.'7

Sometimes, they used extracts from real letters which had been sent to Elvis from fans. The lyrics for the second part of 'I Thought I'd Write To Juliet', for example, were taken verbatim from a letter that was sent to Elvis from a young female soldier called Constance, serving in the Gulf War: 'If I do get home alive, I imagine I will think again,' she wrote. The music itself came organically. When Jacqueline Thomas conjured a siren sound on her cello, it was incorporated into the song.

There was the odd track that Elvis brought in completed, but on the whole they used the same approach that a rock band might take if it were jamming. 'I remember Elvis coming in one day and sitting down and saying, "I've got this really nice little thing I want you to hear",' says Paul Cassidy. 'It was literally a four-bar idea, which subsequently became a little part of 'A Letter Home'. He'd play it on the piano a little bit, someone else would come in with a little riff, and the songs grew.'

The process moved quickly, but it was not without its own particular stresses. It was the first time that any of the Quartet had tried to write original songs, their background being one of interpretation and performance rather than composition, and the emotional vulnerability of providing words in particular proved difficult. 'You can imagine sitting next to one of the greatest lyricists of all time and going, "Your eyes are like the stars," y'know!' Cassidy laughs. 'It was tricky, because you're dealing with another side of each other. If someone comes in and says, "Jesus, sorry, but that lyric's really embarassing," you're touching something else. That was something that we as a quartet had to deal with, that undeniably created a lot of tension.'

By the beginning of March the musicians had all but brought a halt to the writing process, fearing that it would soon become unwieldly. Further time was then spent getting the songs into shape and assembling them in such a way that they would hold together as a unified concept, with a rhythm and a sense of light and shade.

Already, the plan had formulated to record it as an album, but first – as with most classical works – it would have to be performed. The first public flowering of an intense six or seven-month period of work came with the debut performance of this 'work in progress' on 1 July. It took place at the Amadeus Centre before a largely invited audience of about 400 people, including family, friends, and Alan Bleasdale. By the time of the performance the song sequence had been christened *The Juliet Letters* in honour of its original inspiration, and arranged in the order in which it would finally be recorded.

Elvis was shorn of both locks and beard and seemed physically to be something approaching his old self, but he was nervous at the prospect of his first-ever foray into live performance in the classical sphere. And rightly so. 'I caught this feeling at the Amadeus Centre,' says John Woolrich, co-founder of the Composer's Ensemble and a friend of the Brodsky Quartet. 'There was a sniffiness there all right, and quite a lot of "Elvis *who*?".'[8]

The evening was split in two, with an intermission after the opening seven songs, and Elvis stilled any dissenting voices by singing beautifully throughout. He was also unamplified, an acoustic quirk that caused some problems as the adrenalin levels rose. 'We came off for the interval and Elvis just went, "What the fuck?!! What are you doing?? It's so loud!",' recalls Paul Cassidy. 'This was someone who had spent his life in a rock band.'

With an electric instrument, the same noise will emerge unless the volume knob is turned up, which clearly isn't the case with an acoustic instrument. Elvis had been playing with the Brodsky Quartet for six months, but he had never heard them in performance mode, and as soon as he was standing in the middle of the group in concert, the energy levels – and hence the volume – exploded. So did the audience, who gave this unclassifiably seductive music a standing ovation and called them back for an encore, which consisted of the repetition of three songs. They had no other material they could perform together.

Much of the rest of the summer was spent at Dartington Hall in Devon, a sprawling estate that incorporated an arts society. The Brodsky Quartet were in residence at the Dartington International Summer School, an annual gathering which encompassed composing masterclasses, workshops, courses and concerts. It was here, in the fourteenth-century Great Hall on 13 August, that Elvis and the Brodsky Quartet played their second concert in front of their classical peers. It was the same set as the one they played at the Amadeus Centre – the songs and order having been established – but Elvis began the second encore with a new song, the freshly minted 'Favourite Hour', written on piano in a silent rehearsal room. It may have been the most beautiful – if ominous – combination of lyrics and melody he had ever composed.

On either side of the performance at Dartington, Elvis – as plain Declan MacManus – spent time teaching the songwriting class, working diligently and making no attempt to pull rank by explaining who he was. 'He offered a refreshingly new perspective on songwriting,' said John Woolrich, who was a fellow contributor to the course. 'The odd thing was that after two weeks many of our students were still unaware that the talkative guy in horn-rimmed specs, who had been acting as midwife to their hesitant attempts at songwriting, was Elvis Costello.'9 He found the experience and relative anonymity of Dartington energising. It gave him a tiny glimpse into a life he might have chosen, had music not taken him over at such an early age. 'I never went to university, so it was like a little flavour of university life, sitting on the croquet lawn on a sunny afternoon or in the pissing rain,' he said. 'It was very enjoyable and there were lots of great concerts.'10

Played-in and perfected at Dartington, *The Juliet Letters* was recorded quite painlessly in September and early October at Church Studios in Crouch End in London. Produced by Kevin Killen, it was essentially a live recording of the concerts, and the only real technical problem was ensuring that Elvis's voice didn't overpower the instruments in the small studio.

Other than that, it was a case of simply capturing a performance in a room; there was no overdubbing or editing between different takes. 'That's what I love about working with Elvis,' said Killen. 'He takes a lot of chances, and it's always a pleasure to work with someone like that. You know the record is going to be of a certain quality and that vocally the performances are going to be spectacular. They are intense records, both to make and to listen to.'11

As he readied himself for the album's release and a short world tour, Elvis – never happy unless busy – pressed on with other side-projects. Immediately after the album sessions had been concluded in October, he recorded demos of ten cover songs in one day. The songs were a private album for George Jones, following a conversation between Elvis and Jones in *Interview* magazine in which Elvis expressed the hope that Jones might one day record an album of classic songs outside the country genre. Included were Paul Simon's 'Congratulations', Springsteen's 'Brilliant Disguise', Hoagy Carmichael's 'My Resistance Is Low', Gram Parson's 'Still Feeling Blue' and Dylan's 'You're Gonna Make Me Lonesome When You Go', with Elvis backed by Pete Thomas and Paul Riley.

A few days later he renewed his accquaintance with the Count Basie Orchestra, at the Chelsea Arts Ball at the Royal Albert Hall on 9 October. After the embarrassment of his performance with Tony Bennett at the Red Parrot club in 1983, Elvis finally convinced the orchestra he could carry a tune, with versions of 'My Funny Valentine' and 'Lil' Darlin''.

The following week he was due to be in even more exalted company, scheduled to perform 'Positively Fourth Street' at Bob Dylan's fiftieth birthday tribute at Madison Square Garden on 16 October. However, the late addition of the Pope-bashing Irish singer Sinead O'Connor to the bill apparently prompted a last-minute change of heart. 'Catholics, Catholic clergy and Catholic values have become the whipping post for every bigot in America,' said Elvis in a statement. He did not attend the concert, although he later claimed that it was because he was never actually given confirmation of when and where to turn up.

* * *

The Juliet Letters was launched in the appropriately high-brow surroundings of a garden party in The Orangery in Holland Park on 6 January 1993, and released into the shops a week later. It was a truly unique record, fantastically clear and uncluttered-sounding, sometimes very funny, often intensely moving, at times unerringly beautiful, and occasionally falling foul of the basic audacity and ambition of its premise. Above all, after the often harsh vocalisations of *Mighty Like A Rose*, it was a pleasure to hear Elvis singing with such clear, open-throated abandon. It was also nice to hear the Quartet's lyrical contributions; despite what some may have seen as the inhospitable nature of the musical set-up, *The Juliet Letters* was the warmest record Elvis had made since *King Of America*.

The ballads worked best: 'For Other Eyes', 'Taking My Life In Your Hands', 'Why?' and 'The Birds Will Still Be Singing' were beautifully constructed and as emotive as anything Elvis had sung; 'Jacksons, Monk and Rowe', 'Romeo's Séance' and 'Who Do You Think You Are?' were simply great pop songs. At the very heart of the record lay a profoundly moving trilogy: the anti-war lament of 'I Thought I'd Write To Juliet', moving into 'The Last Post' with the sound of an air-raid siren eerily recreated on strings, which then segued into 'The First To Leave', a blasted torch song which wouldn't have sounded out of place on Frank Sinatra's *Only The Lonely*.

Inevitably, there were some misfires. Some of Elvis's more theatrical vocal mannerisms grated on record where they might have worked in concert: 'Swine', 'I Almost Had A Weakness', the opening passage of 'I Thought I'd Write To Juliet' and 'This Offer Is Unrepeatable' tested the listener's patience, while 'Damnation's Cellar' had unfortunate similarities to one of Eric Idle's *Monty Python* compositions. But in general it was a triumphant and seductive record.

Most reviewers concurred. The notices for *The Juliet Letters* were highly complimentary in the main, and not just in the broadsheets and high-brow magazines. *Spin* rated it as 'one of Costello's best', *Newsweek* called him 'a songwriter beyond genre' and *Melody Maker's* perennial fan Allan Jones claimed 'its ambition deserves your perseverance and rewards your time and effort. You know this is an album you're going to be able to live with down the years'.

However, there was a small but predictable amount of sniping here and there at what some saw as pretension and affectation, while others queried

Elvis's motivations. 'To be constantly questioned about the validity of what I'm doing is just tedious,' he later said. 'You can not like it, that's your choice, but to suggest that the things I'm doing are to make myself look more important [is nonsense]. Or the more idiotic criticism you get from classical music critics is that you're doing it to make money.'[12]

With a successful classical record typically selling in the region of 15,000 copies, he had a point. However, Elvis had always been sensitive to poor reviews and, already bruised by the catcalls for *Mighty Like A Rose*, he was more defensive than normal. This was partly because he was especially proud of the unique nature of *The Juliet Letters*, and partly because he felt he was representing four other people who weren't normally thrown to the mercy of fickle pop and rock scribes.

A savage review entitled 'Dead Elvis' in *Vox* magazine raised his ire to the extent that he sent an open letter to the reviewer, Patrick Humphries. Much of it was a slightly childish, aggressive and personal attack on Humphries' writing and apparent lack of intellect, but there was a moment of clarity beneath the rage. '*The Juliet Letters* is not some devious trick, pastiche or bored experiment, it is a beautiful thing,' Elvis wrote. 'To hear it you need ears and you need soul, but consumed as you are by improbable indignation you do not even have the courtesy to acknowledge that many of the songs were written with or by members of the Brodsky Quartet.'

The members of the Quartet appreciated his allegiance, even if it seemed a little reactionary. 'Elvis – bless him – was absolutely adamant that we put across that this was a five-way collaboration,' says Paul Cassidy. 'We were determined to show that we were working together, this was not him sending us some songs to make into a string quartet.'

The world tour kicked off at Glasgow Royal Concert Hall on 22 February 1993 and took in the major points of the globe in a mere twenty-five days: Scotland, Denmark, Germany, England, France, Holland, Italy, Spain, Japan and the USA, ending at the New York Town Hall on 18 March. Each night, Elvis would step out onto the stage with *The Juliet Letters* songbook, which he placed on a music stand throughout the concert. Some saw this – alongside the dinner jacket, bow-tie and theatrical hand and facial gestures – as a rather ridiculous, grandiose affectation, but Elvis claimed the book was there as a tangible representation of their collective efforts, to reinforce the idea that this was a genuine collaboration. But it was also there to hide behind. Elvis had never spent so long on stage without a guitar.

Aside from *The Juliet Letters*, performed in full and in sequence each night, there were extra treats in store for the audiences – a new song by Elvis and Michael Thomas called 'King Of The Unknown Sea', an arrangement of 'Almost Blue', and some handpicked covers: The Beach Boys'

'God Only Knows', the children's song 'Scarlet Ribbons', Tom Waits's 'More Than Rain', Jerome Kern's 'They Didn't Believe Me' and Kurt Weill's 'Lost In The Stars'. The traditional Irish song, 'She Moved Through The Fair', was added to the set especially for the show in Boston on 17 March, arranged by Irishman Paul Cassidy in honour of St Patrick's Day.

The next night, following the final date of the tour in New York, there was an added surprise for Elvis and the Quartet at the post-show party. Outside, a young woman came up to the steward and introduced herself as Constance, the female soldier who had written to Elvis during the Gulf War and whose letter he had used for the lyrics of 'I Thought I'd Write To Juliet'. She had returned safely from the Gulf and the day before the concert had completed her military service. 'That was really spooky,' says Cassidy. 'The more cynical amongst us would say she was Isobel MacGowan from Dumfries, but actually I believe it was her.'

The Juliet Letters material proved to be incredibly forceful on stage. The concerts were almost universally well-received, and audience responses were often ecstatic. It may have had less impact on record, but that didn't necessarily explain why wasn't it shifting more copies. 'I know by the reaction of people that that album could have been really huge,' says Cassidy. 'And [Warners] buried it. They buried it because they didn't understand it.'

Although the record company had been content to let Elvis record the album, they didn't really consider it to be 'proper' Costello product. It was viewed largely as an indulgence, an amusing side-step before Elvis got on with the job of making music with a beat again. 'I actually had someone very senior at Warner Brothers at that time say, "This *Juliet Letters* would be all right if it just sounded more like 'Eleanor Rigby',"' Elvis said. 'I said, "Yeah, but Paul McCartney already made that record. Why would we want to make that again? We're trying to make a record that's *not* like 'Eleanor Rigby'."'[13]

The Juliet Letters reached No. 8 in the UK charts and sold well throughout Europe, but it didn't chart in the States, the first Elvis album containing original material to fail to do so. Elvis – still seemingly convinced that everything he touched had inate commercial potential – thought he knew where to lay the blame.

Even so, it had been a short and very successful world tour. There was certainly scope for many more concerts, but there was something in the format and the songs that seemed to preclude over-kill. *The Juliet Letters* was a very personal statement from five people, and they chose to protect it, to be unwrapped occasionally as a rare and beguiling treat. 'Elvis's shows are always full on,' says Paul Cassidy. 'He doesn't hold back ever. But when you're standing in New York Town Hall without a mike – *that's* heavy duty.'

Chapter Fourteen
1993-95

HE COULD NEVER STAY IN ONE PLACE for long. Just as Elvis was getting to grips with the formal structures of writing and reading music, the weekend songwriting spree and primal demo recordings that he and Pete Thomas had made for Wendy James in Pathway at the end of 1991 had reconnected him with the idea of making louder, simpler music again.

Following the end of *The Juliet Letters* album sessions, Elvis had toyed with an embryonic vision of a noisy record called *Idiophone*, playing everything himself, with Pete Thomas adding percussion. In November 1992, he had gone into Pathway with Pete and cut a few exploratory tracks with just guitar, vocals and drums. With Kevin Killen again roped in on production duties, work soon moved from Pathway to The Church Studios in early December, where Elvis overdubbed bass onto the ultra-raw takes of 'Kinder Murder' and '20% Amnesia' and toyed with an extended rant called 'Poisoned Letter', quite possibly aimed at *Vox*'s Patrick Humphries and his ilk.

Early in these trial sessions, Elvis had realised that his own instrumental limitations were going to hold some of the more involved material back. A chance meeting in a London studio solved the conundrum. Steve Nieve was playing on a session by Sam and Dave stalwart Sam Moore, which included 'Why Can't A Man Stand Alone?', a song Elvis had written specifically for the soul singer. When Elvis popped down to see how the recording was going, he inadvertently ran into the Attraction. The two hadn't seen each other for some years, but Steve had apparently decided that enough time had elapsed since their falling out back in 1987 to let bygones be bygones. 'We got chatting in the break over a tea, and I was invited to a session where Elvis was cutting tracks with Pete Thomas,' said Nieve. 'That was how casually [it] began.'[1]

Although the mood at the first studio session for six years was 'a little formal',[2] according to Elvis, the three-quarters-Attractions trio quickly cut piano, drums and vocal versions of 'Favourite Hour', 'You Tripped At

Every Step', 'This Is Hell' and 'London's Brilliant Parade' at Church Studios. Nick Lowe also popped in to play bass on 'Poisoned Letter'.

It was all slightly chaotic. Elvis had a lot of very beautiful, quite slow material, but after *The Juliet Letters* he wanted to make a raw, rocky record. Producer Kevin Killen was somewhat confused at what was required of him and decided to bow out. Furthermore, there were forthcoming promotional duties and a tour for *The Juliet Letters* to attend to immediately after Christmas. With things in a general state of flux, the *Idiophone* sessions were put on hold until after the spring commitments. By then, Elvis hoped, he would have written some more material and have a clearer idea of the kind of record he wanted to make.

Upon his return from touring the world with the Brodsky Quartet in February and March 1993, Elvis's thoughts quickly returned to the next record. He realised he needed more upbeat material and wrote on guitar throughout the spring and summer, when he spent part of his time in Florence with Cait. It was a month-long working holiday. Cait was taking a doctorate in Classics, and they spent much of their time studying the Italian language and visiting museums and art galleries.

Following the template of the tracks he had recorded before Christmas, the new songs were much simpler than those on *Mighty Like A Rose* and came quickly: indeed, the bare bones of 'Rocking Horse Road', 'Pony Street', 'Clown Strike', 'Still Too Soon To Know', '13 Steps Lead Down' and 'Just About Glad' were all written in a single day, swift work even for Elvis. 'I would work for about half an hour with the guitar cranked up really loud, and make a tape of just anything that came into my head,' he said. 'I did it in bursts, and then I listened to see if any of it was interesting. A lot of it was gibberish.'[3]

However, the stronger material began to rise to the surface. He added 'All The Rage' and 'My Science Fiction Twin', both formed when 'Poisoned Letter' was split into three parts, Elvis keeping many of the words for the former, a bass riff and a snatch of melody for the latter, and discarding the third. 'Sulky Girl' soon followed. Combined with the material that he had attempted to record at Pathway and Church Studios, he now had enough songs for an album.

Elvis demo-ed most of the new songs in Pete Thomas's basement studio, with Nick Lowe on bass. With Mitchell Froom again pencilled in to co-produce, the plan was to make a stripped down combo record, with a number of ballads included. However, there were problems with the band line-up. Lowe regarded himself as strictly a rhythm man, and wasn't particularly at ease playing bass on the slower, more intricate material. When Elvis sent the demos to Froom in Los Angeles, he also felt that some of the songs needed another style of bass playing. The producer had recently been working with Bruce Thomas on albums by Richard Thompson and Suzanne Vega, and tentatively suggested that perhaps the ex-Attraction could provide the kind of inspiration that some of Elvis's new songs required. 'At first Elvis hated the idea,' says Froom. 'But I think he started thinking about it musically and then he came back and said, "Maybe Bruce and I will get together and have a cup of tea or something. And just see".'

Elvis's immediate misgivings had little to do with music and everything to do with personality. After the numerous snipes and counter-snipes between singer and bass player over the last few years, topped off with the bridge-burning *The Big Wheel*, he seriously doubted whether they could pull off being in the same room together again, never mind the same band.

On the other side of the Atlantic, Mitchell Froom also had to do a little coaxing to get Bruce Thomas enthused. However, the bass player's animosity towards Elvis had softened considerably with the knowledge that Steve Nieve had buried the past and was back on board. Eventually the call came from Elvis, who was in Britain at the time. 'He actually rang up in the middle of an earthquake in LA,' Thomas recalls. 'I said, "Look, I do want to talk to you but I'm in the middle of an earthquake at the moment!" He was probably quite pleased to have had an impact.'

Sessions for the new album began at Olympic Studios in London in early August, with Elvis, Pete Thomas and Steve Nieve back in place, and Nick Lowe playing bass. Bruce was due to arrive from Los Angeles a little later. To paraphrase an early Elvis song, Steve chose to be amused rather than disgusted. Elvis was 'exactly as he was before', he recalled. 'He wanted to record without giving anyone a chance to know what they were doing. He was really animated, always moving the microphones or behind the mixing desk pushing all the faders. Normally people do their singing and that's it. It's not like that with Elvis.'[4]

'Kinder Murder' and '20% Amnesia' were already complete, left red-raw and untouched from the very earliest Pete and Elvis sessions at Pathway back in November 1992. The rest of the material came together quite easily. Nick Lowe played bass on the more Attractions-sounding tracks, while Elvis, Steve and Pete quite clearly hadn't forgotten how to conjure up the old magic on songs like 'Rocking Horse Road' and 'Just About Glad'.

The sessions had produced seven songs before Bruce Thomas arrived back on the scene to complete the somewhat accidental reunion. Initially, the mood was 'cautious and respectful'.[5] Nobody wanted the intensity and strained feelings of the *Blood & Chocolate* sessions to resurface this time around. 'We *elected* to get on,' said Bruce Thomas, summing up the general tenor of tolerance and patience – perhaps it was maturity – which characterised the sessions. 'We put a sticking plaster on it.' Elvis also made a concerted effort not to dwell on the past, buying Bach's *Preludes* for Bruce for his birthday and generally making an effort to meet the bass player halfway.

The music fell into place immediately, but then the music had never really been the problem. 'I got this great moment,' says Mitchell Froom. 'I mean, I was an Attractions fan, so I got to see the first rehearsal where the four of them were back in a room together. They'd all gotten the tapes and the first thing they played was 'Sulky Girl', and it took about fifteen seconds for it to sound great. It was just right back. After they played that song they all laughed, saying, "Well, we know how to do this, I guess!".'

From that point on it all went relatively smoothly. It was actually a much easier experience than the making of *Mighty Like A Rose*, and the group quickly knocked off the remaining tracks. The record was finished by October, mixed and sequenced at Sound Factory in Los Angeles by the end of the year, whereupon it was played to executives at the Warners' New Year party. There would, they noted with relief, be no string quartet on this record.

* * *

After visiting Canada with the Brodsky Quartet early in 1994, performing Kurt Weill's 'Lost In The Stars' for a film tribute to the great European songwriter, Elvis undertook heavy promotional duties in Europe throughout February and March. These included The Attractions' first appearance on *Top Of The Pops* for ten years, performing 'Sulky Girl', which reached No. 22 in the UK charts in early March. It was Elvis's biggest hit single since 'Pills And Soap' in 1983.

Finally called *Brutal Youth* after a line from the closing 'Favourite Hour', the album was released on 7 March. Predictably, the critics focused on the return to a more familiar, welcoming sound after *The Juliet Letters* and *Mighty Like A Rose*, while the reformation of The Attractions grabbed most of the headlines. Despite the fact the band only played together on five songs and their name didn't feature on the sleeve, the record was inevitably hailed as a comeback, and Nick Lowe's significant role on the album was all but overlooked.

Brutal Youth was wildly eclectic at heart, much more *Imperial Bedroom* than *Blood & Chocolate* in spirit. It wasn't really a raw record at all, with plenty of surprising little production details buried in many of the songs. However, there were a few typically pulsing moments which were bound to induce a certain amount of nostalgia: the chorus to 'Sulky Girl'; the razor-wire guitar riff and squaddie-baiting squall of 'Kinder Murder'; the shades of 'Radio, Radio' in '13 Steps Lead Down', and the majesterial fade of 'Rocking Horse Road', but they were fewer than many of the rave reviews suggested.

Instead, it was the strange, humourous, slightly off-kilter songs like 'This Is Hell', 'My Science Fiction Twin' and 'Clown Strike' which best summed up the mood of the record. 'Still Too Soon To Know' and 'Favourite Hour' – performed solo on the piano by Elvis – were spare, stark and sorrowful, while 'You Tripped At Every Step' and 'London's Brilliant Parade' were lush, beautiful, compassionate recordings.

The latter in particular was a very personal song: there were mentions of the 'Gates of St Mary's,' the local Catholic primary school in Olympia, where Elvis spent his earliest years; the Hammersmith Palais where Ross plied his trade for so long; and even the Diorama in Euston, where Elvis had first laid eyes on Cait. Elsewhere, there were regretful glances back at youthful bravado in 'Just About Glad', and even a few classic selections from the Costello Book of Puns.

All in all, it was a far more ambitious, melodically broad and warmer record than the lazy *This Year's Model* comparisons often gave it credit for. Nonetheless, there is no doubt that the inclusion of The Attractions and the sense of returning to something fundamental helped the record enormously, and most of the reviews were predicatably euphoric. 'This is an emotional whirlwind,' said Chris Roberts in *Melody Maker*. 'A disciplined stab at perfection, a jaded howl of unabated anguish and a bloody good beat record.' The *NME* awarded it nine out of ten. 'Elvis Costello has made an album that sounds like a debut, with all the fire and fury that entails – and he has brought to it a wise man's brain and wit.' *Q* heard his 'best pop album since 1982', while *CD Review* praised the 'superb melodies, punkish anger, sarcastic wit, creative arrangements, flashes of tenderness, daring and literate lyrics. Although The Attractions don't appear on every track, the old chemistry does.' There were dozens more along similar lines, an outpouring of genuine affection and delight which must have touched even Elvis. It was enough to quickly propel *Brutal Youth* to No. 2 in the UK charts and No. 32 in the States, his best combined placings since *Get Happy!!*. However, the record dropped quickly and in fact did not sell significantly better than his recent releases.

If the album was the appetiser, then the *Brutal Youth* world tour was the proper Attractions reunion. Opening in Vancouver on 3 May with the swift knock-out triptych of 'No Action', 'High Fidelity' and 'The Beat', the spine of each night's set was firmly centred around *This Year's Model* and *Brutal Youth*.

'No Action', 'The Beat', 'You Belong To Me', 'Radio, Radio', 'Lipstick Vogue' and 'Pump It Up' were all regulars, while 'Hand In Hand' and 'This Year's Girl' also made the odd appearance. Almost all of *Brutal Youth* was played every night, while the remaining third of each night's show consisted mainly of classic Attractions material: 'Alison', 'Red Shoes', 'High Fidelity', 'Less Than Zero', 'Clubland', 'New Lace Sleeves', 'Shabby Doll', 'Beyond Belief', 'Party Girl', '(What's So Funny 'Bout) Peace, Love & Understanding', 'Watching The Detectives', 'Accidents Will Happen', and a Merseybeat-style 'Everyday I Write The Book'. *Spike* and *Mighty Like A Rose* were raided for 'Deep Dark Truthful Mirror', 'Veronica' and a rare 'So Like Candy', with the occasional 'Uncomplicated' or 'Honey, Are You Straight Or Are You Blind?' from *Blood & Chocolate*. Rarities included 'Temptation' and a performance of 'Puppet Girl', one of the songs Elvis had written for Wendy James. All in all, it was the closest thing going to a crowd-pleasing, greatest hits set, albeit one that rarely featured 'Oliver's Army' or 'Chelsea'.

Some found great difficulty in reconciling the well-fed, classical music-loving millionaire on stage with the angst-ridden anti-hero who wrote most of these songs in the late '70s. 'Anyone who saw Costello when these songs seemed like fresh wounds couldn't help but recognise how emotionally hollow they seem now,' wrote Greg Kent in the *Chicago Tribune*, after the show at Tingley Park in Illinois on 28 May, claiming that the concert was 'at best nostalgia, at worst hypocrisy'.

It was admittedly a tricky tightrope to walk, but for most observers the undeniable whiff of nostalgia in the setlist was largely nullified by the sheer vigour of the performances. Clearly, everyone involved felt an urgent need to play this music again, even more so considering the rancour that had surrounded the end of the band in the '80s. As they hammered through thirty-odd songs in under two hours each night, with barely a pause in between and little inter-band interaction, it was impossible to feel that this was anything other than a creative collaboration brought on by something deeper and more fundamental than nostalgia or money. It may have been lacking in the trite, on-stage bonhomie of most 'reunions', but then everyone was on-stage for very personal and probably very different reasons. Certainly, there was little sense of someone simply going through the motions. Elvis and The Attractions played for their lives most nights.

The band were in good musical shape and all concerned were managing to survive the early rigours of touring without coming to blows. Elvis and

Pete were thirty-nine years old, almost forty, Bruce was forty-five and Steve thirty-six. Having spent fifteen years on and off the road, they had all finally grown up to a greater or lesser extent, and had other interests outside of music, alcohol and chasing women. Bruce was still interested in literature and increasingly into martial arts, and had combined the two by writing a book on martial arts legend Bruce Lee; Pete Thomas had settled down and was often heard talking about his nine-year-old daughter's progress on the piano; Steve Nieve retreated into his portable computer. Elvis even brought his mother Lilian out to California for a Mother's Day treat to see the show at Concord Pavillion on 8 May. Compared to the madness of old, the US tour was calmness personified.

'I think we're probably less selfish [now],' said Elvis. 'Nobody is going wild. It would be really stupid to think that just because you're playing some of the old songs, you've also got to stay up all night and get drunk. We might have less nervous energy and more physical energy, because we're probably looking after ourselves a bit more.'[6]

Nonetheless, the sense of kinship and comradeship was forever lost. The band were paid as session men, and Elvis seemed rather churlishly reluctant to actually utter the name 'The Attractions', instead referring to the band as 'these gentlemen on stage with me' or similarly vague terminology. 'It was never a band again,' says Bruce Thomas.

Away from the shows, Elvis spent most of his time with Cait, visiting museums, reading and eating well, although it was not always entirely harmonious. Their relationship could be wildly volatile and inconsistent, and there were frequent rows throughout the tour, the rumours of marital discord reaching print in America. And although most of the concerts had been very well attended, audience responses had often been surprisingly muted, given the circumstances. The tour also wasn't helping the record: *Brutal Youth* had slid to No. 195 in the US charts by mid-May and continued its descent thereafter. Neither was there a hint of a hit single which may have helped focus the attention on more current concerns, rather than past glories.

Elvis and The Attractions headed back to Britain in June to play at Glastonbury, the scene of their last British appearance seven years earlier. It was a standard set, notable for the fact that Elvis duly dished out 'Oliver's Army' for the fairweather festival fans and Jake refused to allow any of the performance to be filmed for TV – unlike all the other acts – because permission had not been sought early enough.

It was Jake's last stand, though at the time he probably didn't know it. Following a brief British tour and festivals in Europe throughout July, Elvis and The Attractions took a break for the whole of August. As Elvis turned forty, the indomitable and often fearsome pairing of Riviera and Costello had finally cracked. 'Like Burton and Taylor, [Graham] Taylor and England, and Halpern and Burton's, many great partnerships come to an end,' ran a statement released the following month. 'After seventeen mighty, furious years we have decided to end our working relationship. We remain good pals and do not invite and will not welcome further questions on this matter.'

The off-hand bonhomie of the press release was a smokescreen. The underlying reasons for the split inevitably remained private, mired in nearly two decades' worth of intense personal involvement, but it seemed that the fissure was deep and far from amicable. There were rumours of a backstage bust-up between Riviera and Cait at one of the three Royal Albert Hall shows, which ran between 5–7 July. When Jake showed up for the next British concert at Liverpool Royal Court on the twelfth there were embarrassed glances among the band and the crew, who already knew his fate. By the time July was over 'he was gone', says Bruce Thomas. 'And we never saw him again.'

It is possible that there may also have been some residual tensions at play. 'I think Elvis had to reel in Jake on one or two times – I won't go into details – but let's just say old Mr Riviera was an impetuous sort of person,' says Marc Ribot. Jake had reportedly been unhappy for some time about the direction in which Elvis's career was travelling, while Elvis may have felt that Jake's aggressive style of management didn't sit well with his new classical contacts. He also probably felt that commercially he should be doing somewhat better than he was, especially with *Brutal Youth*, which had sold less than *The Juliet Letters* in the US by the summer of 1994. Indeed, none of Elvis's '90s records had sold more than 200,000 copies in the US.

Neither Jake nor Elvis has ever spoken publicly about their parting of the ways, but Roger Bechirian remained on good terms with Jake and recalls some of the fall-out. 'Certainly, I know Jake would never want to see Elvis for as long as he lives,' says Bechirian. 'He doesn't even buy his records any more. As far as he's concerned, Elvis's ego is so enormous that he needs a truck to drive behind him to carry it, and he [thinks he] just [won't] listen to reason. It hurt Jake tremendously.' A character like Jake Riviera was basically irreplaceable, but in time his role was taken on by Elvis's own management company, By Eleven, under which he started running his own affairs with the day-to-day help of former Riviera-Global assistant Gill Taylor, aided by Chris Difford's elder brother, Lew.

* * *

By the time the tour reached Japan on 17 September, the set had begun to loosen up a little. Elvis was playing a lot of very loud and haphazard solo guitar, a tactic which had begun on the US tour and had increased in Japan, and did little to add to the songs. However, The Attractions had become something approximating the mercilessly well-oiled unit of old, and were more than ready for their first extensive tour of the UK since 1984.

Before the tour kicked off on 3 November, there was a welcome distraction. While working with the Brodsky Quartet in 1992, Elvis had appeared on BBC Radio Four's *Desert Island Discs*, choosing his eight all-time favourite pieces of music: 'At Last', sung by Ross MacManus with the Joe Loss Orchestra, had featured, alongside Beethoven's 'Opus 35'; Sinatra's 'I've Got You Under My Skin'; Mozart's 'Marriage Of Figaro'; The Beatles' 'You Really Got A Hold On Me'; Schubert's 'B-flat Sonata'; 'Dido's Lament' sung by Anne Sofie Von Otter; and 'Blood Count' by Bill Strayhorn and the Duke Ellington Orchestra. He had wanted to include a recording of his son Matthew playing guitar, but feared it would make him cry.

Two years on, Elvis finally got to sing 'At Last' with Ross at a tribute to Joe Loss at the Barbican on 30 October. It was a brief, sentimental journey, directly at odds with the full-throttle Attractions shows. Once again, Elvis was playing a little residency on the tour: four Friday nights at London's Shepherd's Bush Empire throughout November. In between, they were playing theatres and small halls around the 2000 capacity mark, but even then most shows were far from being a sell-out.

There was a significant amount of new blood in the set. 'I Want You' quickly replaced 'No Action' as the opener, a choice guaranteed to grab any audience by the throat. In Manchester and Glasgow, Elvis threw up 'Why Don't You Love Me Like You Used To Do?' and 'Good Year For The Roses' as back-to-back encores, and on the second night in Glasgow on 16 November he acceded to an audience request by playing Leon Payne's 'Psycho', a real note from the underground.

Ultimately, however, the tour was marred by the problems Elvis was having with his voice, which eventually forced him to cancel the show in Exeter on 20 November, and led to walk-outs from some disgruntled audience members in Bristol the following night. In truth, Elvis's insistence on keeping the concerts as raw as possible began to seem slightly self-defeating. It was as though he were pre-empting any criticism of having mellowed by racing through everything as fast and as furiously as possible. With the sound mixes frequently terrible, it was often to the detriment of the material.

Part of his frenzy was aimed at rousing audiences who were tame and usually didn't fill the halls. By the time the tour reached Oxford Apollo on 27 November, Elvis gave up any pretence at civility. 'You can't stand up for sitting down,' he screamed sarcastically during 'I Can't Stand Up For Falling Down', ending it all with 'Good night, God bless, God help you!'

However, by far the most interesting and significant feature of the tour was the inclusion of 'new' songs: at Poole on 8 November, The Attractions showcased two tunes Elvis had written for other people: 'Dirty Rotten Shame' for The Dubliners' Ronnie Drew and 'Complicated Shadows', which had been written for – and was rejected by – Johnny Cash. By the second Friday at the Shepherd's Bush Empire on the eleventh he was also playing 'Poor Fractured Atlas', a slow ballad which he had reportedly written the previous night, with a piano melody based on – or more accurately, stolen from – Beethoven's 'Moonlight Sonata'. The following Friday in London, Elvis opened alone with 'All This Useless Beauty', the song he had written for June Tabor's 1992 record, *Angel Tiger*, and a week later at the final London show he and Steve opened with 'I Want To Vanish', another song written for June Tabor, this time for her *Against The Streams* album. All this was heading somewhere.

* * *

Much of Elvis's schedule in the opening six months of 1995 was tailored to fit around his massive commitment to curate the annual Meltdown Festival at the South Bank Centre at the end of June. During his stay at Dartington Hall in 1992, Elvis had received an offer to become the first non-classical artistic director of the festival. It would prove to be a huge undertaking, but it was both an opportunity and a ringing endorsement he had been happy to accept.

He was certainly no stranger to the South Bank, the hub of London's contemporary arts scene. He had spent an inordinate amount of time there since 1989 watching and listening to classical music, and had recently been commissioned by Graham Sheffield, the Music Department Director at the South Bank, to write a piece for viol and counter-tenor as part of the tercentenary celebrations of Henry Purcell later in the year.

However, Meltdown was on another level entirely. The week-long festival was in its third year, but this was the first time that a non-classical composer had been approached to oversee it: in the previous two years the artistic directors had been British composer and conductor George Benjamin and Dutch composer Louis Andriessen, both little known outside contemporary classical circles. Elvis was sufficiently worldly-wise to be aware that his name was being used as a bait for a bigger audience than a classical festival would usually attract, but he also recognised an opportunity when he was handed one.

The black and white world, 1980.
Credit: Pennie Smith

Touring *Trust* on the 'English Mugs' tour of the US, January 1981.
Credit: Redferns/Ebet Roberts

(Above) Jake Riviera and Elvis, Dublin, June 1983. Credit: Redferns/Keith Morris

(Below) The Coward Brothers: Elvis and T-Bone Burnett
wear their influences on their sleeves, 1985.

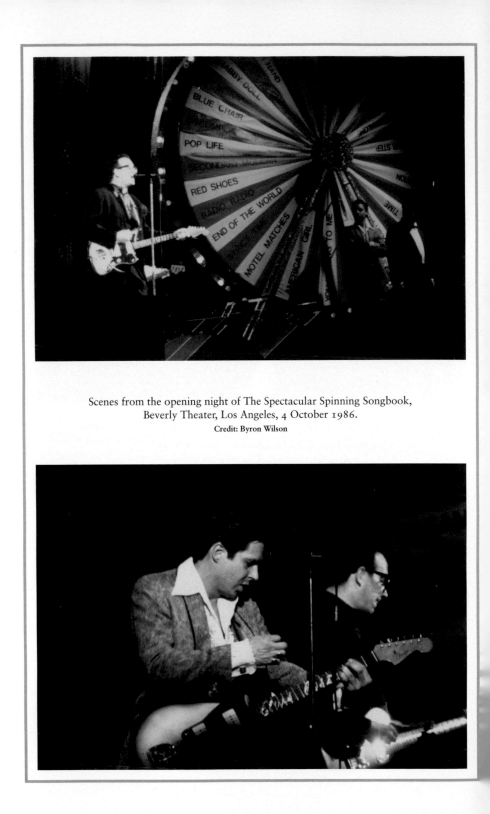

Scenes from the opening night of The Spectacular Spinning Songbook,
Beverly Theater, Los Angeles, 4 October 1986.
Credit: Byron Wilson

The Beloved Entertainer, 1989.
Credit: Redferns/Rob Verhorst

Deep in the 'Beard Years', 1991.
Credit: Redferns/Rob Verhorst

An uneasy truce: The Attractions reunite in 1994.

Credit: Redferns/Keith Morris

Elvis brings *Brutal Youth* to the world in 1994.
Credit: Tony Sacchetti/Mike Bodayle

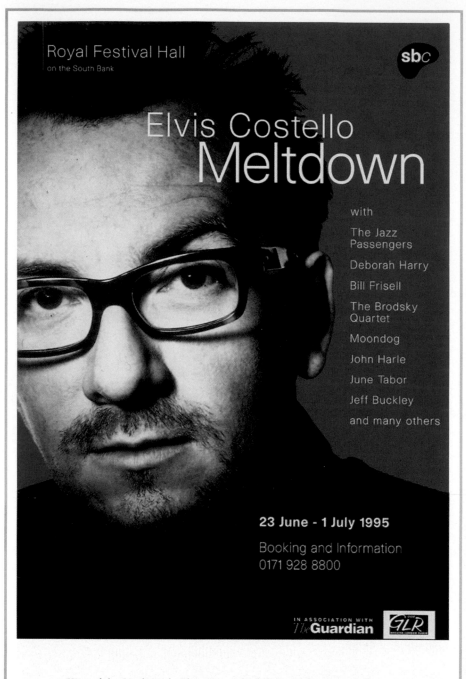

King of the South Bank. Elvis curates Meltdown in the summer of 1995.

Courtesy: The South Bank Centre

The final night of Meltdown, 1 July 1995,
featuring Jeff Buckley *(below)*.
Credit: Mary Ann Hauser

(Above) Elvis and Cait on tour in 1996.

(Below) Bruce and Elvis edge closer to the end of the line.
Note the difference in body language. Credit: Masanori Saito/Keiko Sunata

The master craftsman keeps a keen eye on his star pupil.
Burt Bacharach and Elvis bring *Painted From Memory*
to the stage in 1998.
Credit: Redferns/JM Enternational

The Lonely World, 1999.
Credit: Michel Laake

(Above) The Brodsky Quartet in their original line-up: *(l-r)* Ian Belton, Paul Cassidy, Michael Thomas and Jacqueline Cassidy. Credit: Redferns/Patrick Ford

(Below) The reformed Radiators From Space (Plan 9) in 2004, featuring Philip Chevron *(far left)* and Cait O'Riordan *(far right)*. Courtesy of Philip Chevron

Mr and Mrs MacManus: Diana Krall and Elvis step out in style, May 2003.
Credit: Starfile Agency

'What I wanted to do was bring it to a wider audience,' admits David Sefton who, as Producer of Contemporary Culture at the South Bank, was in charge of Meltdown. 'Elvis was such an obvious choice for the first non-classical composer, from the point of view of somebody who had worked so broadly across so many different worlds and clearly was interested very widely in music.'

For Elvis, this was the chance to finally synthesise all – or at least several – of the disparate strands of his musical interests over the past five or six years. Having had three years to plan the itinerary, he spent the time ensuring that he got it right. Initially, it was simply a case of discussing loose ideas and the range of what might be possible. From making a conceptual wish list, it was then a case of everyone getting together periodically to discuss the options. 'We're obviously going to bring in other kinds of music [aside from classical], as I don't belong to any particular field,' said Elvis at the end of 1994. 'We're still planning it but hopefully it will lead to some new collisions and happy accidents and maybe some further collaborations on my part.'7

Anything seemed possible. Meltdown provided the perfect opportunity for Elvis to express his own feelings on how accessible most of the music he loved could be, and anyone involved in its organisation who felt that he was simply there to puff up his ego and increase his own muscial credentials was swiftly disabused of the notion. 'He was very, very involved,' says Sefton. 'He personally invited a lot of the artists to take part, he was in dialogue with a lot of them about what they would do and the content of what the evening would be. He would sit in meetings and discuss not just pieces of classical music, but specific recordings of pieces of classical music. I mean, Elvis knows more about classical music than the guy who programmes the Proms, I know that for a fact.'

As discussions progressed, Elvis began to focus on what might be realistically possible, as opposed to simply what he wanted to do, which he insisted included a duet of honking horns performing from either side of the Thames. Nobody was entirely sure whether he was joking.

The festival would begin on 23 June, and as it drew closer Elvis upped his usual frantic pace, expecting others to do the same. 'There were times when I was on the phone at 2 a.m. as he had another idea,' sighs David Sefton. 'You kind of think, "Well yes, but I really want to go to sleep now!".'

Elvis also had other varied commitments to squeeze in. On 7 March he was back at the South Bank for another landmark: the performance of 'Put Away Forbidden Playthings', a composition inspired by Purcell's 'Fantazias', written by Elvis for the Purcell tercentenary.

It was in two parts: an instrumental opening and closing section to be played by the viol ensemble Fretwork and a lyric for counter-tenor Michael Chance in the middle. Elvis wasn't playing or singing, but he was in attendance at the Purcell Room to watch the performance of his work, one of six specially commissioned for the event and something he described as 'one of the three most terrifying moments of my life'. He neglected to mention what the other two had been, but he needn't have worried. The performance went smoothly enough for the *Daily Telegraph* to call it 'the loveliest of all six. This seemed a genuine homage'. Elvis would sing the text himself a month later with Fretwork at an AIDS benefit, and would also reprise it during Meltdown.

Following a brief tour of Spain with the Brodsky Quartet between 23 –28 January as part of the *Grande Conciertos 1995* series, Elvis and the Quartet teamed up again on 23 March, for a charity performance with Paul McCartney in aid of the Royal College of Music.

The concert took place at St James's Palace in front of Prince Charles, and required Elvis to set aside his deeply held antipathy towards the Royal Family. However, he studiously avoided meeting the Prince of Wales. 'There's people who want to meet him and it's a big deal to them, but it ain't a big deal to me,' he said. 'I was there at Paul's invitation, not his.'[8] It was Elvis's first public performance with McCartney, and the two duetted happily with acoustic guitars on 'Mistress And Maid' and the old Beatles song 'One After 909'. Having already performed 'I Almost Had A Weakness', 'The Birds Will Still Be Singing' and 'God Only Knows' with the Brodsky Quartet, Elvis then left the building as quickly as he could.

The run-in to Meltdown was further complicated by the release of *Kojak Variety*, which had finally been slotted into Warner's schedule for 9 May, almost exactly five years since it had been recorded in Barbados. The intervening years had done little to perk up an already jaded piece of work, but Elvis was keen to ensure that the record wasn't simply passed over as old news.

To coincide with the album's release, there was a one-off gig at the Shepherd's Bush Empire on 17 May, featuring The Attractions and the two guitarists from the record: Marc Ribot and James Burton. By the time the gig came round Elvis's voice was in trouble after over-energetic performances on Jools Holland's and David Letterman's television shows, and the set never really took flight.

He began with three solo songs to warm up, but thereafter all the songs were from *Kojak Variety* – which wouldn't necessarily have helped to rouse the audience – except for 'Tonight The Bottle Let Me Down' and 'Why Don't You Love Me Like You Used To Do?' from *Almost Blue*, specifically included to showcase James Burton's searing country licks. It ended with predictable encores of 'Alison' and 'Pump It Up'. 'The level of chat among the crowd told a sorry story,' said Max Bell in the *Evening Standard*. 'The concert proved to be a labour of love for both the artiste and the audience – accent on the word labour.' *Kojak Variety* only limped to No. 21 in the UK, and failed to chart in the States.

Elvis was disappointed with both the set and the reaction, but in the months leading up to Meltdown he had become accustomed to dealing with criticism. His stewardship of the festival provided a perfect opportunity for all manner of snipes and jibes, ranging from cries of 'pretentiousness' about the venture from the pop end of the spectrum, to accusations of 'dumbing down' from the hard-line classical fraternity. In the end, most of it boiled down to: *'Who does this guy think he is?'*

'That's the kind of deadening hand of anti-intellectualism,' says David Sefton. 'You're not allowed to experiment, it's the anti-arts stance. The only acceptance comes when you're being told that you're not being very much like yourself, when your name is used as a stick to beat your back with. I think that's the same with any pop star trying to do anything unusual. It's definitely no-win.'

As it was, the final line-up for the festival was hugely appetising to anyone with a thirst for interesting and unique musical adventurism. It was a truly ambitious sweep across the boundaries of modern music, with Elvis seemingly everywhere at once. In the words of David Sefton: 'He knows no fear.'

* * *

Meltdown opened on the evening of Friday, 23 June with a performance by the Rebirth Brass Band, followed by London ensemble Afro Blok, a wall of drummers spanning the entire stage. Then – in the spirit of sometimes wilful collaboration which was to define the festival – the Rebirth Band returned to the stage and the two acts played together.

The main act of the opening night was New York's Jazz Passengers, an eclectic and consciously post-modern collective of saxophones, trombones, vibes and strings, with Marc Ribot's skewed guitar lines thrown in for good measure. Guest vocalist Debbie Harry stole the show early on, before departing to make room for Elvis to sing half-a-dozen songs, including 'Man Out Of Time' and 'God's Comic'. The evening ended with a closing duet between Elvis and Debbie Harry, the long-since abdicated King and Queen of new wave, on Blondie's 'The Tide Is High'. It undeniably became the first high spot of the week.

The National Film Theatre was running a 'Celluloid Jukebox' season, and the next day Meltdown took film as its theme, screening some of Elvis's favourite music movies: two Thelonius Monk documentaries, The Beatles' *A Hard Day's Night*, *This Is Spinal Tap*, Jimmy Cliff in *The Harder They Come* and the Marx Brothers' *Duck Soup* among them. Elvis dropped in to chat about his own videos, and used other film extracts to illustrate his points. He also previewed five minutes – sadly, all that would ever be completed – of the animated feature *Tom Thumb*, for which he was scoring the music.

That evening, Marc Ribot and avant garde pianist Keith Tippett performed 'Music Out Of Film', the kind of event that, for good or ill, could only happen at a contemporary arts festival: Ribot played live guitar over a 1920's Soviet science fiction film called *Aelita, Queen of Mars*, while Tippett improvised over several animated shorts.

Elvis's opening showcase as a performer fell on Sunday the twenty-fifth. In the early evening he took part in 'Waterloo Sunset', a performance of pieces from the Composer Ensemble's 300-strong songbook which included arrangements of works by Shostakovich, Brahms, Lizst, Madness, Brian Wilson, Peter Gabriel and the Pet Shop Boys. Elvis selected a closing version of Ray Davies's 'Waterloo Sunset', before departing for the Queen Elizabeth Hall for a concert entitled 'Old Flowers In New Dirt'.

It was a show of many parts, unashamedly ambitious and illustrating something of the variety and lack of boundaries of his artistic reach. Elvis initially took to the stage alone and played six songs on acoustic guitar, half of which were unrecorded: 'Starting To Come To Me', 'All This Useless Beauty', 'Complicated Shadows', 'Indoor Fireworks', 'Little Atoms' and 'Deep Dark Truthful Mirror'.

Once the venerable gospel quintet The Fairfield Four had performed a selection of gospel standards, Elvis returned with jazz guitarist Bill Frisell. He had worked briefly with Frisell a few years previously on 'Weird Nightmare', a track on a Charles Mingus tribute record, and had later sought him out at the Village Vanguard club in New York.

The songs that had emerged as the strongest in their one brief rehearsal tended to be among the least accessible – and most neglected – of Elvis's repertoire: 'Poisoned Rose', 'Poor Napoleon', 'Baby Plays Around', 'Love Field', 'Shamed Into Love', plus an incongruous cover of 'Gigi', and a new collaboration with Frisell, called 'Deep Dead Blue', where Elvis added words to Frisell's music.

It was a sparse, uncompromising vocal-and-solo-guitar performance, adding extra dimensions to the material, most of which hadn't been heard in concert for many years. Although one-paced and not entirely successful, the concert was put together with just a single rehearsal, an indication of just how confident Elvis had become in trusting his own instincts. 'He takes a lot of risks,' observes Frisell. 'He likes to put himself into situations where he's not sure what's going to happen: to play in that kind of naked circumstance with just guitar and voice, where there's nothing else there to hold things together. He just goes in there wide open and lets it happen, and that's the way you learn the most, rather than trying to mould it into something that you already know.'

When Frisell departed, Elvis played a number of songs with just Steve Nieve on piano. More obvious choices like 'Shot With His Own Gun', 'Just A Memory', and 'Shipbuilding' lined up alongside the recently composed 'Poor Fractured Atlas' and a magnificent reinterpretation of 'Temptation' as a stately ballad. To finish, The Fairfield Four joined Elvis and Steve for an *a capella* treatment of Van Morrison's 'Full Force Gale' and a closing 'That Day Is Done', both ranking among the most emotionally uplifting performances of his career.

It was a truly remarkable evening of music, all the more so when considering the fact that, as artistic director, Elvis was also running around making sure that all the events were going smoothly. 'Seeing him functioning was unbelievable,' says Bill Frisell. 'I couldn't believe how somebody could deal with that much information all at one time.' To add to Elvis's considerations, he learned over the weekend of the cancellation of Friday night's main act, Pakistan's Sabri Brothers, after one of them had been injured in a car crash. On hearing the news, Elvis called Donal Lunny and asked for help in putting together a band of traditional Irish musicians for Friday's show, a concert which would now have to be rehearsed from scratch.

Elvis watched the Brodsky Quartet perform Szymanski and Shostakovich in the Queen Elizabeth Hall on Monday, a little nostalgic reminder of how he came to be there in the first place. The following evening Bill Frisell played again, starting his set solo and then expanding to a trio of trumpet and violin. He included a sweet version of Elvis's 'Sweet Pear', obviously one that didn't make the final cut for their collaboration.

On the night of Wednesday the twenty-eighth, Elvis made the second of his three major contributions to Meltdown as a performer, prefaced by a solo piano recital by Steve Nieve in the Purcell Room.

The main performance took place in two parts in the Queen Elizabeth Hall. For the opening half, Elvis was alongside the Brodsky Quartet, playing a selection of songs from *The Juliet Letters*, but also showing off their expanded repertoire: 'Pills And Soap', Michael Thomas's new composition 'Skeleton', Tom Waits's 'More Than Rain', 'God Only Knows' and Jerome Kern's 'They Didn't Believe Me'. In their own way, they had become as tight a pairing as he and The Attractions had ever been, instinctive, able to improvise and surprise each other.

Perhaps the second set was less sure of itself. The Brodskys were augmented with an eleven-piece chamber orchestra directed by Diego Masson, featuring french horns, clarinets, trumpet, flute and double bass. Interspersed with classics such as 'New Lace Sleeves' and 'Long Honeymoon' were rarities like 'Having It All', 'Punishing Kiss', and the beguiling 'Upon A Veil Of Midnight Blue', arranged by Bill Frisell. Proving there were no grudges left over from the *Goodbye Cruel World* debacle, 'Shipbuilding' had a new arrangement, written by Clive Langer. 'I had a good chat with him,' says Langer. 'It was great to see him. I always found him brilliant to work with, he's interesting and fascinating and he's got a great mind.'

The second set was over-ambitious, with the larger chamber ensemble sounding slightly cluttered after the stripped-down, assured performances of Elvis and the Brodsky Quartet. But nobody could claim that it didn't make for riveting listening. 'I'd be inclined to think more in terms of a "shared path" than the woefully inadequate "cross-over" epithet,' said Robert Cowan in *The Independent*. 'This was quality stuff, and as significant for the development of music now as anything we're likely to hear from the hard-line avant garde.'

On the Thursday, the London Philharmonic Orchestra provided eccentric and compelling entertainment. The day-time Children's Concert featured John Williams's film themes for *Superman* and *Star Wars*, as well as several of Elvis's beloved cartoon tunes. In the evening, guest conductor Gunther Schuller led the orchestra – plus a scratch seventeen-piece jazz band, saxophonist Martin Robertson and violinist Alex Balanescu – through a melange of different music, including a suite from Bernard Hermann's score for the film *Taxi Driver*, Duke Ellington's 'Night Creatures', Mark-Antony Turnage's 'Drowned Out' and Korngold's 'Violin Concerto', as well as the world premiere of Elvis's first orchestral work, a modest three-minute 'thumbprint' called 'Edge Of Ugly'. The latter was slotted into the running order with typical haste. 'He sang it over the telephone to me the other day,' Schuller laughed on the eve of the performance. 'I could tell it was fine. It's very short, a pot-pourri that goes from a fanfare to a waltz, some cartoon music and ends with very fast swing.'9

In truth, 'Edge Of Ugly' was hardly the highpoint of the festival, and left many fans and critics alike desperately disappointed at both its slightness and its brevity. 'Two wacky xylophone motifs and a brass passage resembling the theme tune to *That's Life!* hardly amount to orchestral fare,' sneered Rick Jones in the *Evening Standard*. But then it was never intended to be. The LPO concert as a whole marked the outer limits of the festival's experimentation, a wildly eclectic meshing of styles that took most of the concert to find its feet. By the end, it worked, but only just.

Irish vocal group Anuna began and ended proceedings on Friday night, while in the middle, Elvis played with Donal Lunny and the All-Star Irish Band, thrown together at less than a week's notice after the withdrawal of the Sabri Brothers. They were still deep in rehearsal on the afternoon of the show. It was a fun, necessarily spontaneous evening of polkas and reels, reuniting some of the musicians who had played on the *Spike* sessions in Dublin. It also gave Elvis a rare chance to perform 'Any King's Shilling' and 'Tramp The Dirt Down' in their original recorded format, as well as 'American Without Tears'.

Meltdown's final day was a sprawling affair. The afternoon concert was almost a pastiche of collaborative zeal: John Harle, the London Saxophonic, London Brass, bassist Danny Thompson, and the seventy-nine-year-old, legendary blind New York street musician Louis Hardin, aka Moondog, all performed together. Harle played pieces from his enormously eclectic repertoire for saxophone in the first half, some dating back to as far as the twelfth century; then after a break, Moondog conducted the ensemble through his own compositions using a large bass drum.

Perhaps mercifully, the evening concert returned to 'The Song', dedicated to showcasing a wide range of different voices and types of music back-to-back. It was a finale designed to underscore the broad theme of the festival: that music from all ages and genres exists simply to be heard and felt, and needn't be categorised and pigeonholed. However, for all its ambition, in the end the evening couldn't help but reflect the instincts and personality of the man who had put it together. It was essentially a melancholic choice of material and voices.

It opened with a set from one of Elvis's favourite singers, June Tabor. After the interval a number of performers took the stage, sitting and listening when they weren't called upon to sing. To the backing of viol ensemble Fretwork and the Composer's Ensemble, soprano Patricia Rozario sang pieces by Henry Purcell and William Byrd, vaulting rock singer Jeff Buckley sang Benjamin Britten's 'Corpus Christi Carol' and Purcell's 'When I Am Laid In Earth', Mary Wiegold sang a new composition entitled 'Malicious Observer', which set Elvis's lyrics to a tune written by John Woolrich, and Elvis sang his own recent Purcell tribute, 'Put Away Forbidden Playthings' and John Dowland's 'Can She Excuse My Wrongs?'

The third and final section of the concert involved a rotating bill of Elvis, Tabor and Buckley singing to the backing of Steve Nieve and Marc

Ribot. Elvis sang Randy Newman's 'I've Been Wrong Before' from *Kojak Variety*, the standards 'My Funny Valentine' and 'Glad To Be Unhappy', a version of 'Almost Blue' which merged into 'The Thrill Is Gone', its original inspiration, and a sincere 'Alison', a song that had served Elvis well through the years. At the end, Elvis thanked everyone for taking part in the festival and got as close to emotional as he ever does in public: 'It's been pretty fucking amazing, actually,' he smiled, encoring with a poignant 'I Want To Vanish'. Whereupon he hugged Steve Nieve and went home. It was 1 a.m.

'The final concert ended up running [for] about six hours, which was probably a little long,' says David Sefton. In actual fact, it was a little over four hours, although it had started almost an hour late. Nobody seemed to mind. The final day's concerts were given an extra poignancy by the fact that both Moondog and Jeff Buckley would soon be dead. Moondog passed away in 1999, while the prodigiously talented Buckley drowned in the Mississippi at the age of thirty in May 1997. It was the last time either man performed in Britain, and they were fitting farewells. Buckley, in particular, undoubtedly stole the final show, and at his memorial at St Ann and Holy Trinity Church in Brooklyn on 1 June 1997, Elvis sang a classical piece at the piano in tribute. 'He was fantastic,' he said. 'He gave everything.'

Meltdown proved a considered success. Generally, the ambitious and sometimes eccentric ideas that Elvis put together met with audience approval and enthusiasm, as well as inspiring rather than alienating the musicians he was working with. There was little of the frictions or petty resentments that could sometimes occur when the worlds of pop and classical met, mainly because Elvis – unequivocally – no longer regarded himself as part of any specific musical world, and had both the experience and confidence to follow his ideas through. He had become a consummate collaborator, with an uncanny knack of choosing people who relished the opportunity to experiment.

The festival had been well attended and high-profile – famous visitors included Suggs, Eduardo Paolozzi, Terry Gilliam and Alan Bleasdale. However, there were the inevitable gripes and an underlying sense that Elvis and his robust ego had somehow hijacked the festival. 'I suspect that even Costello's most fervent well-wishers could hardly have been prepared for the paean of self-aggrandisement which characterised the whole ethos of this year's festival,' wrote Antony Bye in the *Financial Times*. 'The oversized programme booklet set the tone, screaming out Elvis Costello in word and image on almost every page.'

It was, however, a two-way trade-off. Elvis wasn't shy about proclaiming his talents, but he had attended every single performance during the festival, taking a personal interest in every detail of the event. Such an unashamedly hands-on approach from a high-profile, no-holds-barred artist was inevitably going to make a dramatic and overpowering imprint on the festival. That, in essense, was the entire point. Ultimately, the South Bank Centre were more than satisfied with the results, both commercially and artistically. 'There certainly, to my memory, wasn't a bad concert,' says David Sefton. 'Some of the shows we did are still some of the best shows of his I've seen. I went on to do seven Meltdowns and I think of all of the people, Elvis was the most hands-on. Everything you could want from a collaborator worked out.'

Elvis was satisfied, too. As well as having direct repurcussions for at least three of his subsequent solo records, Meltdown set in motion a number of small explosions, opening up numerous possibilites which he continues to explore to the present day. In the ensuing months and years some of Elvis's more esoteric sidelines, collaborations and lower-profile projects could be traced back to Meltdown: *Deep Dead Blue*, the limited edition – only 10,000 copies – seven-song memento of the concert with Bill Frisell would be rush-released on 14 August 1995, a permanent record of a concert played with just a single rehearsal. Elvis would work with Frisell again on the songs for the *Painted From Memory* record in 1998, and beyond.

There were numerous other connections: he recorded his own song 'Aubergine' on the Jazz Passengers' next record and performed with Debbie Harry and the band several more times, as well as collaborating with saxophonist Roy Nathanson. He finally cut a version of 'That Day Is Done' that did the song justice on The Fairfield Four's *I Couldn't Hear Nobody Pray* record. He worked with saxophonist John Harle on his *Terror And Magnificence* album, released in October 1996, singing three settings of Shakespeare songs from *Twelfth Night*: 'O Mistress Mine'; 'Come Away, Death'; and 'When That I Was and A Little Tiny Boy'. Elvis also toured with Harle and used him for the recording of his first ballet score, *Il Sogno*, in 2002. He sang on Donal Lunny's *Common Ground* record, while Fretwork recorded his Purcell-inspired composition 'Put Away Hidden Playthings' on their album, *Sit Fast*. Elvis would continue to work with the Brodsky Quartet off and on over the next decade, which would in turn smooth the way for collaborations with Anne Sofie Von Otter.

Perhaps most significantly, and certainly most gratifyingly, Elvis finally realised at Meltdown that there was a huge amount of potential in working as a duo with Steve Nieve. It had only taken eighteen years. Elvis would also work with David Sefton again on an album of songs for Ute Lemper in 1999, and in Sefton's new role at the UCLA in 2002. 'So much came out of Meltdown,' says Sefton. 'It's nice, that's the purpose of it. We made the time and space, he made the time and space, and he was able to do a lot of things that he wouldn't have been able to do otherwise.'

Chapter Fifteen
1995–96

OVER THE PREVIOUS DECADE, Elvis had amassed dozens of songs that had either been recorded by other people, or indeed hadn't been recorded at all. He had become adept at tailoring tunes for other artists, enjoying the craft of writing for another style of voice or musical genre. He was also happy to collaborate with anyone he found interesting, and these diversions had thrown up some excellent results. 'I realised that if I don't address the songs I'd written for other people soon, it'll become an unweildly repertoire,' he admitted. 'It's already something like forty songs.'[1]

There was indeed a vast array to choose from: 'Shadow And Jimmy' (Was (Not Was)); 'The Miranda Syndrome' and 'Shamed Into Love' (Ruben Blades); 'The Other End Of The Telescope' (Aimee Mann); 'Miss Mary' (Zucchero); 'I Want To Vanish' and 'All This Useless Beauty' (June Tabor); 'You Bowed Down' (Roger McGuinn); 'Hidden Shame' and 'Complicated Shadows' (Johnny Cash); 'Why Can't A Man Stand Alone' (Sam Moore); 'Dirty Rotten Shame' (Ronnie Drew); 'Upon A Veil Of Midnight Blue' (Mary Coughlan, also recorded as 'I Wonder How She Knows' by Charles Brown); 'Punishing Kiss' (performed by Annie Ross in Robert Altman's *Short Cuts*); not to mention the collaborations with Paul McCartney, the ten songs he wrote for Wendy James, and a selection he had quietly kept to himself.

Elvis had played many of these songs in concert over the years and had aired a large number of them during Meltdown. Now he planned to make a record using the pick of the litter, under the heading: *A Case For Song*. Elvis's initial ideas for his new record had been heavily influenced by his ongoing involvement in organising Meltdown. He wanted to make a double album, using several different types of musical accompaniment: string quartet, The Attractions, jazz ensemble, gospel quartet, whichever style suited each individual song.

In order to aid the selection process, Elvis had popped up as an unannounced support act for Bob Dylan in the spring, playing solo and testing out new material. In Paris on 24 March, Brixton Academy on 29–31 March, and Dublin on 11 April, he strolled on-stage and played a dozen songs to generally sympathetic crowds.

Opening each night with 'Starting To Come To Me', a spry country shuffle which dated back to the *Mighty Like A Rose* sessions and owed something to Dylan's 'Lily, Rosemary And The Jack Of Hearts', Elvis added several other 'new' or unrecorded songs over the five nights: 'Complicated Shadows', 'All This Useless Beauty', 'Shallow Grave', 'I Want To Vanish', 'It's Time', 'The Other End Of The Telescope' and 'You Bowed Down' had all been written either as collaborations or with other artists in mind, while 'Distorted Angel', 'Poor Fractured Atlas' and 'Little Atoms' were fairly recent compositions – the former had been kicked around with The Attractions at the *Brutal Youth* sessions. All eleven would end up on the next record.

Also debuted on the closing night in Dublin was 'God Give Me Strength', a genuine work-in-progress which at the time of the concert was still being co-written with Burt Bacharach for the film *Grace Of My Heart*. The collaboration had been suggested by the film's musical supervisor Karyn Rachtman, but when a scheduled songwriting session in Los Angeles was scrapped, the pair had to find another way of working together to fit the tight deadline. 'I was in this extraordinary situation where I was coming home from the last show I did with Bob in Dublin at 2.30 in the morning and ringing Burt when it was still afternoon [in LA] and working on the song,' said Elvis.[2]

As an ice-breaker, Elvis had written the plaintive, characteristically Bacharach-esque intro of the song and nervously played it onto Burt's answering machine, fearing it was too close to pastiche. Bacharach loved it, adding his own harmonies and structural changes to the blueprint. In this eccentric manner – using telephone, fax and answerphone, ideas criss-crossing the Atlantic between Dublin and Los Angeles – the track was quickly completed. Then Elvis wrote the words. The minute it was finished, he knew he had a winner. He played it again at Meltdown with Steve Nieve, and at every opportunity thereafter, like a boy eagerly displaying his favourite new toy.

'God Give Me Strength' was one of the songs Elvis had in mind for the next record, but although Meltdown had prepared him for the more esoteric side of the record, The Attractions needed warming up. There had been only two live performances with Elvis in 1995, the second coming at Denmark's Roskilde festival on 2 July, and both had been limited to showcasing old songs and *Kojak Variety* material.

To get inside the material, Elvis scheduled five shows over six nights with The Attractions in New York's Beacon Theatre in early August as 'open rehearsals'. It was another bold and novel idea, although in truth it was also one born of a growing and uncharacteristic amount of uncertainty about what the new record should sound like. In New York, he was hoping to stumble upon something.

Elvis had originally wanted in-demand American producer Brendan O'Brien to produce his new album, but they had failed to agree over budgets. Instead, he decided to reunite the production team of Geoff Emerick and Jon Jacobs, who last worked with him on *Imperial Bedroom* in 1982. The two engineers were in New York to record all the shows between 2–7 August, on hand to capture anything spectacular on tape before they all went into Windmill Lane in Dublin later in the month to begin recording.

Over the residency at the Beacon, Elvis and The Attractions played seventeen new or unrecorded songs: all of the twelve tracks that would eventually make up the album were performed, as well as 'God Give Me Strength', 'Dirty Rotten Shame', 'Almost Ideal Eyes', 'Puppet Girl', and an eight-line fragment called 'Speak Darkly, My Angel'.

Although the concerts were played and performed – and priced – as proper shows, the idea of an 'open rehearsal' was no joke; these were most definitely work-in-progress sessions. During the opening night, the audience were often looking at bowed heads and squinting eyes, as the notes and lyrics placed on music stands on stage were given plenty of attention by each of The Attractions. Gradually, these were dispensed with over the five nights as the band grew into the material. In addition to the new songs, there was the odd nice surprise as well. 'Opportunity' got its first – fairly ragged – airing since the early '80s, while Marc Ribot joined the band on the last night to play on 'Hidden Charms' and 'Pump It Up'.

By the time Elvis entered Windmill Lane in Dublin with The Attractions a week after the final show, he at last had a firmer grasp of the songs he wanted to record for the album. 'I had already changed my mind about the contents of the record several times,'[3] he admitted, but now he had narrowed down the shortlist of suitable songs to around fifteen. The gigs at the Beacon had also convinced him to set aside his initial concept of a double album featuring numerous different styles and forms of instrumentation, and focus on a single album featuring just Elvis and The Attractions.

The sessions proved difficult. Elvis found that some of the songs he had written for others and now wanted to record for himself – such as Aimee Mann's 'The Other End Of The Telescope' – needed drastic rewriting in the studio. He was also finally feeling the pace after the energy-sapping sprint of Meltdown, and was struggling to capture the vocal performances he wanted, while increasingly seeking solace in large amounts of alcohol. His uncharacteristic lack of decisiveness and propensity for self-criticism and self-doubt often infuriated the band, who also found the basic nature of the material problematic.

At least half of the songs being considered were fragile, melancholic ballads, with disappointment and sadness rather than fury at their hearts, and Elvis envisaged the record as largely stripped down, with his voice and Steve's piano to the fore. But progress was slow and the failure of the musicans to get close to the mood of the songs in the studio was made all too clear by the inclusion of live excerpts – taken from one of the Beacon Theatre shows – on 'Complicated Shadows', and several aborted takes of 'God Give Me Strength'.

Geoff Emerick had a long-standing production commitment in the autumn of 1995 to record with Paul McCartney, and the sessions were put on hold in October to await his return. During the break in proceedings, Elvis deliberated about where he wanted the album to go. While doing so, he performed a one-off concert with the Brodsky Quartet at St George's Hall in Bristol on 7 November, and also found time to record a song for a Warner Brothers album of songs inspired by the cult sci-fi show *The X-Files*, cutting the brooding and rather magnificent 'My Dark Life' between the hours of 10 a.m. and 2 a.m. on 22 November with Brian Eno at the helm.

Elvis impressed – and rather annoyed – his collaborator with the sheer wealth of detail he brought to the studio. The session had originally been intended as a chance for the two men to experiment together, but 'My Dark Life' was presented as 'a completely (and minutely) written piece',[4] according to Eno. He ultimately felt rather surplus to requirements.

Elvis and The Attractions reconvened in December and January 1996 to finish recording the album, still provisionally titled *A Case For Song*. During the break in proceedings, Elvis had decided to stop drinking alcohol. It had been a major part of his life for long periods over the last two decades, and had often exacerbated his blackest moods. Increasingly over the past twelve months he felt it was getting in the way of his creative process, while doing nothing to lift a sometimes melancholic disposition. 'I'm not afraid of it,' he explained. 'I drank a lot and some of it inspired some very good songs, and then I got tired of it.'[5]

Rejuvenated and clear-headed, Elvis cut many of his vocal tracks live in this second stretch of recording, while the song list was again revised. He dropped 'Almost Ideal Eyes' – a complex song in two time signatures that he had written with David Crosby in mind – and 'God Give Me

Strength' from the running order, while 'Dirty Rotten Shame' was disregarded after Ronnie Drew – whom Elvis had originally written the song for – decided he wanted to record it for his own album.

With the final track listing reduced to twelve, Elvis decided to play to the songs' strengths, emphasising the beauty of the melodies and the subtleties in the music, rather than succumbing to more obvious arrangements that would merely remind people of past glories. As a result, less and less emphasis was placed on group performances. Pre-recorded loops were used on 'Little Atoms', 'It's Time' and 'Distorted Angel', while Elvis rearranged 'I Want To Vanish' with Steve Nieve, a delicate performance augmented with the Brodsky Quartet, string bass and some clarinet overdubs recorded at Westside Studios in London. Along with a little extra chamber instrumentation on 'All This Useless Beauty', it was the closest the album came to its original blueprint.

Indeed, if Elvis had stayed absolutely true to the material, he would probably have recorded most of the songs with just Steve Nieve, perhaps using the Brodskys and some subtle overdubs. This was primarily an album of simple beauty, melody and voice, and Elvis was becoming increasingly aware that Bruce Thomas, in particular, was playing the songs through gritted teeth. The bass player felt that the essence of The Attractions had been diluted by the arrangements and the production. With a certain inevitablity, towards the end of the sessions the old war wounds began to bleed.

'I think there was a point where Elvis definitely wanted The Attractions to turn into a karaoke machine,' says Thomas. 'He was basically turning the voice up, turning the voice up and turning the voice up. I thought, "Ah, the game is up now".' Although at this stage the atmosphere was one of unarticulated tension rather than explicit antagonism, it would prove to be a bad omen for the forthcoming summer tour.

With the album finished and mixed at Westside and Mayfair studios in London, through February Elvis mopped up some other outstanding business. On the ninth, he met up with Burt Bacharach in New York to record their version of 'God Give Me Strength' for the Grace Of My Heart soundtrack.

The film was a fiction based on the Brill Building songwriters of the '60s and in particular the early years of Carole King, and the song would feature in various states of completion throughout the movie, as though it were being 'composed' in real time. When Grace Of My Heart was finally released in September 1996, the stunning Bacharach/Costello recording would not appear in full until the closing credits, but most critics agreed that the best was saved until last. From New York, Elvis flew to

Nashville to record 'That Day Is Done' with The Fairfield Four for their forthcoming album and to catch some local shows.

Then it was down to album business. The new record – now called *All This Useless Beauty*, the first record Elvis had ever named after one of its songs – was released on 13 May, dedicated to Cait in her new guise as Dr O'Riordan, just a few days before their tenth 'wedding' anniversary. Unlike *Brutal Youth,* this was an Elvis Costello and The Attractions record, the first for ten years. And the last.

It was a seductive, beguiling piece of work. On the title track and 'I Want To Vanish', Elvis had conjured up two of the most beautiful recordings of his career, while the slightly ambient 'Distorted Angel' and 'Little Atoms' were sonically unlike anything he had released, floating on loops and sequenced rhythms. Perhaps most impressively, he sang beautifully throughout, with a measured restraint that could only have been learned from time spent away from roaring over loud rock 'n' roll bands.

However, there was a distinct sense of a band on a leash, and one sometimes wondered why – or indeed, if – The Attractions were playing on the record at all. In the end, only 'You Bowed Down', the berserk 'Shallow Grave' and 'It's Time' featured any hints of the classic, aggressive band perfomances of old. This wasn't necessarily a bad thing, but there was a certain glumness, a sullen quality, in the performances throughout which betrayed the mood in the studio. For all the personal, deeply felt sentiments on the record and the sometimes superlative songwriting, there was a distance at its heart which kept the emotions at arm's length.

Reviews were hit and miss. The *NME* found Elvis 'caught between the Bacharach and the Britpoppers. Curios and cheese baubles sit next to pure gems.' *Rolling Stone* gave the record an A-grade, as though it were a particularly well-constructed history essay. The review in the *Boston Phoenix* seemed to come closest to articulating what Elvis was trying to achieve: 'He has captured better than any singer of his generation the cautious expression, the heartache hiding behind the mask of aggression, the punctured dreams we're all prey to,' wrote Stephanie Zacharek, before going onto describe him as a modern-day Sinatra. It was hyperbolic, but not preposterously so.

* * *

Elvis concluded that the best way to promote an album heavy on quiet ballads was initially to perform the songs with just piano and guitar. As such, the mini-tour kicking off in America on 13 May featured just him and Steve Nieve. Following their emotional and wildly enjoyable performance as a duo at Meltdown, Elvis had established a new rapport with Steve. He seemed to have finally and rather belatedly come to the conclusion that he was considerably more than a band member, and perhaps something close to his musical equal.

With the full Attractions line-up waiting in the wings for the European dates, the May tour was essentially a short, promotional hop, featuring just nine concerts in all with lots of interviews, radio slots, some industry performances and a couple of TV appearances thrown in. The theatres and clubs were small, ranging from just 350 in the Troubadour in Los Angeles to 1300 in the Filmore in San Francisco, and they made for a perfectly intimate evening's entertainment, with Elvis in particularly fine voice on all nights.

The sets were heavy on the *All This Useless Beauty* material, but alongside some of the more appropriate older material best suited for piano and voice there were plenty of surprises. In New York on 22 May, Elvis played an evening show and a late show at the Supper Club, five hours of music in total. Treats included 'You'll Never Be A Man', 'King Horse', 'Black Sails In The Sunset', 'Talking In The Dark', 'Watch Your Step', 'Men Called Uncle' and a great, Motown-inspired new track called 'Unwanted Number', also written for *Grace Of My Heart*.

These were some of the most expressive and enjoyable concerts of his career. Elvis looked happy on stage, impersonating Elvis Presley singing the hits of Bruce Springsteen and Blondie, and during 'God's Comic' recounting a dream in which the Heavenly Father asked him if Alanis Morissette and Dave Grohl were in fact the same person. Far from limiting his options, the stripped-down format seemed to free him to achieve more than he ever could with a full rock band, particularly as a vocalist.

Nevertheless, Elvis would be fulfilling the rest of the tour dates with The Attractions, returning to Dublin to rehearse in early June. Already, *All This Useless Beauty* was dropping down the charts. It had sold poorly in the States, reaching a peak of No. 53, and fared little better in Europe, dipping under the 100,000 sales mark. It limped to No. 23 in the UK.

It was a hugely disappointing showing for an album of songs Elvis held very close to his heart. After *The Juliet Letters* and the commercial failure of *Brutal Youth* he had become increasingly disillusioned with Warners. He felt that they had promoted the new record 'atrociously', abandoning him in the same way that Columbia had done in the mid-'80s. 'I was being told officially from the most senior levels that I was wasting my time,' he said.[6]

His typically bloody-minded idea of releasing a different single in the UK every week throughout July – 'Little Atoms', 'The Other End Of

The Telescope', 'Distorted Angel' and 'All This Useless Beauty' – was probably designed to annoy the record company as much as anything else. In that aim he succeeded, but it certainly didn't come close to providing him with a hit single. Furthermore, ticket sales for the European tour proved to be surprisingly poor.

On the eve of the tour, Elvis taped a BBC TV Special in London on 18 June. Entitled *A Career Revue*, the show looked back to the breadth of Meltdown and finally incorporated many of the elements that Elvis had initially wanted on the album: the Brodsky Quartet; a chamber orchestra; solo slots; duets with Steve, as well as The Attractions. Taped at the BBC Television centre studios, the performance was an exemplary demonstration of the core versatility of Elvis's talents. Broadcast twice on BBC TV in July, it was later released on video in October, when Elvis finally got to use the title *A Case For Song*. It seemed fitting.

The tour kicked off at the Stadium in Dublin on 26 June, opening with just Steve and Elvis. The Attractions joined in halfway through 'Oliver's Army', before things really took flight with a rare performance of 'Miracle Man'. As the tour moved on, the band were playing with much more light and shade – and far fewer decibels – compared to the sometimes extreme *Brutal Youth* shows two years earlier. The song selection was also much more adventurous, with a generous sprinkling of old and new tracks throughout: 'Motel Matches', 'Brilliant Mistake', 'Opportunity' and 'Human Hands' among them. On a Cajun campfire reworking of 'Pump It Up', Steve Nieve even switched to accordion.

But tellingly, the highlights of the shows were usually the sections featuring just voice and piano. In truth, any concept of band unity on- or off-stage had long since evaporated. Elvis broke up the tour to perform alone with Debbie Harry, The Jazz Passengers and The Brodsky Quartet at the Montreux Jazz Festival on 9 July, and fitted in gigs with Steve in Dranouter in Belgium and the Water Festival in Stockholm, performing without the remaining two Attractions. He had his own dressing room and travelled separately to and from concerts, and he and Cait very often stayed in different hotels to the band. Essentially, they would meet at the soundcheck and again at the show, but other than that, singer and band had very little to do with each other.

With Pete Thomas the most laid-back member of the group and Steve finally getting the recognition he deserved as a worthy collaborator in his own right, it was left to Bruce Thomas to play upon the tensions and resentments that had been simmering since the recording of the album. Although he and Elvis had both made genuine efforts to get along, their relationship had an all too easily activated fault line. 'It gradually just deteriorated again,' says Thomas. 'It got into some sort of dysfunctional loop, like when you get back together with your ex and after three months you're fighting over the same things. No matter what we did, we just ended up the same.'

Matters came to a head when the tour reached the Auditorio San Javier in Murcia, Spain on 14 July. The Attractions were playing 'I Can't Stand Up For Falling Down'. 'Elvis did this Wilson Picketty sort of soul declamation, and I just did a little blues lick,' recalls Bruce Thomas. 'The next day on the bus, he said, "By the way, I don't want you camping it up on stage again tonight, blues licks and things like that." I said, "Well, it was just a bit of spontaneous expression. Where's the problem?" Then he said, "Well, there's only room for one star on that stage." And I thought, "Well, that's it." When somebody turns round to you and says that they don't want your input intruding, who would want to play under those circumstances?'

Bruce and some of the road crew immediately took to calling Elvis 'Tex' behind his back, a lightly-coded reference to Texas: The Lone Star State, and a pointed sneer at his apparent reluctance to share any of the limelight. From then on, relations deteriorated rapidly and the mood worsened, to the extent that communication all but ceased between singer and bass player for the rest of the tour. It wasn't the only relationship going through the mill. Bruce Thomas claims that Elvis and Cait were arguing frequently – and audibly – and she even quit the tour on a few occasions, flying back home to Dublin, only to return a few days later. On other occasions, again according to Thomas, she would stay in the hotel after a row, running up an enormous room service bill while Elvis was working.

The concert in Barcelona on 16 July betrayed something of Elvis's furious mood: he walked on-stage nearly an hour late, played 'Veronica' by himself and then performed a perfunctory half-an-hour set with The Attractions before stomping off. It was almost like 1979 all over again. On his return for a three-song encore he shouted, 'Fuck Johnnie Walker and fuck Sold Out,' the sponsors and promoters of the gig respectively. It lasted barely an hour.

In this atmosphere of recrimination and rapidly declining respect, Bruce Thomas chose to air his grievances by sliding into disinterest and unprofessionalism on-stage. Disenchanted with the record they were promoting and tired of the growing sense that this was The Attractions in name but not in spirit, the bass player was beginning to let his personal feelings affect his performances. 'I just lost interest and I suppose it showed in my eyes and my body language,' he admits. 'I was taking the piss out of him, to be honest, singing alternative versions to the lyrics when he was doing his solo set, or forgetting songs on stage. Elvis would turn around and say, "You'd better fucking rehearse!". But I don't have a problem remembering songs, I just have a problem concentrating when I'm not committed anymore.'

Elvis was enough of an old hand to keep on playing through the storm, but there was only so much of this behaviour he was prepared to swallow. '[Bruce] was making lots of embarrassing mistakes, and The Attractions had taken pride in never being erractic,' he said. 'We did set a very high standard and the last thing I wanted it to be was a sorry excuse for it.'7 When the tour reached America, he made the decision privately – then publicly – that this would be the last time around the block for The Attractions. This time he meant it.

The tour rolled into Los Angeles on 25 August like a thundercloud. Bruce gave Elvis a stuffed armadillo as a forty-second birthday present, a fairly pointed indication of how high Elvis ranked in his affections. The next night, Elvis and The Attractions performed the withering 'You Bowed Down' on *The Tonight Show with Jay Leno* in Los Angeles, and Elvis changed the words to incorporate the title phrase from a new song, 'I Should Have Never Walked Over That Bridge I Burned'.

As if the inference wasn't obvious enough, he told Leno he was quitting touring and possibly even recording. Disenchanted with the predictability of playing with a loud rock 'n' roll band, particularly one where only three-quarters of the line-up were committed to the music, his exhaustion and disaffection was palpable. 'I don't think he'll be working with The Attractions again,' admitted a Warners' spokesman the next morning, with some understatement.

Effectively, for the last three weeks of the tour, The Attractions were simply working their notice. Everyone knew it was the end, and by the time the tour dropped anchor in Osaka in Japan on 6 September, the mood had turned unbelievably sour, far worse even than the first time the band had imploded. Elvis and Bruce hadn't spoken to each other for nearly a month, and the expression of animosity had descended to primary school levels. 'In the end I was blowing raspberries at Cait, or she would walk into the lift and stand with her back six inches from my face,' admits Thomas. It was a terribly undignified way to end.

Elvis, for his part, was displaying signs that the whole experience had left him somewhat dejected. In Minneapolis on 18 August, he had walked into his room in the Whitney Hotel and decided that the windows were too narrow, moving instead to the Presidential Suite at the Marquis Hotel at a cost of $2000 a night. Bruce also alleges that Elvis believed the bass player was badmouthing him, feeding snippets of (mis)information and hostile propaganda to Costello fanzines.

It all ended, mercifully, on 15 September at the Kinro-Kaikan in Nagoya. There seemed to be a kind of release, The Attractions ratcheting up the intensity as they neared the finish line, racing down the final furlong with a searing blast of 'The Beat', 'Man Out Of Time', 'Mystery Dance', 'Red Shoes', 'This Year's Girl' and a final – perhaps ironic – '(What's So Funny 'Bout) Peace, Love & Understanding'. Elvis introduced The Attractions one last time and they were gone: 'Good night. God Bless. Sayonara!'

They at least exchanged a tepid handshake after the show. 'Whenever,' Bruce shrugged. 'Yeah, whenever,' replied Elvis. And that was that. There would be no sentimental rapprochement this time. 'You won't see them again,' swore Elvis. 'I had a slight feeling of sadness on the last night that we played. It was like the last night of your childhood. I knew I wouldn't do that again. When somebody is deliberately fucking it up, you have to get rid of them. It's as simple as that.'[8]

Chapter Sixteen
1996–99

ELVIS DIDN'T JUST SAY GOODBYE to The Attractions in Japan, he effectively waved farewell to the notion of taking any further part in the commercial circus of rock 'n' roll for several years. Following the disappointment of *All This Useless Beauty* – which a year on from its release had sold a mere 97,000 copies in the US – and Elvis's less-than-complimentary remarks about his record company over the last couple of years, the relationship with Warners was entering its death throes. 'I'm sick of working as hard as I do for no reward in terms of selling records,' he later said. 'That had to stop.'[1]

Amid allegations that Elvis had stormed into the Warners building in Los Angeles and resigned, it became clear that the next record would be his last for the label. 'I just think he's done all he could do with us and he's looking to start over and find some new blood,' said Warners spokesman Bill Bentley, with the usual corporate diplomacy.

However, Elvis was unwilling to hand them any new material, and it was agreed that his final record for Warners would be a compilation, scheduled for release in the autumn of 1997.

He was exhausted with the limitations of the rock band format, and wouldn't tour again with a band until 2002, so sincere and thorough was his disillusion following the demise of The Attractions. He was also unhappy with his own writing, thinking deeply about the lasting worth of what he was doing and what he had done, and looking at different means of expressing himself. He talked about using electronic instruments in a new way or eventually making instrumental music so expressive it required no explanation. 'I've been troubled by the relationship between word and thought and what use it is to me,' he admitted. 'I'm troubled by what the point is in saying anything else. Why add a single wasted word to the stack of wasted words? My ambition is to write no words at all.'[2]

Preoccupied with a sense of futility, Elvis effectively took a year off, spending some time decompressing at home in Ireland with Cait and considering his options. He was far too creatively hyperactive to sit still for long, but the ensuing eighteen months were largely to be a period of patchwork activity: small pieces, fun collaborations and impromptu live appearances.

Following the derailment of The Attractions in mid-September, there had been some piecemeal classical commitments. Spread thinly throughout October and November, Elvis had participated in a brief UK tour with John Harle in support of the saxophonist's *Terror And Magnificence* album. Part of a line-up which included soprano Sarah Leonard and saxophonist Andy Sheppard, Elvis appeared in Aberdeen, Nottingham, Birmingham, Manchester and London, where his contribution included singing the three songs from *Twelfth Night* that he had performed on Harle's record, plus renditions of John Dowland's 'Flow My Tears' and his own 'Shipbuilding'. It was a rather strange affair and, aside from the show at London's Royal Festival Hall, most of the other dates were sparsely attended and Elvis's involvement passed off virtually unnoticed.

There were two more similarly low-key classical engagments in 1997: three Spanish concerts with the Brodsky Quartet in Malaga, Jerez and Valencia on 8, 9 and 11 January, and the world premiere of his score for the animated film, *Tom Thumb*, on 3 July.

Elvis had written and recorded the original score in 1993, but the film – which was to have been narrated by John Cleese – was never finished. However Paul Pritchard, a member of the studio ensemble who had played at the session, suggested that Elvis might like to adapt the score for a concert performance with a small orchestra, staged by the Academy of St Martin's In The Field chamber orchestra.

Performed in the lashing rain at the Thorndon Country Park in Essex, 'Tom Thumb' was effectively the warm-up act for the main production. Elvis declined to narrate the piece himself, merely introducing his work before leaving the stage and letting children's TV presenter Zoe Ball do the honours. The music was simple, light and often cartoonish, specifically designed to give children an interest in different musical instruments and textures, but Elvis had given the piece his full consideration. 'I try to go against type,' he explained. 'I didn't make Tom Thumb a piccolo. He's a bassoon because he's always trying to be bigger than he is, huffing and puffing.'[3]

Much of the rest of the year was spent in America. There were numerous appearances across the Atlantic, cameos with the likes of The Jazz Passengers, the Charles Mingus Orchestra, Ron Sexsmith, The Fairfield Four and Ricky Skaggs, who hosted a TV show where Elvis performed with George Jones. On that occasion Elvis was – according to Skaggs –

'nervous as a cat' as he sang Jones's 'The Last Town I Painted' and 'The Big Fool Of The Year'. He also played Gram Parsons' 'That's All It Took' and his own 'Indoor Fireworks' on the show. Elvis had written the latter back in 1985 with Skaggs in mind, but the singer passed it up, wary of the song's 'drinking, cheating lines. I wasn't really doing that kind of country,' he explains. What other kind of country is there?

It was all enjoyably hectic, largely free of all the hassles and responsibilities of being in charge of a band on the road. He simply turned up, learned his lines and sang his songs.

However, there was something more significant brewing. During all his many trips to the States in 1997, a collaboration with Burt Bacharach was uppermost in Elvis's mind. Following the undeniable creative success of 'God Give Me Strength', he and Bacharach were now actively planning an album-length collaboration, at Elvis's initial instigation.

Their first public appearance was on the David Letterman show at the end of February, playing 'God Give Me Strength' together for the first time. The following night, Elvis and Burt popped up at the Grammy Awards to co-present an award, and they found time in March to meet again in Los Angeles.

The writing process finally began in May, at Bacharach's home in California. Initially, the plan was for an album partly made up of old Bacharach songs augmented with some co-written songs, satisfying Elvis's instincts as a fan as well as his natural and ever-present inclination to create something new. However, when the two men discovered they were equally driven when it came to writing music, the ambition of the project intensified. 'He's someone who lives like I live,' Bacharach said in the summer. 'Someone who can be writing a tune at four in the morning.'4

When Bacharach played London's Royal Albert Hall on 1 July, Elvis was there, and over the course of the year they came together about four or five times to write, sitting at keyboards or pianos in Burt's music room in Santa Monica or in a suite at the Regency Hotel in New York, trading ideas for days at a time.

Sometimes, Elvis simply provided the words to Burt's music, as on 'The Long Division' and most of 'This House Is Empty Now'. But usually the songs were either a joint dialogue, or created from the process of combining separately composed pieces. Musically, the combination of magpie and fan in Elvis was happy to bend more towards Bacharach's traditional style, and he later expressed delight that many of the more obvious 'Burt' touches were actually written by him. 'Toledo', for example, with its clipped time signature, parping horns and 'Do You Know The Way To San Jose' feel, was essentially a Costello composition.

Having written or presented the basic tracks face-to-face, much of the spade work was done apart. When Elvis was away on a jaunt or back in Dublin, Bacharach would work on the songs, altering harmony or structure or adding a bridge, while Elvis was constantly attending to the words. Lyrically, they had agreed that the songs would be loosely based on the theme of lost love, luxuriating in melancholy. In actual fact, they ended up being much darker than that: tales of infidelity, divorce, despair and obsession. Elvis later claimed the songs were written to order, essentially a craft job; if so, he showed himself to be a terrific actor.

Renowned within music circles as not just a perfectionist but an absolute obsessive, Bacharach was one of the business's hardest task-masters when it came to the formalities of song structure. Although he was impressed with his collaborator, the two embarked on a very amicable but bruising contest, in which the traditional Costello method of cramming as many words as he desired into whatever structure could hold them was given short shrift by his partner. 'He's a very exacting person,' Elvis admitted. 'I've had to really think about what I wanted to say in the lyrics, maybe get rid of the superfluous words.'5

During the composition of 'In The Darkest Place', Elvis had come up with the line 'That is the torch I carry.' Bacharach, however, found the final syllable intolerable, because he felt it didn't fit snugly enough the melody he had written. Left to his own devices, Elvis would more than likely have bent the melody to fit his words, but this time there was no give. Eventually, he went away and changed the line to 'This is the torch I bear'.

This minute pruning of lyrical excesses fitted neatly with Elvis's stated desire to let the music do the talking for much of the time, but even so it was undoubtedly a steep learning curve for him, working out exactly what was and wasn't necessary in a song. 'We had the inevitable arguments, but I mostly went with his judgment,' he admitted. 'I found that the changes he was suggesting weren't just improving a line, but, two or three lines on, would pay off again. The shape of the melody, that's really Burt's bag.'6

Following songwriting sessions in October and four further days in the middle of December, the duo had between ten to twelve songs written and were essentially ready to record. Indeed, they were already talking about touring.

However, their respective schedules dictated that it was going to be the summer of 1998 before they could start work on the record. The fact that Elvis was switching record labels also pushed the recording back. His deal with Warners was dead, and throughout the year Elvis had been looking at the options for a new record company. During October, news leaked out that he had signed with Polygram worldwide, although it would not be officially announced until the New Year.

Crucially, the deal confronted head-on one of the major problems that Elvis had encountered latterly with Warners: that of his growing diversity and his desire to release records outside of the mainstream rock market, without the pressures of trying to shoehorn them into the preconceived company idea of what 'Elvis Costello' represented.

The new deal with Polygram would, in theory, allow Elvis the freedom to release records on Polygram's affiliated labels, specifically designed to cater for – and sell records to – specialist markets. His traditional rock releases would be released on Mercury; a mooted jazz-orientated project would come out on Verve; while classical-leaning work would appear on Decca/London. It seemed the perfect set-up. 'A company that has outlets to accommodate everything from Hanson to Cake, from Bryn Terfel to an Allen Ginsberg record, sounds like a place for me,'7 said Elvis, with uncharacteristic optimism.

At the same time as news was leaking concerning the new deal, Elvis was fulfilling the last part of his contract with Warners. *Extreme Honey: The Very Best of The Warner Brothers Years*, covering songs from 1989–97, was released on 17 October. Featuring tracks from *Spike, Mighty Like A Rose, The Juliet Letters, Brutal Youth* and *All This Useless Beauty,* the only two rarities were the Eno collaboration 'My Dark Life' and 'The Bridge I Burned', a new song based on a bastardisation of Prince's 'Pop Life'.

The latter was significant not so much for its mildly unhinged nature and its kiss-off sentiments – which could reasonably be said to be directed towards both The Attractions and Warners – but for the fact that it was the first recorded collaboration between Elvis and his son.

Matt was now in his early twenties and a jobbing bass player, propagating the fourth generation of MacManus musicians. He had already appeared on the personnel for *All This Useless Beauty*, credited with 'rhythm research' on 'It's Time'. 'Elvis strongly wanted to involve his son,' recalled Pete Thomas. 'What [Matt] did was find out if his impressive collection of Detroit soul and funk had a loop for a song. After a while he came to me with many a loop and we listened to them all together.'8 On 'The Bridge I Burned', Elvis took the father-son partnership further. They produced the song together, MacManus Jr playing bass and providing a drum loop. Also involved was Matt's friend Danny Goffey, the drummer from Supergrass.

The promotion budget provided by Warners for *Extreme Honey* was $1000, a 'calculated insult', according to Elvis, who lamented the 'shoddy treatment' he had received over the past two or three years. Right at the death, Warners' president Stephen Baker tried to stem the flow of bad blood. 'However our relationship ended, everybody here really loved being in business with him,' he said in a statement. 'Whether he was happy or sad or whatever, I was talking to an artist I totally respected, and it was a thrill for me and for Warner Brothers Records.'

For Elvis, comfort probably couldn't have come any colder. Even so, he did his bit for the promotion of *Extreme Honey*, appearing on Clive Anderson's talk show in the UK and playing 'So Like Candy' on David Letterman's show on 18 November in the States, but unsurprisingly the record failed to chart on either side of the Atlantic. Most fans already had the songs, while those with a merely passing interest in Elvis probably didn't even know the record existed.

He was, in truth, travelling very far away from the pop charts, and mainly under his own steam. A short tour of northern Italian opera houses wasn't every record label's idea of sound commercial practice. Nevertheless, Elvis set off at the beginning of 1998, with Steve Nieve in tow. His relationship with both Steve and Pete Thomas had survived the fall-out from the final Attractions tour, and he and Steve had become especially close. 'He is a great friend,' said Elvis. 'We spent so much time touring with The Attractions and he never had the opportunity to show what he could do. He has gained a lot of confidence in the last few years.'9

Elvis remained keen to pursue the potentially rich music the two of them had begun making, and the Italian tour was a romantic undertaking, playing in small theatres with almost perfect acoustics between the 3–16 February. Close reading of the dates revealed that Elvis was using the tour as something of a Trojan Horse, to catch as many shows as he could by Italian opera star Cecilia Bartoli, who was also touring Italy at the same time.

The duo were somewhat under-rehearsed, but as the tour went on they took the chance to mine the deepest seams of Elvis's songbook. In particular, he seemed to have been listening to *Punch The Clock* again: rarely heard obsurities such as 'King Of Thieves', 'Invisible Man', 'Mouth Almighty', as well as 'Kid About It', 'I'll Wear It Proudly', and 'From A Whisper To A Scream' sat alongside versions of Shakespeare's 'O, Mistress Mine', 'Gigi', 'My Funny Valentine' and a new song called 'Bright Blue Times', written for a BBC television series.

It was a genuinely energising experience. Elvis judged the results to be some of the freest and most rewarding shows of his career, and within six months he would receive the Tenco Award, the most prestigious recognition for a foreign musician in Italy. The tour was also a healing process after the desultory mood of the last Attractions tour. The sense of gloom and futility was beginning to lift. 'I've rediscovered a love of playing live and an affection for performing a broad range of my own catalogue,' he said. 'I've got a pride in it that I didn't have a few years ago.'[10]

* * *

On 8 April, Elvis and Cait travelled to New York to appear with a gallery of stars at Burt Bacharach's 'One Amazing Night' tribute concert at the Hammersmith Ballroom in Manhattan. At the show, which also featured Dionne Warwick, Chrissie Hynde, Sheryl Crow and Luther Vandross, the audience were given a brief filmed preview of the pair working together, before Elvis came on and sang one of their new tracks, 'This House Is Empty Now'.

Immediately afterwards, the two men embarked upon their final song-writing – or more accurately, song-polishing – session before they finally began recording the songs in Ocean Way in Los Angeles over June and July 1998. It was one of the hottest summers in living memory, and Elvis cut an eccentric figure in the Californian sun: receding hair brutally shorn and topped off with a straw pork-pie hat, dressed in a thick black leather coat and tinted yellow shades, he was the antithesis of Bacharach's immaculate West Coast cool.

The sessions were split into two. The basic tracks were laid down in the first half of the recording schedule, while the final two-week session was devoted to adding the layers of overdubs and wealth of detail that characterised Bacharach's recordings. There were a few familiar faces at Ocean Way. Elvis had insisted on putting together a core group to hold the songs together – Steve Nieve played keyboards, Greg Cohen bass and Jim Keltner drums, while Kevin Killen was engineer – but although it was a genuine collaboration and a co-production, the songs inevitably leaned far more towards Burt's style than Elvis's. 'There was nothing to be gained in trying to prove the point that we could make some sort of Frankenstein's monster out of the most extreme edges,' Elvis admitted. "The hybrid of 'Pump It Up' and 'What's New, Pussycat' might seem like something of a road crash.'[11]

It was arduous work. Even Elvis found the intensity of Bacharach's focus astonishing, and ultimately the older man called the shots. They were still tinkering with the songs as they arrived in the studio, with Bacharach continuing his zero-tolerance approach to the shape of the songs and especially the lyrics, fussing and fretting over misplaced commas and stray syllables.

Elvis was more assertive in terms of instrumentation: he weaned Bacharach away from the thick synthesiser sound that he had been using since the early '80s and towards more organic, emotionally resonant textures. Many of the vocals were sung live as Burt played piano and conducted the rhythm section of Jim Keltner and Greg Cohen, ensuring that there was an emotional heartbeat at the record's centre.

The lushness of the final album was achieved at the second recording session, where a twenty-four-piece orchestra overdubbed string arrangements written and conducted by Bacharach; female backing singers were added to most of the songs, as well as brass and woodwind; and a whole day was devoted to adding tuned percussion touches. Finished by the end of July, the record was scheduled for a late September release, and Elvis came away from the sessions exhausted but beaming. 'Just watching him work like that has been an inspiration,' he said. 'I'm blessed.'[12]

While Elvis and Bacharach were recording in Ocean Way, Bill Frisell was hard at work in New York on a unique parallel project, recording instrumental versions of the same set of songs at the same time without having the faintest clue what Elvis and Bacharach were coming up with. 'They gave me the music as they had finished writing it,' says Frisell. 'It was just Elvis singing the songs, standing next to Burt Bacharach who was playing the piano. I had this cassette of what sounded like classic songs that no one had ever heard before, it was just amazing.'

Although neither knew what the other was doing, there were odd resonances in the finished project. Frisell might give the melody to the trumpet on a particular song, and later find Elvis and Bacharach had done the same, while Elvis later came and added vocal parts to 'Toledo' and 'I Still Have That Other Girl'.

Called *The Sweetest Punch*, Frisell's album was due to be released on Polygram's jazz label, Verve, at the same time as the main album hit the shops, in order to showcase the duality and versatility of the new songs. However, that plan proved unworkable and eventually it was released on Decca, another arm of Polygram, in autumn 1999, undeniably deadening the impact of the venture.

Painted From Memory – as this dark, regretful record was now aptly called – was released on 28 September 1998 on Mercury. The essence of the record was melody and melancholy, two touchstones which neither artist had much of a problem locating. 'In The Darkest Place', 'Toledo', 'I Still Have That Other Girl' and 'God Give Me Strength' were as good as anything Elvis had written over the last decade, and certainly matched anything Bacharach had done since his '60s heyday. Both 'My Thief' and the title track were truly mesmerising torch songs, worthy of Sinatra at his most forlorn, while 'The Sweetest Punch' zipped along, the one example of Elvis in pop mode.

But there were inevitable problems with the record. At either extreme of the collaborative spectrum, 'Such Unlikely Lovers' and 'The Long Division' strayed into the middle-of-the-road territory covered in Bacharach's terminally over-cooked '80s collaborations with the likes of Christopher Cross, while some of the more inventive wordplay one might have expected from Elvis was missed on a record with such an unvarying mood. The instrumentation could also grate: the polished guitar solo on 'This House Is Empty Now', the Moog-break on 'The Long Division', the keyboards on 'Such Unlikely Lovers', the ultra-smooth, somewhat syrupy backing singers. There was a sense that few writers other than Bacharach would have been able to get such banal textures onto an Elvis Costello record.

In the end, the album was saved as an emotionally involving document by the strength of the songs and Elvis's singing: dramatic, passionate, raw and deeply felt, his live vocals provided the perfect counter balance to the smooth sophistication of the music. His voice wasn't what it used to be: what it had gained in richness, it had lost in crackle. It had widened and loosened, but had lost its laser-like precision and its ability to cut through in the process. It also often wobbled alarmingly, as though there was a whammy bar at the back of his neck.

But those reviewers who desired a more technically accomplished singer missed the yearning at the songs' hearts, and if his voice was sometimes straining at the very top of his register or occasionally even cracking, very few singers could have wrung so much genuine and affecting emotion from songs like 'My Thief' or 'God Give Me Strength', even if it did make for an exhausting listening experience. 'We're not making an easy-listening record,' said Elvis. 'We're making a passionate, emotional record the way we always intended to.'[13]

Even so, Andy Gill in *The Independent* wasn't alone in finding Elvis's voice and vibrato the sticking point. 'The arrangements feature the familiar Bacharach trademark touches – the discreet brass, the piano, the solitary French horn – but it is like trying to gaze at a beautiful vista whilst a huge lorry belches diesel fumes in your face.'

With such a unique collaboration there was bound to be a certain amount of huffing and puffing from the critics. 'Sumptuous arrangements, artful songwriting, timeless sophistication,' said the *Observer*. 'Costello's ballads are top-drawer, showing none of his usual verbal contrivance, while Bacharach's arrangements only occasionally become somnambulent.' The *NME* called it a 'powerful and occasionally elegiac reminder of the art of song', while *The Sunday Times* heard 'a compromise – classic instrumentation with glossy modern production'.

In the States, it was a similar story, most reviews split according to whether they felt Elvis's voice was an attraction or an aberration. *Music Week* called it 'a match made in musical heaven. Bacharach's lush, sweeping sound finds a perfect foil in Costello's frail yet distinctive voice. The enduring appeal of both these artists should pay dividends in the charts.'

Indeed, Mercury were expecting big things commercially from the record. Bacharach was cool again – albeit in a consciously kitsch way – following years of being dismissed as little more than a purveyor of plastic lounge music, while Elvis had a name which still resonated across musical boundaries. 'Every year or two there is an album that crosses several demographics and brings together musical styles that galvanize audiences: we think this is one of those albums,'[14] said Danny Goldberg, the CEO of Mercury. The promotional campaign was aggressive, including dozens of interviews, TV appearances on the *Late Show with David Letterman* in the US and Chris Evans' talk show in the UK, in-store appearances, a proposed television special and, most significantly, a mini-tour of five dates in the US and Britain.

Opening on 13 October at the Radio City Music Hall in New York and ending at the Royal Festival Hall in London on the twenty-ninth, the structure of each concert was virtually identical every night. Elvis began by singing the opening verses of 'Baby, It's You' off-stage, before introducing Bacharach over the PA. Then the two strolled onto the stage, Elvis looking more like an ageing boxing referee than a bobby-sox crooner in his swish tuxedo and bow-tie, Bacharach sliding smoothly behind the grand piano. It was pure showbiz.

The musicians on stage replicated the line-up on the album: Steve Nieve on keyboards and piano, a small orchestra, a band playing traditional rock instruments and three female backing singers. Following 'What The World Needs Now Is Love' – not a sentiment which many people would have expected to hear from Elvis's lips – came the first of three segments featuring selections from the new record: 'Toledo', 'Such Unlikely Lovers', 'This House Is Empty Now', and 'Tears At The Birthday Party'. Then he sang 'I Just Don't Know What To Do With Myself', a song he had been performing live since 1977 but – as he admitted – never with all the right chord changes until now.

Then he left the stage to Bacharach, who played a medley of some of his greatest songs, including 'The Look Of Love' and 'Raindrop's Keep Fallin' On My Head'. Elvis returned after half an hour to sing the rousing 'Make It Easy On Yourself', performing what *Uncut* magazine deemed to be 'one of the most spectacular vocal performances of his life' at the London show.

'Painted From Memory' and 'What's Her Name Today' followed, before Bacharach departed and Elvis and Steve played a short set of Costello songs: a stripped-down 'Accidents Will Happen' was followed by 'Veronica', where the orchestra joined in towards the end and stayed for versions of 'Just A Memory', 'Almost Blue' and 'Alison'. After the opening shows in New York and Washington, Elvis added 'Still Too Soon To Know' to the solo set.

Then Burt re-emerged for the final flourish of 'In The Darkest Place', 'The Long Division', 'My Thief', 'I Still Have That Other Girl' and 'The Sweetest Punch'. The encores were 'My Little Red Book', 'Anyone Who Had A Heart' and a closing 'God Give Me Strength', the latter more than holding its own in such exalted company.

It was all very tasteful and respectful, although at $75 and £50 a ticket it was debatable as to what would have represented value for money. Elvis's short set with Steve and strings was a high point, providing a little grit in the shows, while the suitability – or otherwise – of Elvis's voice remained a moot point. Many were thrilled by the combination of the two unlikely bedfellows, the old-fashioned emphasis on the songs and the voice. Others seemed happy to talk through many of the performances.

In the end, Elvis cared little for what the critics said one way or another. The collaboration with Bacharach had been a piece of wish-fulfilment that was far more personal than merely writing a few songs. Elvis had grown up watching his father singing big, emotive ballads – sometimes Burt's – in a dinner jacket in front of a pop orchestra, and after working with Bacharach he felt he had finally made his own mark on Ross's territory. Hence the eager, non-ironic adoption of all the auxiliary hallmarks of the genre: the tuxedo, the glitz, the occasional lounge singer affectation, the respect for the sanctity of the song. 'It was very much an ambition of mine that one day I might end up doing exactly what [my dad] had done,'[15] Elvis admitted. *Painted From Memory* was a fitting realisation of those childhood dreams.

* * *

Once again, there were ominous clouds on the horizon. Polygram was merging with Universal as part of a take-over deal by Seagram, and there had been a large amount of blood-letting, including the departure of the man who had been instrumental in signing Elvis to the label, Danny Goldberg. The disruption meant not only that the post-release promotion of *Painted From Memory* got caught somewhat in the middle, but also that Elvis's plan to record a rock 'n' roll album in 1999 was shelved. He wasn't going to let any more releases get caught in the corporate crossfire.

Painted From Memory was listed in many of the year-end magazine and newspaper polls as one of the top albums of the previous twelve months. Indeed, it had attracted some of Elvis's best notices of the last ten years, benefiting from the kind of marketing campaign from his new record label that he had so long desired from Warners.

Furthermore, in February, Elvis and Burt bagged a Grammy in the slightly obscure catergory of Pop Collaboration With Vocals for the single of 'I Still Have That Other Girl', beating the motley crew of R. Kelly, Stevie Wonder, Celine Dion and Babyface in the process. Typically, Elvis did his utmost to conceal his pleasure. 'I am sceptical about these things,' he said. 'The first time I was nominated, The Attractions were up against Chic for Best New Artist of the Year. We thought we might be in with a distant chance of second. What won? A Taste of Honey with "Boogie Oogie Oogie"! So I can't take it too seriously.'[16]

Over all, there could be very few music fans in the western world who weren't aware of the album's existence, and yet it proved a huge commercial disappointment, peaking at No. 32 in the UK – his worst-ever chart position for an album of new material – and No. 42 in the States.

Predictably, Elvis pointed the finger at Polygram, but his continuing insistence on blaming record company problems for his lack of commercial success was becoming just a little suspicious. The musical landscape had changed beyond all recognition, and Elvis had for some time been a cult act, albeit one who had flirted with huge, global superstardom and then backed off. He was well-respected and well-rewarded, both renumeratively and in terms of the respect of his peers, yet he also appeared to believe he was living in a halcyon age of songwriting where Burt Bacharach records still got to No. 1 and sold a million copies. It was faintly absurd.

Instead of locking horns with the spirit-sapping forces of the musical industry, Elvis spent most of the year on the road with Steve. Before setting out, however, there were sombre duties to address. Elvis attended Dusty Springfield's funeral on 12 March at St Mary the Virgin Church in Henley on Thames, saying a few words during the service in appreciation for the unique talents of the great soul singer whom he had loved since his teens, and who had recorded a version of Elvis's bespoke composition 'Just A Memory' back in the '80s. Less than a month later, on 10 April, Elvis was at the Royal Albert Hall for a memorial concert for Linda McCartney, who had – like Dusty – recently died of breast cancer. He and Steve were accompanied by the Duke String Quartet on Wings' 'Warm And Beautiful', having already played an emotional 'That Day Is Done' as a simple duet. Again, Elvis spoke movingly, this time recalling how Linda made him feel at ease and calmed his nerves when he had started working with Paul back in 1987. The three-song set ended with '(What's So Funny 'Bout) Peace, Love & Understanding', backed by The Pretenders, and Elvis later joined the ensemble finale to sing backing and play guitar on 'Let It Be', Ricky Nelson's 'Lonesome Town' and 'All My Loving'.

The 'Lonely World' tour kicked off in Amsterdam two days later, coming on the back of a handful of brief collaborations with the pianist following their Italian tour the previous spring.

Which version of the Costello-Nieve roadshow were audiences going to get? A performance together at the Fuji Rock Festival in Tokyo on 1 August 1998 had been disappointing, a mere forty-five minutes in length and almost an apology for the non-appearance of The Attractions. For the first time as a duo they played old standards such as 'Less Than Zero', 'Chelsea', and 'Everyday I Write The Book', songs generally unsuited to the pared-down format. They miscued the ending of 'Chelsea', Elvis fluffed the words to '(What's So Funny 'Bout) Peace, Love & Understanding', and generally the performance was subdued and seemed to lack heart, as if he wasn't really feeling these songs anymore.

In contrast, a brief jaunt around New Zealand, Japan and Australia in February had seen some genuine treats thrown into the sets, some often played just once: 'Baby Plays Around', 'Love Field', 'Pads, Paws And Claws', 'Inch By Inch', 'I Hope You're Happy Now', 'Hand In Hand' and 'Town Cryer' among them.

In the end, it was the latter incarnation which came out of the blocks for the 'Lonely World' tour on the twelfth of April. Elvis and Steve had worked out about seventy songs in all, ensuring that the setlists were open to substantial change every night, but the tour was loosely designed to promote *Painted From Memory*. 'Toledo' was released as a single in April, but predictably did little business, and following the upheavals at the record company, Elvis felt the tour was 'the only way to spread the word about these songs'.[17]

The duo had become an awesome live act, with a huge repertoire not only of songs, but also of moods, textures and emotions. In the absence of Bacharach and his orchestra, the songs were stripped down from their original recorded states and the lush presentations of the concerts the previous October. In many ways this freed them. 'Steve Nieve's stream of inventions and embellishments allowed Costello to take the songs to places they'd never seen before,' said Adam Sweeting in the *Guardian*, reviewing the Albert Hall show on 15 April.

The shows were a Costello fanatic's dream. In Copenhagen on 30 April there were a couple of real rarities: 'After The Fall' and 'Suit Of Lights', while 'Little Palaces', 'Any King's Shilling', 'Waiting For The End Of The World', 'Little Triggers', 'Blue Chair' and 'Rocking Horse Road' also popped up throughout the tour. Each show ended with Elvis singing 'Couldn't Call It Unexpected No. 4' without a microphone, trawling the front of the stage as he serenaded the crowd, like a modern-day John McCormack. Audience reactions were genuinely passionate.

When the tour hit North America halfway through May, the duo incorporated the Charles Aznavour ballad 'She' into the set. Elvis had recorded the song as the theme song for the film *Notting Hill*, a vehicle for Julia Roberts' smile that went on general release at the end of May. His unironic and emotional reading – with vibrato in full effect – was recorded at Abbey Road with a ninety-six-piece orchestra as he gazed at Ms Roberts on the studio cinema screen. 'She' gave Elvis his first Top 20 UK single since 1983 – reaching No. 19 in the summer and yielding an unlikely *Top Of The Pops* appearance, following which the single promptly plummeted.

The US tour ended with a show at the Woodstock Festival on 25 July, a misguided attempt to tap into the nostalgia surrounding the thirtieth anniversary of the original. It was an incongruous place to find Steve and Elvis, but they nonetheless won the Sunday afternoon crowd over with a fourteen-song set which covered most points of his career. No longer merely contrary for the sake of it, Elvis even finished with '(What's So Funny 'Bout) Peace, Love & Understanding'.

* * *

There was a break in live work in August and September, with further dates planned with Steve throughout the final three months of 1999. Culminating with two concerts in Japan on 15 and 18 December, the 'Lonely World' tour would end up being Elvis's most intensive spell on the road since the late '70s, featuring some of his most artistically satisfying shows. During the lull, Universal released a comprehensive double CD *Best Of* collection, which provided Elvis with an unexpected hit record, entering the charts at No. 4, his first Top 10 UK album since *Brutal Youth* five years earlier. While watching some of his old recordings climb the charts, Elvis spent much of his seven weeks off writing new songs.

It was the first time he had written 'for himself' for four years, and also the first time since 1994 that he had used the guitar as his principal compositional instrument. '45' was written on his forty-fifth birthday, an autobiography in three minutes, dissecting late twentieth-century history and his own upbringing in clever nine-year chunks, with just a handful of chords and a classic 1978 melody. 'Alibi' was a long, forensic examination of a lifetime's worth of lame excuses which could have graced *Blood & Chocolate* without sounding out of place. 'I love you just as much as I hate your guts' was the central refrain, and he would add several more over the next two years as the song evolved.

'Heart-Shaped Bruise' and 'I Dreamed Of My Old Lover Last Night' were more traditional tracks, both written from a woman's perspective for a story-in-song cycle that Elvis was developing, provisionally called *The Delivery Man*. The tunes were simple, written on acoustic guitar with instantly arresting country and folk melodies, with shades of *King Of America*.

These songs were firmly within the classic Costello template, but Elvis was also experimenting with computers, samples and beat-boxes for his next record, which he planned to build on a heavy rhythmic base, using technology to explore different rhythmic settings for the songs. He had used computer technology since *Mighty Like A Rose*, but this was very far removed from writing carefully layered orchestral lines. 'I want the music to be driven more by rhythm,' he explained. 'I want to use the same computer technology, but balance the harmony with rhythm. It might mean abandoning the accepted song structure a little bit, but I do think it's possible.'[18]

Partly, his inspiration came from an interest in the deep bottom-end of modern hip-hop and R&B records, whose production he found 'absolutely mind-bending'. And partly it stemmed from a desire to wrest control of the rhythmic rudder of a song, ensuring that it wasn't reliant on the input of other musicians – a legacy of the dog-days of his relationship with Bruce Thomas, perhaps.

The first results of these experimental approaches were startling. 'When I Was Cruel' was downright menacing, with airy, discordant guitar shapes ringing above a slow, rhythmic pulse. The other new songs were sparse, disquieting tracks written from a teacher's and a lawyer's viewpoint respectively, and had more specific starting points: 'A Teacher's Tale (Oh Well)' and 'Soul For Hire' had initially prompted Elvis's summer writing spree, composed to order for the film called *Prison Song*.*

When he and Steve resumed their 'Lonely World' tour in the States the fruits of his summer labour were beginning to appear. Less emphasis was placed on the *Painted From Memory* material, now a year old, and the

---

* The film finally appeared in 2001 with both songs on the soundtrack. Elvis's small role as a 'despairing teacher in a leaky school' seemed to have been cut at the editing stage.

new songs crept in. He performed '45' on *The Tonight Show with Jay Leno* before the tour began, and at the opening night at the Warfield Theatre in San Francisco on 30 September, there were three new songs in the set. 'Alibi' opened – as it would throughout the tour – played without stage lights as Steve and Elvis conjured up a brooding, demi-Attractions sound in the dark with a clattering electro-rhythm, snarling guitar and a full sneer in Elvis's voice. 'I Dreamed Of My Old Lover Last Night' and '45' were also debuted.

By the end of the US tour on 31 October, Elvis had played ten new songs in total. In addition to the above, 'Couldn't You Keep That To Yourself' was a bluesy lounge song, piano-heavy and lyrically wry, that Elvis had had lying around for a while. He was pushed to finish it when a call came from David Sefton at the South Bank asking if Elvis had any songs for an album Sefton was producing for German cabaret chanteuse Ute Lemper. 'Burnt Sugar Is So Bitter' was a stark tale of domestic disharmony co-written with Carole King, while 'Suspect My Tears' was a big, poppy piano song that sounded like a *Painted From Memory* out-take, or at least a nod to Bacharach. 'It's good to go on the road when you've written a few new songs,' said Elvis. 'It's a great opportunity, if you've got the audience's confidence in you.'[19]

Steve and Elvis continued to play a winning combination of old and new songs when the tour reached Britain in November and December. 'Alibi' was still the throat-grabbing opener, usually followed by 'Man Out Of Time' and 'Talking In The Dark'. Then the sets skidded all over the vast expanses of Elvis's career; by the penultimate show of the UK tour in Glasgow on 7 December, he and Steve were playing three-hour concerts which compared favourably with anything Elvis had ever done on a stage. 'An evening shot through with smiles and spit, cries and whispers and history,' raved Damien Love in *The Scotsman*. 'A reminder that the luckiest archeologists of tomorrow will stare at the stretch of Costello's output and wonder – a truly, truly great concert. Absolutely staggering.'

Chapter Seventeen
2000–01

WHILE NEARING THE END of the *All This Useless Beauty* sessions back at the beginning of 1996, Elvis had travelled to Stockholm for two shows on 6 January with Sweden's Radio Symphony Orchestra and Anne Sofie Von Otter, the classical star. It was another exercise in wish-fulfilment for Elvis, who had been an admirer of the Swedish mezzo-soprano since the late '80s and had made no secret of both his love of her voice and his desire to collaborate with her. He was by no means alone in his admiration. 'In the classical world, she is *it*,' says Paul Cassidy. 'She's one of the greatest voices there has ever been.'

That night, a palpably nervous Elvis sang Bill Frisell's arrangement of 'Upon A Veil Of Midnight Blue' and Richard's Harvey's arrangement of 'The Birds Will Still Be Singing' with the Orchestra. Then – apparently unscheduled – he joined Anne Sofie to sing 'Autumn Leaves', 'Baby, It's Cold Outside' and 'Without A Song', with just a piano accompaniment. Later, they sang Kurt Weill's 'Lost In The Stars', and encored with 'My Ship' and 'Every Time We Say Goodbye'.

It was a low-key, fun engagement and both singers enjoyed it immensely. 'There's something about him when he performs that is terribly moving, really,' said Von Otter afterwards. 'I like his voice very much, it has a lot to say, the colour in it. It's a privilege to have got to know him a little bit.'[1] The two became friends. Elvis and Cait went out for dinner with Anne Sofie and her husband and frequently popped backstage after her concerts, and almost a year later, they collided again.

On 2 December 1997, Elvis watched Anne Sofie perform three pieces he had composed for her and the Brodsky Quartet in Paris's Cité De La Musique. Entitled *Three Distracted Women*, the songs – 'Speak Darkly, My Angel', 'Spiteful Dancer' and 'April In Orbit' – had been pieced together over a two-year period. 'Speak Darkly, My Angel' had been performed by Elvis as a song fragment at the Beacon Theatre shows in

New York the previous August, but each had been specially written to suit Von Otter's voice and the Quartet's style.

The Paris premiere was followed by a brief European tour, including dates in London, Madrid and Bologna. In London, Nicholas Williams of *The Independent* rated *Three Distracted Women* as among 'the evening's most substantial offerings – part concert aria, part reflection on the seventeenth-century consort song'.

Ever since, Elvis had been talking to Anne Sofie about the possibility of a recording collaboration. She was keen, and throughout 1999 and into 2000 they discussed suitable ideas and possible songs, exchanging cassettes and letters, finally settling on a non-classical template.

Unlike the collaborations with the Brodsky Quartet and Burt Bacharach, this time Elvis was bringing much more of his own musical background to the partnership, including some of his own songs, both new and old. Von Otter's varied personal tastes included folk music, standards and pop, but it was Elvis who was taking her into his own musical heartlands. On 19 February, he travelled to Stockholm for a few days to make some demo recordings with Anne Sofie. Having worked on ten songs and decided that they were compatible, they both consulted their hectic diaries and set aside time in October to start work on an album.

* * *

In contrast to the concert fireworks of the previous year, 2000 would prove to be a year of few public appearances but much activity behind the scenes, most of it on the classical side of Elvis's increasingly schizophrenic career. With so much varied work, and still uncertain about manouevres within the record company, Elvis again shelved his own plans to record a 'beat' album that year, putting it on hold indefinitely. Instead, throughout the rest of the spring he concentrated primarily on tackling perhaps the most ambitious project of his life.

In January, Elvis had flown to Perugia to attend a production of *Paradiso* by the Aterballetto, a well-established dance company based in Reggio Emilia in north Italy. He had recently been approached by the company to collaborate on their forthcoming production of *A Midsummer Night's Dream*, but Elvis felt ballet lay outside even his range of experience and ambition, conceding that he danced only in his mind. However, he was curious enough to attend, and after watching the performance of *Paradiso* and being 'overwhelmed' by it, he agreed to take on the commission of writing a score for *A Midsummer Night's Dream* (*Il Sogno Di Una Notte Di Mezza Estate*), *Il Sogno* for short.

The work would hold Elvis's attention for the better part of the year. He composed many of the basic themes for *Il Sogno* based on the motifs of Shakespeare's original play, with distant but frequent consultation with the Aterballetto's Mauro Bigonzetti, Nicola Lusuardi and designer Fabrizio Plessi, as well as some help from a bilingual colleague of the company. Elvis speaks passable Italian but it wasn't up to this kind of dense, fine-toothed discussion.

With the preliminary work done, Elvis travelled to Reggio in July with his demos and his piano melodies to ponder the finer details of the production face-to-face with members of the company and the creative team. 'Every aspect from the dramatic outline and choreographic intention to the stage design was examined in relation to the musical content,' said Elvis. 'I then returned home to Dublin to write and orchestrate each scene in the production.'[2]

After ten weeks of intense work at home throughout the late summer, the score began to take shape. Working originally on piano and then transcribing his work into musical notation, the constraints of time meant that, towards the end, Elvis had to begin orchestrating directly from his head onto manuscript paper for the sixty-piece orchestra. All the work was done manually with a pencil. Still, despite all the preparation, there were elements of the process which relied on a combination of serendipity and a degree of artistic telepathy. 'I had to go away and compose and then hope that [they] could make use of what I wrote,'[3] he admitted. At the end of the ten-week stretch of intense activity, Elvis had a score ready for performance later in the year.

As soon as he was finished with the compositional side of *Il Sogno*, recording could finally begin with Anne Sofie Von Otter. Elvis travelled to Stockholm towards the end of September to familiarise himself with the musicians and his surroundings. They were recording at Atlantis Studios, where Abba had cut 'Dancing Queen'; the famous grand piano which had inspired Steve Nieve to add his distinctive part to 'Oliver's Army' many years earlier was still in the room. Now, the pianist finally got the chance to play it.

Steve, ex-Rockpile member Billy Bremner and Michael Blair added subtle touches to the final record, but the core studio ensemble were respected local Swedish players familiar to Anne Sofie, as were the Swedish string quartet Fleshquartet, who also played on a handful of tracks. 'In the end, rather than it being something that I presented her with completely formed, it was a proper collaboration,' Elvis explained. 'Not in writing this time, but in choices: choices of instrumentation, choices of venue, choices of musical background.'[4]

Elvis's role was essentially that of producer and mentor, although he sang briefly on six of the eighteen songs and added a little guitar. He also brought two new bespoke tracks, called 'No Wonder' and 'For The Stars', to the sessions, and with typical collaborative zeal wrote three more while in Sweden. Two of them, 'Rope' and 'Just A Curio', were co-written with Fleshquartet, Elvis adding words to their music. The third was 'Green Song', Elvis adding lyrics to the ensemble leader Svante Henryson's solo cello piece.

The final track selection included the five newly composed songs and four old Costello numbers – 'Shamed Into Love', 'This House Is Empty Now', 'Baby Plays Around' and 'I Want To Vanish', ensuring that Elvis's fingerprints were all over the record. In the end, they decided not to record the *Three Distracted Women* songs that Anne Sofie had sung with the Brodsky Quartet in 1997, believing they were more suited to the stage than the album.

The nine remaining songs were covers of original material by Brian Wilson, Paul McCartney, Tom Waits, Abba, Jesse Mae Robinson, Ron Sexsmith and Kate and Anna McGarrigle. The sound was a loose amalgamation of folk music and laid-back jazz with classical inflections, with some pop touches thrown in. The mood – once again – was autumnal, a restrained, melancholic hue, etched with cello lines, soft piano, double bass and the occasional saxophone or pedal steel.

Overall, recording was a happy process, but there were tensions in the studio, brought about by the intrinsic cultural collisions of the project rather than any personality clashes. Elvis was determined to coax Anne Sofie Von Otter out of her classical stylings: he demanded live vocals rather than compound takes, while experimenting with microphone techniques and shifting song keys to force her into singing quietly, more naturalistically.

But some of the material caused problems: the two Tom Waits covers – 'Broken Bicycles' and 'Take It With Me' – were especially troublesome, primarily because the singer had trouble locating the song's melodies beneath the gruff, eccentric timbre of Waits's voice. 'Any song that Tom Waits sings is difficult for me to imagine that I could ever sing,'[5] she admitted, with some justification. 'Baby Plays Around', meanwhile, was the one Costello song that Elvis had brought to the session at his own instigation rather than Anne Sofie's, and the contours of the melody line gave her some difficulty. With the recording process so much more time-consuming than it is in the classical field, she also found her attention span and patience started to wane after more than a handful of takes on each song.

There were other glitches that only came to light in the studio. Elvis had envisaged singing duets and harmony on many of the songs, but soon found that the blend of voices didn't work on tape. 'With all respect to Elvis,' admitted Anne Sofie bluntly, 'I must say [our voices] don't go together too well.'[6] Instead, they mostly sang in sequence, Elvis coming in to fill the parts where Anne Sofie had left spaces in the songs. 'We developed this idea, I think quite wisely, that the way for me to make an appearance was by taking up the story at a certain point in the song,' said Elvis. 'So there are only a few bars where we actually sing together.'[7] Some may have asked why there was any need for the producer to sing at all. On the final record, even Elvis's brief interruptions – added at Windmill Lane in Dublin and Westside in London in mid-November, away from Anne Sofie's raised eyebrows – sounded utterly inappropriate.

Perhaps the highpoint of the recording – indeed, probably the album itself – was the collaboration with Abba's Benny Andersson on 'Like An Angel Passing Through My Room'. Anne Sofie knew Andersson from old and invited him to the sessions, and he ended up playing piano and synclavier on the new version of his own composition. 'It was amusing; these two high dignitaries of pop smelling each other out,'[8] she said.

The work was swift. They recorded twenty-seven songs in just two weeks, concluding on 21 October. Eighteen would be used for the final record, and Elvis would return to Stockholm in mid-January to mix the record.

Meanwhile, there were more pressing concerns. From Stockholm, Elvis travelled to Italy in the last week of October to put the finishing touches to *Il Sogno*, attending the final rehearsals and the press conference, before the Aterballetto premiered the ballet at the Teatro Comunale in Bologna on 31 October. Steve Nieve was in attendance at the premier, popping along for moral support; it was all a long way away from 'Pump It Up'.

Elvis was terribly excited by the end product. As an artist who was primarily recognised for his ability with words, *Il Sogno* marked the fulfilment of a deeply held desire to write a major work of instrumental music, and he found the final synthesis of music and movement profoundly rewarding. 'I couldn't believe I'd imagined all this music,' he admitted. 'I put things in the music which I hoped were going to be useful in the choreography, and then you see them and think, "Wow, how did he know I meant *that?*" Every time it is what I hoped, but much, much more.'[9]

The review in Italy's *La Stampa* was generally positive: 'Elvis Costello was able to show that he knows cultured music and knows also how to write it, from Debussy, Stravinsky, Mozart, jazz, big bands of the last fifty years, music from cinema and other areas.'

Aterballetto's *Il Sogno* tour then continued through northern Italy over

November and December, reaching France and Germany in 2001, where it was again warmly received. Elvis expressed his desire to capture the score on record some time soon.

* * *

He was back in Stockholm for a few days on 15 January to mix the new album, now called *Anne Sofie Von Otter Meets Elvis Costello: For The Stars*. The next few weeks were taken up with promoting the record, which was being released on Universal's classical label, Deutsche Grammophon. The launch for both the classical and popular music media took place in Vienna on 25 February, where Elvis and Anne Sofie played a live set featuring most of the album with the studio musicians. A little later, ITV screened a *South Bank Show* documentary on the making of the record, and there were numerous joint interviews.

However, no amount of hype could make the record work. Released on 19 March 2001, *For The Stars* was far from successful. Despite the best efforts of all involved, the basic premise failed: to coax a naturalistic, unstudied vocal performance from a classical singing star. Anne Sofie Von Otter had trouble negotiating many of the songs, often sounding stiff, mannered and uncomfortable, while the subdued tone of the record was almost unwavering throughout, washed-out and depressed rather than melancholic.

Elvis's new original songs – with the exception of 'Green Song' and the closing title track, which at least showed a little life – were little better than mediocre, and some of the cover versions wildly ill-judged. Von Otter simply didn't have the kind of grain in her voice necessary to make sense of the sultry, weary sadness of 'The Other Woman', not to mention 'Don't Talk (Put Your Head On My Shoulder)', 'Take It With Me' and 'For No One'. The occasional interjections from Elvis at the top of the mix only proved conclusively that their voices should never have appeared within a mile of each other.

Only on Abba's glacial 'Like An Angel Passing Through My Room', and Elvis's 'Shamed Into Love' and 'For The Stars' did the record really show glimpses of what might have been. In retrospect, it would have been considerably more rewarding and exciting to have persevered with Anne Sofie Von Otter's intial desire to create an all-out pop album. On the up-beat title song, the results were actually quite exhilarating.

Even some of Elvis's closest collaborators and admirers conceded that they found little to love in the record. 'I don't get much relief from it,' admits the Brodsky Quartet's Paul Cassidy. 'It feels like it's in a certain place and it's determined to stay there, and I don't really know why that is. I would have thought that with his imagination and his incredible encyclopedic knowledge of song and music in general that he would have presented her with many more options.'

David Sefton, who by now had left the South Bank to take up a post as Performing Arts Director at UCLA in California, felt that the record stretched to the limits Elvis's ceaseless desire and belief that anything is possible within music. However, there is often much to be taken from a well-intentioned failure. 'The fact that he knows no fear is a positive thing,' says Sefton. 'Ambition and enthusiasm go hand in hand. I think there's nothing wrong with over-reaching.'

Many of the reviews proved the point by lauding the album, too easily enchanted by its charms. Nevertheless, there was an undeniable sense that *For The Stars* marked a natural last port of call for Elvis's roving enthusiasm for joint ventures. His limitless curiousity, ample ego and inate sense of *carpe diem* meant that he was often unwilling to turn down an opportunity to work with someone he admired, but very occasionally he seemed to prolong the collaboration beyond its natural tenure, trying to bring it to life through sheer force of will. *For The Stars* was one such instance.

Without an album of new songs under his own banner for five years, Elvis's core audience were in danger of viewing his designated role in music as the man who ushered non-pop acts into unlikely unions, while the media image of him had very firmly become that of someone hell-bent on chasing down every last musical nook-and-cranny until he had sated his thirst.

The numerous side-projects throughout 2000 hadn't necessarily helped. Aside from writing a ballet score and making an album with a mezzo-soprano, Elvis had played Singleton: The Narrator in New York and London performances of Jazz Passenger Roy Nathanson's 'jazz oratorio', *Fire At Keaton's Bar And Grill*; and Drunkman in Steve Nieve's first-ever contemporary opera, *Welcome To The Voice*.

The latter role demanded a degree of acting ability, while requiring Elvis to sing complex songs in both English and French. He more than coped, although he did hide a lyric sheet inside his rather conspicuous newspaper prop. Dressed plainly in black shirt and trousers, he looked the part: crop-headed, unshaven, distinctly overweight, he attacked it with his usual animated ferocity, acting out the part with abandon while Steve and saxophonist Ned Rothenberg improvised around the score.

The *New York Times* came away from *Welcome To The Voice* with the observation that 'a patch on the border between art music and pop is being cultivated, and Elvis Costello is its chief gardener'. Maybe so, but the pop side of the lawn was becoming distinctly weed-ridden through neglect. Elvis was in real danger of losing his connection with his core audience.

'For the past few years, it has not always been clear what the point of Elvis Costello was,' wrote Jonathan Romney in the *Guardian*. 'He has become an expert at keeping himself interested, diversifying into umpteen left-field projects. It is obviously a healthy move for him, trading in the conventional solo role for gentleman-scholarhood, but he has also come close to being a high-culture dilettante, [and] you sometimes wish he would just come out and, well, entertain us.'

Elvis was coming to similar conclusions himself, even if he would have vehemently disagreed, mostly with absolute justification, with any charges of dilettantism. One of the lasting legacies of his career to date has been his enduring enthusiasms as a fan. In that capacity, he has written sleevenotes for re-issues of albums by Gram Parsons and Dusty Springfield, as well as published appreciations of artists as diverse as Benny Green and The Beatles. A happy knock-on effect of these appetites is the way in which Elvis has helped to introduce his fan base to genres as varied as country, northern soul and classical. On the down side, however, he hadn't made a solo record since 1996, and he was keen to get back to it. 'I know he got sick as being always seen as the arch collaborator and experimenter, I think that definitely wore thin,' says David Sefton. 'You spend twenty years giving interviews as an advocate for everything from country music to contemporary classical music, then in the end you just want to get on with making records.'

Chapter Eighteen
2001–04

'I HAVEN'T A CLUE WHAT I'M DOING,' laughed the dishevelled-looking man as he moved around the stage. Dressed down for the occasion in a floral shirt, combat trousers, trilby and trainers, Elvis was detonating distorted beats and slamming out electric guitar chords, revelling in simply making a noise again.

This was, appropriately enough, Total Meltdown. As part of the Royal Festival Hall's fiftieth anniversary concert, many of the previous Meltdown curators were invited to play sets on the night of 4 May 2001. Eschewing any notions of a 'greatest hits' set, Elvis plugged back into the Meltdown spirit and took the opportunity to experiment with a wild solo set of almost completely unheard material, using electric and acoustic guitars, tape loops and drum machines.

A few months earlier, on the day before Valentine's Day, Elvis had played a charity gig organised by Donal Lunny at Vicar Street in Dublin, where his set had included 'Daddy, Can I Turn This?', 'Oh Well', 'Soul For Hire', and 'Spooky Girlfriend'. At the Royal Festival Hall he added more new songs to the mix: 'Dust', 'Alibi', 'When I Was Cruel', and an encore of 'I Want You', the only previously recorded song in the set.

It was as gloriously shambolic as any work-in-progress offering should be, but there was no mistaking the singularity of purpose behind it all. It may have 'veered erratically between an acoustic guitar and a drum machine and box of tricks designed to make him sound like a one-man band', according to *The Times*, but it was less indulgent than it looked or sounded. Elvis was genuinely exploring ideas for his next record.

Over the course of the year there would be the usual generous scattering of eclectic cameos and dizzying array of guest appearances: a concert in Liverpool in March to launch a local compilation record; two shows at UCLA in April, performing in tribute to legendary folk archivist Harry Smith; jamming on-stage with Roger McGuinn in Dublin in May; organised stage invasions at New York shows with the Charles Mingus

Orchestra and Lucinda Williams in June; and three more performances of Roy Nathanson's *Fire At Keaton's Bar And Grill* in London, Manchester and Rotterdam during the same month.

Elvis also played his second – and last, to date – show with Anne Sofie Von Otter at the Hit Factory in New York on 6 June. It was an industry-only affair, in front of an invited audience of 150 people, mostly sticking to the *For The Stars* material, although Elvis also sang 'Almost Blue' and 'The Birds Will Still Be Singing'.

But the most significant concerts of 2001 took place at the Royal Festival Hall. Following the constructive mayhem of Total Meltdown, Elvis returned for the Meltdown 'proper' on 26 June. This year the artistic director was Robert Wyatt, and Elvis duly sang 'Left On Man', 'Caroline', and of course 'Shipbuilding', at a concert showcasing Wyatt's songs on the twenty-fourth. The explosions of two nights later were another prospect entirely.

Elvis opened the show with 'Alibi' and '45', played solo on acoustic guitar, before launching into the darkest depths of electronic exprimentation with Steve Nieve, turning 'Green Shirt' into a long, meandering piece filled with loops, samples and echo. He was clearly not entirely in control of the differing technical elements on stage, and for much of the time Steve was all but inaudible as the waves of electronica and distorted beats washed over the songs. 'As deep house beats cascade and distant bells sound, with only the occasional lyric, it feels like sitting in on a radiophonic workshop and, well, I think he's getting away from us,' said *The Independent's* reviewer. 'The numbers are darkly anarchic but deeply distancing – there's emotion in there but it's lost in the random bleeping.' The unsettling trio of 'Dust', 'My Dark Life' and 'Spooky Girlfriend' closed the opening set.

After a break, Elvis introduced the Brodsky Quartet for a short period of calm, including 'Pills And Soap' and 'New Lace Sleeves', before returning alone to sing a very rare rendition of 'The Great Unknown'. He then took a deep breath and plugged in his beatbox again for 'Hurry Down Doomsday' and 'When I Was Cruel', two songs which actually seemed to benefit from the additional electronica. He and Steve encored with 'The Bridge I Burned' and a straight, solemn reading of 'Shipbuilding', before the Brodsky Quartet reappeared to run through 'Rocking Horse Road' and 'Almost Blue'.

The real treat of the evening, however, came at the end, when the screen was pulled back to reveal a drum kit and a bass. Pete Thomas and US session-man Davey Farragher stepped out to join Elvis and Steve, and the ensemble lashed into 'Man Out Of Time', followed by seven more classic Attractions songs, only one of which – a deadly, deaf-defying 'Honey, Are

You Straight Or Are You Blind?' – was recorded after 1978. 'It seems he does care after all, handing out sugar lumps for those who've stayed the course,' sighed *The Independent*. 'And thus the devious Costello, grinning like a ferret, triumphs again, drat him.'

After fully five years, Elvis was finally back in band mode, reconnected to the primal impulse of the most basic of beat music. 'I had done some things that were very concentrated and very disciplined, whether it was working with Burt Bacharach or Anne Sofie Von Otter,' he explained. 'And then, suddenly, all the liberties of [rock 'n' roll] appealed to me again.'[1]

The quartet made their second live appearance supporting Bob Dylan at Nowlan Park in Kilkenny on 15 July, although this time there were no new songs in evidence. Instead, it was a unashamed and breathless 'greatest hits' set, beginning with 'Accidents Will Happen' and ending with 'Pump It Up' and '(What's So Funny 'Bout) Peace, Love & Understanding'. With all the linear career landmarks – 'Less Than Zero', 'Alison', 'Lipstick Vogue', 'Chelsea', 'Oliver's Army', and 'Good Year For The Roses' – assembled in order and fired off into the air, this was clearly an opportunity to mould new bassist Davey Farragher around the two remaining Attractions. Inevitably, no offer was extended to Bruce Thomas, although Pete and Steve had initially lobbied to get him on board. In Kilkenny, Elvis chose to respond by playing 'How To Be Dumb'.

Shortly after the Dylan show, Elvis finally went into Windmill Lane in Dublin to record his long-awaited 'beat' album. Essentially, he planned to make a rock 'n' roll record, but one with a tight and inflexible rhythmic pulse at the core of many of the songs, which would then stretch outwards towards the melody and harmony, rather than vice versa.

Whether the songs had been written simply and traditionally on guitar, or their origins had been more rhythmically propelled, melody would be secondary to feel throughout, in the manner of modern hip-hop and R&B records. There had been such a lot of melody, anyway, on *Painted From Memory*, that Elvis was ready to take a rest from it.

Straying into somewhat uncharted waters sonically, he needed a production team who were comfortable with the modern studio technology he wanted to use on the record, such as MIDI and digital. With this in mind, he assembled a young team of engineers and producers in Dublin who could work at speed, with a confident command of the latest possibilities that the studio now offered.

They consisted of Ciaran Cahill, the assistant engineer on *All This Useless Beauty*; Leo Pearson, who had programmed for The Corrs and U2 among others; and Kieran Lynch, who had worked with Shania Twain, which obviously didn't put Elvis off. Broadly speaking, each had a defined role. Cahill took care of the engineering, Lynch oversaw the editing and musical 'housekeeping', while Leo Pearson looked after the rhythm processing, perhaps the most important element of the record.

'If we created a sound and we wanted it twisted a little bit to give it a little more character or a little more grit, Leo usually had that job,' admitted Elvis. 'We tried to work as a team. Obviously, I'm governing the thing, from the point of view I'm writing the songs and I know what I want to hear, but I allowed them responsibilities for different areas.'[2]

Elvis had originally envisaged it as a solo record, but the Dylan show convinced him that he might as well use the band, who were now all in Ireland anyway. Once that decision had been made, the primary production task became finding a way of welding the electronic textures central to the sound of the record with the traditional shape and sound of a four-piece, combo-style band.

Some of the simpler, more traditional songs such as '45', 'Doll Revolution', 'My Little Blue Window', 'Tart', 'Dissolve' and 'Alibi', were laid down with the minimum of fuss, Elvis playing his guitar through a cheap fifteen-watt Roebuck amp, happy with the rough sound it produced as he bounced off the band.

However, other tracks needed a more ambitious and less immediately straightforward approach. 'Leo would start off getting a groove together, picking out some sounds, and we just kept layering,' says Ciaran Cahill. 'There are many different approaches to recording, from putting the band in a room and letting them go at it full-tilt, to looping up something that Pete Thomas was playing.'[3]

The most startling and easily the most successful example of this experimental approach was 'When I Was Cruel No. 2', a seven-minute near-masterpiece which was as sonically adventurous as anything Elvis had ever put on one of his records, using samples, loops and pre-programmed rhythms to create a genuinely unsettling and yet beautiful musical landscape. 'It started with a '60s Italian pop record by Mina,' explained Elvis. 'It's a two-bar loop that's just put through this little kind of kids' sampler, and there's a little bit of backward bass that's also on that.'[4] Over the top, Steve added impressionistic piano, Elvis twanged a baritone guitar and added a mesmerising lyric and serpentine melody, until the track gelled into something wonderous and haunting.

Despite the new, experimental approach to recording, Elvis had been working on many of the songs for some time and he knew exactly the sound he wanted. As a result, the recording sessions were fast and furious. 'Alibi' was recorded in one take, and all the basic tracks were finished by the end of August.

The following month, on 24 September, Elvis was in Avatar Studios in New York with Kevin Killen, laying down brass overdubs for '15 Petals', 'Dust' and 'Spooky Girlfriend', while Bill Ware of the Jazz Passengers played vibraphone on 'When I Was Cruel No. 2'. Elvis also recorded a version of the old Charlie Chaplin song 'Smile', commissioned for a Japanese television programme. 'It just came out of the blue,' he shrugged. ''Smile' is a famous song in Japan, in lots of different renditions, and they just for some reason decided they wanted me.'[5] He cut the song live in a three-hour session with old hands like Marc Ribot and Greg Cohen, as well as a string octet for which he had written and orchestrated an arrangement.

He was pleased to see them all. Both New York sessions took place less than a fortnight after the 9/11 attacks, and Elvis and Kevin Killen discussed at length whether they should cancel the pre-booked studio time, but decided to press on and immerse themselves in music rather than dwell on the alternatives.

While in New York, Elvis also rehearsed with the Charles Mingus Orchestra for shows in Los Angeles. Earlier in the year, in his position as Head of Performing Arts at UCLA, David Sefton had approached Elvis about becoming Artist in Residence for the 2001–02 academic year, beginning in the autumn. Elvis agreed. It was designed as a natural progression from Meltdown, with Elvis engaging on a roughly quarterly basis, with the idea that he would be present at regular intervals throughout the year. 'Really, the template was as loose as that,' says Sefton. 'I didn't really want to impose any real rigours on it.'

The first fruits of the proposed year-long residency were two full concerts with the Charles Mingus Orchestra on 27 and 28 September at the Royce Hall. Elvis had jumped on stage with the Orchestra on several occasions, but this would be the first time that he would lead them through a full concert, as well as the first time that they would be playing adaptations of original Elvis songs alongside their own material. He added 'Long Honeymoon', 'Upon A Veil Of Midnight Blue', 'Stalin Malone', 'Chewing Gum', 'Watching The Detectives' and 'Almost Blue' to the Orchestra's traditional set, without diluting the essence of the ensemble.

The shows were sold out and the two evenings were generally deemed to be a highly successful opening collaboration to his year as Artist in Residence. 'When Costello performed it was not merely as singer, instrumentalist, songwriter or former new wave rocker anthropologizing in the big, sophisticated world of jazz,' ran the review in the LA Weekly. 'It was, instead, as a bona fide bandleader, welding dizzyingly complex tunes to weird lyrics and singing them all like he's squeezing passion from a narrow-necked tube. His fans are forever vindicated.'

Elvis returned to Dublin in the autumn to mix the new record, taking care not to sanitise the tracks: he wanted a raw, densely packed rock record with harsh electronic beats. There was spillage and distortion on some songs, but – as with the making of records as diverse as *My Aim Is True* and *Blood & Chocolate* – any technical imperfections were deemed secondary to the feel of the final recording. 'If something was going down that was passionate and had a vibe and had emotion and carried the message or idea of the music, that's more important,' said Leo Pearson. 'There were other mixes of tracks that were more sonically correct but that just didn't have the same vibe to them. And we want to tip our hat to Elvis for hammering that home.'[6] If the production team of Cahill, Lynch and Pearson had taught Elvis much about the most advanced production practices, he had taught them plenty about the inexact art of making records in return.

The release of the new album was delayed slightly to make way for a short tour that Elvis undertook in January 2002. The Concerts For A Landmine Free World took in Belfast, Dublin, London, Glasgow, Stockholm and Oslo between 13 20 January, and Elvis shared the stage with Emmylou Harris, Steve Earle, John Prine and Nanci Griffith, taking it in turns to sing and play their songs and occasionally joining in on each other's.

Thus he got to duet with Emmylou Harris on heartbreaking renditions of 'Indoor Fireworks' and 'Sleepless Nights', or enjoy the attentions of A-grade ensemble backing vocals for 'American Without Tears'. 'Elvis loved it and he had a great time doing it,' recalls Steve Earle, who was mesmerised by watching Elvis sing at close quarters. 'He's one of the best singers alive. My favourite singers are Costello, David Hidalgo and Aaron Neville – he's *that* good a singer.'

Entitled *When I Was Cruel*, a gloriously self-referential in-joke, the new album was finally released on 15 April 2002, credited to Elvis Costello and The Imposters and released on Island/Def Jam, the hip-hop wing of Universal. This wasn't a nod to Elvis's new-found rhythm method, but rather a bizarre indication of just how much reshuffling had gone on in the record industry in recent years.

The record was accompanied by a feverish media campaign throughout February, March and April which was designed to let everyone know that Elvis was firmly back in the ring. It was not an easy album, nor was it a return to a particular familiar sound in the way that parts of *Brutal Youth* had been. There may have been faint echoes of *This Year's Model* and *Blood & Chocolate* in particular, but it was defiantly more of a fresh departure than a homecoming: an angry, rowdy, bruising, often brilliant affair, bass-heavy and densely rhythmic, with very little of Steve Nieve's trademark swirling organ and stately piano.

It was also consciously far less melodious than most people expected from an Elvis Costello record, again a trait it shared with *Blood & Chocolate*. Only the stuttering '45', 'My Little Blue Window', 'Spooky Girlfriend', 'Tart' and 'Alibi' had tunes which really stuck in the head. This lack of melodic invention did eventually wear the listener out, not least because the record was much too long. *When I Was Cruel* could probably have lost at least a quarter of its sixteen tracks without deadening any of its impact.

The sound of the record was really defined by the sparse, unsettling beats and bleak lyrical visions of 'Dust', 'Oh Well', 'Soul For Hire' and 'Radio Silence'. Mercifully, there was no hint of an artist desperately trying to sound contemporary. The songs had been written to weather the intense rhythms and they did so without the feeling of artificial studio surgery. And in 'When I Was Cruel No. 2', Elvis had a killer song that would grace any *Best Of* collection, a hypnotic crawl through the small, sour vignettes of an industry wedding, Elvis confronting everyone's *sotto voce* sneers and latent hypocrisies, not least his own.

But it wasn't a truly *great* Elvis Costello record. It only sounded like one if you hadn't played a great Elvis Costello record in a while. Nonetheless, it was greeted with predictable fervour by the media, finally happy to hear Elvis making some noise again, with the sneer firmly back in the voice. 'Alone among his peers, Costello forges ahead, his snarl and his relevance intact,' said the *Guardian*. 'These are punchy, throaty, blood-rush tracks which effortlessly overshadow all the little Spiritualiseds, Radioheads and Starsailors blubbing and boo-hooing out there in Poor Me Land,' said *Uncut*. 'The veins at Costello's temples are throbbing again,' reckoned *Q*. It was, truly, the return of the prodigal.

A brief, promotional tour was organised to coincide with the record's release, a precursor to the mammoth world tour scheduled for the remainder of the year. Between 15 and 28 April, Elvis and The Imposters played club gigs in Amsterdam, London, New York, Philadelphia and Chicago, bedding in the new material. It was clear that apart from the *When I Was Cruel* songs, much of the new setlist would revolve around *This Year's Model* and other classic Attractions material. There may have been a degree of spoon-feeding in this approach, but Elvis was also hungry to play a lot of those songs again.

On the opening night in Amsterdam, 'Accidents Will Happen', 'Waiting For The End Of The World', 'You Belong To Me', 'Pump It Up', 'Chelsea' and 'Lipstick Vogue' were all aired, alongside 'Man Out Of Time', 'I Hope You're Happy Now' and 'I Want You'. They stuck to this template throughout the April shows, occasionally adding 'Beyond Belief' or 'Uncomplicated'.

Typically hyperactive, Elvis had another project planned for the two-week gap between the end of the brief April tour and the beginning of the world onslaught in mid-May. He had been keen to capture the *Il Sogno* score on record for some time, and had continued working on the piece since 2000, making significant changes and ensuring that the music was no longer reliant on the dance movements to carry it along.

In the first week of May, he ducked into Abbey Road Studios with conductor Michael Tilson Thomas and the London Symphony Orchestra to record the score. Paul Cassidy dropped in to say hello and was blown away by the strides his friend had made in the past decade. 'Elvis has got a score the size of a table, handwritten by him,' he recalls with amazement. 'We're talking "Second cor anglais, fourth cornet, harp". It was really astonishing. Eight years ago he didn't know what a piece of manuscript looked like, and there he is writing out by hand a fullscap score for 120-piece orchestra.'

As with most classical recordings, the cost of keeping a large orchestra in the studio precluded lengthy sessions, and the work was done quickly. Elvis would spend the next two and a half years searching for a suitable release date.

* * *

The world tour for *When I Was Cruel* kicked off at the Roseland Theatre in Seattle on 18 May and swaggered through North America until 24 June. America had loved the record. 'Costello's latest album makes a master's gifts matter again,' said *Rolling Stone*, while the *New York Post's* Dan Aquilante claimed that 'Costello will not only satisfy his old fans with this record, he's going to win a new generation's devotion'. He wasn't wrong. *When I Was Cruel* had entered the UK charts at No. 17 in April and had continued to sell well, but it was a much bigger story in the States. The record had debuted at No. 20 on the Billboard chart, Elvis's best-ever first-week position, and went on to sell over 200,000 copies. It also gave him a No. 1 record on college radio.

One of the earliest dates on the tour was at the UCLA's Ackerman Grand Ballroom, the second and final instalment of Elvis's disappointing tenure as Artist in Residence at the university. After Meltdown, David Sefton had hoped for great things from the union, but he had caught Elvis just as his musical pendulum was swinging back into a conventional solo career. With a hit college record, Elvis was reaching a new, younger audience, and felt compelled to continue touring to capitalise on his relative success, with the result that the UCLA collaboration did not go to plan: the proposed US premier of *Il Sogno* with Aterballetto at UCLA was cancelled when Elvis's touring commitments meant he would be unable to attend, and overall David Sefton had been dismayed at the lack of focus and commitment that Elvis was able to bring to the flagship plan, which had been heavily publicised in the US.

'To be frank, what happened was that *When I Was Cruel* became a much bigger thing for him and his pop career than had been anticipated or allowed for,' says Sefton. 'He simply ended up doing other stuff. In terms of the record industry, when someone says you're going on tour to Japan because you can sell a lot of records, you can't really say, "No, I'm going to LA to do an esoteric chamber theatre project!". It unquestionably didn't work out.' In the end, Elvis simply brought his touring show to town on 28 May at the end of the academic year. It wasn't anywhere close to what had been planned.

The tour was as close to an Attractions reunion as there was ever likely to be. Davey Faragher had a more laid-back style than Bruce Thomas, but with Elvis, Pete and Steve in place, the sound was inevitably going to lean in that direction. In concert, the *When I Was Cruel* material benefited from Steve Nieve's vast repertoire of textures, deliberately reined in on the record. Elvis was also getting re-acquainted with the tremelo arm and the reverb pedal on his guitar, which couldn't help but evoke reminders of 1978. The echoing beats were still in place, however, ensuring that this band ultimately sounded unlike any other Elvis had toured with.

He was using his older songs to build momentum for his newer songs. In this way, a spectral 'Watching The Detectives' would set the mood for 'Spooky Girlfriend', while 'Brilliant Mistake' lead into 'Tart'. In New York, there was a very rare 'How To Be Dumb' and versions of 'All This Useless Beauty' and 'Clubland'. Elvis also premiered a declamatory new soul song called 'The Judgement' on a few dates on the US tour, written to order for the return-to-the-fray album by soul legend Solomon Burke.

By the time Elvis reached Japan and Australia in the middle of July, the sets were beginning to loosen up. 'High Fidelity', 'Human Hands' and 'God Give Me Strength' all featured at Sydney's Elmore Theatre on the thirteenth, while 'Miracle Man', 'Little Triggers', 'Possession', 'Almost Blue' and 'All The Rage' made appearances over the next few nights.

The band were becoming more subtle and attuned to the delicacies of the material they were serving. They could morph easily from the rabble-rousing racket of 'Honey, Are You Straight Or Are You Blind?' into the downbeat, sample-laden twists of 'When I Was Cruel No. 2', from the dense clatter of 'Uncomplicated' to a gloriously crisp 'Man Out Of Time'; or take flight on extended, echoing codas at the end of 'Watching The Detectives'; '15 Petals' – a somewhat crazed love song for Cait – had also become a highlight, a huge wave of rhythm with an almost muezzin wail at its heart from Elvis.

From Australia they returned to Europe for the first time since April, playing the festival circuit throughout July and August. Festivals had never been Elvis's favourite live experience – the conservative setlists, disinterested audiences, poor sound and time restraints held little appeal for him, but then the money was often spectacular. At the V2002 festival at Chelmsford on 17 August he came face-to-face with the generation gap and didn't like what he saw. 'All these sullen little Thatcher's children, looking up and sneering because we were old,' he sighed. 'We played abominably, it was the longest fifty minutes of my life.'7

The tour proper revved up again in September, with a full European leg kicking off in Dublin on the second, before he returned to the US for his most extensive tour for a number of years. Halfway through the tour Elvis released *Cruel Smile*, a companion piece to *When I Was Cruel* featuring recent live versions, radical re-mixes, two versions of 'Smile', and 'When I Was Cruel No. 1', an entirely different song to its namesake, and almost as magestic. It must only have been left off its namesake album as punishment for its obvious similarities to bygone glories, or perhaps for its near-the-knuckle lyrical admissions: 'Why did you leave your happy home,' he ponders rhetorically, 'So you could sleep with strangers?' It was perhaps a pertinent question.

* * *

Throughout the summer there had been rumours circulating about the state of his 'marriage'. By September, he and Cait had agreed in private to separate permanently. However, the end of their relationship wasn't announced until the end of the US tour, in a brief statement issued on 25 November which stated simply: 'It is regretfully announced that the marriage of Elvis Costello and Cait O'Riordan has come to an end. The parting is amicable and it is hoped that the privacy of the individuals will be respected.'

The statement and unofficial announcements from 'friends' were at pains to make it clear that nobody else was involved in the breakdown of the relationship, instead blaming the disorientating effects of touring. However, by the time the statement was released, Elvis was already involved with Diana Krall, a glamourous, talented and highly successful Canadian jazz artist ten years his junior.

In recent years, Elvis had been a regular attendee of the annual Grammy Awards in New York; back in February, he had co-presented the Song Of The Year award with No Doubt's Gwen Stefani and Diana Krall. '[It's] essentially a beauty and the beast type of presentation,' he joked, looking less than pristine in heavy leather jacket, stubble and loose shirt next to the two blonde women.

However, it would prove to be an auspicious occasion for Krall, a genuine star and previous Grammy winner in her own right. 'I saw him at the Grammys and he was so kind in helping me get over my nervousness,' she said the following month. 'We clicked. And I think he's the coolest guy.'[8] Their meeting seemed to spark Krall's curiousity about someone she knew very little about musically; friends claimed she was smitten, and she seemed inclined to agree. 'It's great,' she said. 'All of a sudden, I'm up at three in the morning and I'm surrounded by Elvis records.'[9]

Their relationship would remain officially unconfirmed until the New Year, but quite quickly, it seems, Elvis's feelings for Krall grew. He attended a recording session with the Brodsky Quartet in November for an album project they were working on, involving a number of performers singing on a string arrangement of one of their own songs. Those involved included Paul McCartney, Randy Newman, Bjork and Elvis himself.

As he was leaving the session, the Brodskys began playing their arrangement of 'Real Emotional Girl' by Randy Newman, a song Elvis loved and had wanted Anne Sofie Von Otter to sing on *For The Stars*. By coincidence, he had just given Diana Krall a cassette tape with Newman's version of the song at the beginning. Without a word, Elvis returned to the microphone and sang the song through. Then he simply burst into tears.

Spurred by the huge upheavals in his private life, Elvis had been writing prodigiously throughout the final leg of the US tour and on into the remaining months of 2002. The new songs were simple piano ballads, directly influenced by the breakdown of his marriage to Cait, and the fact that he had fallen in love with someone else.

For all his forthrightness, Elvis had never really covered clearly expressed emotion terribly well. He'd written dozens of beautiful, emotive songs, but the very simplest declarations of love and regret had never come easy. 'I've always looked for the escape hatch from feeling, the get-out clause,' he admitted. 'That isn't the way I'm feeling right now.'[10] He seemed to be writing directly from his heart, with little desire to edit or disguise or obscure his meanings with codes or double-bluffs. For perhaps the first time in his career, Elvis was facing his own emotions head on, without distance or irony.

Paul Cassidy was one of the first people to hear demos of the songs. 'I am forever touched, because no matter what it is he does, he always sends me a copy of his demos to see what I think,' he says. 'And these songs were the most extraordinary thing you've ever heard. Sixteen tracks of him on an old pub piano. Massive. I'd never heard Elvis like that. I'd never heard anything like it.'

Elvis spent much of December in New York, where Krall had an apartment. In early January he was spotted with her in Nello's restaurant on Madison Avenue, holding hands and sharing lunch. The meeting was widely reported in magazines and papers on both sides of the Atlantic, and by early February the relationship was fully out in the open. The two played together at a charity fundraiser at London's Old Vic on 2 February. Elton John – someone Elvis seemed to have recently discovered an unlikely appreciation for – was chairman of the Old Vic, and during the concert Krall and Elvis duetted on John's 'Sorry Seems To Be The Hardest Word', Elvis singing as Krall played piano.

Clearly in love, Krall admitted to being excited about the upcoming Grammy Awards on 22 February in New York, marking a year since she first met her new man. 'The thing I'm looking most forward to is being with him because that's where we met,' she said. 'It has significance for me almost more than being nominated.'[11] Elvis himself was nominated for three Grammys and arrived for the show a day early, rehearsing with a supergroup including Bruce Springsteen, Dave Grohl, Steve Van Zandt and Pete Thomas, firming up a tribute to Joe Strummer, who had died of a heart attack just before Christmas. The next night they played a punchy version of The Clash's 'London Calling' at the ceremony, as images of Strummer flickered behind them. Under the circumstances, it didn't really matter that he went home empty-handed.

* * *

The batch of ballads he had recently written demanded an outlet. Wanting to get the songs down quickly before he lost his nerve, Elvis booked studio time in New York for April. However, there was one piece of old, unfinished business to attend to before he could begin. To celebrate twenty-five years since they first started recording, Elvis and The Attractions were being inducted into the Rock and Roll Hall Of Fame in Cleveland on 8 March. Elvis had initially been characteristically sceptical about the notion of a Hall of Fame for modern musicians, pondering whether 'putting rock and roll in a glass case would choke the life out of it'.[12] However, in a philosophical frame of mind, he eventually decided that it would be ungracious to decline.

Implicit in the invitation to perform was the tantalising hope against hope that Elvis might reunite The Attractions for one last send-off, much as The Police had agreed to do on the same night. Elvis hadn't forgiven or forgotten that easily. 'I'm not going to get into any phoney reunions or insincere forgiveness,' he said unequivocally. 'I only play with professional musicians. I always speak with respect of Bruce Thomas and his playing but he's a fairly unbearable human being and I don't want to spend any more time with him.'[13]

Nonetheless, Bruce intended to be in Cleveland to collect his award. 'I wrote to his office and said, "Look, I'm not going to cause any bother but I'm going, so deal with it however you want to deal with it. You can't write me out of this one".'

As it transpired there was little time for recriminations. The Attractions were united briefly on stage, but only to collect their awards from Elvis's new friend Elton John, whose speech inevitably focused on Elvis's talents rather than the band's, somewhat understandable given that he had played with The Attractions for less than fifteen of his twenty-five years as a professional musician.

On stage, Elvis clapped Bruce Thomas on the back and admitted: 'This is not the place for airing my petty grievances,' before calling The Attractions 'a great, great band'. 'Thanks for the memories,' said Bruce Thomas, adding 'That's it,' as he walked away. There were no backstage hugs or buried hatchets. It was absolute minimal contact. Thus it was The Imposters who played 'Pump It Up', 'Deep Dark Truthful Mirror'/'You Really Got A Hold On Me' and '(What's So Funny 'Bout) Peace, Love & Understanding' after the handing out of the gongs. Bruce Thomas simply stood in the crowd and watched somebody else being him.

* * *

North was recorded a month later, engineered by Kevin Killen in Avatar Studios in New York during April and May. The city was now effectively Elvis's new adopted home; Waymark was up for sale, and would be sold for €1,300,000 before the end of the year. While in New York, he and Diana Krall joined Willie Nelson on stage at the Beacon Theatre to sing 'Crazy' on 9 April, but for most of the month Elvis was squirrelled away in the studio.

The songs were simple and stark, all whispers and sighs, and needed the subtlest of touches rather than a beat band. As such, most of the record was played in a four-piece, jazz quartet format: Elvis singing, Steve Nieve playing simple piano, Peter Erskine on muted drums and Michael Formanek on bass. The tracks were then augmented with various shades of brass and string colours – a forty-eight-piece orchestra, flutes, French horns. All the orchestrations had been written by Elvis, which he then conducted. He was keen to keep it simple. 'There are strings, but used very sparingly,' he said. 'They might only play three notes on a song. There are only twelve bars of electric guitar in the whole thing.'[14]

The Brodsky Quartet appeared on 'Still', playing live in London while Elvis sang live in New York, brought together in the moment by the magic of technology. Elvis sat at the piano and sang the closing ballad 'I'm In The Mood Again' alone, a very personal ending to his most naked album to date. He recorded quickly, wanting to stay true to the immediacy of the songs.

By the first week of May the record was being mixed, and by the time he went back on the road with The Imposters in July it was ready for release. However, there were no new songs on show until the tour reached the Canadian border, where for four concerts it was just Elvis and Steve on-stage. The stripped-down format allowed them to flex a little, and almost half of North was debuted, as well as 'North' itself, a tongue-in-cheek number left off the album, which espoused the joys of Canada, and one Canadian in particular.

In the end, it seemed to be an album people could either instinctively feel and hear, or which left them cold. After the rowdy and successful When I Was Cruel there was a general feeling that Elvis had failed to capitalise on the renewed momentum his mainstream career had gained. As ever, he had simply followed the music. Very much a mood piece, North's initial impact was minimal; as grey and monchrome as the picture of a forlorn, rain-soaked Elvis on the cover, it was hard to hear any tunes. It was also difficult to escape the nagging sensation that Elvis was showing off to his new girlfriend, displaying his versatility in a jazzy, piano-and-voice template which closely mirrored her own.

However, repeated listenings – which many people failed to afford it – allowed the record's fragile beauty to emerge. Musically and lyrically a less dramatic counterpoint to Painted From Memory, and aspiring to Frank Sinatra's Wee Small Hours territory, North was designed for winter time, late-night-early-morning listening. Elvis's voice was most effective when simmering at the lower ends of both volume and key, but strained and wobbled elsewhere.

The songs themselves were split roughly down the middle: the first six appeared to dwell on Elvis's break up with Cait, while the remaining five celebrated his new-found love for Diana Krall. Domestic detectives looking to apportion blame had plenty of material to sift through, but there was no malice in these songs. Just a genuine, surprised sadness. 'I thought we'd make it all the way,' he crooned on 'You Left Me In The Dark', while on the profoundly affecting 'You Turned To Me' he reflected on being 'betrayed,' before adding, 'Both of us had strayed.' The master of the double bluff hadn't resigned his post just yet.

Much of the lyrical content, however, bordered on the banal, a disappointment for those who had waited twenty-five years for Elvis to bare his soul. In the end, it seemed that trying to articulate the realities of love and loss rendered him as tongue-tied as everybody else, save perhaps for Smokey Robinson and Cole Porter. Some listeners regarded this as a positive. 'He has never sounded quite so human,' said the *Evening Standard*, and many of the reviews agreed. 'With every play this album becomes, like love itself, impossible to fight off,' was the *Guardian's* verdict. There were plenty more positive notices, but again, for many the record stood or fell on whether you enjoyed Elvis's voice stretching itself with difficult, low-key material.

Simmy Richman concluded a quite stunningly personal attack in the *Independent On Sunday* by stating that *North*'s 'only purpose is to serve as a faux-classical showcase for that pompous and preposterous baritone crooning voice. This self-penned, soporific, pseudo-Sondheim sucks. With strings on'. *Time Out* expressed similar sentiments, directing its readers towards *Songs For Swingin' Lovers, In The Wee Small Hours, Only The Lonely* or *Come Fly With Me*. 'Already got them?' it concluded. 'Good. Now rest assured, you don't need this.'

As ever, Elvis took such criticism personally. Having decided to lay his heart on the line, he was stung – if not surprised – by the criticism. 'There's a rather unpleasant English personality trait,' he proposed. 'That of being uncomfortable in the presence of clearly expressed emotion.'[15] Notwithstanding the fact that he had spent an entire career avoiding such 'clearly expressed emotion' until now, Elvis also seemed to overlook the possibility that people simply might not like the record on its own terms.

North debuted at No. 1 on the Billboard Jazz charts and stayed there for five weeks, but it sold poorly, reaching only No. 42 in the UK and No. 57 in the US and notching up a mere 84,000 sales in the US in the nine months following its release. Many of the reviews had inevitably focused on the obviously autobiographical nature of the songs, and Elvis was anxious not to get into detailed discussions regarding the circumstances of the writing of the record. The eleven songs were the first and last statement he was prepared to make about the tectonic shifts in his private life. One interviewer mentioned Cait and he firmly stated his position. 'It's entirely at your discretion to mention her name, but I very much want to be respectful of her independence as a person,' he cautioned. 'And one of the things you have to say when you part with somebody is that they have the right not to be drawn into the consideration of your life. It's really important that I don't say anything that puts her in the public focus. It's not fair, she didn't ask for it.'[16]

North, it seemed, was all the explaining Elvis was going to do. That particular bridge was burned, and there was no remaining contact between the two ex-lovers. It was perhaps telling, though, that Cait had picked up the threads of her musical life after eighteen years, as well as her defunct relationship with some of The Pogues. She remained in Dublin, and joined Philip Chevron's re-formed Radiators From Space (Plan 9) in December for an appearance at Joe Strummer's memorial tribute at the Temple Bar Music Centre in Dublin, and continued to gig with the band into 2004. She also sang the female part for 'Fairytale Of New York' at Shane MacGowan's solo show in the same city a few days earlier. Perhaps most spectacularly, she went on to climb Mount Everest in the early summer of 2004.

Meanwhile, Elvis returned from the *North* tour to make plans for his marriage to Diana Krall. The tour had quite sensibly featured just Elvis and Steve, kicking off in Japan on 1 October. Most of the new record was aired, and the songs seemed to become more effective when played in groups of two or three rather than as a whole, where their similarities tended to merge into one. In concert, with just Steve's piano and Elvis's voice, they were allowed to soar. 'Costello croons with passion and style, conjuring intimacy with a flickering hand, sparking audience participation and backing off the mic to sing without amplification,' said the *Observer,* reviewing the show at Glasgow's Royal Concert Hall on 7 October. 'He has made a middle-aged man in young love look dignified and rather glorious.'

Wedding banns had been posted at Marylebone Town Hall in mid-October, and Elvis and Krall spent much of their time in London, staying at a suite in Claridges and dining at The Ivy while they fulfilled their residency criteria and organised themselves. The marriage finally took place on 6 December, a statement confirming that it was 'a private event with close friends and family in attendance'.

Nonetheless, there was a distinctly showbiz buzz about it all. The wedding took place at the mansion home of Elton John in the Surrey countryside, with Paul McCartney and his wife Heather Mills, David

Letterman and Canada's Consul General to New York, Pamela Wallin, among the 150 guests. The Chieftains were the house band, a safe bet for getting everyone on their feet and dancing. The newlyweds were spotted a few days later, strolling through the Jardin des Tuileries in Paris, before returning to their new home in Nanoose on Vancouver Island in Canada. Elvis was heading north, after all.

* * *

He moved into 2004 with the usual incessant energy of ideas, the customary planned projects and side-steps. Elvis had become increasingly well-connected in TV and film in the States, and in recent years there had been the odd ironic toe dipped into the mainstream, popping up for brief cameos in the Spice Girls film *Spiceworld*, *The Larry Sanders Show* and *Austin Powers: The Spy Who Shagged Me*. It would be fair to say that the camera had always stopped some way short of loving Elvis, and the luckier viewers often blinked and missed him. In 2003 he had – rather nervously – guest-presented David Letterman's show, on which he had appeared numerous times throughout his career; while there remained industry talk of a US television sitcom called *The Arc Angels*, based on a treatment Elvis had written in 2001 with his long-time friend, the US TV producer John Mankiewicz. Elvis had originally composed 'Doll Revolution' and 'Spooky Girlfriend' for the show, which was reportedly being developed by Ron Howard's company Imagine. According to Elvis, the basic plot line was a kind of proto-feminist take on *The Monkees*, and concerned four Russian supermodels who come to the US and become the world's biggest rock band. Nobody was necessarily holding their breath for that one.

More significantly, Elvis made his first appearance at the Academy Awards on 29 February, nominated with his old friend T-Bone Burnett in Best Original Song category for their co-composition 'Scarlet Tide', sung by bluegrass artist Alison Krauss and taken from the Anthony Minghella film *Cold Mountain*. Burnett had already scored a huge hit for Lost Highway records in 2001 by producing the wildly successful soundtrack album for *Oh Brother, Where Art Thou?* and had gone on to launch the DMZ record label in association with celebrated film-makers the Coen Brothers the following year. Elvis sat on the board of advisors at DMZ alongside such luminaries as Sam Shepard, Bono, Tom Waits and Wim Wenders, hence his involvement in the *Cold Mountain* soundtrack and his appearance at the Oscars. Willingly playing second fiddle to Alison Krauss's stunning voice, the erstwhile Coward Brothers reunited to perform 'Scarlet

Tide' in front of a global television audience of a little under a billion people, with Elvis looking oddly adrift, clutching a ukelele and occasionally playing it. It didn't win, but 'Scarlet Tide' became a regular in Elvis's sets throughout the rest of the year.

He was becoming distinctly at ease among the red carpets, popping flashbulbs and the grinning, posed celebrity photo opportunity. He even seemed to be enjoying it. Cait had rarely savoured the limelight and had usually shunned it, but Diana Krall was used to the hot gaze of the cameras and Elvis readily succumbed. He was even seen shopping for CDs with Elton John in Los Angeles.

The newlyweds had a direct influence on each other. Diana Krall's record, *The Girl In The Other Room*, was released in April and debuted at No. 4 in the UK album charts. Elvis had coaxed, cajoled and pushed his wife into composing for the first time, and the record featured six original co-compositions written by Krall and her husband. His fingerprints were evident throughout a record which – though it had far more heart and personality than any of Krall's previous jazz-lite output – was ultimately a strangely mismatched and melancholic experience. Alongside a straight, respectful version of Elvis's own 'Almost Blue', there were covers of songs by Tom Waits, Mose Allison, and Joni Mitchell – Costello favourites one and all.

The cross-fertilisation continued away from the music. After years of effectively managing himself, Elvis signed up with Krall's business team of Macklam-Feldman Management, who also looked after Joni Mitchell, Norah Jones and The Chieftans. It was a further sign that all the important elements of his life and career had moved across the Atlantic.

There were continuing performances with Steve Nieve throughout February and March, including three superb shows with the Brodsky Quartet in Boston, Nashville and New York at the end of February. The collaborative relationship with the Quartet had now lasted longer than the initial incarnation of The Attractions, and continued to yield huge creative bounties.

However, following the gentle, personally fulfilling detour of *North*, the most significant creative development of 2004 was taking The Imposters back into the studio. In early 2003, Elvis had planned to keep running with the impetus created by *When I Was Cruel* by making an impromptu album with the band, playing new songs on tour in the American south and then going into local studios to capture them on tape while the feel was fresh. However, *North* had got in the way, in the nicest possible sense. Elvis picked up on the idea a year later, and his US concerts with The Imposters in March threw up a batch of new – or at least, unheard – songs in the encores.

On 2 and 3 April, Elvis and The Imposters played four sets at Proud Larry's in Oxford, Mississippi, a tiny bar with a stage a mere twelve inches off the floor. It was like the very, *very* old days, the smell of sweat and beer in the air. By the time the gigs took place, Elvis and the band were already recording at Sweet Tea Studios in town, under the auspices of the owner and engineer Dennis Herring. The concerts were necessarily experimental affairs, rowdy, rough and intimate and, in the case of 'Heart-Shaped Bruise', sometimes featuring two arrangements of the same song back-to-back in order to clarify the decisions they had been making in the studio.

Many of the new songs had been culled from the long-mooted *Delivery Man* project, and there was a heavy, bluesy vein running through a significant proportion of them: 'Button My Lip' was a churning reminder to think before you speak, while the ominous 'Needle Time' sounded as though a bastard combination of Bo Diddley and Muddy Waters had sneaked onto the tiny stage and started jamming 'Tokyo Storm Warning'. 'Delivery Man' and Elvis's straight, heartfelt reading of Peter Green's 'Love That Burns' were also coloured deepest blue.

Highlights over the four shows were plentiful. 'Bedlam' was a rowdy riot in six minutes, which would have fitted snugly onto *When I Was Cruel*, while the poppy, piano-laced stripper's song 'She's Pulling Out The Pin' – 'She came out high and kicking/While the band played 'Hey, Good Lookin'' was the prize-winning line – sounded like a refugee from the *Trust* sessions. The reflective 'Nothing Clings Like Ivy' was a kissing cousin to The Beatles' 'She's Leaving Home'; 'In Another Room' was a rolling, sorrowful ballad; while the rollicking upbeat country rock of 'There's A Story In Your Voice' featured Elvis in Dylan mode, reeling off a litany of character faults which by the end amounted to assassination. The two indisputable diamonds in the rough were 'Monkey To Man', a scratchy, instantly catchy re-writing of Darwin's theory of evolution – 'For all of the misery that he has caused/He denies he's descended from the dinosaurs' – and the magnificent 'Country Darkness', a tear wringing country-soul number and close companion to 'Motel Matches'.

Also featured at Proud Larry's were songs that Elvis had performed in concert several times before but had so far left unrecorded: 'Heart-Shaped Bruise', 'Suspect My Tears', 'Unwanted Number' and 'Burnt Sugar Is So Bitter'. As was normal when Elvis was testing out swathes of new material, he peppered the set with treats, rewarding the audience's patience. Mostly, crowd-pleasing candidates from his first three records were the order of the day: a snatch of 'Moods For Moderns' was the trainspotter's favourite this time around. Nothing from *When I Was Cruel* or *North* featured.

Elvis and the band returned to the studio over the following days to continue recording the album for Lost Highway, the ultra-hip branch of Universal Records. The sessions – which featured guest appearances from Lucinda Williams, Emmylou Harris and John McFee on pedal steel – were kept raw and unadorned, with plenty of Steve Nieve magic on Moog, modulators and even the theremin. The rawness of the recordings had shades of *Blood & Chocolate*. 'The same sound system we used in the club [was] set up in the studio,' explained Nieve. 'There are no headphones in sight. If we need to replace a line of vocal or overdub a guitar, or piano, the direct sound on tape goes back down through the monitor speakers to recreate the "spill" of the live band on all the mics, as the overdub is recorded. So even the overdubs have the sound of everyone playing on them, and match up with the original.'[17]

Following the Sweet Tea sessions, Elvis and the band resurfaced at the Hi-Tone Café in Memphis for four more low-key gigs, again pregnant with new material, on 16 and 17 April. The band then went back into the studio, squeezing in a session at a vintage studio in Clarksdale, Mississippi. '[The] studio is an old room with old tiles, and it will give the music a different quality and a different character,' said Elvis. 'It's nice and vivid.'[18]

Then it was on to Europe for a sprinkling of duo shows with Steve Nieve in England, Portugal and Italy. The sole UK show in Bournemouth on 30 April was a strange affair. It was relatively short – a little over ninety minutes in total – and Elvis didn't say a single word to the audience until he introduced Steve at the end of the main set. He then performed 'Nothing Clings Like Ivy' solo at the piano. There were no 'good evenings', 'good nights' or 'thank-yous'. It was all rather odd, although Elvis later claimed that he was suffering from a throat infection. From England, he and Steve travelled on to Lisbon, Porto, Catania and Cagliari, where the shows typically opened with '45', followed by 'Accidents Will Happen', 'Brilliant Mistake', 'Shot With His Own Gun' and 'This House Is Empty Now'. There was an unusually high incidence of *Goodbye Cruel World* material on display: 'Home Truth', 'Love Field', 'Peace In Our Time' and 'Inch By Inch' all featured. He would invariably end with the wracked soul classic, 'The Dark End Of The Street', a song which had also featured heavily in his solo shows back in 1984.

Following the duo shows with Steve, there was a single date with Bill Frisell – a second gig was cancelled at relatively short notice – at the Jahrhunderthalle in Bochum, Germany on 21 May, part of the 'Century of Song' series which also saw Frisell performing with Ron Sexsmith. 'The idea is to feature Elvis's songs, but then also to play songs that mean something to him, like old standard songs,' said Frisell beforehand. 'Knowing him, it could be a huge amount of things to draw from.' In reality, Elvis rather disappointingly chose to play a set which drew almost exclusively from his own back catalogue and – although Elvis and Frisell were playing with a band, consisting of Ron Miles on trumpet, Jenny Scheinman on violin, Viktor Krauss on bass and Matt Chamberlain on drums – there were heavy echoes of their 1995 Meltdown collaboration in the song choices: 'Gigi', 'Weird Nightmare', 'Deep Dead Blue', 'Love Field', even 'Sweet Pear'. However, in the end it proved to be a triumphant – if slow moving – night of music, featuring a smattering of tracks from *North* as well as superb versions of 'Radio Silence' and 'Poor Napoleon'.

The onset of summer heralded more characteristically eclectic twists and turns. He returned to Sweet Tea Studios in Mississippi in late May and June to mix the new record with Dennis Herring, and also recorded a fine cameo on the new album by Los Lobos and a scatty version of 'Let's Misbehave' for the soundtrack to the film *De-Lovely*, in which Elvis – resplendent in white tuxedo and ironic grin – had a small part singing the Cole Porter classic.

More significantly, following shows with Steve and the Metropole Orchestra at the North Sea Jazz Festival in The Hague, on 17 July at Avery Fisher Hall in New York the *Il Sogno* score was performed in full for the first time, played by the Brooklyn Philharmonic Orchestra, the same ensemble who had previously recorded Philip Glass's acclaimed *Low Symphony*. The landmark performance was the last of three New York concerts showcasing the strafing diversity of Elvis's music: alongside *Il Sogno*, the Metropole Orchestra were featured on the thirteenth and The Imposters on the fifteenth. The concerts with The Imposters looked forwards, a taster for a proposed full-blown tour to promote the new record, slated for towards the end of the year. The inclusion of orchestral shows with the Metropole was more of a backwards glance, the result of Elvis's nagging sensation that he hadn't really toured the *North* material as extensively or as sympathetically as he could have, despite the fact that many felt the songs had benefited from the stripped-down duo arrangements.

The performance of *Il Sogno* in New York was particularly satisfying, a prelude to the long-delayed release of the studio recording of Elvis's score made by the LSO in 2002 in Abbey Road. The recording of *Il Sogno* had finally been scheduled to come out in September 2004, released simultaneously alongside the new Imposters record. It was called *The Delivery Man*.

Also on the schedule was *The Secret Arias*, a chamber opera which Elvis had written especially for the Royal Theatre in Copenhagen. Part of a series of works commissioned to celebrate the 200th anniversary of the birth of Danish story-teller Hans Christian Andersen in 2005, the opera explored Andersen's infatuation with Swedish opera singer Jenny Lind. Doubtless there were already half-a-dozen other projects in stages somewhere between a seed in his brain and active pre-planning. However, as a marker of precisely where Elvis Costello was in 2004, the twin release of rock 'n' roll and orchestral works was as accurate a barometer as anything ever could be. As always with Elvis, it was difficult to predict where he might be in a year's time. It would probably be somewhere interesting, a road worth following him down. His sometime collaborator Richard Harvey concedes that Elvis has 'a quarter eye on posterity', and there remains a sense that he is an artist whose almost pathological eclecticism and fearsome drive was born of – and thereafter has been partially driven by – a keen awareness of his own legacy, a desire to ensure that his musical obituary will be as monolithic and far-reaching as humanly possible. That said, one should never underestimate his genuine love of music.

As Elvis turned fifty in August 2004, there appeared to be no blunting of the appetite for musical discovery which had driven him through a professional career now approaching a tenure of three decades, with almost unfathomable twists and turns. A complex character, as contradictory in his impulses and desires as any true artist worth their salt must be; as driven, controlling and frequently as coldly calculated as the breadth of his ambition demanded, Elvis had pushed himself and those around him harder than most to get to this place – a place where he could follow the never-ceasing music in his head to wherever it led, a place where the boundaries disappeared.

'I have to go with what's true to me, and I think the smart people appreciate and respect that I'm doing it for sincere reasons and that I'm not being perverse,' he said in 2003. 'I really believe that it's all the result of curiosity and love. There's a time in life for Hoagy Carmichael. There's a time in life for Claude Debussy. There's a time in life for Jerry Lee Lewis. There's a time in life for Destiny's Child. All of these things have their moment.' [19]

Notes and Sources

Unless otherwise credited in the text or below, all quotations are drawn from the author's interviews, conducted between August 2002 and April 2004. All footnotes are denoted by an * and are listed within the text at the bottom of each page, except in the Prologue, where the sole footnote comes at the end.

PROLOGUE: 'Drunken Talk Isn't Meant To Be Printed in the Paper'
1. *NME*, 27 January 1979
2. *Uncut*, June 1997
3. *Rolling Stone*, July 1982

CHAPTER ONE
1. ASCAP Awards, 20 May 2003
2. quoted in *Let Them All Talk*, by Brian Hinton (Sanctuary, 1999)
3. Letter to *Rolling Stone*, 1979
4. *Rolling Stone*, 11 November 1999
5. BBC Radio One interview with Simon Mayo, 10 November 1994
6. *The Observer*, 18 July 1999
7. *The Face*, August 1983
8. BBC Radio One documentary, 29 February 1992
9. *Rolling Stone*, 11 November 1999
10. ibid
11. *The Face*, August 1983
12. BBC Radio One documentary, 29 February 1992
13. *Melody Maker*, 13 May 1989
14. *The Times*, 2 March 2002
15. *Record Collector*, September 1995
16. *Rolling Stone*, 11 November 1999
17. *Folk Roots*, July 1989
18. *Liverpool: Wondrous Place*, by Paul Du Noyer (Virgin, 2002)

19. *Folk Roots*, July, 1989
20. *The Face*, August 1983
21. *Liverpool: Wondrous Place*, by Paul Du Noyer (Virgin, 2002)
22. ibid
23. ibid
24. *Folk Roots*, July 1989
25. *Across The Great Divide*, by Barney Hoskyns (Pimlico, 2003)
26. *Vanity Fair*, November 2000
27. *Folk Roots*, July 1989
28. BBC Radio One documentary, 29 February 1992
29. ibid
30. *Folk Roots*, July 1989
31. *The Face*, August 1983
32. *Folk Roots*, July 1989

CHAPTER TWO
1. *Across The Great Divide*, by Barney Hoskyns (Pimlico, 2003)
2. *Record Collector*, September 1995
3. ibid
4. BBC Radio One documentary, 29 February 1992
5. ibid
6. *The Face*, August 1983
7. *NME*, 27 August 1977
8. *Trouser Press*, December 1977
9. BBC Radio One documentary, 29 February 1992
10. *Melody Maker*, 25 June 1977
11. BBC Radio One documentary, 29 February 1992

CHAPTER THREE
1. *Melody Maker*, 25 June 1977
2. *Folk Roots*, July 1989
3. *Melody Maker*, 25 June 1977
4. *Record Collector*, September 1995
5. *My Aim Is True*, CD notes.
6. *Record Collector*, September 1995
7. *My Aim Is True*, CD notes.
8. ibid
9. ibid
10. *NME*, 27 August 1977
11. BBC Radio One documentary, 29 February 1992
12. ibid

13. ibid
14. *My Aim Is True*, CD notes
15. *The Dark Stuff*, by Nick Kent (Da Capo Press, 1994)
16. ibid.
17. BBC Radio One documentary, 29 February 1992
18. *Trouser Press*, December 1977
19. *Record Collector*, September 1995

CHAPTER FOUR
1. *Melody Maker*, 25 June 1977
2. BBC Radio One documentary, 29 February 1992
3. Interview with author, August 2002
4. *Record Collector*, September 1995
5. *The Face*, August, 1983
6. BBC Radio One documentary, 29 February 1992
7. *My Aim Is True*, CD notes/Trouser Press, December 1977
8. *NME*, 27 August 1977
9. *Sex & Drugs & Rock 'n' Roll: The Life Of Ian Dury*, by Richard Balls (Omnibus, 2000)
10. *Village Voice*, 29 March 2000
11. *NME*, 27 January 1979
12. *The Independent*, 25 June 1995
13. ibid.
14. *NME*, 27 January 1979
15. *NME*, 27 August 1977
16. *NME*, 27 January 1979
17. *Tom Snyder* TV Show, 1981
18. *This Year's Model*, CD notes

CHAPTER FIVE
1. *Record Collector*, September 1995
2. *GQ*, April 1994
3. *The Guardian*, 30 August 2003
4. *GQ*, April 1994
5. *MOJO*, October 2003
6. *NME*, 18 March 1978
7. BBC Radio One documentary, 7 March 1992
8. *NME*, 30 October 1982
9. *Rebel Heart*, by Bebe Buell with Victor Bockris (St Martin's Griffin, 2001)
10. *Armed Forces*, CD notes

11. *Record Collector*, September 1995
12. *Rebel Heart*, by Bebe Buell with Victor Bockris (St Martin's Griffin, 2001)
13. *NME*, 30 October 1982
14. BBC Radio One documentary, 29 February 1992
15. *Record Collector*, September 1995
16. *Rebel Heart*, by Bebe Buell with Victor Bockris (St Martin's Griffin, 2001)
17. *Associated Press*, 7 October 2003
18. *Armed Forces*, CD notes
19. BBC Radio One documentary, 7 March 1992
20. *MOJO*, October 2003
21. ibid

CHAPTER SIX
1. *Rolling Stone*, 17 May 1979
2. ibid
3. ibid
4. ibid
5. ibid
6. BBC Radio One documentary, 7 March 1992
7. *Rolling Stone*, July 1982
8. *NME*, 9 July 1979
9. *NME*, 30 October 1982
10. *Rebel Heart*, by Bebe Buell with Victor Bockris (St Martin's Griffin, 2001)
11. *Get Happy!!* CD notes
12. *Uncut*, July 1998
13. *Record Collector*, September 1995
14. ibid
15. *The Face*, August 1983
16. BBC Radio One documentary, 7 March 1992
17. ibid
18. *NME*, 30 October 1982

CHAPTER SEVEN
1. Interview with author, August 2002
2. *Record Collector*, September 1995
3. *Trust,* CD notes
4. ibid
5. *The Face*, August 1983

6. *Almost Blue* CD notes
7. *Record Collector*, September 1995
8. *Melody Maker*, 13 May 1989
9. *The South Bank Show*, London Weekend Television, first broadcast November 1981
10. ibid
11. ibid
12. ibid
13. ibid
14. *Girls Girls Girls* CD notes
15. *The Face*, August 1983

CHAPTER EIGHT

1. *Record Collector*, September 1995
2. Interview with Maureen Droney, *Mix-online*, October 2003
3. BBC Radio One documentary, 7 March 1992
4. *Grammy Magazine*, 19 February 2003
5. *Imperial Bedroom*, CD notes
6. *NME*, 30 October 1982
7. ibid
8. *Rock Lives: Profiles and Interviews*, by Timothy White (Henry Holt and Co., 1990)
9. *Record Collector*, September 1995
10. Interview with David Jensen, *GLR*, 21 July 1983
11. *Record Collector*, September 1995
12. *Punch The Clock*, CD notes
13. Interview with David Jensen, *GLR*, 21 July 1983
14. *Chet Baker: Deep In A Dream*, by James Gavin (Chatto and Windus, 2002)
15. *NME*, 8 October 1983
16. *Punch The Clock*, CD notes

CHAPTER NINE

1. *Rebel Heart*, by Bebe Buell with Victor Bockris (St Martin's Griffin, 2001)
2. *Hot Press*, 1987
3. *Goodbye Cruel World*, CD notes
4. BBC Radio One Documentary, 7 March 1992
5. *Record Collector*, September 1995
6. ibid
7. *Rebel Heart*, by Bebe Buell with Victor Bockris (St Martin's Griffin, 2001)

8. ibid

9. *Record Collector*, September 1995

10. *Hot Press*, 14 December 1984

11. *Melody Maker*, 1 March 1986

12. ibid

13. ibid

14. BBC Radio One documentary, 14 March 1992

15. Pete Thomas, ibid

16. *Record Collector*, September 1995

17. BBC Radio One documentary, 14 March 1992

18. *Rolling Stone*, Issue 471, 1986

19. *NME*, March 1986

20. *The Independent On Sunday*, 31 January 1988

CHAPTER TEN

1. *Blood & Chocolate* CD notes

2. BBC Radio One documentary, 14 March 1992

3. ibid

4. *Mix*, 1 May 1999

5. *The Independent On Sunday*, 31 January 1988

6. *The Pogues: The Lost Decade*, by Ann Scanlon (Omnibus, 1988)

7. *Melody Maker*, 13 May 1989

8. *Blood & Chocolate* CD notes

9. *LA Times*, 4 October 1986

10. *Blood & Chocolate* CD notes

11. BBC Radio One documentary, 14 March 1992

12. ibid

13. *New York Observer*, 16 August 1999

14. *Blood & Chocolate* CD notes

CHAPTER ELEVEN

1. *Folk Roots*, July 1989

2. BBC Radio One interview, 1989

3. *New York Times*, 8 February 1989

4. BBC Radio One documentary, 21 March 1992

5. *Chicago Tribune*, 11 June 1989

6. Interview with Michel Lavidiere

7. ibid

8. *Hot Press*, March 1989

9. *Melody Maker*, 13 May 1989

10. *Spike* CD notes

11. Quoted in *ECIS*, April 1990 issue
12. *NME*, 18 February 1999
13. *Sunday Times*, 11 June 1995
14. *The Dark Stuff*, by Nick Kent (Da Capo Press, 1994)
15. *Aberdeen Evening Express*, 4 May 1988
16. *The Times*, 2 March 2002

CHAPTER TWELVE
1. *The Times*, 13 March 1993
2. *Mighty Like A Rose* CD notes
3. *Kojak Variety* CD notes
4. *Creem*, 1991
5. *Mighty Like A Rose* CD notes
6. *Daily Telegraph*, 15 March 2001
7. *Time Out*, June 1991
8. *Record Collector*, October 1995

CHAPTER THIRTEEN
1. *The Guardian*, 15 January 1993
2. *Q*, March 1993
3. ibid
4. *Q*, April 1994
5. *Q*, March 1993
6. *Hot Press*, April 1994
7. The *Guardian*, 15 January 1993
8. The *Times*, 13 March 1993
9. The *Independent*, 20 June 1995
10. The *Guardian*, 15 January 1993
11. *Mix*, 1 May 1999
12. Interview with author, August 2002
13. ibid

CHAPTER FOURTEEN
1. *New York Observer*, 16 August 1999
2. *Brutal Youth* CD notes
3. The *Independent*, 24 February 1994
4. *New York Observer*, 16 August 1999
5. *Brutal Youth* CD notes
6. The *Guardian*, 21 June 1994
7. Interview on BBC World Service, November 1994

8. *NME*, 20 May 1995
9. *The Times*, 28 June 1995

CHAPTER FIFTEEN
1. *Arena*, July/August 1995
2. *Entertainment Weekly*, spring 1996
3. *All This Useless Beauty* CD notes
4. *A Year With Swollen Appendices*, by Brian Eno (Faber & Faber, 1996)
5. *The Big Issue*, 1 December 1997
6. ibid
7. *Associated Press*, 19 December 1997
8. *The Independent*, 28 October 1997

CHAPTER SIXTEEN
1. *Q*, February 1998
2. The *Irish Times*, 4 April 1998
3. *The Independent*, 26 June 1997
4. The *LA Times*, 12 April 1998
5. Electric Ballroom Radio Show, 24 March 1998
6. The *Guardian*, 19 September 1998
7. BPI newswire, 30 January 1998
8. Interview with Francesco Calazzo, printed in *Beyond Belief*, March 1997
9. Interview with Damon Coward, Bologna, printed in *Beyond Belief*, October 2000
10. Woodstock.com
11. *Associated Press*, 29 October 1998
12. The *Guardian*, 19 September 1998
13. amazon.com, 6 October 1998
14. *Daily Variety*, 6 August 1998
15. *New York Post*, 9 October 1998
16. The *Sunday Herald*, 11 April 1999
17. Woodstock.com
18. The *Sunday Herald*, 11 April 1999
19. *Entertainment Weekly*, October 1999

CHAPTER SEVENTEEN
1. The *Guardian*, 1 March 1996
2. Programme notes for *Il Sogno*

3. Interview with Damon Coward, Bologna, printed in *Beyond Belief*, October 2000
4. *Dallas Observer*, 5 April 2001
5. *Phoenix New Times*, 12 April 2001
6. *Expressen*, 1 December 2000
7. The *Daily Telegraph*, 15 March 2001
8. *The Independent On Sunday*, 11 February 2001
9. Interview with Damon Coward, Bologna, printed in *Beyond Belief*, October 2000

CHAPTER EIGHTEEN
1. The *Boston Globe*, 21 April 2002
2. *Mix*, 1 May 2002
3. ibid
4. ibid
5. Interview with author, August 2002
6. *Mix,* 1 May 2002
7. *Word*, April 2003
8. The *Detroit News*, 22 March 2002
9. ibid
10. *Word*, April 2003
11. *Daily Star*, 23 February 2003
12. *Word,* April 2003
13. ibid
14. *Providence Journal Bulletin*, 11 July 2003
15. The *Guardian*, 19 September 2003
16. The *Guardian*, 30 August 2003
17. stevenieve.com, 7 April 2004
18. *Clarksdale Press*, 15 April 2004
19. ASCAP Awards, 20 May 2003

Index

'King Of The Unknown Sea' 235
'King Of Thieves' 158
Kingston, Rhode Island 211
Kinks, The 16, 74, 88
Knetchel, Larry 213, 217, 219, 224
'Knocking On Heaven's Door' 44
'Knowing Me, Knowing You' 190
Kojak Variety (album) 218, 248–9, 253, 258
Korngold, Erich 252
Kraftwerk 101
Krall, Diana 302–3, 304, 306, 307–8, 309
Kramer, Billy J. 14
Krauss, Alison 308
Krauss, Viktor 312
KSHE, St Louis 111–12
Ku Klux Klan 134

L
LA Times 85, 149, 188, 190, 191, 192, 203
LA Weekly 296
'Labelled With Love' 131
Lahinch, Co Clare 167
Lala, Jim 112
Lancaster University 85
'Land Of Give And Take' 144
Landmine Free World, Concerts For A 297
lang, k.d. 203
Langer, Clive 116, 123, 124, 153, 154, 155, 156, 157, 207, 252
Larry Sanders Show (US TV series) 308
'Last Boat Leaving' 20, 36, 93, 204
'Last Post, The' 234
Last Resort, The (TV show) 204n
'Last Time You Were Leaving, The' 193
'Last Town I Painted, The 270
Lauder, Andrew 87, 120–1
'Leader Of The Gang' 162
'Leader Of The Pack' 75
'Leave My Kitten Alone' 186, 205, 212, 217
Led Zeppelin 29, 96
Lee, Bruce 243
Lee, Peggy 9, 12
'Left On Man' 293
Leicester De Montfort Hall 152
Lemper, Ute 255, 283
Lennon, John 113, 131–2
Leno, Jay 266, 283
Leone, Sergio 187
Lerwick, Shetland Is 205, 225
'Less Than Zero' 58, 61, 71, 75, 76, 81, 87, 242, 280, 294
'Less Than Zero (Dallas Version)' 68
'Let Him Dangle' 200, 204, 210, 213
'Let It Be' 280
'Let Them All Talk' 154, 158, 161
'Let's Misbehave' 312
'Letter Home, A' (Costello) 231

Letterman, David 248, 273, 277, 307–8, 308
Lewis, Huey 56, 192
Lewis, Jerry Lee 313
'Like A Rolling Stone' 145
'Like An Angel Passing Through My Room' 288, 289
Lil' Darlin" 233
'Lily, Rosemary And The Jack Of Hearts' 258
Lind, Jenny 312
Lindersmith, Jim 112
'Lip Service' 52n, 68
'Lipstick Vogue' 52, 68, 69, 92, 93, 97, 146, 162, 242, 294, 299
'Little Atoms' 250, 258, 261, 262, 263
Little Feat 35, 38
'Little Goody Two Shoes' 136
'Little Palaces' 20, 182, 190, 281
Little Richard 176
'Little Sister' 131
'Little Triggers' 93, 281, 300
Live Aid 174
Liverpool 193, 292
    Cavern Club 26
    folk scene in 21, 28, 29
    The Medium Theatre 21–2
    Royal Court Theatre 152
    SFX School in 20
    Temple Bar, Dale Street 24–5
    Toxteth 11
    West Derby 19–30, 58
Liverpool FC 16, 17, 19, 20
'Living In Paradise' 36, 68
Living In The USA (album) 116
Lizst, Franz 250
Los Lobos 165, 177, 312
Loder, Kurt 3
London
    Abbey Road Studios 116–17, 281, 299, 312
    AIR Studios 143, 208
    Albany Theatre 128
    Alexander Street (Stiff Records) 55–6, 62–3
    Am-Pro Studio, Shepherd's Bush 121
    Amadeus Centre, Maida Vale 228, 231–2
    Archipelago Studios, Pimlico 117
    Beaulieu Close, Twickenham 12, 13, 31, 41
    The Big One at the Apollo 162
    Brown's Hotel, Kensington 42
    The Canteen 155–6
    Chelsea Arts Ball 233
    Church Studios, Crouch End 233, 237–9
    The Clarendon 121
    Cypress Avenue, Whitton 48, 79, 88
    Dingwalls 76, 77

332

333